In this book, Christoph Bluth provides an original analysis of one of the most perplexing periods of Soviet foreign and military policy – the build-up of strategic forces from the death of Stalin to the SALT I agreement. Bluth outlines Soviet strategic arms policy in this period, identifies the principal interest groups involved and studies a number of critical decisions taken in relation to strategic bombers, strategic nuclear forces based at sea, ballistic missile defence and the military uses of space.

Strategic arms policy in the Khrushchev period exhibited a number of apparent paradoxes which the author explains. As well as examining external threat assessment and wider foreign policy, he pays particular attention to the rôle of domestic factors such as Khrushchev's endeavours to shift resources away from the military industries to agriculture and the production of consumer goods. Bluth is therefore able to demonstrate how domestic priorities and internal power struggles account for some of the seeming inconsistencies of military and foreign policy.

Given current reassessments of the nature of the Soviet military threat and the revival of interest in the Khrushchev period, this book is most topical. Using source material hitherto unavailable, Bluth combines, for the first time, an analysis of foreign, military and domestic policy. *Soviet strategic arms policy before SALT* will, therefore, be of interest to a wide range of students and specialists of Soviet affairs, strategic studies and international relations.

SOVIET STRATEGIC ARMS POLICY BEFORE SALT

Soviet and East European Studies

series list continues on p. 314

SOVIET STRATEGIC ARMS POLICY BEFORE SALT

CHRISTOPH BLUTH

Lecturer in International Politics,
Department of Government, University of Essex

CAMBRIDGE UNIVERSITY PRESS

Cambridge New York Port Chester
Melbourne Sydney

Published by the Press Syndicate of the University of Cambridge
The Pitt Building, Trumpington Street, Cambridge CB2 1RP
40 West 20th Street, New York, NY 10011–4211, USA
10 Stamford Road, Oakleigh, Victoria 3166, Australia

First published 1992

Printed in Great Britain at the University Press, Cambridge

A catalogue record for this book is available from the British Library

Library of Congress cataloguing in publication data
Bluth, Christoph.
Soviet strategic arms policy before SALT/Christoph Bluth.
    p.   cm. — (Soviet and East European studies)
Includes bibliographical references and index.
ISBN 0 521 40372 3 (hardback)
1. Strategic forces – Soviet Union – History – 20th century.
2. Soviet Union – Military policy. 3. Nuclear weapons – Soviet Union –
History – 20th century. I. Title. II. Series
UA770.B592 1992
358'.1754'0947 – dc20   91–13574

ISBN 0 521 40372 3 hardback

For Alison

Contents

Tables

Acknowledgments

My thanks are due first of all to Professor Lawrence Freedman who provided constant guidance and inspiration for this work throughout my period of study.

A number of other people have, through conversations or correspondence, provided invaluable advice and suggestions. Among those who shared their expertise with me I would like to acknowledge Hannes Adomeit, Roy Allison, Alexander Dallin, Christopher Donnelly, Raymond Garthoff, Andrew Goldberg, Arnold Horelick, David Holloway, Michael MccGwire, Robbin Laird, Margot Light, Carl Linden, Pat Litherland, Robert Nurick, Stephen Meyer, Alex Pravda, Stephen Shenfield, Paul Stares, Kosta Tsipis, Notra Trulock, Adam Ulam, Peter Vigor, Nicholas Wheeler and Kimberly Zisk.

I would like to thank the Soviet Studies Centre of the Royal Military Academy, Sandhurst for allowing me to use their library facilities. I acknowledge financial support from the Central Research Fund of the University of London and the Department of War Studies, King's College London for a research trip to the United States.

This work could only be completed because of the constant and loving support of my wife Alison Williams-Bluth to whom this volume is dedicated.

CHRISTOPH BLUTH
December 1991

Abbreviations

ABM	Anti Ballistic Missile
ADM	Atomic Demolition Munition
ASAT	Antisatellite
BMD	Ballistic Missile Defence
CC	Central Committee
CIA	Central Intelligence Agency
CPSU	Communist Party of the Soviet Union
FOBS	Fractional Orbital Bombardment System
FY	Fiscal Year
GCD	General and Complete Disarmament
GKO	Gosudarstvenii Komitet Oborony (State Committee for Defence)
ICBM	Intercontinental Ballistic Missile
IISS	International Institute for Strategic Studies
INF	Intermediate Nuclear Forces
IRBM	Intermediate-Range Ballistic Missile
MIRV	Multiple Independently Targeted Reentry Vehicle
MLF	Multilateral Force
MPA	Main Political Administration
MRBM	Medium-Range Ballistic Missile
MT	Megaton
NATO	North Atlantic Treaty Organisation
NIE	National Intelligence Estimate
NPT	(Nuclear) Non-Proliferation Treaty
OKB	Opytno Konstruktorskie Biuro (Experimental Design Bureau)
PRO	Protivoraketnaia Oborona (Anti-Rocket Defence)
PSO	Protovosamoletnaia Oborona (Anti-aircraft Defence)
PTBT	Partial Test Ban Treaty

PVO-S	Protivovozdushnaia Oborona Strany (Anti-air Defence of the Country)
R&D	Research and Development
RV	Reentry Vehicle
SAC	Strategic Air Command
SAINT	Satellite Inspector
SALT	Strategic Arms Limitation Talks
SAM	Surface-to-Air Missile
SED	Sozialistische Einheitspartei (Socialist Unity Party)
SIPRI	Swedish International Peace Research Institute
SLBM	Submarine-Launched Ballistic Missile
SRF	Strategic Rocket Forces
SS	Surface-to-Surface
UN	United Nations
USA	United States of America
USSR	Union of Soviet Socialist Republics
VPK	Voenno-promyshlenniia kommissiia (Military Industrial Commission)
VVS	Voenno-Vozdushnye Sily (the Air Forces)

Part I

Soviet strategic arms policy: the general framework

1 Introduction

Since the end of the Second World War, the global confrontation between East and West has been a central feature of international relations. One of the key aspects of this confrontation has been the growth in Soviet and US military power. The question as to how and why the Soviet Union and the United States, who were allies in the war against Germany, came to be opponents facing each other in a monumental global power struggle which threatened to plunge the world into a nuclear holocaust is the main issue of Cold War history. The growth of Soviet and US strategic nuclear arms which has resulted in a situation where both sides have more than 10,000 nuclear warheads targeted against the other is frequently referred to as the arms race, implying that both superpowers are engaged in a competition to acquire greater and greater arsenals of increasingly sophisticated weapons of mass destruction. One of the principal tasks of strategic studies is therefore to explain the evolution and nature of the arms race, if indeed there is such a phenomenon, and investigate the factors which cause it to occur.

There is a large academic literature devoted to strategic theory and various models which are designed to explain the pattern of strategic arms deployments. While a number of sophisticated models explaining the interactions of various factors, such as the international situation, threat perceptions, strategic theory, foreign-policy goals and the interests of various bureaucratic institutions (the defence industries, the services in the armed forces, etc.) have been developed, most of the detailed application of such models has been confined to the examination of how strategic arms policy is made in the United States. By comparison, less attention has been paid to how such decisions are made in the Soviet Union. This study examines the build-up of strategic forces in the Soviet Union from the death of Stalin to the SALT I agreement. It thus concerns itself with the Soviet side of the arms race. It addresses the fundamental nature of the Soviet nuclear challenge at the beginning of large-scale strategic deployments.

The main emphasis of this study is on the Khrushchev period. There are a number of reasons why, despite the considerable body of literature which exists on all aspects of Soviet foreign and military policy under Khrushchev, a reconsideration of this period is in order. First of all, most of the important studies were written at a time when the data available on Soviet force deployments during the period was still comparatively scant. Although even now many questions are still unanswered, we have much more sophisticated and detailed information about the numbers and kinds of weapons developed and deployed by the Soviet Union; we know more about their capabilities, we are able to classify missiles into various modifications and planes into various prototypes, we have information about the dates of various flight tests, the accuracy of the missiles and the explosive power of their warheads. Much of this information was classified at the time when the principal studies of Soviet strategic arms policy under Khrushchev were written.[1] The same applies to the availability of Soviet military literature. The path-breaking study of Arnold Horelick and Myron Rush based itself almost exclusively on citations from *Pravda* and *Izvestiia*.[2] Thomas W. Wolfe's study of *Soviet Strategy at the Crossroads*, which is primarily based on the classic exposition of Soviet military strategy edited by V. D. Sokolovskii again makes wide use of newspapers, and some very limited use of other military literature (mainly the journals of the Main Political Administration *Kommunist Vooruzhennykh Sil* and *Voenno-Istoricheskii Zhurnal*, but not any of the then available journals of the services or *Voennaya Mysl'*).[3] The first and so far the only systematic analysis of a wide range of the Soviet military literature from the late Fifties and the first half of the Sixties was undertaken by Roman Kolkowicz in his book *The Soviet Military and the Communist Party*.[4] The focus of Kolkowicz's study, however, was rather narrowly confined to Party–military relations.

Some of the most important Soviet military literature has only become available more recently. The journal of the air defence forces, for example, has only recently received much attention. More importantly, previous studies of the Khrushchev era did not have the articles from the classified military journal *Voennaya Mysl'* at their disposal. At the time when a selection of *Voennaya Mysl'* articles from 1959 to 1973 were made available (in translation), the focus of scholarly attention had largely shifted to more contemporary issues. Those recent studies which have made use of the declassified translations have in the main sought to draw inferences for more contemporary issues in Soviet military policy.[5]

The advent of *new thinking* and *glasnost'* has encouraged a more open re-examination of Soviet history by Soviet scholars; some of those involved in Soviet policy-making at the time have written their own accounts and become more accessible for interviews. Among the new materials available for this study are the memoirs by Andrei A. Gromyko,[6] the former Foreign Minister, the long-delayed biography of Marshal Malinovskii,[7] an article by Fyodor Burlatsky on the Khrushchev period,[8] the interviews with leading Soviet politicians and military personnel in the television series *The Nuclear Age* and statements made by Soviet participants at a conference on the Cuban Missile Crisis.[9] This new evidence has to be treated with some caution since, despite a greater degree of openness not all the false interpretations of the past have been swept away. Furthermore, the intellectual framework of the *new thinking*[10] is now used to re-interpret Soviet history and thus imposes a new interpretation which, while quite different from the old, is not necessarily correct and does not necessarily improve our understanding of Soviet history.[11]

The limitations imposed on this study are those which generally confront students of Soviet military affairs. There is still no access to Soviet archives and documents. In particular, there is no access to Soviet data on military hardware deployed during the period in question – an issue on which articles even in the classified military press are conspicuously silent. Despite these limitations, a new look at the Khrushchev period based on the rich source material now available seems warranted.

Since the classic studies of Soviet miltary policy in the Sixties were written, a good deal of work has been done on various aspects of the Khrushchev period. The study by Carl A. Linden[12] showed that the picture of a relatively unified, centralized policy-making process had to be revised substantially and that during the Khrushchev period there was a great deal of conflict over the direction that the Soviet Union should take in terms of its political process, its economic priorities and its foreign relations. Based on a meticulous study and comparison of Soviet sources, Michel Tatu enhanced Linden's work and extended it partially into the Brezhnev period.[13]

While a much more sophisticated analysis of Soviet domestic policy of the Khrushchev period has thus been undertaken, the application to the fields of foreign and military policies has so been very restricted. Linden and Tatu devoted only limited attention to foreign policy. Perhaps the most ambitious study so far which seeks to link divisions within the Party over domestic and foreign policy to specific issues in the conduct of Soviet foreign policy is that of the *Berlin Crisis 1961* by Robert Slusser.[14] As far as the study of military policy is concerned, little work has been done to link the policy disputes in the Communist Party and the associated power struggles with military policy. The work by Roman Kolkowicz and Michael Deane on Party–military relations has recognized divisions among the military, and divisions between the Party and the military. But it does not consider to any extent the consequences of divisions within the Party leadership, nor are broader conclusions about the evolution of Soviet military doctrine and Soviet strategic arms policy drawn.

The extension of the framework of analysis established by Linden, Tatu and Slusser is therefore the task of this study. Although its primary focus is the Khrushchev period, the analysis is extended somewhat into the early Brezhnev period, up until the conclusion of the SALT I Treaty. The reason is that the Soviet strategic arms build-up, especially as far as ICBM deployment is concerned, did not get seriously under way until after the fall of Khrushchev. The shifts in policy which then took place help to determine the extent to which the build-up observed in the Brezhnev period can be traced back to decisions of the Khrushchev period. The manner in which the internal controversies were carried out and partially resolved under Brezhnev also throws important light on the nature of the debates during the Khrushchev period.

As a preliminary to this investigation, let us briefly review the empirical data on the development of Soviet strategic power and consider the various interpretations of Soviet strategic arms policy that have been advanced.

The development of Soviet strategic power

The purpose of this section is to give a general outline of the development of strategic nuclear forces in the period 1953–1972, leaving for later consideration the analysis of operational doctrines and requirements. It provides the basic data of the phenomenon under study. Deployment patterns themselves may yield clues about policy, and these will also be examined here.

When Stalin died in 1953, the Soviet Union had a limited stockpile of atomic bombs and, by American standards, only obsolescent bombers from which to deliver them (the range of the TU-4 was insufficient for two-way missions to the continental United States). However, the comprehensive research and development programme initiated by Stalin to produce nuclear weapons and improved delivery vehicles continued to progress. In August 1953 the USSR exploded a thermonuclear device. Among the new developments were a new twin-turbojet medium-range bomber (the *Badger*) and two modern types of heavy bomber with intercontinental range (the four-jet *Bison* and the multi-turboprop *Bear*). These developments led to fears in the United States that the Soviet Union might be on the brink of a mass-production programme of long-range bombers resulting in a 'bomber gap'. In 1955 the Soviet Union still possessed no delivery systems of intercontinental range, while the United States had 1,309 bombers which could deliver 2,310 warheads (plus 698 warheads deployed on forward bases). American fears of the emerging strategic nuclear capabilities of the Soviet Union were dramatically heightened by the Soviet launch of the first earth satellite (Sputnik) in October 1957, which demonstrated to all the world that the Soviet Union possessed the technology to develop intercontinental ballistic missiles.

However, these fears turned out to be unwarranted. The first generation ICBM (the SS-6) was never deployed in more than token numbers. By 1960 the Soviet Union had deployed a total of four ICBMs and 145 strategic bombers. The low number of strategic bombers produced is indicative of a definite decision not to seek to overcome the large American strategic advantage by the method most obviously within Soviet technological capabilities. This would appear to be in direct conflict with the arms-race paradigm and thus requires explanation. The same applies to the decision not to deploy the SS-6 in large numbers, especially in light of its symbolic status as demonstrating that the Soviet Union had become a global power rivalling the United States.

The development of Soviet military power, in particular the capability to deliver nuclear strikes, was far more impressive in the European region. In 1955 the Soviet Union had 1,296 bombers for use in a regional theatre, 25 battlefield nuclear missiles and a total estimated stockpile of 324 warheads, implying that many of the bombers would be used with conventional weapons. By 1960 a total of 200 medium-range land-based missiles had been deployed (SS-3 and SS-4), thus providing a considerably enhanced nuclear capability against Western Europe. In addition the number of battlefield nuclear missiles had been doubled (although this hardly constituted a large-scale deployment) and nuclear submarines were carrying 36 medium-range sea-based missiles. There had been no increase in the number of medium-range bombers, but the stockpile of warheads had jumped to 1,328 (of which 294 were designated for intercontinental delivery and 1,034 for regional deployment). The deployment of medium-range missiles continued and by the time Khrushchev left office there were 705 such missiles deployed, while the number of bombers had been reduced to 880 and the number of medium-range sea-based missiles had grown to 105. The emphasis on medium-range systems can be partially explained by the fact that they had strategic significance in view of US forward-based systems, particularly in Western Europe. Nonetheless, given the perceived requirement to be able to target the continental United States and thereby make the American homeland vulnerable, and the existing capabilities for producing long-range systems (especially bombers, but also ICBMs), this emphasis in the allocation of resources needs further analysis before a satisfactory explanation can be given.

Second- and third-generation missiles with intercontinental range, the SS-7, SS-8, SS-9, SS-11 and SS-13, were already in development in the late 1950s. The deployment of SS-7 and SS-8 missiles did not get under way until 1962 but, by the time Khrushchev left office, the number of ICBMs deployed had risen to 224. The third-generation missiles were not deployed before 1965.

The first test-flight of the SS-7 took place in 1961. The decision to proceed with its development must therefore have been taken around the time of the first Sputnik launch in 1957. Test flights of the SS-8 and SS-7 (modification 3) also took place in 1961, while the first test flights of third-generation missiles occurred in 1964 (SS-9) and 1965 (SS-11). Crucial decisions, therefore, were taken in 1961: the decision to proceed with the deployment of the SS-7/8 which began in 1962 (after about half the average period between the first test flight and deployment of Soviet ICBMs), and (most likely) the decision to proceed with the development of the SS-9. Looking at the number of second-generation missiles (SS-7/8) deployed, we see a sudden jump in numbers between 1963 and 1964 coinciding with the appearance of the SS-8 and the third model of the SS-7, which had twice the megaton yield of the earlier model. No more than 23 SS-8s were ever deployed. On the face of it it appears possible that the Cuban missile crisis in 1962 may have influenced the increased deployment in 1963/64, but the increased production capacity must have been available earlier and therefore the data would also support the contention that a programme which already existed before 1962 was merely carried out as planned as soon as the SS-8 and SS-7 mod.3 became available (although not many SS-8s were deployed in the event). If one bears in mind that the missile programme of the Kennedy Administration made public on 28 March 1961 started a deployment goal of 600 Minuteman ICBMs and a total of 1,298 missiles of intercontinental range (including the submarine-based *Polaris*), it is quite evident that the expansion of the Soviet ICBM programme decided on in 1961 did not in any sense constitute an effort to match American plans such as would be predicted by the arms-race paradigm.

After the fall of Khrushchev, in 1964–65, the level of ICBM forces remained very nearly constant. The military budget also fell during this time. One could argue from the data that the deployment of second-generation missiles had now been completed and that the Soviets were waiting for the third generation of missiles to become available. At the end of 1964 the SS-9 mod.2 was tested (the mod.1 which was tested earlier in 1964 was deployed after the mod.2), 42 silos had been prepared for the SS-9, and, as I have already mentioned, in 1965 the SS-11 had its first test flight. These facts alone suggest some definite decision in 1963 at the latest to proceed with some SS-9 deployment, subject to satisfactory test flights. Deployment of both missiles began in 1966. The SS-9, a rather large missile with a 20-megaton warhead, was deployed at a constant rate of 42 missiles per year, with deployment levelling off at about 290 SS-9s. The SS-11, a rather smaller missile, was deployed in very large numbers, reaching 720 in 1970, by which time the deployment of the even smaller, solid fuelled SS-13 had begun.

The SS-11 entered service in 1966. It was at first deployed more slowly than the SS-9 but, by 1967, the SS-11s were more than double the number of the SS-9s.

The SS-11 was a missile of variable range and thus also played an important rôle as a long-range theatre missile. We can briefly summarize Soviet theatre-missile deployment as follows: by 1960 200 land-based missiles of medium range had been deployed (the SS-3 and SS-4) together with 50 short-range missiles and 36 medium-range missiles deployed on submarines. The number of medium-range bombers had remained constant. The Soviet Union under Khrushchev continued to build up its INF forces; in 1961, the SS-5 entered service and, by the time the First Secretary was ousted, there were 705 missiles of medium-range deployed, and 105

Table 1 *The development of Soviet ICBM deployment 1960–1972*

Year	SS-6	SS-7/8	SS-9	SS-11	SS-13	Total
1960	4	0	0	0	0	4
1961	4	46	0	0	0	50
1962	4	71	0	0	0	75
1963	4	87	0	0	0	91
1964	4	196	0	0	0	200
1965	4	220	0	0	0	224
1966	4	220	72	48	0	344
1967	0	220	114	236	0	570
1968	0	220	156	520	0	896
1969	0	220	198	644	15	1077
1970	0	220	240	720	40	1220
1971	0	220	280	950	60	1510
1972	0	210	290	970	60	1530

Sources: Robert P. Berman, *Soviet Air Power in Transition*, Washington: Brookings Institution 1978; Robert P. Berman and John C. Baker, *Soviet Strategic Forces*, Washington: Brookings Institution 1982; Lawrence Freedman, *U.S. Intelligence and the Soviet Strategic Threat*, London: Macmillan 1986; International Institute for Strategic Studies, *The Military Balance* (all editions from 1960–61 to 1970–71); C. G. Jacobson, *Soviet Strategy–Soviet Foreign Policy*, Glasgow: Robert Maclehouse & Co. Ltd. 1972; Michael MccGwire, *Military Objectives in Soviet Foreign Policy*, Washington: Brookings Institution 1987; Robert S. McNamara, 'Statement of Secretary of Defense Robert S. McNamara before a Joint Session of the Senate Armed Services Committee and the Senate Subcommittee on Department of Defense Appropriations on the Fiscal Year 1966–70 Defense Program and the 1966 Defense Budget', declassified (US Department of Defense, 1965); Mark E. Miller, *Soviet Strategic Power and Doctrine: The Quest for Superiority*, Advanced International Studies Institute 1982; *Nuclear Weapons Databook*, 'Soviet Nuclear Weapons' (Working Paper), Washington: National Resources Defense Council 1986; Scientific American, *Progress in Arms Control?*, San Francisco: W.H. Freeman 1979; Stockholm International Peace Research Institute, *Armaments and Disarmament in the Nuclear Age*, Cambridge: MIT Press 1976; Edward L. Warner, *The Military in Contemporary Soviet Politics: An Institutional Analysis*, New York: Praeger 1977

Note on the sources
To obtain the basic data for the Soviet strategic arms build-up during the period under discussion proved a more difficult task than anticipated. This is primarily due to the fact that, during the earlier part of this period, means of reconnaissance were not as highly developed as they are now and many of the fundamental data were under dispute as they could not be established

with precision. For this reason the *Military Balance* published by the International Institute for Strategic Studies, for example, which is relied upon as a basic and comprehensive source by many researchers in the field of strategic studies, published numbers for Soviet ICBMs and SLBMs which with hindsight appear to have been rather unreliable and are not broken down sufficiently precisely into the various categories of missiles, such as we would expect today. While the information provided about present levels of strategic missiles and warheads is very detailed and assumed to be reliable, until very recently, there has been very little interest in arriving at more precise figures for the early years of the Soviet strategic weapons' programme. The most detailed and informative survey of the development of Soviet strategic power published recently is that by Robert P. Berman and John C. Baker. (According to experts interviewed in the United States, it is generally believed that Berman and Baker had access to classified information for the preparation of their study. It is certainly indisputable that the sources which they cite themselves do not contain much of the information they provide.) The main drawback of Berman's and Baker's study is that their figures are given at five-year intervals (except for the SS-9, where figures are given for every year), which is insufficient for our study. To assemble the information in the table given above, the figures by Berman and Baker were taken as a baseline and the intermediate figures were reconstructed on the basis of the other sources listed above. The underlying assumption was that the principal sources, i.e. Berman and Baker, US Government statements (in particular Posture Statements for various Financial Years by the US Defence Secretary) and the studies based on them such as Freedman's and Warner's books yield a consistent general picture. Comparison with more recent publications, such as Michael MccGwire's book, confirm the accuracy of the result given in this chapter. One exception is the recently compiled *Nuclear Weapons Databook*, which presents figures completely at variance with all other sources. Thus the table for ICBM deployments states that only 2 SS-4s were deployed (although the figure 4 is the one given in the accompanying text), and gives 1963 as the first year of SS-7 deployment (although this also is contradicted in the accompanying text). The number of Soviet strategic bombers listed is also very different. On the whole the figures given in the *Nuclear Weapons Databook* are so inconsistent with other sources that they have been ignored here. Figures for the period before 1960 were considered too unreliable to be included here; in any event the deployment of strategic nuclear missiles did not start before 1960.

medium-range sea-based missiles (some of which had the capability to strike the United States through forward deployment), while the number of bombers had been reduced to 880.

Intermediate-range nuclear forces were also central to the Soviet military-force posture with regard to China. A medium-term solution to this problem was achieved by the designation of part of the

Table 2 *The development of Soviet SLBM deployment 1960–1972*

Year	SS-N-4/SS-N-5	SS-N-6	Total
1960	36	0	36
1961	36+	0	36+
1962	36+	0	36+
1963	117	0	117
1964	117	0	117
1965	117	0	117
1966	117	0	117
1967	117	0	117
1968	117	32	149
1969	117	128	245
1970	117	224	341
1971	117	320	437
1972	96	464	560

The figures for SLBMs given in Miller are incompatible with any conceivable configuration of submarines. The data in Berman and Baker and SIPRI on the number of missiles of submarines were used to calculate the number of SLBMs – in the absence of any other information it was assumed that the maximum number of SLBMs was deployed on every submarine.

SS-11 force to regional targets. By 1975 350 SS-11s were deployed in this manner (120 in the Far East). Regional targets could, of course, also be covered by SLBMs; in 1975 there were 89 SS-N-4/N-5 and 480 SS-N-6 medium-range SLBMs (these figures do not include those which could reach US territory by virtue of forward deployment). The importance attached to these targets can be seen by the fact that the SS-11 and the SS-N-6, despite their designation for regional targets, were counted as ICBMs in the Strategic Arms Limitation Agreement (SALT I) and therefore limited Soviet strategic deployment options.

Another significant observation is concern about the survivability of ICBMs emerging in 1962. The SS-6 was deployed above ground and, together with its support buildings, was extremely vulnerable. Attempts were made to provide some concealment for the SS-7/SS-8 missiles, but they were also deployed in a soft configuration, enabling comparatively rapid reload but providing little protection against an accurate nuclear attack. As US strategic power shifted in emphasis from bombers to missiles, this vulnerability became critical because of the short warning time and the absence of ballistic missile defences. The first step towards hardening was the

Table 3 *Soviet deployment of bombers with intercontinental range 1960–1972*

Year	TU-20 Bear	MYA-4 Bison	Total
1960	60	100	160
1961	70	120	190
1962	70	120	190
1963	70	120	190
1964	70	120	190
1965	80	120	200
1966	90	110	200
1967	90	110	200
1968	90	110	200
1969	90	110	200
1970	100	90	190
1971	100	40	140
1972	100	40	140

The numbers for strategic bombers were basically derived from the IISS *Military Balance*, after comparison with Berman and Baker.

deployment of ICBMs in so-called 'coffins' in 1962, with three launchers per site. Subsequently, underground silos were constructed; the silos for the SS-9 and SS-11 were hardened to withstand a pressure of 200–440 psi. By the time the fourth-generation missiles arrived, this had been improved to 4000 psi. Evidently, for non-mobile ICBMs survivability was given preference over reload capability.

The development of an anti-ballistic missile system was apparently initiated in 1957. In 1962, the SAM-5 missile, code-named *Griffon* was deployed around Leningrad. A second-generation ABM intended for deployment around Moscow, code-named *Galosh* by NATO, was shown on Red Square three weeks after the fall of Khrushchev on 7 November 1964. The Soviet Union did not develop a nationwide ABM system, but accepted a restriction to 200 launchers (later reduced to 100) in the ABM Treaty of 1972.

The Soviet Union and the arms race

The existence of an arms race between the United States and the Soviet Union appears to be an assumption which underlies most of the literature on nuclear strategy and arms control. The classic study by Lincoln P. Bloomfield et al. on Soviet strategic arms and disarmament

Table 4 *Estimated megatonnage deliverable by Soviet missiles 1960–1972*

Year	ICBM	SLBM	Total
1960	20	126	146
1961	158	126+	284+
1962	233	126+	359+
1963	281	468	749
1964	866	468	1334
1965	1010	468	1478
1966	2495.6	468	2963.6
1967	3494.2	468	3962.2
1968	4604	490.4	5094.4
1969	5570.8	557.6	6128.4
1970	6498	624.8	7122.8
1971	7528.5	692	8220.5
1972	7552.5	709	8261.5

Table 5 *Estimated throw weight of Soviet ICBMs 1960–1972*

Year	Throw weight total (in thousand pounds)
1960	32
1961	193
1962	280
1963	336.5
1964	718
1965	802
1966	1594
1967	2264
1968	3110
1969	3731
1970	4290
1970	5007
1972	5107

policy under Khrushchev is entitled *Khrushchev and the Arms Race*. Such well-known theorists as Hedley Bull, Herman Kahn, Thomas Schelling and Herbert York formulated their thinking in the framework of the arms-race paradigm.[15] The arms-race paradigm interprets strategic arms policy as an interactive process between different protagonists, in this case the Soviet Union and the United States. Although there have been academic critics of the notion of the arms race, and there are certainly different viewpoints as to its

Table 6 *USSR military budget 1960–1970*

Year	Defence budget (in billion roubles)	Defence budget (percentage of total budget)
1960	9.3	12.7
1961	11.6	15.2
1962	12.6	13.9
1963	13.9	15.9
1964	13.3	13.4
1965	12.8	12.6
1966	13.4	12.7
1967	14.5	13.2
1968	16.7	13.5
1969	17.7	13.2
1970	17.9	12.4

These figures are only given up to 1970 because official figures given in later years are not comparable, possibly due to a different method of calculation.

Table 7 *Soviet regional power 1960–1970*

Landbased missiles							
Year	SS-3	SS-4	SS-5	SS-11	SS-12	SS-14	Total
1960	48	200	0	0	0	0	248
1965	28	608	97	0	0	0	733
1970	0	508	90	290	54	29	971

Bombers			
Year	TU-4	TU-16	TU-22	Total
1960	296	1000	0	1296
1965	0	775	105	880
1970	0	550	174	724

dynamics, the arms race as a fundamental concept in the interpretation of the military East–West relationship has very strongly permeated popular thinking, as can be witnessed by newspaper articles, spy novels and films.

The existence of a fundamental political conflict between two major powers (representing two blocs) which has a significant military component, in the context of the rapid development of fundamentally new military technologies, may in itself have been sufficient to give rise to the perception of an arms-race pattern. The

Table 8 *Total military manpower of the Soviet Union 1960–1972 (in thousands)*

1960	3623
1961	3000
1962	3600
1963	3300
1964	3300
1965	3150
1966	3220
1967	3220
1968	3220
1969	3300
1970	3305
1971	3375
1972	3375

The figures for the total manpower of the Soviet Armed forces are also taken from the *Military Balance*.

attempts by the Soviet Union to break the American nuclear monopoly, the endeavour on both sides to develop intercontinental delivery vehicles for nuclear weapons and the more or less overt competition in the development of space technology all combined to strengthen this perception. It is very striking, therefore, how strongly Soviet strategic arms policy under the Khrushchev leadership departed from expectations rooted in the arms-race concept. When the *Bison* jet bomber made its first appearance at the 1954 May Day parade, this event immediately gave rise to discussions in the US intelligence community about production rates and projections of future force sizes which resulted in the postulation of a 'bomber gap'. At its root was the expectation (in the absence of more precise information) that the Soviet Union would engage in 'arms race type behaviour', i.e. that it would maximize bomber production to close the then existing gap between Soviet and US intercontinental range bomber capabilities and then surge ahead unless the United States in turn increased the number of bombers available to the Strategic Air Command. This, however, did not occur. US intelligence estimates of Soviet bomber production had to be continually revised downwards, as Lawrence Freedman has pointed out:

> The Soviet output was found to be modest. This new evidence started to be assessed in August 1956. By the spring of 1957 the

estimates of Soviet bomber production had begun to slide. By the November 1958 NIE the 1956 estimates had been cut by three-quarters; by November 1959 the projection for mid-1961 was only 19 per cent of what it had been in 1956.[16]

Indeed, by 1960 the Soviet Union had deployed only 100 *Bisons*. The period of 1957–61 is characterized by the 'missile gap', whose defining features was American uncertainty about Soviet ICBM capabilities which was intensified by exaggerated Soviet claims in the wake of successful satellite launches beginning in 1957. These claims notwithstanding the Soviets had only deployed four of their first-generation ICBM by 1960; in 1961, the first second-generation ICBM started to be deployed but, to quote Lawrence Freedman again,

> The leisurely pace at which they deployed their SS-7 and SS-8 ICBMs did not give much support to assertions that they were interested in attaining numerical parity with the US, let alone a first-strike capability.[17]

By the middle of 1964 the United States had a lead of 4:1 over the USSR with regard to ICBMs and SLBMs: 200 ICBMs and no long-range SLBMs had been deployed by the USSR.

This study will argue that Soviet strategic arms policy under Khrushchev may not fit the expectations of the arms-race paradigm and that therefore an alternative explanatory framework must be found which does not seek to interpret Soviet strategic arms policy solely in terms of the interaction with the West. Why did the Soviet Union allow the United States to develop such a substantial margin of superiority? The argument I intend to develop states that there were factors involved unrelated to the interaction with the United States, that Khrushchev pursued a conscious political choice in favour of a minimum deterrent posture, and that Soviet strategic arms policy was shaped in a political struggle between Khrushchev and his opponents over a wide range of foreign and domestic policy issues.

After the fall of Khrushchev there seems to have been a determined effort to achieve parity in strategic nuclear weapons and thus strategic arms policy after the fall of Khrushchev bears closer resemblance to the arms-race pattern.

There are considerable differences of view among scholars about what drives military policy in general and weapons acquisition in particular. The following constitutes a survey of various possible motivating factors in the formulation of strategic arms policy, which may or may not constitute an arms-race type behaviour.

Soviet strategic arms policy and foreign-policy objectives

One reason why the arms race paradigm, has found such universal acceptance consists in the patterns of political justifications in the West for defence spending and strategic force planning; they are invariably based on scenarios of the opponent's capabilities which need to be matched in some way (although in more recent debates more complex arguments based on political symbolism and perceptions have been advanced). The underlying assumption is that the arms race is driven by the Soviet Union and that the West is merely trying to keep pace. The underlying motivation lies in an expansionist Soviet foreign policy, which is driven by an ideology that sees itself in fundamental conflict with other prevailing philosophies and has as the final objective the domination of the world.[18]

This is perhaps the most extreme formulation of a spectrum of views all of which see the Soviet Union as continually seeking to gain the military and strategic advantage. At one end of the spectrum of possible threat scenarios the Soviet Union is seen as seeking a first-strike capability against the United States. Some analysts have gone as far as to suggest that the Soviet Union is preparing to initiate a strategic nuclear war against the United States.[19] At the other end it is seeking a strategically advantageous position for political and regional gains in the global power game (while avoiding direct military conflict with the United States). The strategy of containment assumed the fundamentally aggressive character of Soviet foreign policy.

It is a paradox of Soviet foreign policy during the time of Khrushchev's leadership that while on the one hand eschewing a determined build-up of Soviet strategic forces, and maintaining an emphasis in declaratory policy on détente and peaceful co-existence, the Soviet leadership under Khrushchev quite overtly attempted to exploit strategic power for the attainment of foreign-policy objectives. This was most notably the case during the Berlin crisis when from 1958 to 1961 Khrushchev put pressure on the Western allies with a series of ultimata with the apparent objective of removing any Western presence from West Berlin. The culmination of missile diplomacy was the Cuban Missile Crisis of 1962 when it was put to its ultimate test.

Thus on the surface this explanation for Soviet strategic arms policy appears to be plausible and seems to be confirmed by Soviet behaviour in disarmament and arms-control negotiations in which the Soviets showed no real preparedness to inhibit the growth of their strategic arsenal.

In terms of the models of decision-making developed by Graham T. Allison, the view just outlined would interpret Soviet strategic arms policy in the framework of the *rational-actor* paradigm which sees the government as a rational, unitary agent responding to the international situation on the basis of strategic objectives conceived within a well-articulated general set of goals.[20] As Allison describes it, according to the rational-actor paradigm:

> Soviet force posture (i.e., weapons and their deployment) constitutes a value-maximizing means of implementing Soviet strategic objectives and military doctrine.[21]

This fits in well with the image of the Soviet state as a totalitarian structure under effective central control by a leadership that allows no deviation from the prescribed path. Every action in foreign and military policy is interpreted as a tactical step designed to further the general goals based on a calculation of the correlation of forces. In its most extreme formulation this view is tautologous in nature, because it is not susceptible to empirical refutation. Since virtually any foreign-policy action by a state can be interpreted as being designed to strengthen the power of that state, and tactical retreats as well as advances are conceivable in the framework of the gradual achievement of the victory of world socialism, both overtly hostile political manoeuvres (e.g. an arms build-up) and conciliatory gestures (e.g. concessions in arms control) can be interpreted as fitting into a fundamentally offensive political strategy.[22]

A closer analysis of Soviet policymaking shows that the fundamental assumption that the rational-actor paradigm is particularly suitable to explain Soviet decision-making is not tenable. Furthermore, the interpretation of Soviet foreign-policy objectives as described above turns out to be at best partially correct. While some of the contradictions of Soviet policy may have owed their origin to Khrushchev himself, it is a serious question to what extent he was not always the master of events and was at times driven to certain policies as the result of power struggles with the military and the supporters of different economic and foreign policies. While it is true that the above characterization of Soviet policy objectives which derive from an ideologically motivated expansionism accords with the views held by *some* Soviet policymakers, the dominant objective for Khrushchev was the maintenance of the status quo in Western Europe and the pursuit of peaceful coexistence and détente.

This study will therefore investigate to what extent the contradictions between Khrushchev's foreign-policy objectives, such as they can be discerned, and his actual foreign-policy behaviour and the shifts in policy at various times can be shown to be a reflection of the power struggles within the Presidium and were also influenced by domestic-policy objectives. Furthermore, as has already become clear, the attempt to explain strategic arms policy on the basis of foreign-policy objectives fails for the simple reason that the strategic arms policy pursued did not match the foreign-policy goals assumed by this explanation. Indeed, not unlike foreign policy, strategic arms policy under Khrushchev exhibited a number of paradoxes. On the one hand, nuclear strategic forces were declared to be the main weapon of a future war, and their enormous destructive potential was used to justify cuts in conventional forces. On the other hand, Khrushchev was unwilling to make available resources to build a substantial fleet of bombers with intercontinental range or a credible ICBM force. Indeed, from a purely empirical standpoint it is questionable whether Soviet strategic arms policy under the Khrushchev leadership actually fits the arms-race paradigm as such.

The argument will be pursued in a conceptual framework which takes into account the critiques of Allison's analysis of decision-making.[23] The rational-actor model applies in so far as Khrushchev did have a discernible set of objectives in foreign and military policy which competed with that of his opponents. However, as has been explained above, there seem to be contradictions between Khrushchev's apparent security-policy objectives and his conduct of foreign policy, and between his missile diplomacy and his strategic arms policy. One explanation is that security policy at times became the instrument to pursue certain political objectives unrelated to the concerns of national security as such. The organized process paradigm plays a rôle in so far as a study of the weapons-acquisition process shows the constraints imposed on leadership decisions by a highly bureaucratic structure. The governmental (bureaucratic) politics paradigm is a partially valid description of decision-making in Soviet strategic arms policy, as the decisions made can be shown to be the results of compromises achieved between various institutional actors who were pursuing their own organizational interests.[24]

The attempts to exploit strategic power for political gains were not as apparent under Khrushchev's successors. The dominant political objective that emerged in the pursuit of strategic parity with the United States was that of political parity, i.e. the recognition of Soviet superpower status equal to that of the United States with an appropriate rôle in global affairs. This again is not necessarily compatible with the interpretation which sees the major impetus for the arms race coming from the Soviet Union if in the 1960s the Soviet participation in the arms race extended only to catching up with the United States.

The arms race as an action–reaction phenomenon

As the Soviet Union and the United States began to deploy nuclear weapons and intercontinental delivery means in the mid-Fifties, it was soon recognized by a number of people that the arms race would quickly produce a strategic stalemate, i.e. that both sides would retain an assured second-strike capability which would make any first-strike scenario prohibitive. Furthermore, it would also make the arms race an exercise in futility since there was ultimately no escape form the stalemate. The continued build-up of strategic arsenals therefore requires an explanation. To this end US Defence Secretary Robert McNamara introduced the concept of the 'action–reaction phenomenon':

> What is essential to understand here is that the Soviet Union and the United States mutually influence one another's strategic plans. Whatever their intentions or our intentions, actions – or even realistically potential actions – on either side relating to the build-up of nuclear forces necessarily trigger reactions on the other side. It is precisely this action–reaction phenomenon that fuels an arms race.[25]

The propensity of military planners to base themselves on 'worst-case scenarios', resulting in the procurement of greater forces than required, is frequently cited as considerably enhancing this dynamic. The continuous advancement in weapons technology provides additional momentum. If the 'action–reaction' process itself is a result of rational actors seeking to provide for the perceived requirements of national security, the organizational process gives it further impetus. The underlying assumption in McNamara's exposition was that the principal goal of both superpowers consisted in the preservation of a credible second-strike (i.e. assured destruction) capability. The action–reaction phenomenon, in other words, served as an explanation for the dynamics of the arms race even if neither side was seeking superiority.

Critics such as Albert Wohlstetter have pointed out that the underlying assumption about the objectives of the two sides may be false or incomplete, and that this explanation ignores a multitude of other factors affecting force planning.[26] It seems particularly inappropriate if Soviet strategic arms policy under Khrushchev did not conform to the arms-race model in the first place. Indeed, in some sense one can describe Soviet strategic arms policy under Khrushchev as an 'action–inaction' phenomenon. 'Best-case' scenarios, based on the exaggeration of Soviet capabilities and their implication for the strategic balance, were used as a justification for restricting military expenditure. Nonetheless, it is difficult to deny that some aspects of strategic arms policy were influenced by an action–reaction dynamic. The US ICBM build-up gained a great deal of momentum from the 'missile gap', even though it continued even after the 'missile gap' had been exposed as a myth. The partial reversal of Khrushchev's policies announced in January 1960 and the increases in the Soviet defence allocations in 1961 were substantially influenced by the strategic arms programme of the Kennedy Administration announced in 1961. For this reason, some analysts have taken a view that a significant shift in Soviet military policy took place and that the Soviet strategic arms build-up can be substantially traced back to this shift.[27] A closer analysis of the debates in 1961 shows, however, that the Soviet 'reaction' was more significant in the conventional sphere. Another hypothesis which has been advanced is that a major revision in the ICBM programme took place in 1963 as a result of the Cuban missile crisis in October 1962. There is evidence that for a period after the crisis Khrushchev's opponents were in a strong position and some significant decisions about third-generation ICBMs were made, but the Soviet strategic arms build-up of the 1960s was a more complex process which cannot be completely explained as a reaction to the humiliating retreat forced on Khrushchev. The classic example of the action–reaction phenomenon is, 'of course, the deployment of ballistic missile defences, the development of MIRVs and the renunciation of large-scale BMD deployment as signified in the ABM Treaty.

Domestic influences on strategic arms policy

The continued strategic arms build-up by the United States even after the 'missile gap' had been exposed as fictitious serves as a good demonstration for the theory that strategic arms policy is not governed by external threats or requirements of security, but rather by factors of domestic policy. In this model the armed services, the defence industries and the political bureaucracy constitute large and politically and economically powerful institutions, whose institutional interest demand continuing large defence expenditures. The construction of threat scenarios and technological progress are the instruments of this interaction of vested interests which result in the build-up of ever-increasing arsenals of weapons systems that become more complex and expensive. President Eisenhower coined the phrase 'military–industrial complex' to describe this phenomenon.

Desmond Ball has argued in a detailed study of the strategic missile programme of the Kennedy Administration that force-level decisions were not primarily based on analyses of Soviet capabilities or requirements for the implementation of US strategic doctrine, but rather resulted from a complex interaction of pressure from the military and political conflicts between Congress and the Administration as well as within the Administration.[28] Another instructive example of this phenomenon is American decision-making on ballistic missile defence in the late Sixties.[29]

In this model the arms race is to some extent considered to be an illusion. The driving force is not the *interaction* between protagonists, but rather the interests of domestic institutions. The interaction is important only in so far as it serves to legitimize the demands of the 'military–industrial complex'. In this respect, the persistence of external threats and a tense international climate is in the mutual interest of the military-industrial institutions in both superpowers.[30]

The concept of the 'military–industrial complex' as a loose coalition of interest groups who benefit from the continuation of the arms race is a standard part of Soviet explanations of the arms race. It fits in with the Soviet ideological perspective that capitalism is the main source of international tension. The notion of a 'military–industrial complex' in the Soviet Union, however, is not compatible with the standard view presented in the Soviet literature. If the Soviet Union itself is a 'rational actor' without a military–industrial complex then a real arms race exists in which the Soviet Union is forced to participate. Nonetheless, in the Soviet Union different interest groups also exist, and the interaction of institutions with their own vested interests is an important factor. In domestic policy, Khrushchev's priorities consisted in the restructuring of Soviet industry away from the heavy metal industries, relieving the shortage of manpower in the economy by reducing military manpower and reallocating resources of consumer goods production and agriculture. Khrushchev had very clear priorities which differed from the consensus which surrounded him and which he attempted to impose on the military. The early stages of Soviet strategic arms policy (prior to 1961) were therefore significantly influenced by the particular interests and ideas of the national leader.[31] These policies met with very considerable opposition. It is possible to determine a loose political alignment of those who supported continued investment in heavy industries, increased defence expenditures and a more aggressive foreign-policy stance, which included certain figures in the Presidium, defence industrialists and the military. A weakness of existing studies of Soviet military policy of the period consists in their underlying assumption that Khrushchev was more or less in control of policy. Indeed, the standard studies on Khrushchev's military policy do not mention his main political rival, Frol Kozlov, by name even once.[32] A principal argument of this study will be that the inconsistencies in Soviet policy can at least partially be explained by shifts in power from one faction of the Presidium to another at various times.

The controversies about the direction of Soviet industrial investment and allocations of resources to the military continued in the post-Khrushchev period. This study will argue that the 'military-defence-industrial' alignment together with their supporters in the Presidium won a partial victory, allowing the build-up of Soviet strategic forces which occurred in the latter half of the Sixties.

This study therefore argues that the hitherto standard explanations are not adequate to account for Soviet strategic arms policy in the period 1957–72. The political context in which strategic arms policy was formulated was one in which Khrushchev was attempting to redirect the priorities of the Soviet economy and society as a whole. In this he was opposed by the institutional interests affected by his policies. The perception of the international environment influenced the formulation of security policy in so far as it exercised a legitimizing function for Khrushchev or his opponents. The interaction between the priorities of the 'national leadership' and the institutional conflicts they engendered is therefore shown to be a principal determinant of strategic arms policy during the Khrushchev period.

The standard approach to the subject of this study is to analyse Soviet foreign-policy objectives and security interests in the post-war era. The military policy which is defined within the parameters of such constraints is then analysed in terms of the evolution of military doctrine and its adaptation to the nuclear age. It is shown, however, that this approach does not allow one to construct a picture that is either consistent within itself or a coherent explanation of the observable empirical evidence. A further analysis of the political process in the Soviet Union is necessary.

Chapter 2 describes the decision-making process in the Soviet Union and introduces the principal institutional actors and identifies the main sources of conflict in domestic policy. Chapter 3 deals with the formulation of foreign policy, while the evolution of Soviet military policy is analysed in Chapter 4. One interest group which plays a particularly significant rôle is the military establishment. It is therefore necessary to identify the constitutional interests arising from the various branches of the military establishment and their interaction with the political decision-making process (Chapter 5). Having established the broad outlines of Soviet strategic arms policy in the period under study and identified the main trends of policy as advocated and pursued by the principal interest groups involved in part I, a more detailed study of a number of critical decisions is undertaken in a series of case studies of the principal areas in part II: strategic bombers (Chapter 6), ICBMs (Chapter 7), strategic nuclear forces based at sea (SLBMs) (Chapter 8), ballistic missile defence (Chapter 9) and the military uses of space (Chapter 10).

The standard sources for such a study are an analysis of the empirical data (Soviet force deployments, Soviet foreign-policy behaviour), speeches, articles and books on foreign policy, speeches on military policy, Soviet military writings etc.

A thorough re-examination of the fundamental objectives of Khrushchev's policies, what he sought to achieve for the Soviet people and the political struggles his attempt to substantially alter the direction of Soviet domestic and foreign policies engendered result in a picture of Soviet strategic arms policy and its interpretation in terms of East–West relations that is in certain fundamental aspects quite different from that prevalent in the existing literature. However, this study will argue that the approach taken in this study permits the resolution of many of the questions and contradictions and provides a coherent explanation for the pattern of Soviet deployments and the force posture which emerged.

2   Decision-making in the Soviet Union

Introduction

The analysis of Soviet strategic arms policy in the 1960s and, in particular, that of the factors which led to the massive Soviet build-up during that decade in the established literature has been dominated by an approach based on the assumption that the main determinants of decision-making are the fundamental foreign-policy objectives of the Soviet Union, the international environment and the threat perceptions to which it gives rise, the technical capabilities and the economic potential of the Soviet union. These result in the particular articulation of CPSU military policy (military doctrine and strategy) which constitutes the determinative framework for strategic arms policy. Even on the basis of such restrictive assumptions an analysis of the process of decision-making in strategic arms policy, the principal institutional actors and the weapons-acquisition process is expected to yield valuable insights into the evolution of the Soviet force posture. This study will seek to go significantly further by raising the issue of to what extent institutional interests and differences about the Soviet domestic political agenda within the policymaking elite played a part. Much of the existing literature on Soviet military policy under Khrushchev assumes that domestic factors were largely irrelevant given the great degree of control over policy exercised by the party leadership and the central planning apparatus. It is true that the domestic sources of influence on security policy are quite different in the Soviet Union in comparison with Western democratic societies. The Soviet leadership did not have to take much account of public attitudes to security policy. Nevertheless it can be demonstrated that within the Soviet leadership itself there were deep divisions about the fundamental direction of economic and industrial policies which had profound implications for foreign and military policy. Furthermore, various institutions had vested interests which were in conflict with each other or with the policies of the Party leadership and thus these institutions sought to bring their influence to bear on the policy process. In this chapter, we shall describe the various institutions involved in decision-making and the weapons-acquisition process in general. This will allow us in later chapters to reconstruct these processes with respect to a number of important policy areas and key decisions in strategic arms policy.

Soviet decision-making: an analysis of the institutions

The Politburo

Policy formulation in the Soviet Union during the period under discussion was dominated by the Communist Party and in particular by its leadership in the Politburo. The Politburo (called the Presidium from 1953 to 1966) was formally elected by the 240-member Central Committee but the real power relationships were reversed since the Central Committee was largely appointed by the Politburo. The Government, headed by the Premier and the Council of Ministers, played the subordinate rôle of policy implementation. However, during the 1950s and 60s the relationship between Party leadership and Government was by no means constant. When Malenkov assumed the leadership of the Soviet Union in 1953 after Stalin's death, he resigned his post as First Secretary of the Central Committee of the CPSU (the equivalent of which was subsequently generally considered to imply the leadership position) and became Premier instead. Indeed, his policies had the general aim of strengthening the rôle of the government. Khrushchev became First Secretary, but was then considered to be only No. 5 in the hierarchy of power. When Malenkov was forced to resign in 1955 and Khrushchev assumed the leadership, Bulganin was appointed as Premier but, in the wake of the conflict with the 'anti-party' group which Bulganin allegedly supported, he was removed from this position in August 1958 and Khrushchev became the leader of both the Party and the Government.[1] His opponents, however, were critical of this concentration of power and his successors restored the principle of collective leadership with L. I. Brezhnev assuming the Party Leadership, A. N. Kosygin that of the Government and N. V. Podgornii becoming Chairman of the Presidium of the Supreme Soviet of the USSR.

While at first state administrators had equal representation with political leaders in the Politburo, the Party gradually began to assert greater control over the Government, as Brezhnev became more powerful, and instead of career specialists, more and more Party generalists tended to be appointed to the Council of Ministers.[2] Thus during the Brezhnev era we witness the apparently contradictory tendencies of increased and tightening Party control and, at the same time, a devolution of authority to government technocrats. The latter aspect may have been necessitated by the rigidity of the bureaucracy created by the centralized control of policy and the resulting dampening of innovation in a stable system governed by strict adherence to Party orthodoxy. It was also unavoidable due to the increasing complexity of society and the organization of industrial production, in particular military production.[3]

The Politburo was thus the central decision-making agency concerned with all areas of national importance. It was therefore ultimately in control of defence policy; it determined the main lines of policy, it took the major resource allocation decisions, approved budgets and was the final arbiter of any controversies that could arise. At times the Politburo became involved directly with the development and procurement decisions for particular weapons systems: Khrushchev, for example, described his various interventions on ICBM development, naval construction and nuclear aviation in his memoirs.[4] During the Strategic Arms Limitation Talks in 1974 special sessions of the Politburo (which normally met once a week) were convened to consider certain proposals. The Politburo's rôle in defence and foreign affairs was strengthened even more when in 1973 the Ministers of these departments as well as the head of the KGB were made full members.

It is clear, however, that given the central rôle of the Politburo and therefore the enormous range of areas in which it supposedly exercised its controlling and administrative function, it could only pay superficial attention to most defence issues which were resolved somewhere else in the bureaucracy and then routinely approved. Certain projects, because they were particularly important or expensive, might have been given closer attention. Controversial issues, especially if they involved questions of budgetary allocation, possibly fell into this category. During Khrushchev's time, for example, there was considerable controversy and political in-fighting with regard to resource allocation, in particular as it affected the defence industries. As we shall discuss later in more detail, the different factions made their views known in the Presidium and no doubt the controversies which raged there had very considerable effect on the development of Soviet military programmes.

The Defence Council and Main Military Council

At the end of World War II, the combined General headquarters which directed the overall strategic command (*Stavka*) was dissolved and replaced by the Higher Military Council. The precise functions of this body are not known, although it is generally believed that it combined those of the *Stavka* with the State Committee for Defence (GKO: *Gosudarstvenii Komitet Oborony*) which was responsible for the organization of economic resources for the war effort until 1945. In the late 50s, the Higher Military Council was described as

> the collective organ composed of members of the Politburo, military and political leaders of the army and fleet.[5]

In the early 60s, the Higher Military Council was apparently split into two different bodies: the Defence Council and the Main Military Council.

The Defence Council (*Sovet Oborony*) has been described as 'essentially a subcommittee of the Politburo', which may have been true in practice, but, according to the 1977 Constitution, it was a State and not a Party institution.[6] Its composition was determined by the Presidium of the Supreme Soviet. Like the Politburo Brezhnev chaired the Defence Council, which at one time included Premier Kosygin, former President Podgornii, Marshall A.A. Grechko and Party Secretary D. Ustinov. The chiefs of the General Staff and the Warsaw Pact apparently were also members.[7] The Defence Council thus contained the top political leadership of the Soviet Union, and it is probably a correct interpretation that during Brezhnev's time it was designed to ensure Brezhnev's domination of defence policy.[8]

The Defence Council concerned itself with military policy in the broadest sense, including questions of internal and external policy of the economy, ideology and diplomacy of the state. It also dealt with decisions regarding the defence industries, important weapons developments and procurement, budgetary questions and manpower levels. It provided the guidelines at the start of the planning process and prepared recommendations to the Politburo with regard to the finalized plans submitted by the defence industries and the Ministry of Defence.

Some light was thrown on the function of the Defence Council when it became apparent during the SALT I negotiations that it was the chief instrument whereby the political leadership involved itself in the process. It appears that the Defence Council resolved the final policy decisions with regard to SALT on behalf of the Politburo.[9]

Given its high-level membership the Defence Council played a key rôle with regard to military policy, including the approval of military and strategic doctrine, the overall force posture, a review of final plans, approval of procurement programmes and budgets. Even so, given the many other responsibilities of its members, there was an obvious limit to the extent of their involvement in defence matters, and thus many questions were resolved elsewhere in the bureaucracy before they reached the Defence Council. Western observers have expressed doubt that the Defence Council has the administrative resources for much independent analytical work and it seems that it was thus largely dependent on input from other parts of the bureaucracy, in particular, of course, the military.[10]

The Main Military Council was responsible for the detailed aspects of military policy as well as the command and control of the armed forces. It is thus generally assumed by Western observers that in war-time the Main Military Council would have assumed the rôle of the *Stavka* and the Defence Council that of the GKO.[11]

The Central Committee Secretariat

The administrative support for the work of the Politburo was provided by the Secretariat of the Central Committee of the Communist Party which was responsible to a great extent both for the flow of information to the Politburo as well as overseeing the implementation of policies, and was 'consequently at the central node of policy- and decision-making' according to Arthur Alexander.[12]

The Party Central Committee elected secretaries (about ten in number) who, under the leadership of the General Secretary (or First Secretary from 1952 to 1966), were responsible for the work of the various departments of the Secretariat. Under Khrushchev all the secretaries were also members of the Politburo; a general review of the rôle of the Secretariat after his fall led to a strengthening of the position of the Politburo *vis-à-vis* the Secretariat by a reduction of the latter's representation from 10 to 5.

The Secretariat had three departments that dealt with defence matters. The Main Political Administration of the Soviet Army and

Navy had a dual status as a department of the Central Committee Secretariat and as a directorate in the Ministry of Defence. It was responsible for Party political work in the armed forces. The Administrative Organs department dealt mainly with personnel matters. Finally, there was the Department of Defence Industry which was responsible for the implementation of party policies with regard to weapons development and production. It was under the supervision of the Secretary for heavy industry and defence production. This post was held by Brezhnev from 1957 to 1960. After a time of confusion of authority Dmitri F. Ustinov took up this position in the Secretariat when Brezhnev became General Secretary. In 1976 Ustinov became Minister of Defence, and, although he was not formally removed from the Secretariat, his functions were taken over by Iakov Riabov.[13]

It is not clear to what extent the Secretariat was capable of functioning as an independent decision-making agency. On the one hand it would follow the policy guidelines laid down by the Politburo and the Defence Council; on the other hand the Secretariat departments were probably to some extent allied to and dependent on the ministries which they supervised. A general similarity of view was probably generated by personnel transfers between Secretariat and ministries, and regular cooperation in drafting policy documents. Differences could arise, however, if there were differing viewpoints in the ministries, and the Secretariat would have had more of an overall perspective. On the whole, however, it seems that in general the Secretariat cooperated with and represented similar views to that of the defence-production ministries.[14]

The Ministry of Defence

The Ministry of Defence was the primary government agency responsible for the implementation of CPSU military policy. Structurally, there were three different loci of decision-making within it: the centralized activities of the ministry itself, the General Staff and the five branches of the armed services. Although technically the ministry was a government agency, it stood apart from other ministries by virtue of the fact that it was dominated by the military and thus in some sense represented a different constituency which may be argued to have formed an interest group of its own.[15] Since Leon Trotskii's removal from the post of Minister of Defence in 1925, his successors tended to have been career officers, with the important exception of Dmitri Ustinov who was a civilian. The Minister had three deputies – the Chief of the General Staff, the Chief of the Warsaw Pact and a deputy involved with administration. The protocol rank of a First Deputy Minister was also held by the Chief of the Main Political Administration.

The basic position of the Ministry of Defence in the defence industry was that of the consumer. Production of military hardware was the responsibility of other ministries which were subordinated to the Council of Ministers. From 1970 on there was an armaments directorate established in the ministry probably responsible for 'a link between force planning, and weapons procurement'[16] as well as supervision of research and development programmes in the ministry and the armed services.[17] It was first headed by General Alekseev, who had been chairman of the scientific-technical committee of the General Staff and then, after his death in 1981, by Army General V. Shabanov. While detailed planning was the task of the General Staff, the central Ministry organs provide guidance and control of these activities.

The central rôle in the weapons acquisition process was occupied by the General Staff. Its position was considerably enhanced after the fall of Khrushchev, and its importance tended to increase during the seventies when the then Chief of the General Staff Ogarkov was second in command to the Minister of Defence Ustinov,[18] whereas in the past this position was held by the Chief of the Warsaw Pact. The General Staff has been described as the 'brain of the army', responsible both for the formulation of military doctrine and the coordination of its practical application.

> The General Staff comprehensively analyzes and evaluates the developing military-political situation, determines the trends in the development of the means of waging war and the methods of their application, organizes the training of Armed Forces and ensures their high combat readiness to repel any aggression.[19]

While Khrushchev was himself very actively involved in the debate over military doctrine, since his ouster

> there has been very little evidence of overt attempts by the party leadership to establish new directions in Soviet military doctrine. Rather, what has occurred has been a ratification by the party leadership of the precepts of the new doctrine spelled out by military spokesmen in the early 1960s . . . The party leadership has been content to make very general pronouncements on what the Soviets call the 'political content' of their military doctrine: assertions about its 'defensive nature' and warnings about the destructiveness of nuclear war.[20]

It is not surprising therefore that the General Staff played an important part in the SALT negotiations.[21]

There were a number of agencies within the General Staff involved in the weapons procurement process. The main operations directorate was concerned with the formulation of military policy in general and the determination of the broad lines of future policy, force posture and weapons development. The central financial directorate dealt with the problem of reconciling military requirements with the availability of funds: technical advice on proposed weapons systems was provided by the scientific-technical committee which apparently was involved with the planning of military-related research in the Soviet Union and the Warsaw Pact countries. Arthur Alexander speculates that it may have had

> the overall responsibility for managing scientific-technical committees formed to review and follow each proposal and project throughout the R&D process.[22]

Most of the direct work of the General Staff with regard to weapons procurement took place in the armaments directorate.

The General Staff did not, in general, either propose new weapons systems or give the final approval for them. Its rôle was rather to process all requests and proposals, fitting them in with overall procurement budgets and military policy, thus serving as a locus for the resolution of inter-service rivalry with regard to resource allocation. A good example of this is the debate over the deployment of ABM systems. General Zakharov, Chief of the General Staff, was an ardent critic of ABM deployment and a strong supporter of increasing the ICBM capability of the Soviet Union. The debate was naturally also an institutional competition for the allocation of resources between the Strategic Rocket Forces and the PVO-S. It appears that the support of the Chief of the General Staff for the case of the Strategic Rocket Forces was an important factor in the decline of support for the ABM deployment.[23]

The military services themselves[24] initiated most of the requests for new or improved weapons systems, as well as providing an estimate for the number required. Each of the service commands was in charge of the weapons and equipment development within their own service, and the bureaucratic institutions in the General Staff involved with weapons procurement were to some extent mirrored by analogous institutions in each of the services. They also had direct links with the defence industry, i.e. the research institutes, the design bureaux and industrial plants, to which they submitted their requirements within the approved framework. Military representatives were sent to defence-industry installations to monitor directly the progress of weapons development and production, a form of quality control which was taken very seriously.[25]

The Council of Ministers

The Council of Ministers was at the top of the administrative structure of the Soviet government. The Council itself had more than 100 members representing all the various ministries, state committees, chairmen of the Councils of Ministers of the Union Republics etc. It was therefore the Presidium of the Council of Ministers that exercised the real responsibility for policy. It consisted of the Premier (or chairman) of the Council of Ministers together with his deputies. The Council of Ministers was responsible for the industrial aspects of the 'military–industrial complex'.

Khrushchev attempted to introduce many changes in the way in which things were being done in the Soviet Union, but none seems as radical as his assault on the Council of Ministers. In 1957 he launched a drive for decentralization. The central ministries were dissolved and their executives sent to the provinces (sovnarkhozy). The cure for the problems of the economic planning bureaucracy turned out to be much worse than the disease. The defence industries, however, were exempt from decentralization, and, although after Zhukov's fall they were formally disestablished and converted into state committees, responsible for a collegial body rather than a single minister, they remained largely intact and continued to be directly responsible to the Council of Ministers.[26]

The Military-Industrial Commission

The Military-Industrial Commission (VPK: *Voenno-promyshlenniia kommissiia*) was an agency of the Council of Ministers responsible for co-ordinating the various organizations in the military, the Party and the government involved with the procurement and production of weapons. Its chairman was deputy chairman of the Council of Ministers Leonid V. Smirnov, and it was central to the co-ordination and planning of military R&D. The defence industries submitted their proposals to the VPK, where they were to be studied for their technical feasibility, production requirements and impact on other sectors of the economy. The VPK also studied funding arrangements, production methods and time-tables. Some research institutes of the Academy of Sciences were apparently under VPK control, which shows how the VPK was involved with all aspects of military R&D everywhere in the Soviet Union, and, to some extent in the Warsaw Pact countries. The VPK would draft a document with regard to a weapons development proposal, which constituted the decision binding on all parties involved after approval by the Council of Ministers.

The defence-industrial ministries

The defence industry of the Soviet Union was controlled by (at least) nine ministries subordinate to the Council of Ministers through the VPK and supervised also by the Defence Production Department of the Central Committee Secretariat. These included:[27]

The Ministry of Defence Industry (conventional weapons)
The Ministry of Machine-Building (ammunition)
The Ministry of Medium-Machine Building (nuclear warheads)
The Ministry of General Machine Building (ballistic missiles and
    space vehicles)
The Ministries of Radio Industry and Electronics Industry
    (electronic systems, radars and computers)
The Ministry of Shipbuilding Industry (naval vessels of all kinds)
The Ministry of Aviation industry (aircraft, spare parts, some
    weapons for aircraft, airbreathing missiles)
The Ministry of the Means of Communication
    (telecommunications)

In contrast to the civilian industry, which had great difficulty in meeting its targets, the defence industry had generally a very generous allocation of resources and a surplus capacity which was used for civilian purposes when not otherwise needed. Indeed, Brezhnev claims in 1971 that

> 42 per cent of the total volume of the defence industry's production
> is for civilian purposes.[28]

Even if this statement was correct, which is difficult to verify, Brezhnev omitted to refer, as Adomeit and Agursky have pointed out,[29] to 'the other side of the coin', namely the involvement of civilian industry in production for the military. In particular the

Ministry of Motor Industry (motor vehicles, armoured vehicles etc.), the Ministry of Chemical Industry (chemical weapons and fuel), the Ministry of the Electrical Engineering Industry (electrical equipment) and the Ministry of Instrument-Building were of importance here. The production equipment for military industries also came from the civilian industrial ministries and almost all the research institutes, universities and the Academy of Sciences dealt with military programmes.

The structure of the Soviet defence industries has been identified by Mikhail Agursky, who himself at one time worked in the Soviet defence industry, as follows:[30]

1 The First Department which dealt with all matters concerning personnel and secrecy.
2 The Technical Department which was responsible for the technical policy with regard to production.
3 The Supply Department.
4 The Department of Construction.
5 The Department of Technical Training.
6 The Finance Department.
7 The Department for Scientific and Technical Information.
8 Departments concerned with coordinating the production in plants which manufacture similar products.

While mass production took place in some sections of the industry, as, for example, in the Ministry of Machine-Building, small-scale and serial production was the dominant mode in most sections of both the military and civilian industry (accounting for over 80 per cent of the gross industrial volume).[31] This applied for almost the entire ship-building, missile and aircraft production, for example.

Attached to the defence production ministry were the experimental design bureaux (OKB: *Opytno konstruktorskie biuro*). They played a key rôle in military R&D. In contrast to the civilian industry, which could choose between various design organizations, the military production plants were assigned to particular design bureaux and thus the latter occupied quite a dominant position. Agursky and Adomeit pointed out that

> in the military industry the documentation which the design bureau hands down to the plant assumes the force of law.[32]

The OKB also had their own workshops for the building of prototypes. They were run by the designer, who was usually well known for his outstanding technical expertise and achievements and who exercised a degree of autonomy within his OKB quite out of keeping with the normal mode of Soviet administration. Some of the well-known designers were aircraft designers Iakovlev and Mikoian, and missile designers Korolev, Iangel and Chelomei.

The weapons acquisitions process: a summary

Requirements for new weapons systems usually originated from the respective service organizations by means of a 'tactical-technical requirements document' produced by the armaments directorate. Sometimes, however, a requirement came from high up, in the General Staff, for example, or even the political leadership itself. Ideas and proposals for new weapons systems could also originate from the design bureaux themselves. Aircraft designer Tupolev, for example, had frequent contact with Khrushchev, explaining his new designs and ideas. Khrushchev described Tupolev as acting like

> a businessman dealing with a good customer. 'Here's my product', he was saying. 'If you want it and can afford it, I can build it for you.'[33]

Given the requirement for a new weapon, the question of budgetary and materials allocation for its development of production thus arose in a climate where competition for resources was intense. On the basis of preliminary design work a proposal was formulated, reviewed by the scientific-technical committee and eventually delivered to the minister's office. After a further review by a ministerial collegium it was submitted to the VPK where its resource requirements, its impact on the economy and other military programmes were considered before a VPK decision was formulated.

A parallel process took place in the military sector, where a proposal was first considered by the armaments directorate of a particular service, and then moved up to the General Staff. The culmination of the process was the submission to the Defence Council and the Politburo for final approval.

Arthur Alexander emphasizes that the system had a built-in tendency to conservatism. Proposals which were likely to incur disapproval or which were too controversial tended to be stopped before they went too far up.[34] Problems connected with production facilities and resource allocations were often resolved within the bureaucracy before a proposal reached the leadership. The result of the attitudes engendered by the need to travel smoothly through the bureaucracy was an emphasis on using designs similar to those that were approved in the past, improving on weapons that have been established in manufacture and use, rather than introducing revolutionary new ideas.

Another interesting feature was the competition between various design bureaux. Before a production decision was taken, prototypes produced by various design bureaux were tested and several options of fulfilling a certain mission requirement could be available.

This feature was particularly evident in ICBM developments, which also show that certain design bureaux seemed to specialize in particular technologies. The Iangel bureau specialized in large boosters, used in missiles with large throw weight such as the SS-9 and SS-18. The Nadiradize design group specialized in solid-fuel technology and a third design group produced lighter missiles like the SS-11. Aircraft design bureaux showed similar patterns of specialization; the Mikoian design bureau, for example produced aircraft whose performance characteristics always emphasized altitude and high speed.

The decision to develop a weapon and make funds available for its design and the construction of a prototype was frequently distinct from that to produce and deploy it. The latter was often taken after the testing of several competing prototypes, based on the information with regard to the performance and costs derived from these experiments. A number of ICBMs for example, were developed and tested but either never deployed or only deployed in very small numbers, presumably due to a disappointing performance of the prototype and various technical difficulties.

It is important to emphasize that not only technical considerations were involved, however. The political agencies involved in the decision-making process were the ones who ultimately held the purse strings and had to adjudicate between competing claims for scarce resources coming not only from various parts of the military establishment, but also from the civilian sector. In reconstructing particular decisions to produce and deploy certain weapons systems the bureaucratic organization of the weapons-acquisitions process is therefore only one aspect. Internal politics and personalities will be important, as they were particularly in Khrushchev's time, when other priorities (e.g. agriculture, consumer goods production) became major goals of an influential political faction. The international environment and threat perceptions will play a rôle, since a situation of external tension tended to strengthen the hand of those seeking to increase the level of military expenditure. The analysis of the bureaucratic structures thus provides the setting in which the interaction of these various factors and the institutional actors may be studied.

3   Strategic nuclear power and foreign-policy objectives

The objectives of foreign policy

The early post-war Western literature on Soviet foreign policy is characterized by a remarkable degree of consensus on the objectives of Soviet foreign policy. Daniel Yergin describes it as

> an image of the Soviet Union as a world revolutionary state, denying the possibilities of coexistence, committed to unrelenting ideological warfare, powered by a messianic drive for world mastery.[1]

Not all specialists in Soviet foreign policy would have expressed it in those terms. For example, while many experts may have surmised that the policy of 'coexistence' was merely a ruse, it was nonetheless an element of declaratory Soviet policy which was progressively filled with greater substance. However, although there was already developing a diversity in the interpretation of Soviet foreign-policy objectives, there was a large consensus that the Soviet Union was fundamentally expansionist and that therefore Soviet military power represented a deep threat to the West. Another remarkable feature of the literature at the time is the relatively unsophisticated approach to the process of Soviet foreign policymaking. A pervasive assumption of much of the writing of the period seems to be that the Party Leader, Khrushchev, was in complete control of foreign policy. Thus there was little appreciation of the domestic sources of foreign policy; it was largely interpreted as being entirely defined by external factors and objectives.

The revisionist literature on the Cold War, the beginning of which can be dated to the publication of Gar Alperovitz's study on *Atomic Diplomacy* in the mid-Sixties, developed an entirely different framework for the interpretation of Soviet foreign policy.[2] It has been described by Daniel Yergin as one which

downplayed the role of ideology and the foreign-policy consequences of authoritarian domestic pratices, and instead saw the
Soviet Union behaving like a traditional Great Power within the
international system, rather than trying to overthrow it.[3]

There is now a large literature on Cold War history from what are
called the 'traditional' and 'revisionist' perspectives (and attempts at
finding a synthesis). Most of the 'traditionalist'/'revisionist' debate
concerns itself with the period prior to Stalin's death and is therefore
outside the scope of this study. Nonetheless, one of the central
underlying issues, i.e. the influence of Soviet ideology on the
objectives and conduct of Soviet foreign policy, is of crucial importance also in the post-Stalin era.

The ideological basis of the view of the Soviet Union as a world
revolutionary force is the Marxist–Leninist vision of a world Communist society which involves the abolition of the nation state and a
classless society without political hierarchies and, naturally, without
war. The Leninist understanding that because of the different stages
of development in the capitalist countries socialism will not win in
all of them at once, but, in fact, only in one or a few at first, however,
implies that there will of necessity be a period of coexistence
between socialist and capitalist states. The issue of the nature of such
coexistence is central to the question of the Soviet attitude to military
force as an instrument of policy towards other states and the
non-socialist states in particular.

Although the dominant scenario for the victory of socialism in the
capitalist countries was that of domestic revolutions, in the Leninist
view the socialist countries would support such revolutions, if need
be by means of forceful intervention. The first practical example of
such an endeavour was the Soviet–Polish war of 1920, which began
as a defensive war; after the Polish defeat in the Ukraine, Lenin,
against Trotskii's advice, decided to move into Poland with the
intention of bringing about a revolution in Warsaw and even Berlin.
The war failed in these objectives and Lenin was forced to retreat.
This experience led Lenin to the view that Soviet troops should never
again be used directly to support a revolution in another country.[4]

Nonetheless, it is clear that Lenin considered wars between
socialist and capitalist states at least possible. Here Lenin introduced
the doctrine of the 'just war' which is quite different from what is
known as the 'Just War Tradition'. To decide whether a war is 'just'
or 'unjust', the issue of who is the aggressor is quite irrelevant.
Rather, it depends on the class interests of the parties; a war which

furthers the interests of socialism is just, while a war which furthers the interests of imperialism is by definition unjust.[5]

There is some dispute in the Western literature as to whether there was a a Leninist doctrine of the 'inevitability of war'.[6] It seems quite clear that Lenin taught the inevitability of war between capitalist states.[7] Capitalism develops unevenly, resulting in the upsetting of the economic balance as one capitalist country develops more than another; the restoration of the balance is impossible without crises, conflicts and war. Pechorkin, writing in 1960, analysed the Leninist doctrine of the inevitability of war in the following terms:

1 World wars are inevitable if the whole world is capitalist.
2 Wars between capitalist countries are inevitable even if there exist one or several socialist countries alongside the capitalist system if the socialist countries are still economically weak. In such a situation there remains the real possibility and even probability that the socialist countries will be drawn into war and that such wars become world wars.
3 Wars become impossible after capitalism has completely and finally disappeared from the world stage.[8]

From 1916 onwards we find more explicit statements about the inevitability of conflict between capitalism and socialism. One of the best-known statements was made by Lenin to the 8th Party Congress in 1919:

> We are living not only in a state but in a system of states, and the existence of the Soviet republic side by side with imperialist states for a prolonged period is unthinkable. At the end, either one or the other will win. And before this happens a series of the most frightful collisions between the Soviet republic and bourgeois states is inevitable.[9]

Later Soviet commentary has played this passage down, claiming that it referred to the context of civil war and the Allied intervention where such clashes appeared quite likely, while at the same time denying that it referred to war between socialist and capitalist states.[10] Nevertheless the notion of a violent confrontation with capitalist states culminating in the ultimate destruction of capitalism and the establishment of world socialism appears to be inherent in Lenin's thinking. It was frequently reasserted by Stalin, who stated quite explicitly in 1952:

> The fate of the world will ultimately be decided by the outcome of inevitable conflict between the two worlds.[11]

Much of Soviet literature (including some of Lenin's writings) does not appear to make a fine distinction between the 'inevitability of war' between capitalist countries and that involving the Soviet Union, or even between inter-state wars and other kinds of violent conflict (such as civil wars). Certainly the emphasis on the 'war-like' nature of capitalism seems to imply that ultimately the Soviet Union would become involved; the notion that the Soviet Union had the means to prevent the capitalists from unleashing war against it did not appear in the Soviet literature until the Sixties. *Izvestiia* in 1929 quoted Lenin as referring to

> the inevitable attack against the Soviet state on the part of the capitalist encirclement.[12]

If the advent of nuclear weapons and their potentially catastrophic effects on all belligerents were to have any effect on Soviet thinking about war, one would expect some moderation with respect to the doctrine of the 'inevitability of war' between Capitalism and Socialism. In 1951, the international legal theorist E. A. Korovin stated in what Margot Light has judged 'a zealously pro-Stalin book':

> Now, when capitalism has ceased to be the only all-embracing world economic system, when the camp of socialism is becoming more and more united and powerful, war engendered by capitalism has ceased to be a fatal, inevitable phenomenon. War can and must be avoided now.[13]

The debate after Stalin's death about the 'inevitability of war', could not possibly have such political significance as it did if it only referred to intra-capitalist war which would not involve the Soviet Union. A challenge to the orthodox view came in an article by M. Gus in a Leningrad journal *Zvezda* in November 1953. After expounding the Leninist doctrine of the uneven development of capitalism and the resulting inevitability of war, he went on to say:

> Experience has shown and proved that we are in a position to prevent war, and to paralyse the action of this law.[14]

Again one can draw at least the inference that the kind of war which according to Gus could now be prevented would also involve the Soviet Union since the article refers to 'world wars'.

Gus's denial of the doctrine of the 'inevitability of war' was immediately attacked by the then chief of the Agitation and Propaganda Section of the Central Committee of the CPSU, V. Kruzhkov.[15] An article in *Krasnaia Zvezda* by Colonel G. Federov in January stated categorically:

> In this connection it must never be forgotten that as long as capitalism exists wars are absolutely inevitable. Only with the destruction of the last system of exploitation – capitalism – will wars become impossible.[16]

A direct refutation of Gus by V. Tereshkin was published in the same journal, while *Voennaia Mysl'* also published an article reaffirming the inevitability of war.[17]

It is clear that this question had become a political issue which must be seen in connection with Malenkov's attempts to reduce international tension, downplay the likelihood of war and emphasize the dangers of atomic war. It thus became part of the policy debates which accompanied the struggle for the post-Stalin leadership. The general arguments deployed by Malenkov's supporters in this debate were that the destructiveness of atomic weapons and the existence of long-range means of delivery meant that no country was invulnerable to attack. Mikoian, for example, spelt out in no uncertain terms that this was a reference to the continental United States.[18] A war fought with such destructive weapons, however, threatened not just capitalists, but the entire world, with a holocaust. Therefore

> Atomic and hydrogen weapons in the hands of the Soviet Union are a means for checking the aggressors and for waging peace.[19]

There was considerable opposition to Mikoian's and Malenkov's views which became particularly apparent in March 1954. Kaganovich stated that the collapse of colonialism should drive the imperialists towards war. Khrushchev, in a similar vein, declared that the reactionary forces of capitalism were preparing a new war in order to overcome their difficulties; Molotov and Bulganin also emphasized the aggressiveness of the capitalist states. H. S. Dinerstein has shown that the war of words between the Malenkov faction and its opponents imposed restraint on both. Thus Malenkov and his supporters were unable to repeat their earlier assertions that an atomic war would result in the destruction of the whole of civilization (i.e. including the Soviet Union) and only spoke of the destruction of capitalism as the result of war. Their opponents on the other hand were restrained from directly attacking the thesis that there was a state of mutual deterrence which could even in the long term restrain the United States from attacking the Soviet Union. Dinerstein shows that only as Malenkov was about to be demoted in 1955, did direct attacks on these views appear in the Soviet press.[20]

After the fall of Malenkov in 1955, the tone of the statements by

Khrushchev and Bulganin changed. For example, Bulganin described 'mutual destruction' as the only alternative to 'coexistence'. The principle of the 'inevitability of war' was finally rejected by the 20th Congress of the CPSU in 1956. To appreciate the significance of this move, we must introduce another concept, that of 'peaceful coexistence'.

As we have pointed out above, the Leninist view of the uneven development of monopoly capitalism implied that there would be a period of time in which socialism and capitalism coexisted in the world. Lenin saw an emphasis on 'peaceful coexistence' as a means of reassuring the capitalist countries of the essentially peaceable nature of Russia in order to obtain a *peredyshka* (breathing-space) to enable the economic reconstruction of Soviet Russia after the revolution.[21] The notion of 'peaceful coexistence' was used by Stalin to describe a temporary state of unspecified duration whch was necessary given the balance of forces in the world and could last for a long period of time, but was not as such considered to be a goal of Soviet foreign policy. Interestingly, Stalin always put inverted commas around the expression *mirnoe sozhitel'stvo*. Even later Soviet interpretation described Stalin's view of 'peaceful coexistence' as a 'truce between inevitable wars'.[22] It legitimized the establishment of diplomatic relations with capitalist countries and must be seen in connection with the principle of 'socialism in one country' enunciated by Stalin shortly after Lenin's death in 1924, according to which the victory of socialism in just one country is possible even if other capitalist states at a higher level of development remain in existence. This thesis, which was publicly adopted at the 14th Party Congress, marks the beginning of the emphasis on according priority to the development of socialism in the Soviet Union and her interests in general, rather than the world revolutionary movement, on the grounds that the Soviet Union provides the basis for world revolution.

The 20th Party Congress at which the campaign of destalinization was initiated adopted fundamental revisions of the Soviet doctrine of world revolution, the inevitability of war and peaceful coexistence. It was categorically declared that war was not inevitable. The (allegedly) Leninist principle of peaceful coexistence was declared to be the general guiding principle of Soviet foreign policy.

Although the principle of peaceful coexistence had by no means acquired the status of an eternal principle, and did not imply a renunciation of the general goal of world revolution, it did amount to a recognition that Soviet foreign policy would be predicated on avoiding war with the West for a long time to come. It did not eliminate the class struggle, nor did it amount to a renunciation of the ideological struggle with the West; on the contrary it implied a strengthening of the ideological struggle and the opposition to capitalism. It did however clearly mean that war with imperialist states could not serve as a means to promote world revolution and the ideological struggle with imperialism. The principle of 'peaceful coexistence' was strengthened at the 21st Party Congress in 1959 when it was stated that the victory of socialism in the Soviet Union was 'final' without the end of capitalism and that now the real possibility existed to eliminate the threat of world war. Instead of a military competition or arms race, Khrushchev advocated an economic competition between socialist and capitalist countries, confident that this would prove the superiority of socialism.[23]

Pechorkin's article on the issue of the inevitability of war reveals that the Khrushchev leadership felt obliged to justify its apparent revision of Leninist doctrine. When outlining the various stages of the relationship between socialism and capitalism in the world (as described above), Pechorkin is attempting to establish that Lenin said nothing about the intermediate stage when capitalism still exists but there are a number of socialist countries which are quite powerful. This leaves open the possibility that the 'inevitability of war', which apparently still is given when a number of relatively weak socialist states have come into existence, no longer prevails when the socialist camp has become strong enough. In other words, the fact that the Soviet Union has now become a very powerful socialist state makes the avoidance of war possible. Pechorkin also discusses Khrushchev's admonition to his critics that we now live in a time where Marx, Engels and Lenin are no longer among us and we just interpret their words creatively, with proper evaluation of the concrete historical situation of the present time. This is evidently a rebuttal of critics of Khrushchev's revision of the thesis of the 'inevitability of war' which gives an indication of the extent of the revision and the existence of opposition in the Soviet Union to it.[24] A central reason for this revision was pointed out by Beliakov and Burlatskii in *Kommunist*:

> A world war with the employment of thermonuclear weapons would make no distinctions between front and rear. It would lead to the complete destruction of the main centres of civilisation and the wiping out of whole nations, and would bring immeasurable

disaster to the whole of humanity. Only madmen could wish for such a catastrophe . . . It is obvious, therefore, that modern nuclear war of itself could in no way be a factor which would hasten revolution or bring nearer the victory of socialism. On the contrary, it would throw back humanity, the world revolutionary workers' movement and the cause of building socialism and Communism for many dozens of years.[25]

At the 22nd Party Congress in October 1961 it was confirmed that peaceful coexistence was not the general line of Soviet foreign policy, the thesis that war was no longer inevitable was strengthened to state that war was not even desirable or permissible to advance the movement towards world socialism and that the peaceful transition from Capitalism to Communism was possible and to be preferred to armed revolution. It was also asserted that Communism could be built in the Soviet Union while there were still capitalist states in the world.

According to Pechorkin's analysis, the crucial difference between the time of Lenin and Stalin, when the Soviet Union was still relatively weak and war was still inevitable, lies not merely in the growth of the economic and military power of the Soviet Union and its achievements in science and technology, although these are also important factors, but also in the formation of a socialist camp which involves a number of socialist states. In other words, the existence of socialism in one country was not sufficient to neutralize the threat from imperialism in order to avert the inevitability of war.

The relations between socialist states were governed by different principles given the Marxist-Leninist belief that socialist states share class interests and that therefore the conflicts of interest inherent in relations between capitalist and socialist states do not arise. Relations between socialist states were governed by the principle of 'socialist internationalism'. They were characterized not by 'peaceful coexistence', but by 'friendship' and 'fraternal aid'. The use of force in the Hungarian crisis in the aftermath of the 20th Party Congress was justified on the basis of 'fraternal aid' even though officially there is respect for the principle of non-interference in the internal affairs even of socialist 'brother states'. The Brezhnev doctrine and the concept of 'limited sovereignty' were not formulated until the Czech crisis of 1968.[26]

The concept of 'peaceful coexistence' also did not imply that the transition from capitalism to socialism in individual countries would necessarily take place without violence, or that the Soviet Union would not support violent revolution.[27] Furthermore the Soviet

Union was still pledged to the support of wars of national liberation. In summary, Soviet thought distinguishes four types of war: nuclear world war, local war, civil war in the advanced capitalist states and national liberation wars involving underdeveloped countries. The first two categories of war are, according to the principles of 'peaceful coexistence', avoidable and to be avoided, i.e. not suitable as instruments of promoting the transition from capitalism to socialism. The latter types, while less preferable than a peaceful transition to socialism, are not necessarily avoidable and are legitimate instruments of world revolution.[28]

Nuclear war as an instrument of policy

What implications do these doctrinal developments have for the use of strategic nuclear weapons as instruments of policy and/or war?

The first point is that strategic nuclear weapons cannot be used directly, as instruments of pressure or warfare, to promote world revolution. Herein lies the essence of one of the central disagreements between the Soviet Union and the People's Republic of China. The Chinese leadership did not entirely condemn the principle of 'peaceful coexistence', but rather advocated a somewhat more restricted form. It rejected the notion, however, that 'peaceful coexistence' should be the general line of the foreign policy of socialist states. It also rejected the substitution of a military competition with an economic competition. From the Chinese perspective the armed struggle was still the central means of promoting the world revolution: Mao's dictum that 'power comes from the barrel of the gun' was seen as still applicable in the nuclear age. As a result, the Chinese also had a different view on the principle of the inevitability of war. In the Chinese perspective, the only form of war which could and should be avoided was a world war. All other types of war were still to be considered inevitable and legitimate means to bring about the revolution.

Of particular significance is the fact that the Chinese urged the Soviet Union to use its strategic nuclear force as an instrument to advance socialism in the world. In the late Fifties/early Sixties, as the Soviet leadership was claiming superiority in strategic nuclear weapons, the Chinese leadership wanted them to translate this superiority into political gains. As we shall discuss in more detail, there was a sustained effort during the late Fifties and early Sixties by the Soviet leadership to do precisely that, but in a considerably more restrained fashion and with far more modest goals than advocated by the Chinese. The question remains, however, to what extent the doctrinal changes with regard to the legitimacy of war as a political instrument informed the actual policies of the leadership, in particular given Khrushchev's sometimes aggressive foreign policy, such as manifested in the ups and downs of the Berlin Crisis in 1958–62. This issue shall be examined in more detail later.

The use of strategic nuclear weapons is legitimate then first of all for the defence of the national territory of the Soviet Union. In all the Soviet political and military literature this is constantly given as the main reason and justification for the arsenal of Soviet strategic nuclear arms and Soviet military power in general. On a more general level, Soviet strategic nuclear forces are the central element of a military power which serves the prevention of nuclear war.

Nuclear weapons also served to defend the socialist system as such and thus the integrity of the socialist camp or, as it would have been put in the West, Soviet domination over Eastern Europe. This was the first element of extended deterrence in Soviet thought.

The second thought of extended deterrence related to wars of national liberation. Soviet military power prevented the imperialists from fully employing their military power and thus helped to cut off 'the imperialist export of counterrevolution'.[29]

Interconnected with all these objectives was the standing of the Soviet Union in world politics. Its military power meant that there was no important problem in international politics that could be resolved without Soviet participation – at least such is the image of itself which the Soviet leadership sought to promote.

The Soviet image of war and the rôle of war as an instrument of policy has, like Soviet policy in general, its roots in and derives its justifications from Marxist-Leninist ideology. As the Sokolovskii authors point out:

> War, teaches Marxism-Leninism, is a socio-historical phenomenon arising at a definite stage in the development of class society.[30]

Lenin also adopted the principle of Clausewitz:

> As applied to wars the main thesis of dialectics . . . consists of the fact that *'war is simply a continuation of politics by other* (namely violent) *means'* . . . And it was always the point of view of Marx and Engels that *every* war was a continuation of the politics of the given interested powers – *and of the various classes* within them – at a given time.[31]

The question which poses itself in the nuclear era is whether the destructiveness of nuclear weapons is such that war can no longer serve as the instrument of politics. Adherence to the Leninist view of the Clausewitz dictum was eroded by Malenkov's thesis of the mutual destructiveness of nuclear war in 1954 and subsequently by the revision of the doctrine of the inevitability of war outlined above. Nonetheless, Soviet military writings during the Sixties restated the validity of the Clausewitz dictum. Thus we find in Sokolovskii:

> It is well known that the essence of war as a continuation of politics does not change with changing technology and armament.[32]

This concept is elaborated at great length in the chapter on the 'Nature of Modern War'. One military expert who at various times threw doubt on the continued validity of the Clausewitz dictum in the nuclear age was Nikolai Talenskii in articles published in 1960, 1964 and, most explicitly, in 1965:

> In our days there is no more dangerous illusion than the idea that thermonuclear war can still serve as an instrument of politics, that it is possible to achieve political aims by using nuclear weapons and at the same time survive, that it is possible to find acceptable forms of nuclear war.[33]

This assertion was strongly contradicted in an article by E. Rybkin from the MPA published in *Kommunist Vooruzhennykh Sil*. Rybkin strongly reaffirmed the validity of the concept of war as the continuation of politics. Other articles in the military press have supported this view.[34] Some Western analysts have drawn the conclusion that the Soviets believe that nuclear war can serve as a practical instrument of policy.[35] The most extreme formulation of this view has been stated by Richard Pipes:

> As long as the Russians persist in adhering to the Clausewitzian maxim on the function of war, mutual deterrence does not really exist.[36]

A close reading of Rybkin's article shows that this is a misunderstanding. While it is stated clearly that if war should break out, it would be a consequence and a continuation of a political struggle, at the same time Rybkin acknowledges that nuclear weapons have changed the relationship between war and politics. Thus Rybkin states:

> War is always the continuation of politics, but it cannot always serve as its weapon.[37]

The controversy about whether the Soviets consider nuclear war as a practical tool of politics has obscured the real meaning of the debate between Talenskii and Rybkin. Talenskii denied the possibility of victory in thermonuclear war and advocated an understanding of 'mutual assured destruction', whereas the majority of military writers, including Rybkin, defended nuclear warfighting and the possibility of victory in a nuclear war. Nonetheless, Rybkin shows awareness of the destructiveness of nuclear weapons, and this cannot be taken to imply the advocacy of a military force structure designed for the initiation of nuclear war for political purposes. This is confirmed in the 1972 edition of *Marxism-Leninism on War and the Army*:

> Western sociologists and authors on military subjects confuse two closely interconnected yet different questions, namely, the theoretical question of the essence (content and character) of nuclear war and the practical question of whether it can serve as an effective instrument of policy-making.[38]

Strategic weapons and foreign policy

In this section, we shall endeavour to establish two general propositions: (1) that the Soviet leadership under Khrushchev attempted to exploit strategic power for the attainment of foreign-policy objectives; (2) that, in view of the Soviet inferiority in strategic arms, the Soviet leadership allowed a false and exaggerated image of Soviet strategic power to arise.

The first attempt by the Soviet leadership to use nuclear weapons to political advantage occurred during the Suez crisis in November 1956. The Soviets declared that

> We are fully determined to crush the aggressors and restore peace in the Middle East through the use of force.[39]

What amounted to a demand for British–French withdrawal was accompanied by the 'rattling of rockets'. At the same time the Soviet Union attempted to enlist the United States in a co-operative effort, as the states in possession of powerful armies and navies as well as nuclear weapons, to deal with the crisis. The United States rejected the Soviet proposal for joint US-Soviet intervention and let it be known that any missile attack on Britain or France would meet with US retaliation.

The effect of the Soviet action is not entirely clear, but it is generally agreed that American pressure was the predominant factor in bringing the Suez intervention to an end. The Soviet threat was never put to the test, but the general failure of Soviet diplomatic efforts during the entire affair and the swift American reaction to the missile threat support the interpretation that the Soviets were unlikely to engage in military action against Britain and France. As Malcolm Mackintosh has observed:

> The Soviet Union's behaviour during the Middle Eastern crisis of 1956 provided no evidence that she would go to the help of a non-Communist ally with no common frontier with the Soviet Union, even if that ally was attacked while in receipt of Soviet arms.[40]

In October 1957 the Soviet Union claimed that Turkey was planning a military attack on Syria and threatened unspecified countermeasures. Although there was internal unrest in Syria such an attack was evidently never planned in the first place. A similar situation arose in 1958 in Iraq when there was a military coup, and Lebanon and Jordan asked for and received direct military aid (including marines and troops) from the USA and Britain. The Soviet Union threatened vague countermeasures against any intervention in Iraq, which again had not been planned. In the same year Khrushchev announced support for Chinese attacks on the islands of Quemoy and Matsu, and said that any attack on China would mean war with the USSR. His support did not, however, translate into tangible assistance, and he left it suitably unclear what would constitute an attack on China. The Chinese failed in their objectives.

One of the most notable foreign-policy ventures was the Berlin Crisis that began in 1958. From 1958 to 1961 Khrushchev put pressure on the Western allies with a series of ultimata with the apparent objective of removing any Western presence from West Berlin. Although the Soviet Union had a clear local military superiority, and for some time there was a degree of uncertainty with regard to the global strategic balance, the Western allies refused to yield and despite various threats Khrushchev was never prepared to risk an actual military confrontation.

Before discussing at greater length the objectives of Khrushchev's missile diplomacy, let us describe the general features of its conduct.

The period of 1957–61 is characterized by the 'missile gap', whose defining features were American uncertainty about Soviet ICBM capabilities which was intensified by exaggerated Soviet claims. The 'missile gap' was preceded by the 'bomber gap'. The

Bison jet bomber made its first appearance at the 1954 May Day parade, immediately giving rise to discussions in the US intelligence community about production rates and projections of future force sizes. Fears about a growing Soviet strategic bomber capability were enhanced by a display on Aviation Day in Moscow on 13 July 1955, when the same group of nine to ten planes passed the reviewing stand three times, giving the impression of 29 operational planes.[41] The difference between the 'bomber gap' and the later 'missile gap' was, however, that the Soviets did not encourage inflated Western estimates of their bomber strength – quite the reverse. During General Twining's visit to the Soviet Union in 1956 Defence Minister Marshal Zhukov explained to him that their estimate of the number of Soviet bombers was inflated; it is clear that the thrust of Soviet efforts during the Twining visit was directed at undermining the impression which had arisen during Aviation Day in 1955. Although this was greeted with considerable scepticism by American experts, nonetheless there was no discernible effort to make political gains out of Soviet bomber capabilities.

The first successful test of a Soviet ICBM was announced on 26 August 1957. On 4 October 1957, the USSR surprised the world by the launch of Sputnik I, thus demonstrating that it possessed the technology to develop ICBMs. The link between space achievements and strategic missile technology was immediately made by Khrushchev when he declared:

> We now have all the rockets we need: long-range rockets, intermediate-range rockets and short-range rockets.[42]

In November 1957, after the launch of Sputnik II, Khrushchev made a statement which amounted to a claim of having a stockpile of up to 20 ICBMs.[43] These statements were clearly directed at a Western audience and were designed to convey the impression of a shift in the balance of power by suggesting that this spectacular technological breakthrough, the development of the intercontinental rocket, rendered bombers obsolescent and thus negated American strategic superiority. The American response was conditioned by uncertainty about the real state of Soviet ICBM capability. Thus no attempt was made to refute Soviet claims in this regard; official statements concentrated on emphasizing that overall US military capabilities, supported by the power of the Strategic Air Command, were still far superior to the Soviet Union. As a precautionary measure, SAC was raised to higher levels of alertness.

In the period from November 1958 to October 1959 a number of public statements were made, designed, it seems, to create the impression that the Soviet Union was rapidly proceeding with the production of ICBMs. Thus, for example, in his speech to the 21st Party Congress in February 1959 Khrushchev declared:

> When we say that we have organized the serial production of intercontinental ballistic missiles, it is not just to hear ourselves talk.[44]

Military leaders, such as Defence Minister Malinovskii, K. S. Moskalenko and V. I. Chuikov emphasized that the armed forces had been equipped with intercontinental missiles. The Soviet leadership was careful not to cite any precise numbers, but rather contented itself with claiming rough equality with Western strategic capabilities and disparaging any Western claims to superiority.

Khrushchev's statements became more far-reaching in their implications by the end of 1959. In November 1959 he stated:

> We have now stockpiled so many rockets, so many atomic and hydrogen warheads, that, if we were attacked, we would wipe from the face of the earth all of our probable opponents.[45]

Some of Khrushchev's statements appear to indicate a belief in the nuclear rocket as a 'country busting' wonder weapon. Thus in May 1959 he expressed the conviction that West Germany could be 'put out of commission' by exploding eight warheads with yields between three and five megatons over its territory.

In order to increase Western uncertainty over the number of Soviet ICBMs deployed, Khrushchev and Malinovskii claimed that it was possible to camouflage and completely conceal rocket launchers. Nevertheless, the data gathered from the overflight of the Soviet Union by U-2 spyplanes, although never complete enough to be conclusive, began to convince a large section of the US intelligence community that the reason why the U-2s never came back with pictures of Soviet ICBMs was because there were none to be photographed.[46] The SS-6 was large and unwieldy and hard to conceal, despite Khrushchev's and Malinovskii's statements. Before the debate within the US intelligence community on this issue could be resolved, however, the shooting down of a U-2 by Soviet air defence in May 1960 put an end to the flights.

This event made the U-2 overflights public and thus raised in the minds of Soviet policymakers the possibility that the game might now be up; although the Soviet Union did not admit to its lack of rocket facilities, public pronouncements now tended to stress, instead of Soviet capabilities, the mutually disastrous consequences of war. Horelick and Rush comment:

> The retreat in Soviet strategic claims that was evident after the U-2 incident continued and became even more pronounced in the winter of 1961.[47]

The main elements of Horelick and Rush's interpretation of Khrushchev's missile diplomacy can be summarized as follows:

1 The Soviet leadership embarked on a deliberate policy of deception, making exaggerated claims directed at a Western audience about their deployment of first generation ICBMs.
2 The purpose of these claims was to reap the political benefits of a substantial deployment of ICBMs even though they had decided not to deploy the SS-6 in large numbers, namely to deter an attack by the United States, to support the claim of the Soviet Union to be one of the two major world powers and to allow the Soviet Union to put pressure on the Western powers in the settlement of certain political issues favourable to Soviet interests, notably with regard to Berlin, Cuba and Southeast Asia.
3 There were certain dangers inherent in this policy of strategic bluff: it presupposed that the bluff would never be called. While the West could discover the truth about Soviet capabilities (and did), the USSR could not easily risk finding out how far the West could be pushed. The policy proved to be unsuccessful since the West, albeit uncertain about Soviet strategic force capabilities, was willing to accept high risks to resist even apparently minor concessions (particularly with regard to Berlin).
4 In the aftermath of the U-2 affair Soviet claims with regard to their strategic capabilities began to exhibit greater restraint as public statements in the US began to indicate a growing confidence that there was no Soviet strategic missile superiority after all. The myth of the missile gap finally collapsed after September 1961 when Joseph Alsop, until then a strong critic of 'understated' estimates of Soviet missile strength, published an article confirming that the USSR was now believed to have no more than a handful of ICBMs and Deputy Defence Secretary Roswell Gilpatric affirmed in October 1961 in a series of speeches the wide margin of superiority of the US strategic forces.

The Horelick and Rush interpretation does not, however, account for all aspects of Soviet missile diplomacy. In order to interpret Soviet statements in the proper context, one needs to take note of the fact that during the period under consideration in this study, it was common practice by Soviet political and especially military writers to claim Soviet superiority against the West, even when such superiority obviously was non-existent and also in classified military writings which were clearly not intended for a Western audience. Whereas their Western counterparts are more prone to emphasize Western vulnerabilities and Soviet advantages in order to justify new weapons programmes, the admission of such weakness appears to have been politically impossible in the Soviet system. The Horelick and Rush interpretation, according to which Soviet strategic claims declined as the 'missile gap' was losing credibility, does not entirely fit the facts. Even Horelick and Rush themselves find that in March 1961, when according to their scheme Soviet missile claims were 'retreating to parity', Khrushchev made a statement which echoed his previous bold claims:

> The Soviet Union has the world's most powerful rocketry and has produced the quantity of atomic and hydrogen bombs necessary to wipe the aggressors from the face of the earth.[48]

It is true, of course, as Horelick and Rush assert, that Soviet leaders were always careful not to make claims which were so well defined and so obviously false that they could be directly refuted. There were also shifts in the nature of Soviet strategic superiority claims. The launch of Sputnik obviously suggested claims of technological superiority while, at a later stage, when the uncertainty about Soviet ICBM deployments still persisted, there were claims of quantitative superiority. After the decline of the 'missile gap' nuclear tests involving warheads of very large megatonnage were used as evidence of Soviet military strength, while there was a renewed emphasis on the political strengths of the socialist system as the source of superiority over capitalism. Nonetheless, bold (and knowingly false) statements about Soviet missile capabilities continued, as for example in Defence Minister Malinovskii's speech at the 22nd Party Congress in October 1961.[49] Indeed, a more recent study[50] has shown that claims to strategic superiority continued during the post-Khrushchev period. A thorough analysis of public statements by Soviet leaders on the strategic state found that in the period 1964–68, 49 per cent of statements claimed superiority, 23 per cent parity and 28 per cent were ambiguous (or 'not ascertainable'). In the period 1969–1970, 24 per cent claimed superiority, 49 per cent parity and 27 per cent were ambiguous. The authors of the study draw a number of conclusions. The first is that there seemed to be a strong *inverse* relationship between the actual strategic situation and Soviet claims. At the time when the Soviet Union was in a strategically inferior position, the Soviet leadership sought to conceal its vulnerability by getting the greatest possible political benefit about planned capabilities such as the ABM, the mobile ICBM and FOBS. As Soviet strategic capabilities approached parity and the Soviet Union was about to enter negotiations on strategic weapons with the United States, public statements moderated a great deal.

A further weakness in the thesis of Horelick and Rush consists in the interpretation that the United States and the Western Alliance were the principal audience for these claims. It is true, of course, that the top political and military leaders in the Soviet Union were aware of the real state of Soviet military power. Nonetheless, it is evident that the claims with regard to Soviet strategic capabilities served an internal legitimizing function for Khrushchev's policies. In order to defend the failure to keep up with the United States, it was necessary to considerably exaggerate Soviet capabilities; this is evidently what Malinovskii did during his speech to the 22nd Congress. This was the result of a compromise, whereby Khrushchev made certain concessions to the military, while in turn Malinovskii gave general support to Khrushchev's policies and aided and abetted in the illusions that Khrushchev fostered.

Another aspect of this is the relationship between claims to superiority and the assertion of parity and 'mutual assured destruction'. In 1960, Major General Nikolai Talenskii published an article in *International Affairs* emphasizing the generally catastrophic nature of nuclear war.[51] Khrushchev's own statements in 1960 referred to the large number of casualties a war would entail on both sides and hinted darkly at the catastrophic consequences for our Noah's Ark, the Earth.[52]

This is contrasted by Horelick and Rush with previous statements, such as his speech to the Supreme Soviet in January 1960, when he stated

> We would have many losses, but . . . the West would suffer incomparably more.[53]

As the study of later statements has shown, however, claims to parity can be made at the same time as other statements claim superiority. Statements claiming parity and emphasizing the mutual destruction resulting from nuclear war are also part of the internal debate on military policy. Horelick and Rush themselves suggest that:

> The main political reason for this retreat in the Soviet public assessment of the strategic balance is not hard to discover. Khrushchev's disagreement on world Communist strategy with the Chinese Communists, and with Mao Tse-tung personally, had erupted in a violent dispute with the representative of the Chinese People's Republic at the Rumanian Communist Party Congress in June, 1960. Talensky seems to have been continuing this polemic in his article by warning the Chinese Communist party, which had criticized leaders who were fearful of war, that 'to depreciate the peril of rocket-nuclear war is criminal'.[54]

The polemic between Khrushchev and Mao, however, also reflected a division within the Soviet leadership itself, and Khrushchev's remarks (as well as the expression of his views by Talenskii) were clearly directed against the conservative faction in the Presidium led by Frol Kozlov. It is therefore not necessarily correct to interpret them as a retreat in 'missile diplomacy' directed at the West. Nonetheless, the Cuban missile crisis does indicate that a time did come when more drastic measures to deal with the adverse strategic balance appeared necessary. The failure of the Cuban missile venture had significant consequences for strategic arms policy and the whole concept of 'missile diplomacy'. To see what they are, it is necessary to discuss the objectives of Soviet foreign policy and the use to which strategic nuclear power was put in supporting it in some greater detail.

The evolution of Soviet foreign-policy objectives

The early post-Stalin era

Even Stalin's foreign policy, which has frequently been interpreted as being fundamentally expansionist was, by the early Fifties, characterized by an emphasis on the consolidation of Soviet power in Eastern Europe and preservation of the status quo. In the aftermath of Stalin's death in March 1953, the main preoccupation of the Soviet leadership consisted in the prevention of the complete collapse of the Soviet regime, as different institutions with political power in the Soviet Union asserted themselves. Malenkov and Beriia managed a coalition between the various groupings on the basis of a flexible and adaptable approach and the abolition of the rule of terror.

Stalin's policy of industrialization which had resulted in an overemphasis on heavy industry and a neglect of agriculture and consumer-goods production presented his successors with great economic difficulties which had potential significance for internal political stability. This problem was exacerbated by the fact that Stalin had forced his industrial priorities also on Eastern European countries which, in combination with the policies of repression and the forced export of goods to the Soviet Union, resulted in considerable discontent and a threat to Soviet rule, as witnessed by the riots in East Germany in June 1953.

The main foreign-policy priority which emerged in the early months was the reduction in international tension to permit the consolidation of the Soviet regime as well as that of the East European regimes and to prevent the development of an integrated Western alliance system. Malenkov and Beriia saw the German problem as being the key to a policy of détente in Europe and thus began to lay the groundwork for a policy aimed at a united and neutral Germany. This policy, however, which threatened the Ulbricht group in East Germany, encountered a great deal of opposition and was derailed by the events in East Germany on 16 and 17 June 1953 as well as the power struggle within the Kremlin which resulted in the elimination of Beriia.

The main feature of the correlation of political forces in the Soviet Union consisted now in the concentration of power in the governmental bureaucracy led by Malenkov on the one hand and that of the Party led by Khrushchev on the other. Initially the domestic priorities of Malenkov and Khrushchev were not so far apart: Khrushchev's main preoccupation was agriculture, while Malenkov continued his efforts to redirect economic priorities from heavy industry to light industry, consumer-goods production and agriculture. However, as Khrushchev began gradually to undermine Malenkov's efforts to make the government the dominant institution in the Soviet Union and strengthened his hold on the Party and the Party's influence in policymaking, his opposition to Malenkov's policies began to crystallize. One particular reason for Khrushchev to support the emphasis on heavy industry lay in the need for heavy agricultural machinery necessary for his ambitious schemes. The central issue was not related to policy, however, but to power, and on his path to becoming the most powerful leader in the Soviet Union Khrushchev forged alliances with those interest groups in the Party, the bureaucracy and the military whose interests were threatened by Malenkov's policies.

In the foreign-policy arena, it soon became evident that the main thrust of Malenkov's policy was directed at the reduction of international tension and in particular improved relations with the United States. He declared that a thermonuclear war would mean the destruction of world civilization.[55] He vigorously condemned the Cold War and emphasized the threat of devastation posed by a nuclear war both to the Soviet Union and the United States. The centrepiece of the policy towards Germany was the proposal for the creation of a pan-European system of collective security in which the two Germanys should participate separately on a temporary basis before reunification. German reunification, however, was only possible if Germany would be neutral.

The most direct confrontation of Soviet and Western views on the future of European security took place at the Foreign Ministers Conference in Berlin from 25 January to 18 February 1954. The Western representatives found the Soviet proposals unacceptable because they appeared to be clearly designed to prevent the creation of a European Defence Community and the incorporation of the Federal Republic of Germany in the NATO Alliance. The United States and the People's Republic of China were only to have observer status in the proposed collective security system which would have resulted in the dissolution of NATO and the effective exclusion of the United States from European affairs. While these proposals went far beyond what the Western Allies could have accepted, the Soviet Union, on the other hand, could clearly not accept the notion of a reunified Germany as part of a Western Alliance.

As the power struggle between Malenkov and Khrushchev intensified, Khrushchev and his supporters adopted a more hostile approach to foreign policy, emphasizing international tension, the hostility of capitalism and the danger of war. A particular focus of their attack was 'Capitalist encirclement' and US military bases. This rhetoric appeared to have been aimed more at priorities in Soviet economic policies, however, and there is no evidence that Khrushchev's growing power resulted in any fundamental changes of foreign policy, despite the (by September 1954) evident shift of decision-making from the government sector controlled by Malenkov to the Party Institutions under Khrushchev.[56] The rejection of the EDC plans by the French National Assembly was interpreted in Moscow as a great success of their foreign policy, an impression which persisted until the ratification of the Paris Treaties in 1954 which resulted in the rearmament of West Germany in the context of the Western European Union. These developments were effectively used by those opponents of Malenkov warning of the dangerous state of the international situation and the need for a greater defence effort.

When Malenkov was forced to resign as Chairman of the Council of Ministers in February 1955, the Party apparatus and Khrushchev assumed a dominant position in the Soviet political hierarchy. It is remarkable how rapidly Khrushchev moved towards a far more conciliatory line in foreign policy based on peaceful co-existence once Malenkov was out of the way. Thus Dinerstein notes

> an almost total absence of statements on the war danger during the rest of 1955 and 1956. The official Soviet line . . . was that prospects of peace had greatly improved.[57]

This provides a strong indication that Khrushchev's support for the 'hawks' was motivated by political expediency. His priorities now were the reorientation of the economy towards greater effectiveness, establishing the new priorities demanded by the institutional allies who helped him to power, as well as to improve agricultural and consumer-goods production. To achieve economic and political stability, a period of consolidation was necessary which required the absence of international tension and external political pressure.

Part of this process of political and economic stabilization involved the consolidation of Soviet power in Eastern Europe. Khrushchev's strategy was rather complex. On the one hand it involved a more relaxed approach. Different paths to socialist construction were recognized as legitimate. The principle of non-interference in internal Party affairs was established as a fundamental rule of the fraternal relations between socialist countries. Genuine friendship and co-operation were to be the hallmark of relations between socialist countries. Nonetheless, while allowing a greater degree of freedom in internal affairs, Khrushchev did to some extent impose his own priorities on other Eastern European countries, such as the transfer of power from governments to the parties and the re-orientation of investment towards heavy industry. Furthermore, there was no question that the priority of Soviet interests and the leadership rôle of the Soviet Union had to be recognized.

The most startling departure from Stalinism was the change of Soviet policy towards Yugoslavia. With a strong denunciation of Stalinist policy Khrushchev attempted to win Yugoslavia back to the socialist camp, without much success. The process was revealing, however, about Khrushchev's Eastern European policy in general and about policy disagreements in Moscow. Molotov led the opposition against Khrushchev's foreign policy and his Yugoslavian policy in particular, but he was defeated by the Central Committee and did not survive very much longer as Foreign Minister.

The foreign policy pursued by Khrushchev went beyond Malenkov's version of peaceful coexistence. It advocated a policy of co-operation between East and West to mutual advantage and, while renouncing war as an instrument of policy between the two blocs, advocated competition in the economic and technological spheres. The Austrian State Treaty of 1955 which led to the withdrawal of Soviet troops, and the Geneva conference which signalled a more serious Soviet approach to disarmament, contributed to a general atmosphere of détente, known as the 'spirit of Geneva'.

What was not as well understood in the West at the time was that détente with the West was to go hand in hand with the consolidation of Soviet power in Eastern Europe. The formation of the Warsaw Pact was one important element of this policy. There was also a definite shift in Soviet policy towards Germany. Instead of promoting proposals which held out the possibility of reconciliation, the policy pursued from early 1955 was based on the permanence of the division of Germany, and aimed at integrating East Germany firmly into the East European Alliance system. This strand of Soviet policy was dramatically illustrated in 1956 when the Khrushchev leadership intervened in Hungary to prevent its defection from the Warsaw Pact. In the West, where Soviet domination over Eastern Europe was still interpreted as a fundamentally aggressive posture which had given rise to the Cold War in the first place, this action did much to destroy the spirit of détente, confirmed the previously held image of the Soviet Union as fundamentally aggressive and thus reinforced the need for a strategy of containment. This interpretation was not entirely correct and the Hungarian intervention did not in fact mark any shift in Soviet policy towards the West.[58]

The intervention demonstrated three important aspects of Soviet foreign policy. First of all, it delineated the limits of Soviet tolerance of dissent in Eastern Europe. Secondly, it proved that 'extended deterrence' worked for the Soviet Union despite US strategic superiority – the West was not willing to risk armed confrontation over Eastern Europe. The third principle was a consequence of the second, namely that a *de facto* recognition of spheres of influence was emerging. Much Soviet political effort during the following fifteen years was expended towards the objective of making this a *de jure* acceptance.

The Berlin crisis

This effort was a principal motivating factor of the events which, on the surface at least, most strongly contradict Khrushchev's declared commitment to peaceful coexistence and détente with the West. They are collectively referred to as the second Berlin crisis which lasted from 1958 to 1961. Khrushchev launched the crisis on 10 November 1958 when he declared that

> The time has obviously come for the signatories of the Potsdam Agreement to renounce the remnants of the occupation régime in Berlin and thereby make it possible to create a normal situation in the German Democratic Republic.[59]

This statement was followed on 27 November 1958 by what amounted to an ultimatum that if negotiations with the other three Western powers with responsibility for the occupation regime did not result in an agreement within six months, the Soviet Union would transfer its powers in Berlin to the government of the GDR which would exercise its rights as a sovereign power, in particular with regard to access routes to West Berlin. Finally, it was proposed that West Berlin should become a demilitarized 'free city'.

The ups and downs of the Berlin crisis over the following years did not indicate a single set of objectives pursued with any degree of consistency. However, some general lines of policy can be discerned. Khrushchev's own account of his objectives is quite clear and consistent with the known facts:

> Therefore we came to the conclusion that we should work out a peace treaty which would consolidate the status of Germany as fixed by the Potsdam agreement. The Potsdam agreement was considered a temporary solution pending the Allies' conclusion of a peace treaty with Germany. Our proposal would have legitimized the provisional *de facto* situation and made it permanent. We were simply asking the other side to acknowledge that two irreconcilable social-political structures existed in Germany, Socialism in East Germany and capitalism in West Germany. We were asking only for formal recognition of two German republics, each of which would sign the treaty. According to our proposal West Berlin would have special status as a free city.[60]

It is clear that the issue of Berlin was central to Khrushchev's efforts to secure Western recognition of the division of Germany. The status of West Berlin was related to the stability of the East German regime which was challenged as long as the border between East and West Berlin remained open; thus West Berlin posed a threat to the stability of Soviet control in Eastern Europe and the Soviet sphere of influence which had assumed a central place in the Soviet conception of their own security. But Khrushchev's pressure tactics could also serve wider political purposes, such as a demonstration to the Chinese and their sympathizers in the Presidium in Moscow that he was pursuing an active foreign policy with regard to the West without having to run a serious risk of war. The negotiations which Khrushchev hoped would take place could be used to prevent the planned equipment of the Bundeswehr with nuclear weapons (albeit with warheads under American control) and inhibit the economic and political integration of Western Europe – objectives of Soviet foreign policy which had been pursued so far with little success. As Carl Linden has convincingly argued, one of the goals pursued by Khrushchev's Berlin policy was a summit meeting with the United States, which would enhance Khrushchev's prestige and allow the Soviet Union to be seen as a world power whose participation in the resolution of major international problems was necessary.[61]

The fundamental dilemma of Khrushchev's policy lay in the fact that the objectives which were seen as important to Soviet security were perceived as aggressive, i.e. as threatening the security of West Berlin and the Federal Republic of Germany in particular for whom the links with West Berlin were seen as fundamental to its own legitimacy. The manner in which Khrushchev pursued his policies also substantially contributed to the perception of Soviet aggressiveness. As on previous occasions, Khrushchev was not prepared to go very far down the road of military confrontation to test the limits of Western resolve and therefore lacked the means to achieve his objectives.

At the 21st Party Congress in January 1959, a rosy picture of détente with the West was painted. Khrushchev described a secure future for the Soviet Union and the steady growth of Communist power and influence. There was now no chance that the progress of the revolution could be reversed. At the same time the rejection of the inevitability of war, as has been pointed out, was advanced to new heights. Even more dramatic was the announcement that the 'capitalist encirclement' of the USSR had now come to an end.

The Berlin crisis began to subside in 1959 when it became evident that Khrushchev had miscalculated with regard to Western reaction. The Western Allies maintained their unity on the central issue and the other three occupation powers were not prepared to make any concessions. By March 1959 Khrushchev had to withdraw his ultimatum, and had to be satisfied with proposing a draft peace treaty and the agreement for a summit meeting between the four powers in May 1960.

Meanwhile, Khrushchev was already preparing further advances in his policies of reform and détente. His policy of widening personal contacts and co-operation with the West reached its culmination in a meeting with President Eisenhower at Camp David in September 1959 Khrushchev returned confidently, stating that responsible people in the United States, including President Eisenhower, were against war. On the basis of this assessment he tried to extract the maximum support for his foreign policy.

There is no doubt that in response to Khrushchev's speech to the Supreme Soviet in January 1960, in which the practical consequences of his military and economic policies were spelt out in greater detail, his opponents began to gather their forces. It was not merely the military but, as John Dornberg put it,

> a conglomerate coalition of guardians of Communist orthodoxy, members of the military establishment and cold warriors.[62]

Among the most powerful hardliners who had already at times forced a toughening of the stance towards the West were Mikhail Suslov and Frol Kozlov. The rival faction in the Soviet leadership argued strongly in favour of developing Soviet military strength and was opposed to this new view of a more permanent peaceful coexistence. Instead they supported the Chinese view that the Soviet Union should use its military strength to pursue a more aggressive strategy against capitalism and bring about its collapse. It seems that the attitude to China was also a major point of contention within the Soviet leadership as the dispute with China widened into a bitter confrontation, and Kozlov supported the Chinese in some of their arguments with Khrushchev, particularly with regard to the posture *vis-à-vis* the West.[63]

The first opening for the Kozlov faction came in May 1960 when the U-2 spy plane of Gary Powers came down over Sverdlovsk.[64] The incident was a blow against Khrushchev's policies particularly since Eisenhower claimed personal responsibility for the overflights. At a

Central Committee meeting three days after the U-2 incident the Party Secretariat was drastically reduced in size and Frol Kozlov was put in *de facto* control over it. Three men who were in no sense Khrushchev protégés were promoted to full membership in the Party Presidium: Dmitri Polianskii, Nikolai Podgornii and Aleksei Kosygin, the last being also appointed First Deputy Prime Minister.[65] Confirmation of the significance of the U-2 incident for Khrushchev's leadership was provided by Khrushchev himself in an interview with A. McGehee Harvey from *Life* after his fall from power:

> [Khrushchev] said that his own idea always had been to have our two countries live together peacefully and compete economically, not militarily . . . And he said: 'Things were going well until one event happened. From the time Gary Powers was shot down in a U-2 over the Soviet Union, I was no longer in full control.' . . . He said unequivocally that his decision-making powers were weakened after the U-2 crisis in the spring of 1960 and that he was no longer calling the shots. He explained that 'those who felt America had imperialistic intentions and that military strength was the most important thing had the evidence they needed, and when the U-2 incident occurred, I no longer had the ability to overcome that feeling.'[66]

Another indication that Soviet foreign policy had slipped away from Khrushchev's hands was provided by the first invitation to Mao Tse-tung in three years to visit Moscow. Mao refused but the invitation itself indicates how far policy was swinging away from the Khrushchev line.

The U-2 incident occurred just before the Four Power Summit was to take place in Paris. Khrushchev did get the Presidium's approval to go to Paris, but it is not clear what his mandate was. The summit failed because of Khrushchev's insistence on an apology for the U-2 incident which Eisenhower refused to give. According to his memoirs, Khrushchev himself dictated his typed opening statement at the summit on the plane to Paris, replacing the initial draft. The line pursued at the summit according to this account was Khrushchev's own idea.[67] In view of Khrushchev's own persistent attempts to downplay the implications of the U-2 incident and leave Eisenhower a way to save face, however, this account appears to be somewhat implausible (Khrushchev does not reveal anything about the content of the supposed initial draft of his statement).[68] All the indications are that the tough line was imposed on Khrushchev by the Presidium. Another interesting question relates to the presence of Rodion Malinovskii on the delegation. This was decided only a day before the Soviet delegation left, according to Khrushchev in order to match the presence of US Defence Secretary Thomas Gates on the American team.[69] Nonetheless, there was speculation at the time that Malinovskii's rôle consisted in watching over Khrushchev on behalf of the Presidium. This interpretation is quite plausible given that Malinovskii had used the U-2 incident to align himself with Khrushchev's opponents and advocate policy changes.

Khrushchev's behaviour during the abortive meeting in Paris was exceedingly bellicose, with its demands for apologies, threats of missile attacks on U-2 bases and the cancellation of Eisenhower's visit to Moscow. It is evident that Khrushchev was exasperated both by Eisenhower's approach to the meeting and his failure to extract even the faint shadow of an apology. His aggressive demeanour belied the fact that he was still seeking an accommodation with the United States, but that the Khrushchev line was no longer the line of the Communist Party of the Soviet Union. This became evident during Khrushchev's stopover in East Berlin on his return to Moscow, where he accused Eisenhower of perfidy, but then went on to suggest that the summit should be reconvened in six or eight months. In the meantime he declared that the Soviet Union would not seek to

> aggravate the international situation and bring it back to the worst times of the Cold War.[70]

According to Michael Beschloss

> Premier Otto Grotewohl was so disgusted by Khrushchev's timidity that he refused to see him off at the airport.[71]

On his return to Moscow it became clear from comments in *Pravda* that not everyone in the Soviet Union was willing to let passions cool for a while and then resume business with the United States.

Khrushchev's loss of control over the direction of economic, military and foreign policy continued throughout 1961, albeit punctuated by sporadic recoveries. As will be discussed in more detail elsewhere, he was forced to accept a compromise on the 'combined arms doctrine' and the troop reductions. In the arena of arms control, a principal vehicle for a policy of détente, the test ban negotiations were scuttled as Khrushchev yielded to military pressure to abandon the moratorium on nuclear testing.[72] All this took place in the context of the increase of defence expenditures and the extensive measures to improve the US strategic force posture and combat readiness by the new Kennedy Administration announced in May 1961. After the June meeting with Kennedy at Vienna Khrushchev reactivated the Berlin crisis by declaring another ultimatum in a televised speech on 15 June. He stated that the Soviet Union would sign a separate peace treaty with East Germany by the end of the year if negotiations with the West for an all-German treaty were not concluded satisfactorily. One principal motive for the Berlin campaign consisted, as Khrushchev describes with great candour in his memoirs, in the threats to the stability of the East German regime by the ever-increasing number of people leaving via West Berlin. By July more than 10,000 people were leaving the GDR, imposing great strains on the East German economy, given that many of those people had played an important part in East German industry. Another problem, according to Khrushchev's memoirs, consisted in the free access by West Berliners to shops in East Berlin where they bought top-grade consumer goods, particularly food, at very cheap prices, thus depriving GDR citizens.[73] As Robert Slusser has argued in his very detailed analysis, two different policy objectives developed in the Soviet policymaking establishment. The maximum objective consisted in an all-out endeavour to dislodge the Western powers from West Berlin. The minimum objective was to stabilize the GDR by cutting off the movement of people from East to West Berlin.

Khrushchev's memoirs provide an intriguing insight into the fact that the objective of stabilizing the GDR was actually incompatible with the declared objective of Soviet policy:

> Of course, even if we had a peace treaty, it wouldn't have solved these problems because Berlin's status as a free city would have been stipulated in the treaty and the gates would have remained open.[74]

It has therefore been suggested by some Western commentators that the Soviet Berlin campaign was to a large extent a cover operation to induce Western acceptance of the closing of East Berlin's border by the wall on 13 August 1961.[75] If so, it was very effective, because, as Robert Slusser has shown, the erection of barriers which were followed by the wall caught the West, whose strategy was exclusively aimed at countering the Soviet maximum objective, completely by surprise.[76] The evidence seems to be quite clear, however, that the Soviet leadership, while pressing its declaratory policy and underlining it by nuclear and conventional threats, was not decided on what it would ultimately settle for. According to Slusser's analysis, the decision to go for the minimum objective was made at the beginning of August, after much pressure to that effect by the East German leader Walter Ulbricht. Slusser argues that this point marks the beginning of a deliberate cover operation to divert attention from the plans for the wall, because official Soviet statements now made explicit that the status of West Berlin could be settled *after* a peace treaty had been signed, thus providing a basis for the view held in the West that the closing of access between East and West Berlin would not happen until after negotiations had taken place for a treaty.[77]

The wall, which can be seen primarily as a defensive measure to inhibit the stream of refugees into West Berlin, was later seen as a stabilizing influence, thus leading to the resolution of the Berlin crisis. Tension over Berlin continued for some time and, on 27 October, there was a sixteen-hour confrontation of American and Soviet tanks at a Berlin checkpoint. But, during the 22nd Party Congress, on 17 October, Khrushchev had already lifted the ultimatum and retreated from the idea of making Berlin a free city.

It goes without saying that Khrushchev's demands at various points of the Berlin crisis were underlined by missile threats. Averell Harriman reported an interview in which Khrushchev said:

> 'Your generals talk of maintaining your position in Berlin with force. That is bluff. If you send in tanks, they will burn and make no mistake about it. If you want war, you can have it, and remember it will be your war. Our rockets will fly automatically. . . .' And his colleagues echoed like a chorus, automatically.[78]

Statements about country-busting weapons were designed to have a similarly intimidatory effect. But it is important to point out that the foreign-policy objectives pursued by Khrushchev, even in the Berlin crisis, were rooted in his vision of peaceful coexistence and economic and ideological rather than military competition with the West. Although the manner in which these objectives were pursued would have suggested a crash effort to bring Soviet military power in line with the exaggerated claims for it, Khrushchev's policy objectives were achievable and compatible with the maintenance of a minimum deterrent.

There is evidence that this did not apply to Khrushchev's political opponents. The decision to resume nuclear testing was taken in Khrushchev's absence and can be seen in context with the suspension of troop reductions. It was announced that the new powerful weapons with 20-, 30-, 50- and 100-megaton yield and new rockets were to be tested.[79] A clear association was made with recent Soviet space flights. It is remarkable, however, that none of the official Soviet statements indicates any attempt to use these measures to apply new pressure either towards Soviet political objectives in Berlin or arms control. As the *Survey of International Affairs* has commented:

> The motive behind the choice of this moment to resume testing was taken by opinion generally all over the world as the desire further to increase the pressure on the western alliance . . . Yet seen in retrospect, the Soviet test-programme was to serve less as a means of pressure on the west than as a smoke-screen to distract attention from the Soviet abandonment of its much-heralded plan to sign a treaty of peace with East Germany before the end of year.[80]

Not only that but, again as Robert Slusser has argued, the decision to end the moratorium marked a shift towards a policy eschewing any form of negotiation with the United States and building up Soviet military strength instead. There is also clear evidence that the Chinese were informed of the shift in policy on the moratorium in advance and they strongly supported it in official statements. The pro-Chinese faction in the Soviet Presidium had regained the ascendancy and clearly sought to undermine Khrushchev's endeavours to keep negotiations with the West on Berlin and arms control going. Slusser concludes his detailed review of the events in early August 1961:

> behind the Soviet decision to resume testing . . . [lay] the temporary ascendancy of a faction in the Soviet leadership which believed wholeheartedly in the paramount need for close Soviet–Chinese collaboration, just as it believed equally wholeheartedly in the need for irreconcilable opposition to the United States.[81]

Khrushchev managed to recover to some extent before the Party Congress in October 1961, but the period of late August 1961 provides an interesting insight into the political objectives of his opposition. They consisted in a far more hostile stance towards the West, and a build-up of both conventional and strategic nuclear power, while eschewing Khrushchev's bold missile diplomacy.

The Cuban missile crisis

The clandestine emplacement of medium and intermediate-range missiles in Cuba in October 1962 was soon another Khrushchevian policy move which on the face of it appeared in direct contradiction to his détente policies. As Carl A. Linden has pointed out:

it . . . bore the earmarks of the classic Khrushchevian tactic – the sudden and bold initiative aimed at setting opponents off balance and producing a quick and decisive advantage in political struggle. It also aimed at accomplishing much with little, namely, with the fairly limited number of intermediate-range ballistic missiles involved in the operation.[82]

Although Soviet missiles were introduced to Cuba to deter an American attack on the island, there was a more important objective, i.e. a dramatic and perceptible shift in the strategic balance. The mix of MRBMs and IRBMs (the latter with a 200-mile range, thus being able to target a large area of the continental United States) is a clear indication that this interpretation is correct. This action was not just directed at the West and the United States in particular, but also against Khrushchev's critics at home who were pressing for higher defence expenditures and a more determined build-up of strategic power.

The idea was to install the missiles in secret and present the world with a *fait accompli* that would be difficult to challenge. But the plan went wrong in that the Americans discovered what was going on far too soon and instituted a naval blockade around Cuba. They also threatened further military action if the missiles were not removed, the clear implication being that the USA was willing to risk an escalation even to the level of all-out nuclear war. The result was a humiliating defeat for the Soviet Union and the withdrawal of the missiles from Cuba.

The American reaction to Khrushchev's action was curious in so far as it violated the normal tacit rules of superpower diplomacy as they seem to have been observed since. Khrushchev's action was not illegal, and Khrushchev could point to the precedence of US missiles in Turkey, as well as to US hostile (and illegal) actions against Cuba to argue the need for deterrence against American attacks. Furthermore, the attempt to redress the strategic balance – one of the main motivating factors for Kennedy's actions – was also not only not illegal, but even to be expected. American actions, on the other hand, such as the imposition of a blockade, were clearly illegal; and constituted an act of war. What gave Soviet actions an aura of illegitimacy was the clandestine nature of the operation, as Raymond L. Garthoff has pointed out

> I have recently asked a number of the 1962 policymakers what they think the American position would have been if the Soviet Union and Cuba had announced plans for a limited deployment of Soviet

missiles in Cuba (the forty launchers planned, for example, were not discrepant from the forty-five launchers the United States had deployed in Italy and Turkey). All believed it was much less likely that the U.S. government would have sought, or been able to compel reaction of the Soviet decision and preclude deployment.[83]

The presently orthodox explanation for the success of the stance taken by the US states that it was not so much the result of American nuclear superiority, but rather of local conventional superiority.[84] While there is some merit in this argument, it misses the essential point. The dynamics of the Cuban missile crisis cannot be understood without the underlying threat of global thermonuclear war. Khrushchev's first letter to Kennedy, which offered the withdrawal of missiles in exchange for a pledge not to attack Cuba bore the hallmarks of a man consumed by fear.[85] The source of this fear was evidently not that some Soviet ships might be sunk in the Caribbean, but that the Soviet Union and the United States might get involved in nuclear war.

From this point of view, as Garthoff has argued, American local conventional and global-strategic superiority, while undoubtedly constituting a significant factor, was not decisive for the outcome of the crisis. The principal factor appears to have been that the American administration set itself a minimum objective – the removal of missiles and bombers from Cuba – and, although it was also deterred from escalating to nuclear war (or inducing Soviet escalation by, for example, bombing the missile sites), it was determined to pursue this objective regardless of costs and risks, while at the same time keeping the danger of escalation to a minimum at every stage. It is interesting that the minimum objective was never in doubt or subject to dispute within the US Administration, even though at the outset it was not clear by what means it would be achieved. The clandestine deployment of Soviet missiles in Cuba was perceived as a political challenge to the United States which could not be allowed to succeed at *any* cost, regardless of the actual military value of the missiles. According to Garthoff's account, based on his own participation as an officer in the State Department and interviews with past participants, the Soviets could have driven a much harder bargain for the removal of the missiles.[86] It is interesting to compare the Cuban missile crisis with the Berlin crisis, because in the two cases the balance of local conventional power was reversed. Nonetheless, the minimum objective of the three occupation powers – not to be dislodged from West Berlin – was pursued with unwavering determination, as a result of which declared Soviet policy objectives were not achieved. It can be argued that while the overall strategic balance again was an important background, the decisive factor was that of political will.

Instead of redressing the imbalance in strategic power, the Cuban missile venture resulted in making it more apparent, and the Soviet military, as will be discussed elsewhere, drew appropriate conclusions from this. The importance of the Cuban missile crisis lies in the fact that it constituted the greatest test of Khrushchev's missile diplomacy and marked its ultimate failure. In the future, the usefulness of strategic nuclear power as a direct political instrument was heavily circumscribed. Another result of the stark reality of being at the brink of nuclear war was a greater awareness of the need for accommodation between the superpowers. As Khrushchev regained greater control of Soviet foreign policy in April 1963, a general relaxation of tension ensued marked by the conclusions of the Partial Test Ban Treaty.

Arms control and détente after the Cuban missile crisis

It is a commonly held view that the Cuban missile crisis and the direct confrontation with the dangers of missile diplomacy resulted in a shift in Soviet foreign policy towards an energetic pursuit of détente and arms control.[87] This interpretation is misleading in some respects. To put it into a proper context, some general remarks about Soviet arms-control policy are in order.

For over three decades there have been negotiations to control nuclear weapons, mostly between the United States and the Soviet Union who are in possession of very substantial nuclear arsenals. At the height of the Cold War, when arms-control negotiations began in the 1950s, the United States approached the issue of arms control and disarmament from the perspective that the growth of the nuclear arsenals was perceived as potentially dangerous and leading to an unstable superpower relationship. These threats to strategic stability were seen to be the consequence of the technical characteristics of particular weapons systems and the mode of their deployment. The purpose of arms control was to inhibit the unchecked growth of strategic arsenals and achieve a state of military stability between the superpowers, as well as inhibit the spread of nuclear weapons to other nations.

The Soviet Union approached disarmament and arms control from a more political emphasis. Finding itself in a position of grave military inferiority in the mid-Fifties, Soviet disarmament policy was designed to address the military threat as well as its political roots. The military goals pursued were the reduction of the risk of a surprise attack and constraining Western military power while allowing the Soviet Union to achieve at least strategic parity. Among the issues of security policy which concerned the Soviet Union particularly were its recognition as a superpower equal to the United States, the recognition of the post-war status quo in Europe, the limitation of American military influence in Europe, the restraint of the growth in the military strength of the Federal Republic of Germany and the prevention of access to nuclear weapons by the West German military. The Soviet Union was also using disarmament as a propaganda weapon to prove itself as a 'peace-loving nation' and brand the members of the NATO alliance as warmongers who were engaged in a dangerous arms race which threatened the world with nuclear annihilation.

Not all of these objectives proved to be compatible. The proposals for General and Complete Disarmament (GCD) had significant propaganda potential, but proved to be non-negotiable. The unwillingness of the Soviet Union to accept the necessary verification procedures and to agree on realistic time-tables for the step-by-step reduction in forces or to negotiate seriously on partial measures of disarmament was interpreted in the West as signifying a lack of serious intent on the part of the Soviet Union. Clearly, this sort of disarmament was incompatible with the way in which the Soviet Union perceived its own security interests, as can be seen by Khrushchev's frequent boasting about Soviet military strength; his 'missile rattling' was designed to have certain political effects but was clearly negating potential benefits from Soviet disarmament proposals. Given the massive strategic superiority of the United States until the late Sixties, it is not surprising that the Soviet Union was not eager to conclude agreements that would effectively prevent it from achieving parity with the United States.[88]

However, from this emphasis on the political effect of disarmament proposals emerged a more sophisticated two-pronged approach to arms control. While publicly proclaiming that GCD was the only solution, the Soviet Union became more interested in partial measures of arms control. An explicit description of this two-pronged approach has been given in a report by the former Soviet arms control expert and representative at the United Nations Arkady

Shevchenko, who defected to the West, of a conversation with Khrushchev where he admitted that the proposals for General and Complete Disarmament were made for propaganda purposes; he did not expect the West seriously to completely disarm, nor did he believe such a course would be a realistic option for the Soviet Union. However, Khrushchev added that one could make disarmament proposals for political effect and pursue serious negotiations at the same time.[89]

From the Soviet point of view, the advantage of certain forms of arms control in military terms lay in their potential to restrain the growth of Western military power and prevent the spread of nuclear weapons to non-nuclear powers (with China and West Germany particularly in mind). The political value lay in the pursuit of relaxation of tensions and détente with the United States and thus the achievement of a more favourable international climate. The Soviet leadership wanted to reach these political objectives without having to restrain its own build-up of strategic forces.

Negotiations for a nuclear test ban began in 1958, involving the Soviet Union, Britain and the United States. Western and Soviet perspectives in issues of verification (the Soviets insisted for a long time that national technical means of verification would be sufficient for all environments) and in on-site inspections in particular, the relationship of a test ban to GCD and control procedures ensured that progress was extremely slow. The forum shifted from direct negotiations to the Eighteen Nations Disarmament Conference, involved a period of tacitly agreed and uninspected testing moratoria and eventually shifted back to a trilateral conference. The underlying reason for these problems apart from Soviet sensitivity about on-site verification in a cultural environment where all military matters are surrounded by great secrecy, was the stark fact that a complete test ban was not in the Soviet interest given the American advantage in nuclear weapons technology. Nonetheless, the negotiations could be made to serve a variety of political objectives.

A significant shift in the Soviet position seemed to occur in 1962, before the Cuban missile crisis, after a series of atmospheric tests which seems to have provided the Soviet Union with most of the information they needed and thus made a limited test ban more viable from their viewpoint. Thus Soviet statements in August and September 1962 no longer insisted on a link between a test ban and GCD, indicated the willingness to accept a partial test ban and, in terms of general disarmament, the retention of a 'nuclear umbrella' during the first phases of a disarmament programme.[90]

It is true that the Cuban missile crisis was followed by a retreat from a more aggressive style in Soviet foreign policy and greater activity in the pursuit of a test-ban treaty. This can be partly explained by the profound failure of Khrushchev's tactics which forced him to adopt a much more cautious approach. Arms control opened up an important and perhaps the only promising path to a policy success for Khrushchev in relations with the United States. But it is important to bear in mind that the Cuban missile crisis resulted in considerably enhanced influence for Khrushchev's opponents who advocated a much more hardline approach in relations with the West, albeit in a more consistent and cautious manner. This accounts for the appearance of a 'thaw' in East-West relations in the aftermath of the missile crisis at a time when Khrushchev's objectives were largely frustrated.

There are clear indications to this effect both in domestic and foreign policy. The clearest signals in domestic terms were the retreat of the anti-Stalin campaign and Khrushchev's inability to pursue his economic policies. The creation of a Supreme Sovnarkhoz in March 1963 was perhaps Khrushchev's most obvious and humiliating defeat. In foreign policy, attempts at rapprochement with China and greater hostility towards Yugoslavia (expressed in terms of seeing 'revisionism' rather than 'dogmatism' as the principal danger for the Communist movement) were clear indicators that Khrushchev was no longer in charge.[91]

Attempts at greater rapprochement on the test-ban issue proved fruitless, partly due to a misunderstanding about the number of on-site inspections to be allowed per annum.[92] As Glenn T. Seaborg recalls in his account of the test-ban negotiations, at the end of 1962:

> the high hopes that both President Kennedy and Premier Khrushchev seemed to have entertained that the world's brush with catastrophe might hasten a test ban agreement were, for the moment not realized. The situation was to get worse before it got better.[93]

Essentially, the talks got bogged down on the issue of the number of annual on-site inspections with the Soviet side offering a maximum of 'two or three', while the American negotiators came down to a minimum number between eight and ten. By the beginning of April 1963 the discussions had gone around in circles to such an extent that the Soviet negotiator pronounced them to be 'a waste of time'.[94]

Despite such a pessimistic prognosis, there was a significant shift in April 1963 which manifested itself by greater Soviet flexibility and resulted in very rapid progress towards the conclusion of arms-control agreements.[95] This remarkable change coincided with Khrushchev's political recovery as a result of the illness of his main opponent in the Presidium, Frol Kozlov. Kozlov suffered a stroke on 10 April and, from then on, Khrushchev rapidly regained a much greater measure of control of the policy process. Khrushchev's first initiative on the test-ban issue involved a conversation with Norman Cousins in which Khrushchev attempted to finally bury the misunderstanding about the number of inspections which had clouded the talks and basically invited the West to present fresh proposals, despite subsequent belligerent outbursts on Khrushchev's part. By early July 1963 Khrushchev had publicly declared his support for a three-environment test ban, albeit linked to a non-aggression pact between NATO and the WTO. On 15 July three-power negotiations resumed, the non-aggression pact issue was dropped and the partial test-ban treaty banning nuclear tests in the atmosphere, the ocean and outer space was signed. Other indications of greater Soviet flexibility in arms control were the Soviet acceptance, announced by Gromyko on 19 September 1963, that during a general disarmament process some nuclear missiles might be retained right until the end. At the same time the Soviet Union agreed with the United States not to orbit nuclear weapons in space (although no formal treaty was concluded) and accepted safeguards at the Vienna Conference of the International Atomic Energy Agency to prevent the military use of fissionable materials by recipients of aid in the construction of nuclear power stations.

To sum up, contrary to a widespread perception, the détente of 1963 of which the conclusion of the PTBT was the most visible symbol was not directly a consequence of the Cuban missile crisis. Although the missile crisis marked the end of missile diplomacy and thereby contributed to a relaxation of international tension, Soviet foreign policy hardened in the first six months after the events of October 1962. The shift towards détente in 1963 strongly correlated with the recovery of Khrushchev's political position. The move towards the conclusion of a PTBT did not represent a dramatic shift, but rather a natural evolution of the Soviet position which had already moved towards the acceptance of a three-environment test ban prior to the Cuban missile crisis. The experience of this crisis may have impressed upon Khrushchev a greater sense of urgency to succeed with the negotiations. But the momentum of the negotiations after April 1963 was primarily due to the fact that Khrushchev was in a much stronger political position than before Cuba.

Soviet foreign policy in the post-Khrushchev period

Khrushchev's departure was not followed by radical shifts in foreign policy; the most obvious change was the manner in which policy was to be pursued. The main emphasis was on the consolidation and management of Soviet achievements, the prudent and gradual strengthening of the international position of the Soviet Union and the defence of her interests in the world. With regard to China, there was a brief phase in which rapprochement was attempted, but evidently the Soviet leadership was not prepared to pay the price China demanded, and Soviet policy came to be dominated by political, ideological and military containment of China.

The more gradualist approach meant that the Soviet leadership would not engage in campaigns like the Berlin or the Cuba crisis. As was to be expected, it was not as concerned to achieve an accommodation with the United States, and a hardening of policy towards the US (which was also influenced by the bombing of North Vietnam) occurred, while at the same time the lines of communication were kept open. Soviet policy towards Western Europe evolved in the direction of ending the confrontation in Europe and establishing a system of collective security while marginalizing American influence and containing the Federal Republic of Germany. At the 23rd Party Congress of the CPSU L. I. Brezhnev defined the goals of Soviet foreign policy in the following terms:

1 Ensuring, together with other socialist countries, favourable international conditions for the construction of socialism and communism.
2 Consolidating the unity and cohesion of the socialist countries, their friendship and brotherhood.
3 Supporting the national liberation movement and engaging in all-round cooperation with the young developing states.
4 Consistently standing up for the principle of peaceful coexistence between states with differing social systems.
5 Giving a resolute rebuff to the aggressive forces of imperialism.
6 Safeguarding mankind from another world war.[96]

West Germany had always been central to the Soviet Union's post-war policy towards Western Europe and, as such, to its arms-control policies. This was evident also in the post-Khrushchev period. The main targets of Soviet policy in the negotiations for a Nuclear Non-Proliferation Treaty (NPT) in the Sixties apart from China was the American policy for the dissemination of nuclear technology within the Alliance and *Multilateral Force* (MLF) which would allow the European Allies, in particular West Germany, a degree of participation in nuclear control. The NPT became possible eventually because the MLF lost support within the NATO alliance and fell by the wayside, and the Soviet Union compromised on the nuclear consultation arrangements envisaged by the NATO Nuclear Planning Group.

The achievement of strategic nuclear parity with the United States by the end of the Sixties was a prerequisite for Soviet interest in strategic arms limitations agreements (SALT). SALT was designed to preserve a stable balance between the superpowers and, at the same time, give political recognition to the equality of the Soviet Union with the United States.[97] The treaties did not inhibit most planned American and Soviet deployments. However, they were part of a much larger process of détente which involved a Conference on European Security (CSCE), the tangible results of which were the regularization of the status of West Berlin, the mutual recognition of the status quo in Europe, and arms control between the superpowers, thus resulting in a very considerable relaxation of tension.

From the Soviet perspective détente was the result of a shift in the correlation of forces in favour of socialism. The Soviet Union was now emerging as a truly global power. It was no longer possible for Western governments to relate to the Soviet Union from a position of strength. By containing the aggressiveness of imperialism, a relaxation of tension would result; arms control would serve to manage East–West relations on the basis of parity and would restrain any efforts by the United States to return to a state of military superiority. It would also restrain American attempts to inhibit Soviet endeavours to form relationships with nations in the Third World and support national liberation, while at the same time limiting the dangers arising out of improved Sino-American relations. Improved trade relations with Western Europe and thus access to Western technology constituted another important benefit perceived by the Soviet leadership.[98] The systematic build-up of strategic nuclear power to achieve parity with the United States was a prerequisite for the foreign policy conducted under Brezhnev, and strategic arms policy under the post-Khrushchev leadership thus was well in line with the foreign-policy objectives which were pursued.

Conclusion

The analysis of Soviet foreign-policy objectives in the post-Stalin era provides a very good test for one particular model which seeks to explain Soviet strategic arms policy as the purposeful pursuit of military superiority, either to achieve global domination or even for more limited political objectives. The general foreign-policy line pursued by Khrushchev, the development of Soviet doctrine on the use of war as a political instrument and the actual strategic arms policy pursued all fundamentally contradict this model. Some of the tactics of intimidation used by the Khrushchev leadership, however, appear to confirm it since they could only succeed if the West believed the claims made for Soviet strategic power. This ambiguity is reflected in the debate between the realist interpretation of international relations which ignores domestic sources of foreign policy and interprets the interaction between states in terms of power and their position in the international system and those who emphasize the dominance of domestic political factors and decision-making processes.[99]

The notion that international relations are governed by potentials of power and the national interests of its members, which do not derive from internal social requirements, but rather from the structure of the international environment, is particularly untenable in the Soviet case.[100]

The interaction between domestic-policy priorities and the position of a state in the international system is well described by David Easton's systems theory of international relations, which defines political interactions in terms of the 'authoritative allocation of values for a society'.[101] The values of Soviet society are defined by Marxism–Leninism as interpreted by the Communist Party. Khrushchev's policies can be described as an attempt to redefine the basic values of Soviet society. The manipulation of the perception of the external 'threat' for political purposes and the extent to which Khrushchev relied on bluff to advance his foreign policy are indications that the likelihood of war with the West, i.e. the imminence of an external military threat, was perceived to be quite low. The post-Stalin period in the Soviet Union was marked by a process of institutional power realignment. This was accompanied by a redefinition of societal values and the resulting policy objectives, both in order to legitimize the new leadership and to address the policy dilemmas facing the Soviet Union in terms of its economic development, the threat to Soviet security and its rôle in the world.

These realignments produced two alternative paths for the future of the Soviet Union, both of which, in terms of the information available to the Soviet leadership at the time, appeared in principle feasible, but with quite distinct consequences for the nature of Soviet society and its relations with the external environment.

One of these paths was promoted by a loose coalition of interest groups based on resistance to the changes in the ideological basis of Soviet foreign and domestic policy which Khrushchev appeared to be instituting, alongside the advocacy of certain directions in internal policy – a priority on heavy industry and military production – which was associated with a certain line in foreign policy – greater hostility towards the West in context of the pursuit of the international class struggle, a closer relationship with the People's Republic of China, a greater emphasis on the development of the armed forces, including conventional forces, opposition to arms control and the continued reliance on force as the main source of the stability of the Soviet system.

Khrushchev, on the other hand, sought to change the direction of domestic policy by relegating the competition with the West to the economic and political spheres, pursuing a policy of détente and shifting economic resources away from the military–industrial sector in order to develop an economic base within the Soviet Union capable of providing for the needs of the Soviet people, thus justifying the socialist system by its economic performance and enhancing internal stability through political and economic success.

The distinction between different perspectives on the significance of domestic politics in the explanation of international behaviour is obscured by the fact that a state's position in the world can itself be an important factor in its domestic politics. As the post-Stalin period demonstrates,[102] the conduct of foreign policy plays an important rôle in the political manoeuvring for power within the ruling group. Khrushchev's missile diplomacy not only promised spectacular foreign-policy successes which would have enhanced his prestige as a leader of the Soviet Union, but also it would have justified his reliance on nuclear weapons and the associated, controversial policies involving the reorientation of economic priorities and reductions in conventional forces. The conduct of foreign policy cannot be explained solely on the basis of foreign-policy objectives and their relation to the Soviet position in the international system per se, given their contradictory nature. It can be correlated to some extent, however, to Khrushchev's domestic political objectives, both in terms of his own position as leader and his domestic-policy priorities.

While on the one hand Khrushchev intended to use foreign policy as a means to achieve greater room for manoeuvre in his ambitious domestic-policy schemes, there was clearly a feedback process whereby foreign and domestic policy influenced each other. The failure to achieve his domestic-policy objectives and his resulting loss of influence meant that forces within the Soviet leadership that espoused ambitious foreign-policy objectives more in line with the 'military superiority model' were able to push Khrushchev into a quite aggressive stance. The whole story of the nuclear test moratorium is quite a good example, where arms-control policy was driven by domestic-policy forces which eluded Khrushchev's control. On the other hand, the failures of Khrushchev's foreign-policy ventures had their effect on his ability to pursue his domestic policies, and were a contributory factor in his ultimate downfall.

The evidence adduced in this chapter confirms the primacy of domestic political priorities. This is not to deny that Khrushchev himself had ambitions for the Soviet Union to be a, and if possible, even *the* leading world power. Nonetheless, it is also evident that the general line of seeking détente and peaceful co-existence and shifting the East–West competition away from the military was, despite some of Khrushchev's tactics, the dominant influence on his strategic arms policy. We have already observed that the post-Khrushchev foreign policy also does not fit the 'military superiority model'. However, military power was the main basis for the Soviet claim to superpower status. A sustained build-up of Soviet strategic power is consistent with this observation.

4   Soviet military doctrine and policy

In the Soviet Union the implementation of a military policy designed to achieve certain political objectives is based on a systematic understanding of the nature of warfare and the means and strategies for the achievement of military objectives. The image of a future war is central to the formulation of policies which result in a certain force posture and the detailed operational plans to be carried out in the event of conflict.

The advent of nuclear weapons and long-range means of delivery transformed the nature of warfare. In terms of their implications for military strategy, the principal protagonists in the East–West confrontation which, in military terms, was ultimately based on nuclear weapons all underwent a similar learning process about the implications of strategic nuclear forces. This involved an evolution from the perception of nuclear warfare as simply conventional warfare with increased firepower, to the reliance on the nuclear weapon as a decisive weapon, to the view that if war breaks out it should be kept at a conventional level for as long as possible and the reliance on nuclear deterrence in the context of assured mutual destruction.

A study of the evolution of military doctrine is thus essential to explain the evolution of Soviet strategic forces. Given the secrecy about military affairs in the Soviet Union and the restrictions on military writings which prohibit, for example, the discussion of specific Soviet military systems and deployment options, and the propaganda element in all Soviet publications of the period, any conclusions reached from the military literature must be interpreted in the light of the nature of the Soviet force posture and the resulting military options which may in turn yield clues about the content of the military doctrine and explain its development. As we shall see, the 'nuclear revolution in Soviet military affairs', as it is called, was not an autonomous development of military thought, but was subject to interference by the Soviet leadership based on extraneous political imperatives. On the basis of the evidence provided both by military writings – the articulation of military thought – and the evolution of the strategic force posture – the implementation of military policy – this chapter seeks to arrive at a coherent account of the evolution of Soviet military policy and its relationship to strategic arms deployments in the period under consideration.

The principles of Soviet military doctrine

Soviet military policy is based on a highly developed structure of military thought known as *military doctrine* (voennaia doktrina). Soviet military writers give the following definitions of *military doctrine*:

> Soviet military doctrine is a system of scientifically based views and directions of the state on questions of its military policy, the organization of the armed forces and the preparation of the country for the triumphant waging of war in defense of the interests of the Soviet Union and the countries of the Socialist community.[1]

Likewise,

> Under military doctrine we understand a system of leading views in the state about the character of war in given concrete historical conditions, the definition of the task of the armed forces and the principles of their organization, and also the means and form of armed struggle which result from the war aims and the socio-economic and military-technical capability of the country.[2]

Military doctrine represents the policy of the Soviet Party and Government in the military arena. As such, it has the status of a state law.[3]

> In considering the content of military doctrine we usually distin-guish between its political and military-technical principles. The political principles include the propositions revealing the socio-political essence of the war which the imperialists can unleash upon the Soviet Union the character of the political objectives and the strategic tasks of the state in it and their influence on the construc-tion of the armed forces and the methods of preparing for and waging war . . .
>
> Military doctrine and strategy are a reflection of the policy of the state in the military field. Defining the general political objectives of the Soviet state and objectives in war by this very process the CPSU leadership also determines the political principles of military doc-trine . . .

The correct determination and understanding of the character of a possible war in which the Soviet Armed Forces will become involved, and also knowledge of the armed forces and the military-economic capabilities of the probable enemy are the initial point of Soviet military doctrine.[4]

The sources, the ideological and methodological basis of Soviet military doctrine and strategy are: Marxist–Leninist teachings on war and the army; Leninist principles of the defense of the Socialist homeland which serve as the basis of CPSU and Soviet Government policy in the resolution of all tasks of military organization, economic, moral and scientific-technical capabilities of the state, data of military science and materialist dialectics which scientifically substantiate the character of war and preparations for waging it successfully in a specifically military respect.[5]

The systematic study of military affairs is called *military science* (voennaia nauka). It is a unified system of knowledge about the waging of war, based on Marxism–Leninism.[6] Issues which therefore concern military science include the character of a future war, the laws of war, preparation of the country and the Armed Forces for war and the methods of conducting a war.[7] The theory of building up the armed forces (*stroitel'stvo*) (mobilization, manning and deployment of forces, reserves) and their structure, military economics, the rear services and military history are also aspects of military science.

The application of military science to military operations is known as *military art* (voennoe iskusstvo), described in the Soviet military literature in the following terms:

The theory of military art, as the most important element of Soviet military science, studies and elaborates actual methods and forms of armed combat . . .

The theory of military art consists of strategy, operational art, and tactics, each of which represents a whole field of scientific knowledge. Strategy, operational art, and tactics are interrelated, interdependent and supplement each other. Among these, strategy plays the predominant role.

The military art of the Services of the Armed Forces, based in a single military strategy, common to all of the armed forces, incorporates the operational art and tactics of these Services of the Armed Forces.[8]

Military strategy (*voennaia strategiia*) is thus the most important of three aspects of military art.

The theory of strategy deals with the use of all military forces and means of a country in a war. This means that one of the problems of military strategy is the development of general foundations for the utilization of various services of the armed services and the coordination of their efforts aimed at the achievement of a common military and political objective. At the same time the theory of strategic utilization of each of the services of the armed forces, resting on a common basis of a unified strategy, works out concrete forms and methods of application . . .

The content of strategy is not constant. Its nature changes depending on the definition of the subject of strategy which has built up at a given time, the problems put to military strategy by the state policy, and possibilities of the material and moral type, i.e., the forces and means placed at the disposal of strategy.[9]

The distinction between military strategy, operational art and tactics has been described by Marshal A. A. Grechko in the following manner:

While strategy encompasses questions dealing with the preparation and use of the Armed Forces in war, operational art involves resolution of problems of preparing for and waging joint and independent operations and combat actions by operational formations and Services of the Armed Forces in individual theaters of military operations. With regard to tactics, operational art occupies a dominant position. It determines tactical missions, and the role and place of tactical operations by units and formations in achieving operational goals.[10]

The following are aspects of the theory of military strategy:

the laws governing armed conflict which are inherent in strategy;
the conditions and nature of a future war;
the theoretical foundation of preparation of the country and of the
     armed forces and the principles of military planning;
the fundamentals of civil defence;
the methods of conducting armed conflict;
the basis of the material and technical support for armed conflict;
the bases of leadership of military forces and of the war in general;
     and
the strategic attitudes of the probable opponents.[11]

Despite this hierarchy of concepts which can be clearly discerned from Soviet military writings, it is important to point out that these distinctions are not always clearly maintained. In particular, the distinction between *doctrine* and *strategy* is at times confused; since one is the implementation of the other, their content is often similar. While in principle military doctrine therefore defines the basic principles of military art, the results of the work of military science (in particular military strategy) are used to formulate military doctrine.[12]

The revolution in Soviet military affairs: 1953–1959

Soviet military writers divide the historical development of Soviet military doctrine into the following periods:

1 The early period, 1917–1941
2 The Great Patriotic War and the post-war period under Stalin, 1941–1953
3 The revolution in military affairs, 1953–1959
4 The modern period

The modern period is not subdivided by Soviet authors, but one could distinguish three phrases in the period under consideration:

(i)   The Khrushchev period, 1960–1964
(ii) The strategic build-up, 1964–1968
(iii) The development of a capability for controlled conflict, 1969–1973[13]

During the time of Stalin, the formulation of military doctrine was the exclusive preserve of Stalin himself; as a result military writing could only take place strictly within the parameters thus defined. Soviet military doctrine in this period emphasized a number of factors declared to be decisive for the outcome of a war. They were known as the 'permanently-operating factors' which were established by Stalin in Order No. 55 on 23 February 1942.[14] H. S. Dinerstein explained Stalin's understanding of war in the following manner:

> Stalin's position was that war was a massive social phenomenon in which two or more societies were pitted against one another. In this contest all the strength and weakness of the societies came into play. It was not a gladiatorial contest in which the superior skill of one man, or the accident of, say, a man stumbling over a stone, could determine the outcome. Since war is a social phenomenon, the laws of society were applicable to it. In the special context of warfare, what were known as the 'permanently operating factors' would determine the outcome.[15]

In Stalin's own words, the permanently operating factors were:

(a) the stability of the rear
(b) the morale of the army
(c) the quantity and quality of divisions
(d) the armament of the army
(e) the organizing ability of the command personnel[16]

The *permanently operating* factors were described in contrast to *temporary* factors (in particular, the rôle of a surprise attack such as the German attack on the Soviet Union in the Great Patriotic War); the latter were considered only of transitory significance and would not ultimately determine the outcome of war. Of particular significance is the fact that under Stalin military doctrine was not revised to take account of the advent of nuclear weapons. Although Stalin obviously recognized that atomic bombs were important, since a great effort was made to break the American atomic monopoly, it was denied that nuclear weapons would by themselves suffice to produce victory, and their significance was played down. This may be due in part to the limited stockpile of atomic weapons in existence at the time, and also to the Western lead in this area. It is important to note, however, that the existence of nuclear weapons did not significantly affect the Soviet understanding of the nature and rôle of war or its strategy during the Stalin era.

A new debate on military science was opened after Stalin's death in March 1953 by an article published in the September 1953 issue of the journal *Voennaia Mysl'* by its then editor Major General Nikolai Talenskii 'On the Question of the Character of the Laws of Military Science'.[17]

Talenskii's article has sometimes been interpreted by Western analysts as 'questioning the validity of Stalin's permanently operating factors'.[18] This, however, is not quite correct. It is true this article constituted a critique of Stalinist military science, but Talenskii's argument was a more subtle philosophical one. It concerned Stalin's assertion, that military science, as a sociological discipline of learning, was subject to a fundamental or basic law, and that this law was best expressed in terms of the permanently operating factors. Talenskii's criticism consisted in saying that this approach was methodologically unsound; the permanently operating factors could by definition only be specific principles of military science, rather than its basic law. Talenskii's own proposal for a basic law of military science was as follows:

> Victory in modern war is achieved by the decisive defeat of the
> enemy in the course of armed conflict by successive strikes increas-
> ing in force, on the base of superiority in permanently operating
> factors, which decide the fate of war, and on the base of the com-
> prehensive use of the economic, moral–political and military possi-
> bilities in their unity and interaction.[19]

Talenskii thus still accepted that the permanently operating factors
were decisive for the outcome of the war, but he assigned them a
different rôle in the systematic analysis of military science. A more
radical departure from Stalinist military doctrine consisted in the
suggestion that under certain conditions war might not be long and
protracted, but could instead be decided in a short time:

> Proceeding from the understanding of contemporary world wars as
> protracted wars, the basic law in the given formulation does not
> exclude the possibility of decisive defeat of one enemy or another
> under well-known circumstances, in a limited period of time.[20]

This was a veiled reference to nuclear weapons, as became clear
through later writings. It must be understood, however, that
Talenskii went merely so far as to say that in exceptional circumstances surprise could be a decisive factor.[21] Another departure from
orthodoxy consisted in the suggestion that the same laws of warfare
applied to capitalist and socialist states. Again this radical argument
was somewhat mitigated by the assertion that since Soviet military
science is based on Marxism-Leninism, socialist states are in a much
better position to recognize and apply these laws; thus, while in
Talenskii's views the laws of war which determined how victory
could be achieved were the same for both sides, this did not apply to
the *recognition* of these laws where the socialist countries had a
distinct advantage over the imperialist countries.[22]

Although Talenskii's article must have reflected a discussion
among Soviet military strategists, he nevertheless overstepped the
boundaries of what was acceptable at the time, and he left the
Military History Department of the General Staff and the editorship
of *Voennaia Mysl'* the following year.

Nonetheless, his article sparked off a vigorous debate among the
Soviet military, as manifested by at least forty published replies
which expressed various points of view.[23]

One focus of the debate was the question of whether there was
such a thing as 'a basic law' of military science which had universal
application. Related to this was the issue of the definition of the
boundaries of military science as a field of knowledge. A particularly
explicit critique of Talenskii's views was given by Colonel R. Zverev:

> [Talenskii views the] . . . armed conflict apart from its dialectical interdependence with the social and political aspect of wars, and this leads to a non-Marxist, non-scientific point of view on the nature and character of war, and on the nature and character of the rules of military science, and reduces military science to a mere military art . . . He [Talenskii] thinks that the armed conflict exists in general without a human being as the representative of a definite social structure, of definite classes, that a bare military science exists, a naked strategy, a naked operational art, a naked tactics, naked, eternal military rules which are the same for all. Such things do not exist in nature. This attempt to 'work out' 'a pure military science, one and the same for all times and peoples' is idealistic in essence and should be decisively rejected.[24]

In what Herbert Dinerstein has interpreted as the 'resolution' of the Talenskii debate by the editors of *Voennaia Mysl'* in April 1955[25] they came firmly down in favour of a more restrictive view of the content of military science arguing that military science could not include

> the whole complex of questions of war as a social and historical phenomenon.[26]

The editors agreed with Talenskii that the laws of war were of a general nature, valid for capitalists as much as for socialists. However, capitalist military experts, lacking the intellectual framework of Marxism-Leninism, were unable to properly understand and interpret the laws of war. Thus different systems of military science existed, even if one could not claim that there were different kinds of objective laws. The resolution of the controversy about a basic law of war was none-the-less unsatisfactory, since the editors of *Voennaia Mysl'* expressed the view

> that it is not yet possible to propound any final and definite formulation of the basic law.[27]

As a result the conceptual issue of whether the laws of war are reducible to one basic law and its content remained uncertain (itself a radical change from the situation under Stalin where all fundamental issues were considered resolved and the basic principles laid down). Talenskii's methodological approach never came to fruition. As S. N. Kozlov later explained in a historical view of the evolution of Soviet military doctrine:

> The existence of a general law of military science was considered self-evident, and it was only necessary to formulate it. This they were unable to do.[28]

Nevertheless, Talenskii's principal purpose was accomplished. The rigid boundaries of the permanently operating factors had been shifted. The professional military could legitimately debate the issue of the requirements for victory without having to assume that the Soviet Union would win any war merely because of the superiority of its social system.

Another controversy of interest was the rôle of surprise. Talenskii's article did not recognize surprise as a decisive factor in war:

> It is well known that the influence of surprise on the course of military operations can be significant. But as a result of the correct actions of a commander, the effect of an enemy surprise attack can be to a greater or lesser degree paralyzed by a system of measures, worked out by Soviet military science.[29]

However in October 1953 an article appeared in *Voennaia Mysl'* in which 'the appearance of new forms of armament of enormous destructive and devastating action' was described as sharpening the danger of surprise attack.[30] While warning in no uncertain terms about the dangers of ignoring the threat, the author, Colonel Nenakhov, nonetheless insisted:

> Surprise of attack was and remains a transitory factor not deciding the fate of wars.[31]

Raymond Garthoff has pointed out that October 1953 is the first time that a specific reference to thermonuclear weapons occurred in the Soviet military literature.[32] In the discussion following these articles in September/October 1953 the factor of surprise was generally given an enhanced degree of importance in the nuclear age, but was not recognized as decisive. There were some indications however in 1954 that the understanding of a surprise attack as a factor in war was developing still further. At the end of 1953 the study of nuclear weapons and combat under conditions of nuclear use was ordered by the Ministry of Defence, leading to radical revisions in the teaching and research programme of the General Staff Academy. A series in *Krasnaia Zvezda* in early 1954 on the significance of nuclear weapons was a further sign that the rôle of nuclear weapons in a future war was now becoming a major and central issue in Soviet military thought.[33]

The debate advanced significantly by the publication in February 1955 of an article by Marshal of the Tank Troops Rotmistrov, 'On the Role of Surprise in Contemporary War' which the editors of *Voennaia Mysl'* had at first refused to publish, presumably because of its controversial aspects, but then, with unprecedented self-criticism, reversed their decision. This probably occurred at the instigation of Marshal Zhukov; it is reported that on the event of his succession as Minister of Defence in February 1955 he gave a secret address to leading officers in which he criticized Stalinist military theory and emphasized the need for a new study of military affairs.

The significance of surprise in modern war was explained by Rotmistrov in the following terms:

> Surprise attack with the employment of atomic and hydrogen weapons and other contemporary weapons now assumes new forms, and is capable of leading to significantly greater results than in the past war. One may frankly say that under the circumstances of the use of atomic and hydrogen weapons surprise is one of the decisive conditions for achievement of success, not only in battles and operations, but even in wars as a whole. In certain cases surprise attack with the mass use of new weapons can provoke the quick collapse of a state whose capability for resistance is low as a consequence of the basic failures of its social and economic structure, and also of an unfavorable geographic location.[34]

If surprise can prove decisive, it follows that it would be of crucial importance for the Soviet Union to deny the aggressor the advantages gained from surprise. How can this be done? What is required is for the Soviet Union to seize the strategic initiative:

> The duty of the Soviet armed forces is not to permit an enemy surprise attack on our country, and in the event of an attempt to accomplish one, not only to repel the attack successfully, but also to deal the enemy counterblows, or even pre-emptive [uprezhdaiush-chie] surprise blows, of terrible destructive force. For this the Soviet army and navy possess everything necessary.[35]

Rotmistrov sharply distinguished pre-emptive action from preventive wars, denying that the Soviet Union had any intention of attacking anyone.

There are many indications that Soviet military doctrine at this time incorporated a policy to be prepared for pre-emptive military action. Thus the editors of *Voennaia Mysl'* stated in March 1955 as part of their self-criticism for holding up the publication of Rotmistrov's article:

> We cannot ignore the lessons of history and we must always be ready for pre-emptive actions against the perfidy of the aggressors.[36]

Similarly, the editorial of the May issue stated:

The matter goes beyond the exhaustive clarification of the significance of the surprise factor and the study of cases and examples of the employment of surprise in recent wars. The task is the purposeful elaboration of all aspects of this question, especially the elaboration of ways and means to prevent an enemy surprise attack and to deal the opponent pre-emptive blows on every scale – strategic, operational and tactical.[37]

General B. S. Shatilov (deputy head of the Main Political Administration), writing for the general public in May 1955, stated:

It would pay the immoderately warlike generals and admirals of the imperialist camp to remember that atomic weapons as well as surprise action are double-edged weapons and that it is hardly sensible to jest with them.[38]

Reading all the various statements by Soviet military authors on the importance of surprise, one detects a deep underlying anxiety about the Soviet defence posture, This is not surprising, given that the Soviet Union was vulnerable to US strategic bomber attack, as well as to attack from forward bases, while it had only limited means to attack the continental United States. At the time of Stalin's death in 1953 the USSR had a limited stockpile of atomic bombs and only obsolescent bombers of limited range to deliver them (the TU-4) (their range was insufficient for two-way missions to the United States). In August 1953 the USSR exploded a thermonuclear device. It was not until 1954 that nuclear weapons were beginning to be integrated into the Soviet armed forces and their training.[39] Although a new twin-turbojet medium-range bomber (the *Badger*) and two modern types of heavy bomber with intercontinental range (the four turbo-jet *Bison* and the multi-turboprop *Bear*) were in development, in 1955 the Soviet Union still possessed no delivery systems of intercontinental range, while the United States had 1,309 bombers which could deliver 2,310 warheads (plus 698 warheads deployed on forward bases). The Soviet Union could deliver a total of 324 warheads on systems with regional range. The preponderance of American military strength was very alarming for the Soviet military and explains in part their deep worry about a surprise attack and hence the move to a policy of pre-emptive attack.

In this context, the military leadership was deeply concerned by the military policy pursued by the party leadership under Malenkov, whose foreign policy was aimed at the reduction of international tension and improved relations with the United States. In stark contrast to the position taken by military leaders Malenkov propounded the view that the international situation was improving, and that the armed forces of the Soviet Union had everything necessary to rebuff any aggression, implying therefore that the danger of war was receding. At the same time he emphasized that nuclear weapons had a very radical impact on the nature of war and the military posture that should be adopted by the Soviet Union. He declared that a thermonuclear war would mean 'the destruction of world civilization'.[40] It was no longer to be taken for granted that socialist countries would prevail in a war with the capitalist countries. He vigorously condemned the Cold War and emphasized the threat of devastation posed by a nuclear war both to the Soviet Union and the United States. He thus moved away from the notion of the 'inevitability of war' as long as capitalism existed and more towards the notion that a long-term, accommodation with capitalism was necessary. The military force posture to be adopted as a result was that of a 'minimum deterrent', rather than developing an all-round war-fighting capability such as envisaged by the military leadership. As will be discussed later, in the chapter on Party–military relations, the position taken by the military on the rôle of nuclear weapons was also influenced by the institutional interests of the military which were clearly threatened by the policies which Malenkov pursued.

An important turning-point in the evolution of Soviet military doctrine was the 20th Congress of the CPSU in 1956, when Khrushchev launched his campaign of de-stalinization with his Secret Speech, as a consequence of which the military leaders could now explicitly break with Stalinist military thought. Khrushchev himself introduced a significant change in Soviet thinking about war. Noting Lenin's thesis of the inevitability of war while imperialism still exists, Khrushchev claimed that the situation had now changed because of the existence of the world socialist camp which had the means to prevent aggression.

> As long as capitalism survives in the world, the reactionary forces representing the interests of the capitalist monopolies will continue their drive towards military gambles and aggression, and may try to unleash war. But war is not fatalistically inevitable. Today there are mighty social and political forces possessing formidable means to prevent the imperialists from unleashing war and if they actually try to start it, to give a smashing rebuff to the aggressors and frustrate their adventurist plans.[41]

The Congress called for a new examination of all aspects of military science.[42] Military history facilities, which had been reduced after Stalin's death, were re-organized and re-vitalized. In May 1957, an important conference of the Soviet Armed Forces was convened which concerned itself with various aspects of military science and, in particular, with problems of military art (primarily strategy). This was the first of a whole series of seminars and studies about the impact of nuclear weapons initiated apparently at the behest of the Presidium, and many of the most senior Soviet military leaders from the General Staff, military academies and the military districts participated. The new formulation of military doctrine and science which emerged from these debates was presented in a group of papers published in a series of articles in *Voennaia Mysl'*; they are referred to as 'The Special Collection'.[43]

A good indicator of the trends of Soviet military thought during this period is the development of the notion of 'permanently operating factors' into that of the 'decisive factors' in contemporary war. As has been pointed out above, Talenskii did not reject the notion of the 'permanently operating factors' as such. Rotmistrov emphasized the importance of temporary factors, such as surprise, but did not go as far as denying the decisive nature of permanent factors:

> Surprise attack by itself still does not and cannot provide complete victory in war or an operation, it only creates a condition which must be skillfully exploited . . . while considering surprise as one of the most important conditions of achieving success and recognizing its ever-growing role, it is necessary to note that this circumstance in no measure contradicts the thesis on the permanently operating factors which decide the fate of wars. They continue in contemporary circumstances to have primary significance for achieving a complete victory over the enemy.[44]

This may appear to be in contradiction with some of Rotmistrov's other statements. The issue was clarified in another article published by Rotmistrov in *Voennyi Vestnik* where he accepted that a surprise attack with new weapons can under certain circumstances be a *decisive* factor; nonetheless he stated:

> Surprise cannot, however, yield a conclusive result, cannot bring victory, in a war with a serious and strong enemy.[45]

The period 1953–55 was marked not by the rejection of the concept of the 'permanently operating factors', but rather by the refinement and re-definition of the concept in order to develop it into a practical guide in military thought. Garthoff has pointed out that during this period at least 57 reaffirmations of the thesis of the 'permanently operating factors' could be found in Soviet writings.[46] The Party

Congress in 1956 proved to be a major turning-point. From now on the concept of 'permanently operating factors' was no longer used. As Garthoff has shown, however, the existence of 'decisive factors' which determined the outcome of a war continued as an important tenet of Soviet military doctrine, and their content was not much different from the 'permanently operating factors'. One of the reasons for dropping the latter term was its association with Stalin and his 'personality cult'. For example, a book review in *Krasnaia Zvezda* criticized adherence to 'the old way' (i.e. the five permanently operating factors) as defining the conditions for success in a modern war.[47] The criticism was directed at the rigid way in which these factors were treated. As the authors of this article stated:

> It would have been more correct to talk about the moral-political, economic and military factors and seek a comprehensive elucidation of their place in securing victory in war.[48]

Another article in *Krasnaia Zvezda* a month later stated likewise:

> We have had attempts to reduce all military theory to I.V. Stalin's propositions on the permanently operating factors determining the course and outcome of war. This proposition essentially reproduces Lenin's ideas on the conditions of victory over aggressors. However, it does not completely exhaust the question of the factors determining the course and outcome of modern war. It would be possible for example, to show that it does not include such important factors as the preparation of troops, their organization, the military art, the state of the military theory of the warring armies, and others. It is impossible also not to note that in present conditions the significance of the surprise factor has grown.[49]

Among the 'decisive factors' continued to be the 'stability of the rear', a principal aspect of which was the economic potential of the country to sustain the war effort.[50] Soviet military writers in 1958 frequently expressed the view that

> The socialist system of the economy . . . gives our state an enormous superiority over any capitalist state in relation to the economic and morale potential of the country and to its utilization to achieve victory in war.[51]

This view was also expressed by General Colonel N. A. Lomov, a Professor of Military Sciences and an important author on military doctrine, in 1962:

> The *economic potential* plays a very important role in deciding the fate of a war. The military strength of a state depends directly on the

> economic possibilities of a country ... The economic potential
> acquires particular significance and the conditions of stormy devel-
> opment of new means of armed combat. The successful conduct of a
> modern large war cannot depend on the timely accumulation of
> strategic reserves of the state. A solid economic foundation is
> essential, especially in case of prolonged war, to satisfy the military
> needs of the state on the basis of continued production.[52]

The 'morale potential' constitutes another decisive factor. Soviet
superiority in morale is asserted on the basis that a state with an
advanced social and political structure (i.e. a socialist state like the
USSR) will conduct a 'just war' in contrast to an imperialist state
whose armed forces will be engaged in an aggressive and unjust
war. The military leaders of capitalist countries cannot rely on the
lasting morale of the entire society, as the policy of the leadership
does not express the interest of the people – hence it cannot be a
just war.

> Such a strategy leads to an over-evaluation of the purely military
> factors, to adventurism in military art, to overestimating the role of
> one or another weapon, arm or element of the armed forces.[53]

The Soviet concern with morale is clear from the military literature
and the efforts at political education, it is also interesting to observe
the reference of overestimating the role of particular weapons, an
indication that the importance of morale is not diminished by the
existence of nuclear weapons.[54] Thus Major General Pokrovskii, an
expert in military technology, stated that

> atomic weapons create a situation in which the morale factor acts
> still more strongly than in ordinary war.[55]

The 'quantity and quality of divisions' and the 'armament of the
army' are two of the permanently operating factors which require
some redefinition in the nuclear age. Marshal Zhukov described
them in his statement on the decisive factors in war in 1957 in the
following manner:

> the success of war depends on a series of factors, in particular the
> technical level and condition of the arms of the armed forces, the
> combat ability and mastery of the troops, the art of the supreme
> command, commanders, and operational-tactical office cadres, and
> the main thing – whether the people and the army recognize the just
> aims of the war because of which the government has led them into
> the given war . . . The factors which have been noted above display
> their decisive influence on the character of the war and the means of
> its conduct.[56]

The term 'military potential' was also used to describe the factors enumerated by Zhukov.

A very succinct summary of the new Soviet thinking about the conduct of war was given by Marshal of the Tank Troops Pavel A. Rotmistrov in an article published in *Voennaia Mysl'* in February 1958 entitled 'On Modern Soviet Military Art and its Characteristic Features'. He described the influence of nuclear weapons on military thought thus:

> Earlier, particularly before World War I, it was considered that the appearance of new weapons and fighting equipment exerts influence above all on methods and forms of waging battle, i.e., on tactics, and hence on strategy. This concept was correct while the operational range of new weapons was limited to the battlefield and their destructive power was comparatively small. During World War II, tanks and aviation, which were rapidly developed after their appearance in World War I, began to influence not only tactics but operational art directly. The case is quite different with atomic weapons, which possess vast destructive powers, and with their carriers: intercontinental ballistic missiles; long-range aviation; surface vessels and submarines armed with rockets which make it possible to deliver crushing attacks on objects hundreds and thousands of kilometers away; rockets for operational-tactical purposes; and atomic artillery. These new types of combat equipment influence strategy, operational art and tactics simultaneously.[57]

The military effect of modern weapons systems was described in the following terms:

> Aviation and rocket attacks against enemy military and economic objectives expand immeasurably the zone of military operations, eliminate the boundary between the front and the rear and impart a universal and an exceedingly decisive character to an armed struggle. The use of rockets of various designations with atomic and thermonuclear warheads, long-range deviation and submarine makes possible the destruction of strategic objectives in enemy territory regardless of their distance from the front line. The destruction or disruption of the normal activities of important economic and entire industrial areas, transport junctions, and political and administrative centers of the enemy during a war can place the enemy in a very difficult situation and exert serious influence on the course and outcome of the war as a whole.[58]

Rotmistrov emphasized the vital task of developing Soviet military strategy to cope with warfare in the nuclear age where military action could extend to the entire area in which forces were present, including the command and control centres, and strategic reserves would be such that prolonged resistance would become impossible.[59]

The emphasis in Rotmistrov's article is on counterforce targets: command and control centres, enemy nuclear forces and strategic reserves. Although Rotmistrov's discussion presupposes a certain degree of resemblance with conventional warfare in so far as he assumes the action of mass armies and prolonged combat operations, the possibility of a short war as a result of the total strategic attack on the enemy with nuclear weapons is clearly hinted at in the above quotation. Operations in contemporary war, according to Rotmistrov, will be different from World War II in that the process of encirclement of large enemy groupings in a small area will be more difficult owing to the high dispersion and mobility of forces. The modern offensive operation in his view is characterized by the growing importance of attacking enemy reserves.[60] Rotmistrov also envisaged that mass-annihilation weapons would be used to break through a defence:

> Modern defense fulfills those tasks confronting it only when it is able to withstand the massive blows of the enemy's atomic weapons and does not permit a breakthrough by his tank groups. Consequently, a most important characteristic of modern defense is its high degree of antiatomic and antitank stability. The effort of the defender to protect his forces from destruction by atomic weapons necessitates their dispersion.[61]

The article also stressed a combined arms approach and the continuing importance of the infantry,[62] despite the recognition that enemy forces might be destroyed in a very short time by the co-ordinated use of new weapons systems.[63]

During the Fifties the Soviet military still conceived of a nuclear war as basically a more destructive version of World War II. But, as we have already mentioned, in May 1957 a conference of the Soviet Armed Forces on military science initiated a secret but wide debate among the military about the nature and strategy of war in the nuclear age, followed by a series of seminars. As Army General S. Ivanov described it:

> Under the leadership of the CPSU Central Committee the elaboration of a new military doctrine in the main was complete at the beginning of the 1960s. Subsequently its individual propositions were developed and refined.[64]

As we have already pointed out, the internal studies on military doctrine and strategy in the nuclear age resulted in the 'Special

Collection' of articles which were published in *Voennaia Mysl'* beginning in 1960. The conclusion of these studies was a radically different view of a future war, which was now primarily seen as a strategic nuclear exchange which might be quite short in duration. It should be pointed out that the articles reflected a compromise between those who thought that nuclear weapons made traditional theatre campaigns obsolete and those who took a more traditional view, according to which large armies, air and naval forces would still be required despite the enormous destructive potential of nuclear weapons (the use of which from the very beginning in a major war was considered inevitable). The ideas expressed in the *The Special Collection* were broadly in line with those of the book *Voennaia Strategiia* edited by Sokolovskii and published in 1962.[65] The *revolution in Soviet military affairs* was exemplified by the creation of a new military service – the Strategic Rocket Forces (SRF) – in December 1959, which replaced the Ground Forces as the pre-eminent service in the Soviet Armed Forces.[66]

Military doctrine and strategic arms policy

The establishment of the SRF, which became the pre-eminent service in war-time (instead of the Ground Forces) was accompanied by a revision in Soviet military doctrine announced by Khrushchev which was not in conformity with the military thinking which had resulted from the debates in the 1950s. In a speech before the Supreme Soviet in January 1960 Khrushchev declared the primary importance of nuclear weapons and missiles. He emphasized that many of the traditional armed forces, such as air forces, surface navies and large standing armies, were becoming obsolete, that the initial phase of a nuclear war would probably be decisive and that such a war would be of short duration. However, he was confident that the Soviet Union would be able to survive such a war, even if it was attacked first, particularly if it took advantage of its size to camouflage and disperse its weapons. He also believed that the 'Imperialist camp' was deterred by the strength of Soviet military forces and then announced a reduction in manpower in the Soviet armed forces from 3.6 milion to 2.4 million men. He claimed that nuclear firepower would more than make up for the reduction in manpower.

As we shall see in chapter 5, Party–Military Relations, there was intense dissatisfaction in the professional military with the stance

Khrushchev took and, as a result of a weakening of his position in the Party, he was forced in 1961 to enter a compromise with Defence Minister Malinovskii, which involved the general recognition that all branches of the armed forces were still of importance in modern war, that multi-million-man armies were still required, a suspension of the troop reductions and an increase in the 1961 budgetary allocations of the military. In return, Malinovskii offered emphatic support to many of the general themes of Khrushchev's defence policy, such as the primacy of strategic nuclear missile forces.

This fundamental compromise is echoed in the military writings of the period, especially the Sokolovskii volume on military strategy published in 1962, which are firmly based on the nuclear revolution in military affairs, but still exhibit elements of more traditional military thought. The following discussion outlines some of the basic issues, to some extent, but by no means exclusively, on Sokolovskii's *Voennaia Strategiia*.[67]

According to Sokolovskii

> In its political and social essence *a new world war will be a decisive armed clash between two opposed world social systems.*[68]
>
> ... *a future war, from the point of view of means of armed combat, will be above all a nuclear rocket war.* The basis of waging it will be the mass use of nuclear rockets by all services of the armed forces, but primarily by the Strategic Rocket Troops.[69]
>
> ... we have concluded that the Armed Forces of the Soviet Union and the other socialist countries must be prepared above all to wage war under conditions of the mass use of nuclear weapons by both belligerent parties.[70]
>
> A future world war will require of the Soviet Armed Forces, of the entire socialist camp, the use of the main military forces, from the very outset of the war, literally in the very first hours and minutes, in order to achieve the most decisive results in the shortest time possible.[71]

There is general agreement in the military literature of the period that a future world war would be an all-out nuclear war, fought by a socialist against an imperialist coalition; it will be a war fought without restraints, and at issue will be the existence of the socialist or the imperialist camp.

Global thermonuclear war differs from the transitional forms of warfare in its strategic objectives:

> The question arises of what, under these conditions, constitutes the main military-strategic goal of the war: defeat of the enemy's armed forces, as was the case in the past, or the annihilation and

destruction of objectives in the enemy interior and the disorgani-
zation of the latter?

... both of these goals should be achieved simultaneously ...
Two main factors are at the root of this solution of the problem: first,
the need to decisively defeat the aggressor in the shortest possible
time, for which it will be necessary to deprive him simultaneously
of his military, political and economic possibilities of waging war;
second, the real possibility of achieving these goals simultaneously
with the aid of existing means of armed combat.[72]

An important feature of contemporary war in this understanding is
the decisive nature of the initial period of the war. This raised a
number of important questions. The first one is that of how to deal
with the threat of a surprise attack. As N. Lomov explained:

Therefore Soviet military doctrine considers it to be the most
important, most urgent, and foremost task of the armed forces, to
maintain constant combat readiness, in order to repel a surprise
attack by the enemy and scuttle his criminal plans. To stop the
nuclear attack of the opponent and take the strategic initiative on
one's own hands is therefore one of the main tasks in the initial
period of war. A particularly important role on the solution of this
task is played by the strategic rocket troops as well as the troops of
the air defence of the country.[73]

Despite some denials[74] a number of such statements from the early
Sixties (such as that by Lomov quoted above) reflect a policy of
preemption. Thus Malinovskii referred in his speech to the 22nd
Party Congress in 1961 to

the readiness of the Soviet Armed Forces to break up a surprise
attack of the imperialists.[75]

The Sokolovskii volume stated:

Since modern means of combat make it possible to achieve excep-
tionally great strategic results in the briefest time, *the initial period of
the war will be of decisive importance for the outcome of the entire war.*
In this regard the main problem is the development of methods for
reliably repelling a surprise nuclear attack as well as methods of
frustrating the aggressive designs of the enemy by the timely
infliction of a shattering attack upon him. A satisfactory solution of
this problem is determined primarily by the constant high level of
combat readiness of the Soviet Armed Forces, especially the Strategic Rocket Forces.[76]

As Thomas Wolfe has argued,[77] these statements and, in particular,
that from the Sokolovskii volume, are somewhat ambiguous in what

precise action is envisaged. It must be kept in mind, however, that the Sokolovskii authors argue very clearly for counterforce *and* countervalue strikes:

> The basic method of waging war will be massed nuclear-rocket attacks inflicted for the purpose of destroying the aggressor's means of nuclear attack and for the simultaneous mass destruction and devastation of the vitally important objectives comprising the enemy's military, political and economic might . . .[78]

Similarly Malinovskii described in his 1962 pamphlet *Soviet Views on Targeting*:

> The objectives of crushing nuclear attacks, together with groupings of the armed forces of the enemy, will be industrial and administrative centers, communications centers, and everything that aids war.[79]

Given the picture painted by the Sokolovskii authors of a massive missile attack requiring virtually all forces in order to be successful, and since it appears unlikely that they were envisaging strikes at empty missile sites or bomber bases, this would point in the direction of preemption. However, the ambiguity on Soviet statements may reflect uncertainty in the Soviet military leadership as to whether preemption or launch-on-warning would be the most effective strategy. An article by Glagolev and Larionov published in *International Affairs*, for example, seems to suggest a policy of launch-on-warning:

> The first rockets and bombers of the side on the defensive would take off *even before the aggressor's first rockets, to say nothing of his bombers, reached their targets*.[80]

Preemption is a technologically demanding strategy, requiring an effective counterforce capability. Furthermore, it is a high-risk strategy which runs counter to post-war examples of Soviet risk-taking, such as in the Berlin crisis or the Cuban missile crisis.[81] Launch-on-warning is even more technologically demanding, since it requires an efficient capability to detect the launch of nuclear missiles, an ICBM force with effective counterforce capabilities to eliminate the remaining enemy nuclear forces and the capability to have a large percentage of the force on a high-alert status for the duration of a crisis at least, but perhaps over longer periods.

The most significant constraints for operational planning in the early Sixties were most likely those imposed by early warning capabilities. The first Soviet early warning satellite was launched in

1967 (Kosmos 159), but even partial operational status for a satellite-based early warning system was not achieved until 1977. In the absence of Over-the-Horizon radar technology, warning time of an American missile attack would be very short – of the order of ten minutes. Berman and Baker estimate that missiles with storable liquid fuels could be launched within 4–8 minutes. If the SS-7 and SS-9 with hot ignition had response times at the upper end of this interval, then a launch-on-warning strategy, while perhaps still theoretically feasible, would be based on very short decision times; the margin was so small that the possibility of being overwhelmed by a surprise attack must have appeared very real. Furthermore, as Berman and Baker have pointed out, this problem could not easily be overcome by having a large number of missiles on alert in a period of crisis:

> the USSR's inability to maintain, without great expense, a large number of missiles on combat alert arose from the fact that the gyroscope in its guidance systems – necessary to induce stability in the missile – rotated on metal ball bearings, not on the gas-actuated bearings found on U.S. missile systems. The guidance system thus needed some time to warm up before a missile could be launched. And in any sustained period of holding a missile ready for immediate launching, the entire guidance system would fail because the ball bearings, which were mass produced to less than perfect tolerances, would fail under such continuing stress. If guidance systems could not be held on alert for more than 12 hours, and 10 per cent of a force of ICBMs had to be put on alert each day, 20 per cent of the guidance systems would have to be replaced on the first day and the entire force of ICBMs would be incapacitated after five days. Clearly, as its reliance on ICBMs increased, the USSR could not afford lengthy alert rates.[82]

Indeed, a realistic appraisal must have led to the conclusion that the lack of early warning facilities and other technical problems might force the adoption of operational plans based on preemptive strikes, in light of the vulnerability of Soviet ICBMs at the time. (This does not perhaps apply with equal force to the threat from intercontinental bombers which were more susceptible to air defence and, due to lesser flight speeds, would be subject to a greater warning time.)

An important consequence which flows from these considerations is that the relevance of the industrial potential of a country does not so much lie in the capability to sustain production during the war, but rather in the preparation for the initial period of the war, as was pointed out in the Sokolovskii volume.[83]

The issue which is important for our discussion here is whether the requirements of the strategy can explain subsequent attempts to deploy a missile force which was capable of implementing it. Michael MccGwire has pointed out that the missiles designed by the Korolev design bureau failed to meet the operational requirements for a strategy of preemption because their engines used non-storable fuels, thus involving an operationally unacceptable response time. (This applies *a fortiori* for launch-on-warning.) The cancellation of the planned series production of the SS-8 and the decision to curtail the development of the SS-10 could be explained on this basis.[84]

The shift in American defence policy in 1961 announced by the Kennedy administration and the resultant strategic missile programmes involving the Polaris SLBM and the fixed-site Minuteman ICBM force (with 600 Minuteman projected in Kennedy's March 1961 speech – this number was doubled in Kennedy's FY 1963 budget speech) changed Soviet targeting requirements. The Minuteman were deployed in hardened silos and therefore required a hard-target kill capability which could only be achieved with much greater accuracy and a much larger number of missiles. The SS-9 which was the first third-generation ICBM to be developed was interpreted by some Western observers as a 'silo buster'.[85] Although it was the most accurate ICBM so far developed by the Soviet Union, and as a high-yield weapon was in principle suitable to attack hard targets, its large size meant that it could not be produced in large numbers rapidly enough to pose an effective counter against the emerging Minuteman force.

The main rôle in countering the large number of American Minuteman missiles was therefore given to the SS-11 since the SS-11 was more comparable to the Minuteman in size and payload (the first modification carried a warhead of yield 0.95 MT). The SS-9 was deployed at a constant rate of 42 missiles per year, levelling off at a total of about 280 missiles, while 720 SS-11 ICBMs had been deployed by 1971; both missiles were deployed in hardened silos.[86] It is therefore apparent that the force posture which emerged by the end of the 1960s was geared to make a launch-on-warning policy operationally feasible.

Some statements in the military literature indicate a concern with early warning systems. Thus Sokolovskii and Cherednichenko wrote in 1966:

> Along with the increased possibilities for surprise attack, the possibilities are growing for the timely detection not only for the

beginning of an attack but also of the beginning of the direct
preparations by the enemy of an attack, that is, there are possibilities of preventing a surprise attack.[87]

The article does not specify the means of preventing a surprise
attack, but apart from diplomatic action a preemptive strike must be
under consideration. However, the article then goes on to speak of a
'*retaliatory* nuclear strike . . . directed at frustrating a nuclear attack
[emphasis added]', suggesting a policy of launch-on-warning. A
similar ambiguity can be detected in the third edition of the
Sokolovskii volume:

> However, possibilities of averting a surprise attack are constantly
> growing. Present means of reconnaissance, detection and surveil-
> lance can opportunely disclose a significant portion of the measures
> of direct preparation of a nuclear attack by the enemy and in the
> very first minutes locate the mass launch of missiles and the take-off
> of aircraft belonging to the aggressor and, at the right time, warn the
> leadership of the country about the impending danger. Thus
> possibilities exist not to allow a surprise attack by an aggressor, to
> deliver nuclear strikes on him at the right time.[88]

The explanation for this ambiguity may be that the Soviet military
leadership was moving towards a posture of launch-on-warning, but
was still uncertain about the capabilities for its implementation. The
trend towards launch-on-warning is confirmed by the scenario
developed in a Soviet manual on the *Design and Testing of Ballistic
Missiles* by V. I. Varfolomeyev and M. I. Kopytov (translated by the
Joint Publications Research Service in 1970) where the United States
strikes first. The first Soviet missile strike is a launch-on-warning.
The manual also indicates a preference to launch as many ICBMs as
possible during the first launch because of the threat to ICBM
survivability by a coordinated American first strike.[89] An analysis of
the military literature would thus appear to confirm the conviction
expressed by a number of analysts that in the late Sixties a shift from
preemption to launch-on-warning occurred.[90] This is further confirmed in an article by the Commander of the Strategic Rocket Forces,
Marshal of the Soviet Union N. I. Krylov published in *Voennaia Mysl'*
in 1967:

> With the presence in the armament of troops of launchers and
> missiles which are completely ready for operation, as well as
> systems for detecting enemy missile launchers and other types of
> reconnaissance, an aggressor is no longer able suddenly to destroy
> the missiles before their launch in the territory of the country

against which the aggression is committed. They will have time during the flight of the missile of the aggressor to leave their launchers and inflict a retaliatory strike against the enemy. Even in the most unfavourable circumstance, if a portion of missiles is unable to be launched before the strikes of the missiles of the aggressor, as a result of the high degree of protection of the launchers from nuclear explosion, these missiles will be retained and will carry out the combat missions entrusted to them. Thus, in modern conditions, with the presence of a system for detecting missile launches, an attempt by the aggressor to inflict a sudden preemptory strike cannot give him a decisive advantage for the achievement of victory in war and, in any case, will not save him from great destruction and losses.[91]

The changing image of a future war

By the end of the Khrushchev period the image of a future war as understood by the Soviet military had begun to change to include the possibility that the early phase of a war in Europe might involve only conventional weapons. Michael MccGwire thus refers to

> a flurry of Soviet articles . . . in 1964, discussing the possibility that a war might start with a conventional phase of indeterminate duration and even speculating on the possibility of a protracted conventional war . . . in 1965 the Warsaw Pact exercise 'October Storm' began with a conventional phase.[92]

In early 1965 General S. M. Shtemenko stated that Soviet military doctrine did not exclude the possibility of warfare restricted to conventional weapons or remaining on the level of tactical nuclear weapons in the framework of so-called 'local wars'. An article by the authority on Soviet military doctrine, General N. Lomov went significantly further. Referring specifically to the NATO doctrine of *flexible response*, Lomov said that such warfare might take place in Europe, fought with conventional weapons, but not excluding the use of tactical nuclear weapons. He stated:

> the probability of escalation into a nuclear world war is always great and might under certain circumstances become inevitable.[93]

The clear implication was that escalation was not necessarily inevitable, and that the Soviet Union should prepare to fight such wars. Earlier, in December 1964, Marshal P. A. Rotmistrov had criticized a NATO proposal for a belt of ADMs along the border on the grounds that this would preclude any war from remaining non-nuclear.

Clearly the possibility of fighting with conventional weapons only was already envisaged.[94] E. Rybkin wrote in July 1966 in a review of a book by N. V. Pukhovskii:

> historical experience has shown that only two local wars have turned into world wars . . . The author [Pukhovskii] says further that 'it is entirely possible' that the aggressor will use nuclear weapons in a local war. This is a correct statement. But again, it is doubtful that this would 'immediately' turn the war into a world war. Everything depends on the specific conditions. In any case, it is in the interests of the Soviet Union and of all progressive mankind to put an end to local war, or to limit it and defeat the aggressor with limited forces.[95]

In the view of Michael MccGwire

> During the second half of 1966 the full realization emerged that, given the appropriate Soviet strategy and contrary to the doctrinal conclusions of 1959, it was no longer inevitable that a world war would lead to a nuclear strike on Russia.[96]

This meant that avoiding such escalation could become a positive objective of Soviet military policy.

It would appear, however, that MccGwire has overstated the degree of conviction during this period that escalation to the strategic level could be avoided. Such a conviction, if it was held by the Soviet military, could not find much comfort in the NATO doctrine of *flexible response*. The German defence minister Kai-Uwe von Hassel and, at a later date, the British defence minister Denis Healey had both stressed that NATO must be prepared for the early use of tactical nuclear weapons and that the nuclear threshold must not be too high, since NATO's conventional forces would be unable to contain a full-scale attack by the Warsaw Pact for very long.[97] The third edition of the Sokolovskii volume gave a full and accurate account of West German reservations with regard to the strategy of *flexible response*.[98] It was also clear that during the Sixties (and early Seventies) British and West German reservations prevailed over the American interpretation of flexible response, and the force levels that would have been needed to implement the American concept were not achieved.

The doctrine of the 'sword' and the 'shield', which was critically analysed in an article in *Voennaia Mysl'* in June 1966, envisaged the conventional forces as the 'shield' which would hold the aggressors at bay while the sword of theatre nuclear weapons would be made ready.[99] But these theatre weapons included weapons which were capable of reaching Soviet territory. Thus an objective analysis of NATO strategy and force posture would not have supported the view that escalation could easily be avoided.

Soviet military literature does not support MccGwire's hypothesis of such a decisive shift. Thus, in 1968 a *Voennaia Mysl'* article describes the following scenario of a future war:

> [the United States] does not exclude the possibility of opening military operations even in the main theaters, with the use of just conventional means of destruction. Such a beginning of war can create favorable conditions for the movement of all nuclear forces to regions of combat operations, bringing them into the highest level of combat readiness, and subsequently inflicting the first nuclear strike with the employment in it of the maximum number of missile launch sites, submarines and aircraft at the most favorable moment.[100]

This sounds very much like the 'nuclear sword' being made ready under the cover of the 'conventional shield'. In 1969 the editor of *Voennaia Mysl'*, General V. Zemskov stated:

> in a nuclear war, if one breaks out, the combatants will use from the very beginning all the available forces and means at their disposal, above all strategic nuclear means.[101]

This article also recognizes the possibility of different variants of war. Another variant is 'a war by stages' which begins with a conventional phase and escalates by various steps to a general nuclear war. Again the purpose of the conventional phase is seen as a preparatory stage for nuclear war. It also mentions the possibility of a protracted conventional war. Soviet military literature, however, recognizes that protracted conventional war is only likely if the forces of the adversaries are roughly equal. The only realistic chance of ultimately avoiding escalation, however, must lie either in an inconclusive end to the conventional war or else in a *blitzkrieg* where the enemy is overrun before escalation can occur. This conventional *blitzkrieg* scenario, however, does not feature in the Soviet descriptions of the conventional phase in the pre-SALT period, nor are the Soviets particularly struck by an inconclusive end to a war. The dominant scenario is clearly that of an all-out nuclear war, with a pre-nuclear war phase as another variant. This has one important consequence: Soviet military writings in the period under consideration do not endorse concepts of controlled escalation or intra-war deterrence such as were to be found in American strategic thought. Thus Captain Iu. Nepodayev pours scorn on NATO concepts of the 'nuclear threshold' or escalation control.[102] This is understandable if the expectation that escalation to the strategic level can be avoided is very low.

A similar description of different variants of a world war, which most likely begins with a strategic nuclear strike but might also begin with a conventional phase, is given in an article by Marshal N. Krylov in November 1967.[103] Soviet military literature before 1973 is still preoccupied with how to fight under conditions of nuclear war. General Major S. Shtrik, although writing on aspects of conventional warfare in January 1968, nonetheless states categorically:

> Modern world war, if launched by the imperialists, will undoubtedly be a nuclear war.[104]

Likewise, Chief of the General Staff Matvei V. Zakharov wrote in *50 Years of the Armed Forces of the USSR*, published in 1968:

> Our military doctrine holds that a new world war, if the imperialists unleash it, will be a decisive clash of two social systems and it will draw into its orbit the majority of the countries of the world . . . It will be a thermonuclear war according to the nature of the means of armed conflict used in war. The nuclear weapon will be the main and decisive means of waging world war, and the rocket will be the main means of delivering it on target. At the same time all other kinds of weapons and combat equipment will find broad application in war. World war might be unleashed by the aggressor by a surprise nuclear attack directly on the Soviet Union and other socialist countries, or it might arise as the result of the escalation of a local military conflict into a world war.[105]

It seems impossible to accept that Zakharov should simply expound old military doctrine. To the contrary, this was the standard version of current doctrine at the time.

It is therefore by no means clear that the decisive shift in Soviet military doctrine which MccGwire asserts did in fact take place in the Sixties. What one discerns is an increasing realization of the possibility of a conventional phase and limiting escalation, with the Soviet force posture being more adapted to dealing with such a situation. Thus the efforts of the professional military to retain the support of the leadership of a large standing army and an all-round development of military capabilities were now being supported by a convincing rationale.

The emergence of a more sanguine perspective on a future war was indicated most openly for the first time in an article by General S. Ivanov which appeared in *Voennaia Mysl'* in 1969. Ivanov reiterates the fundamental tenet of Soviet military doctrine that

> All of this leads to the conclusion that a new world war, if the aggressors succeed in unleashing it, will more than likely be a nuclear war. Strategic missile weapons of unlimited range will be used . . .[106]

Nonetheless, Ivanov completely discounts the possibility of a successful first strike:

> With the existing level of development of nuclear missile weapons and their reliable cover below ground *and under water* it is *practically impossible* to destroy them completely and consequently it is also impossible to prevent an annihilatory retaliatory attack. Along with this modern means of early detection make it possible to reveal the initiation of an enemy nuclear attack and to carry out the necessary retaliatory measures in a timely manner.[107] [Emphasis added]

In considering the possibility of a conventional attack by NATO forces, Ivanov states confidently:

> The availability of a tremendous nuclear missile potential by the Soviet Union and the United States has had great influence on changing the views relative to the possible character of a war between the two coalitions. There is too great a risk of the destruction of one's own government and the responsibility to humanity for the fatal consequences of the nuclear war is too heavy for an aggressor to make an easy decision on the immediate employment of nuclear weapons from the very beginning of a war without having used all other means for the attainment of its objectives.[108]

Despite Ivanov's perfunctory affirmation of official military doctrine, he here portrays a very different image of a future world war. While the aggressiveness of imperialism has not decreased, the dangers of nuclear war and the reality of nuclear parity force the imperialists to employ conventional forces. The Vietnam War serves as an example to show American reluctance to use nuclear weapons:

> Numerous examples are known of so-called local wars in different regions of the world which are being unleashed and waged by the imperialists for the attainment of determined political objectives. In these wars, despite the major military failures, the imperialists have not decided to employ nuclear weapons.[109]

Ivanov then cites the NATO doctrine of 'flexible response' to show that the United States also envisages

> the conduct of other types of wars – with the use of only conventional means of destruction or with the limited employment of nuclear weapons . . . In other words in the conduct of a limited nuclear war the territory of the United States does not suffer. Therefore such a concept of the U.S. Government and military leaders is advantageous to them and they are advocating it.[110]

This article thus confirms Michael MccGwire's thesis that the Soviet military developed a concept of the sanctuarization of superpower territories as a consequence of mutual assured destruction capabilities, although Ivanov also shows awareness of the dangers of escalation and the possibility that the attempts to confine a war to limited selective nuclear strikes may fail.[111] Ivanov's article, however, is rather exceptional for its times, and the majority of articles appears to reflect a view closer to the official military doctrine as outlined above.[112] Only in the time after SALT I, with nuclear parity being more secure and NATO moving towards adopting a posture of keeping the nuclear threshold as high as possible, could the Soviet Union feel more confident that nuclear attacks on Soviet territory might be avoided in case of war.

Strategic force goal: superiority or parity?

Much Western discussion on Soviet military policy has focussed on the question of whether the Soviet Union was attempting to achieve a meaningful strategic superiority over the NATO Alliance. The Soviet military literature during most of the period under discussion is quite unambiguous on this subject: military superiority is absolutely necessary. Stalinist military science expressed this as 'superiority in the permanently operating factors', a formulation which was also supported by Nikolai Talenskii in his 1953 article,[113] but the commitment to superiority endured well into the nuclear era. A good summary of Soviet views on this matter is given in an article by V. Kulakov published in *Voennaia Mysl'* in January 1964:

> The Soviet Union in a minimum period of time not only put an end to the monopoly of the US over the atomic weapon and developed the atomic and hydrogen bomb, but it also in a few years moved ahead of all countries in the development of rocket technology. The achievement by the Soviet Union of military-technical superiority over the United States was a historically necessary victory of our

> economics, science and technology over the economically and militarily strongest country of capitalism . . . Thus superiority in nuclear rocket weapons is the decisive factor of military-technical superiority. At the same time, conventional weapons, which are likewise being constantly improved, will also continue to play their part . . .[114]

The 'achievement by the Soviet Union of military-technical superiority over the United States' was, of course, purely fictional. This points to the main difficulty in determining the meaning of superiority in the period under discussion: while, according to the military literature, it was a central goal of Soviet military policy (and one which had already been achieved, but needed to be maintained), it was in fact not attained. In so far as the political leadership wished to use Soviet military power as a policy tool, claims of superiority had a political function and fall into the same category as Khrushchev's exaggerated claims regarding Soviet ICBM capabilities. To admit inferiority would, of course, have been impossible for any political or military leader; the intrinsic superiority of the socialist system in political, economic, moral and military terms is fundamental to Soviet ideology.

Khrushchev appeared to endorse the need for military superiority in principle. The notion of forcing the imperialist bloc to accept the principle of peaceful co-existence was predicated on the assumption that the socialist countries

> have a rapidly growing economy and surpass the imperialist camp in armaments and armed forces.[115]

The claim to have achieved superiority, of course, implied that there was no need for a particular effort to increase military strength. Many statements by Khrushchev, even if they do not explicitly claim superiority, fall into this category, as does the claim by Malinovskii in his speech to the 22nd Party Congress in 1961 that the Soviet Union possessed already a surplus of nuclear missiles.[116] Khrushchev also introduced another subtle ambiguity into the discussion about superiority by making the distinction between superiority in quantity and quality. This is well illustrated in the article by Kulakov:

> Thus, the most important natural tendency of development in military affairs is the constant change in the qualitative and quantitative relationship between the mass of men and technical equipment, with the latter assuming ever greater importance in this

relationship. In the revolution in military affairs this tendency has been demonstrated very graphically and thoroughly. As a result of the abrupt qualitative leap in the development of sources of firepower and means of delivering it, and also the appearance of other latest technical equipment, there has been created the possibility of decreasing the number of personnel of the armed forces directly engaged in combat operations for the direct destruction of the enemy and in fact increasing their firepower.[117]

Kulakov essentially reiterates Khrushchev's position here. The attainment of military superiority, according to Khrushchev, could be achieved while at the same time carrying out manpower reductions and re-allocating resources from the military to other sectors of the economy.

The Sokolovskii authors take the necessity of superiority simply for granted; military and technical superiority (in addition to moral superiority which is a given in the Soviet Union since its wars are always just) is one of the prerequisites for victory in war, and Soviet military literature does not, on the whole, anticipate any other conceivable outcome should war come.[118] In the second edition, the Khrushchevian distinction between quantity and quality is deliberately robbed of its purpose (which was to substitute quality for quantity) by stating that quantitative *and* qualitative superiority over the probable aggressor was fundamental.[119]

One important issue in the debate in the 1960s about the rôle of war as an instrument of policy in the age of nuclear weapons in which Major-General Nikolai Talenskii and Lieutenant-Colonel E.I. Rybkin were two prominent protagonists was the possibility of victory. Whereas Talenskii, who was then associated with the arms-control community centred around the Academy of Sciences, providing an influential connection between the Disarmament Committee of the Academy and the Ministry of Defence, and had been a regular participant in the *Pugwash* meetings, advocated the view that nuclear war would lead to mutual destruction and could not serve as an instrument of politics, thereby denying the possibility of a victor in a nuclear confrontation. Rybkin, who was at that time attached to the Main Political Administration of the Soviet Army and Navy, defended the view that victory in a nuclear war was not impossible and depended not merely on the character of the weapons employed, but also on the more general correlation of forces:

> Any a priori rejection of the possibility of victory is harmful because it leads to moral disarmament, to a disbelief in victory and to

fatalism and passivity. It is necessary to wage a struggle against such views and attitudes.[120]

The commitment to victory in Soviet military thought has a very important consequence. It means, as has already been pointed out, that while the Soviet armed forces serve a function of deterrence (i.e., of preventing the imperialists from unleashing war), should war come, the objective is nothing short of victory. Intra-war deterrence was not part of Soviet military thought of the period (which is understandable given the scenario of nuclear war current at the time).

A strong defence of the need for military-technical superiority in addition to moral superiority was mounted by Lieutenant Colonel V. M. Bondarenko, in an article published in *Kommunist Vooruzhennykh Sil* in September 1966, where he stated categorically:

> Military-technical superiority is such a correlation of the quantity and quality of military matériel and weapons, of the level of troop training in their use and also the effectiveness of the organizational structure of the army, that a given side has the advantage over a real or potential opponent and can defeat him.[121]

Bondarenko's article, however, does not appear to constitute a call for a quantitative increase in the nuclear strategic arsenal. In his view, the Soviet Union already possesses superiority over the United States:

> However, the real state of affairs is such that our superiority in the latest kinds of military equipment has become a reality. 'Successes in the development of the economy, in science and technology,' said the General Secretary of the CC of the CPSU, Comrade L. I. Brezhnev at the reception in the Kremlin in honour of the graduates of military academies, 'have allowed us to create a powerful, qualitatively new material-technical base for equipping the Armed Forces, the Soviet Army with sufficient quantities of the latest military technology and preserve the superiority over the armies of the imperialist states.'[122]

Bondarenko is not necessarily claiming a quantitative superiority for the Soviet Union, but quotes Brezhnev's assertion of a quantitative sufficiency which, together with the qualitative factors, results in Soviet superiority. The emphasis in Bondarenko's article is thus on maintaining the qualitative, i.e. technological edge in order to prevent the emergence of a qualitatively new weapon which could upset the strategic balance.[123]

Some Western analysts have taken various statements in the Soviet literature on the need for military-technical superiority and the possibility of victory in a nuclear war and have argued that the Soviet leadership believed it could fight and win a nuclear war, and thus strives for strategic superiority.[124]

These arguments have confused two issues: the requirements for a successful military defence posture, and the rôle of military force in foreign policy. (The latter issue has been discussed in chapter 3.) Statements in the military literature which appear to imply that the Soviet military leaders believe they could fight and win a nuclear war must not be taken at face value, since they also maintain that they already have such a superiority, which was patently not the case (either in quantitative or qualitative terms), or that the Soviet economic and industrial base was stronger, which was also far from true. It is axiomatic, like a principle of faith, that the Soviet armed forces are in a position to successfully deal with any threat, regardless of the objective realities. But to assert that the Soviet Union would successfully emerge from even the worst-case scenario of an all-out nuclear attack (thus refusing to admit that there might be contingencies that the Soviet armed forces might not be able to cope with) is not the same as advocating the *initiation* of nuclear war. The military literature also continuously observes that the purpose of Soviet military power is to prevent the imperialists from unleashing war in the first place.[125] However, if the task of the Soviet military leadership is to develop a strategy to cope with the decisive clash between two fundamentally opposed social systems, in the event that war should come, then it is not unreasonable for them to believe that they must be in the possession of military-technical superiority in order to defeat imperialism.

It must be added, of course, that it was also in the institutional interest of the military to emphasize this factor in the battle for resource allocations. The terms in which these debates are conducted in the Soviet Union, as far as the political military literature is concerned, are very different from analogous debates in the West. In the West, supporters of increased military spending frequently assert the inferiority of the Western Alliance in a crucial area of military capabilities. Typical examples are the 'bomber gap' and the 'missile gap' in the Fifties/early Sixties and the debates about Soviet conventional superiority in Central Europe. The debate about ICBM vulnerability in the Seventies ('the window of vulnerability') fits into this mould. Soviet military writers, on the other hand, may emphasize the imperialist threat and elaborate on it in various ways, they may call for greater combat readiness and, obliquely, hint at the need for greater military spending, but they will never admit to Soviet inferiority in any respect.[126]

If we take at face value the assertions of Soviet military writers that military-technical superiority is necessary to deter an attack by the imperialists and, should war come, to defend the Soviet Union adequately and defeat the enemy, the issue arises of the military capabilities needed to implement such a policy, and what 'superiority' would mean in terms of strategic arms policy. We have already discussed the requirements for a strategy of preemption. 'Superiority' in this case would imply the capability to eliminate American nuclear delivery systems, other military targets as well as administrative and economic centres. As Michael MccGwire has pointed out, this did not require a numerical superiority if the strategy of area devastation by large warheads was pursued;[127] hence the emphasis on qualitative superiority.

The deployment of Minuteman ICBMs in hardened silos required a different approach. As MccGwire has explained

> Until the Soviets realized that they could achieve comparable results by striking at the Minuteman launch-control centers (there was one for every ten launchers), they had to plan to target each Minuteman silo with at least one missile.[128]

The requirements for 'superiority' as we have explained it here obviously changed as the strategy shifted from preemption to launch-on-warning, since in the latter case only those nuclear forces held in reserve (i.e. not used in the first wave of the attack) would have to be targeted. In the Soviet understanding of the initial phase of a nuclear war involving the use of strategic strikes, the proportion of missiles used in the first strike would be quite substantial. Nevertheless the SS-11 was not a very effective weapon against the Minuteman force owing to its limited accuracy.[129] Soviet plans to attack American nuclear forces were further complicated by the substantial US SLBM force. The fact that a massive missile attack on the continental United States would not in itself end the war was recognized in the article by Major General V. Zemskov:

> Simultaneously with the infliction of nuclear strikes, a struggle will develop in the sea and ocean regions with the goal of destroying surface and underwater forces of the navy, as well as in the air for repulsing nuclear strikes of the enemy.[130]

The ability of Soviet ASW capabilities to eliminate the entire US SLBM force before the missiles could be launched was (and remains) very much in doubt.[131] Again we see a gap between the ambitions embodied in military doctrine and capabilities.

Nonetheless, deployment patterns are in conformity with the attempt to achieve such capabilities. Thus, by 1970, the Soviet Union had deployed a total of 1,220 ICBMs, 341 medium-range SLBMs and 190 bombers of intercontinental range. This compares with 1,054 ICBMs, 616 long-range SLBMs and 501 strategic bombers deployed by the United States. The 720 SS-11s could be targeted against a substantial number of Minuteman silos – enough to cover a proportion of ICBMs held in reserve as well as a large range of soft targets after an American first strike, but not nearly enough for a first strike. The 240 SS-9s provided a substantial capability against the Minuteman control centres (of which there were 100); assuming that the centres were hardened to withstand a pressure of 1,000 p.s.i. and a reliability of 75 per cent, an accuracy of 0.5–0.75 nautical miles and yield of 20 MT. Berman and Baker estimate that 79–100 of the Minuteman control centres could be destroyed in a first or second strike.[132] The solid-fuelled SS-13 was designed as a mobile system to build up a strategic reserve; the failure of this programme (for technical reasons – mostly due to the inability to meet the high requirements for the guidance of solid-fuel rockets) may have reinforced a decision to develop long-range SLBMs to create a strategic reserve potential like that possessed by the United States. Although a detailed comparison between Soviet and American forces reveals that by quantitative and qualitative criteria Soviet strategic forces could still be considered lagging somewhat behind, the slight superiority in the number of ICBM launchers gave some credibility to the Soviet claim to have achieved parity with the United States.

The question of superiority was placed into a different context by the negotiations for the limitations of strategic arms.[133] Among the civilian arms-control experts, 'parity' had become the major principle of Soviet military policy. This became also the official policy of the political leadership, and political commentary in the Soviet press explicitly denied that the SALT accord would give the Soviet Union superiority.[134] The argument continued on the lines that the growth in Soviet military might, on the other hand, have forced the United States to recognize the reality of parity.

The shift in the correlation of forces which established the state of parity described in the political literature also found some echo in the military literature. Thus Raymond L. Garthoff has stated:

> By 1969, the Soviet military leadership had reached the conclusion that strategic superiority in the sense of a first-strike option permitting escape from a crushing retaliatory strike was not possible for either side in contemporary conditions. They recognised that, with the existing level of development of nuclear missile forces, it had become impossible in practice for an attacker to destroy such forces completely and consequently that it had also become impossible to prevent an annihilating retaliatory strike. In other words, a kind of 'nuclear balance' in terms of capabilities for mutual destruction had come into being.[135]

As we have seen, Marshal Krylov in 1967 expressed the view that a preemptive strike which would completely disarm the enemy was impossible, and that therefore nuclear retaliation could not be avoided by striking first – a statement which amounts to an acceptance of mutual assured destruction.[136] The article by General S. Ivanov spelt out the objective realities of mutual assured destruction.[137] The term 'nuclear balance' is to be found in an article by Major General V. I. Zemskov.[138] However, it is clear that there was military opposition to strategic arms limitation.[139] Nonetheless, even in those articles which indirectly sought to raise doubts about the wisdom of SALT by emphasizing Western aggressiveness to an unusual degree there seems to be some recognition of a nuclear balance and strategic deterrence. Lieutenant Colonel T. Kondratkov, for example, while still alleging that there are in the West 'fervent advocates of nuclear violence on an unrestricted scale' concentrates his attention on those who do not reject nuclear war in principle, but who seek to fight limited nuclear wars owing to the catastrophic consequences a full-scale nuclear war would have for the capitalist system.[140] In this view, the fact that Western strategists are forced to seek ways of limiting nuclear warfare is an expression of the reality of mutual assured destruction as a result of strategic parity.

After the 25th Party Congress in 1976, references to the need to maintain military-technical superiority largely disappeared from the Soviet military press. Some Western analysts have interpreted this not as an indicator that the military doctrine of the 1960s was no longer in force, but that the Soviet leadership was now attempting to conceal it.[141] The official line was given in a speech in Tula by L. I. Brezhnev in January 1977 which recognized the reality of nuclear deterrence and denied that the Soviet Union was pursuing superiority with the intention of seeking a first strike. The concepts of 'parity' and 'equal security' have been fundamental to Soviet declaratory policy since then.

Conclusion

Although by the end of the 1950s the military leadership of the Soviet Union had come to appreciate the fundamental changes in the nature of warfare due to nuclear weapons and long-range delivery vehicles, the notion that more traditional means of warfare would become obsolete and that nuclear firepower could replace conventional forces and permit a substantial reduction in military power was a change in military doctrine imposed by the political leadership.

There was also, however, a fundamental discrepancy between this emphasis in the military doctrine proclaimed by Khrushchev and the implementation of strategic arms policy. Khrushchev's priorities for the Soviet economy required not merely economies in conventional forces, but also limited the commitment of resources to the development of a substantial strategic nuclear force. For some time the substantial 'missile gap' developing between the United States and the Soviet Union was concealed by the exaggerated claims made on behalf of Soviet strategic nuclear capabilities. But, by the autumn of 1961, it became apparent that the United States enjoyed a substantial strategic superiority over the Soviet Union.

After the fall of Khrushchev, the all-round build-up of military capabilities was emphasized, which included a determined programme to achieve strategic nuclear parity with the United States. At the same time there was increasing recognition of the possibility of limited wars and conventional phases in a war with the West. By the time the Soviet Union had achieved strategic nuclear parity with the United States, as codified in the SALT agreements, the Soviet Union moved to a policy of limiting any conflict in Central Europe, if possible, to the conventional level.

In the post-Khrushchev period, we therefore find a better correlation between official military doctrine and the implementation of strategic arms policy. To explain how the deployment of Soviet strategic forces fitted in with the military doctrine in more detail with regard to specific systems, we shall consider a number of case studies in Part II.

5 Party-military relations and strategic arms policy

Introduction

The Soviet military undoubtedly played a central rôle in the determination of Soviet military policy and strategic deployments. It was also an important political factor: Khrushchev's alliance with military leaders was of decisive significance during his power struggles with his opponents; his conflict with them contributed significantly to his downfall. As Khrushchev was introducing new military and strategic doctrines, his relations with the military leadership were again crucial in determining the extent and, more importantly, the limitations of his ability to implement his plans. The institutional interests of the military and the constraints which the Party attempted to impose again played a significant part in the debates about military doctrine and the evolution of the Soviet force posture. This chapter will chart the course of Party–military relations in the post-Stalin era. It will focus in particular on the political struggle between the professional military and the political leadership over the formulation of military doctrine, and the various means the political leadership used to strengthen its control over the military, in particular through the Main Political Administration. It will show how various developments in Soviet military doctrine were influenced by the respective institutional interests of the military and the political leadership and then seek to analyse their effect on Soviet strategic arms policy.

Party-military relations after the death of Stalin

Stalin's death resulted in an intense power struggle not only between the Soviet leaders who survived him, but also the powerful institutions of the Soviet Union whose factional interests had until then been suppressed. An early casualty of the manoeuvring for positions among the leadership were the security organs; as Beriia's execution testifies they represented such a grave danger for the rest of the leadership that they took no chances. As the Party and Government bureaucracies became instrument in the intense battle for the control of power in the Soviet Union between Malenkov and Khrushchev, the military leadership, which under Stalin had been kept under varying degrees of tight control and denied any political rôle what-soever suddenly found itself in a key position.

Despite this situation, Malenkov pursued social and political objectives which turned out to be in direct conflict with the institutional interests of the Soviet military. He attempted to shift resources from heavy industry to agriculture and consumer good production, thus adversely affecting the defence industry. He also called for an end to the 'Cold War', emphasized the suicidal nature of nuclear war and pursued peaceful co-existence and détente with the West.

The institutional interests of the Soviet military which were threatened by Malenkov's policies were:

1 Maintenance of large expenditures to preserve existing military programmes and the institutional power of the military.
2 A high level of investment in heavy industry as the necessary prerequisite for a defence industry capable of serving the perceived industrial requirement of the Soviet military.

As a consequence the military perceived itself to be in conflict with Malenkov not merely directly with regard to its institutional interests, but also with a wider range of policy issues. To justify the maintenance of a high level of military expenditure, some degree of international political tension is politically required. For this purpose, the opponent is described as dangerous and aggressive, bent on destroying the socialist camp, promoting the arms race and the 'Cold War'.

The defence budget

This became the most direct point of conflict between the military and the Malenkov leadership. The 1953 defence budget which was passed in late August 1953 provided for a reduction from 113.8 billion to 110.2 billion roubles in allocated, and from 108.6 to 102.9 billion roubles in actual expenditure. This trend continued with the 1954 budget which allocated 100.3 billion roubles to defence.[1] There is no question that this was disturbing to both the military and some elements of the party leadership, in particular since Malenkov also used some of the national contingency funds to sustain his consumer-goods programme. These funds were reserved for national emergencies, one of which would be a war situation.

Foreign policy

The reduction of international tension and, especially, improved relations with the United States were the centrepiece of Malenkov's foreign policy, since only a reduction in the perception of the imperialist threat could justify the economic policies he was pursuing, in particular the reduction in defence allocations. An interesting indicator of the rôle of external-threat scenarios in Soviet domestic policies during the Malenkov period is the perception of the likelihood of war, as Herbert Dinerstein has demonstrated.[2] Thus Malenkov emphasized the sufficiency of Soviet armed forces to meet any threat, while at the same time defending the view that nuclear weapons had a very radical impact on the nature of war and the military posture that should be adopted by the Soviet Union. As we have already pointed out in Chapter 3, he declared that a thermonuclear war would mean the destruction of world civilization.[3] It was no longer to be taken for granted that socialist countries would prevail in a war with the capitalist countries. He vigorously condemned the Cold War and spoke of the threat of devastation posed by a nuclear war both to the Soviet Union and the United States. He thus de-emphasized the inevitability of war as long as capitalism existed, tending more towards the notion that a long-term accommodation with capitalism was necessary. While condemning 'aggressive circles' in the West at the same time he proclaimed that a decline in international tension had been achieved, that the danger of war was receding. He advocated a *minimum deterrent*. This was in stark contrast to the Khrushchev faction which stressed the likelihood of war with the West on the basis of the orthodox line of the inevitability of war owing to the aggressive nature of capitalism; Khrushchev stated that

> the reactionary forces of the capitalist countries impede in every way the weakening of tension in international relations[4]

Bulganin, taking a similar line, concluded:

> The most important thing in military affairs is the uninterrupted perfection of the armed forces.[5]

Evidence for the rôle of the emphasis on the likelihood of war in the power struggle is given by the fact that Khrushchev's views changed quite dramatically once the struggle against Malenkov had been won. It is clear that the attempt to paint a picture of rising international tensions served a specific function between Malenkov and the Khrushchev faction which was allied with the military.

Economic policy

We have already described the debate about the direction of Malenkov's economic policies. A clear view from the military on this issue was expressed in the journal *Voennaia Mysl'*:

> Heavy industry is the foundation of foundations of our socialist economy. Without heavy industry it is not possible to ensure the further growth of light industry and the productive forces of agriculture, and the furthering of the defence capabilities of the Soviet state.[6]

Initially the military raised its voice against Malenkov's policies only very cautiously. However, it eventually became apparent that the issue of heavy industry was central to the power struggle for the leadership of the Party. By late 1954 a definite alliance had been forged between the military and the Khrushchev faction, resulting ultimately in Malenkov's downfall in 1955.

Marshal Zhukov: the reassertion of the professional military

Malenkov's downfall resulted in a considerable enhancement of the position of the military in the Soviet Union. This was clearly indicated by the advancement of Marshal Zhukov to the position of Defence Minister and that of Marshal Bulganin to that of Premier. On 11 March 1955 eleven generals were promoted to Marshal, and the media reflected the greater self-assertion of the military. Having become aware that it was in a crucial position of power in the struggle between Khrushchev and Malenkov, and having succeeded in promoting its views on the international situation, defence allocations and the rôle of heavy industry, the military, under the leadership of Marshal Zhukov, attempted to use this power to further other objectives. These consisted in widening the military's freedom from political controls in the exercise of its professional rôle, increasing the military's rôle in the formulation of military doctrine and strategy and enhancing the military's standing in society, in particular with regard to the events of the Great Patriotic War.

Military doctrine

During the time of Stalin, the formulation of military theory and strategic doctrine was the exclusive preserve of Stalin himself. As Maj. Gen. S. Kozlov later expounded in a vigorous attack on Stalin's 'personality cult':

> Any further development of military theory depended on his pronouncement – direct or implied. If there was no opinion from his authority on a certain problem of military theory, either working it out was not undertaken at all, or, at best, there was an attempt to fit the problem under one of his remarks, even if it were far removed from the subject or made with regard to a completely different matter.[7]

In the usual manner, Kozlov invoked Lenin's authority to repudiate Stalin's:

> Stalin, in an intolerable manner, tried to diminish the importance of Lenin as the real founder of Soviet military science and to ascribe that role to himself . . . the role of military art was reduced to the organizing capabilities of command personnel.[8]

Thus, in the words of Kozlov, Stalin saw himself as the 'genius leader' while looking down on the masses as 'cogs in the wheel'. Kozlov vividly describes the 'stifling atmosphere' Stalin created around himself:

> Stalin himself often brought forth the well-known thesis which gives the decisive role to strategy in relation to the other parts of military art. This indisputable methodological principle required that the art of tactics and operations be developed in conformity with the aims and principles of strategy. At the same time, even for the more or less wide circle of leaders, strategy remained a secret and taboo subject, the prerogative and the product of the creative genius of one man. Thus for the subordination of the parts of the military there was practically no guiding and determining source, except the most general directives, often bordering on abstractions . . . Therefore strategic theory was mainly reduced to the study of strategic operations which, as a matter of fact, differed in content from operations on a front level in only a few, primarily quantitative aspects.[9]

According to Kozlov, the year 1952 (one year before Stalin's death) witnessed a discussion on the rôle and place of military-technical sciences in the system of military fields of knowledge and of military pedagogy. In 1953 there was a debate about the nature of the laws of military science. After the death of Stalin, changes in military-scientific methodology and military-theoretical thought did not take place at once.

> The spirit of quotation of dogmatism, contained by inertia to dominate the first years of scientific work.[10]

Nonetheless, the well-known article by Major-General Talenskii which appeared in *Voennaia Mysl'* in September 1953 sparked off a debate about military doctrine the principal features of which were the rejection of the Stalinist 'military science', the acceptance of the importance of 'strategic surprise' and the significance of nuclear weapons.[11] The central target of the attack was the effort by Stalin and other Party leaders to assume all authority for the definition of military strategy and doctrine by their formulation of 'military science'.

There was some resistance to the new ideas emerging from this debate. The problem was not only the difficulty of absorbing new ideas in a system that conditions its members to adhere to an official line, but also the emerging conflict between the military and Malenkov. Malenkov himself was attempting to introduce profound changes in the Soviet understanding of the rôle and nature of war in the nuclear age and, as we have seen, this issue was central to the military's conflict with the Malenkov leadership. It was therefore not very opportune for the military itself to admit to changes in the understanding of the nature of military strategy as a result of the advent of nuclear weapons, even if Talenskii did not go nearly as far as Malenkov.[12]

For this reason, the debate did not get properly under way until 1955 when Marshals Sokolovskii and Rotmistrov published articles which went much further than Talenskii in rejecting Stalinist military science.[13] We have already discussed the fact that Rotmistrov's article 'On the Role of Surprise in Modern War' was withheld from publication by *Voennaia Mysl'* until after Malenkov's fall in January 1955, a fact which was criticized in the journal itself.[14] The speed with which the restraints on the internal military debate were removed after the ouster of Malenkov may be an indication that the predominance of the need to oppose Malenkov's policies was suddenly replaced by other institutional objectives, such as reasserting a greater rôle for the military in the formulation of military doctrine.

After April 1955 there was scant reference to the permanently operating factors in the Soviet press; by 1957 Rotmistrov's and Sokolovskii's critique was close to being official orthodoxy. A book review in *Krasnaia Zvezda* criticized adherence to 'the old way' (i.e. the five permanently operating factors as defining the conditions for success in a modern war).[15]

The second period of the debate on military strategy, according to Kozlov, was the years 1954–60, in which firepower was recognized as the new chief factor. However, the

> new quality of nuclear weapons was not fully recognized until new delivery vehicles (rockets) became available . . .[16]

It is important to note the way in which the military reasserted its right to participate in the formulation of military strategy and doctrine. From 1955–57, there was virtually no interference from the Party in this debate because the Party was too preoccupied with its own internal conflicts and Khrushchev relied on the support of Marshal Zhukov.

The issue of professional autonomy

Marshal Zhukov was determined to use his enhanced standing after the fall of Malenkov to achieve professional autonomy for the military and get rid of the elaborate system whereby the Party exercised control over it. What Zhukov was seeking was not the total abolition of the institutions of Party control, but rather their confinement to political education and morale-building, to prevent them from interfering with military affairs which were to be strictly the domain of the military commanders.

In the years 1955–57 the Party was unable to mount any effective resistance to Zhukov's reforms. There was a whole cluster of reasons: the internal power struggles within the Party, involving the process of de-stalinization which was launched by Khrushchev in 1956, the reduction of the authority of the security organs, which made the Party leadership more dependent on the military, particularly as a result of the unrest resulting from the de-stalinization campaign which led to the Hungarian crisis. As Raymond Garthoff has pointed out:

> The period from February, 1955, to October, 1957, may best be understood in terms of an alliance between Khrushchev and Zhukov . . . Khrushchev was building his personal power within the

Party, and the power of the Party within the state; Zhukov was exercising his authority in developing Soviet military thought and training, and in building a modern military establishment.[17]

Zhukov's central targets were the *Main Political Administration of the Army and Navy* (MPA) and its network of political officers (*zampolits*), the Military Councils (at district levels) (which tended to undermine the authority of a district commander who could be easily outvoted by members not committed to the military) and Party and Komsomol organizations at all levels. Zhukov's first major success consisted in restricting the role of the MPA:

> In September of 1955 the Party Central Committee defined the role of the Main Political Administration and the content of its activity in connection with the examination of the statute pertaining to the Ministry of Defence. The statute indicated that the Main Political Administration was the leading Party organ *on questions of Party-political work among troops.*[18]

In order to constrain it further, Zhukov recreated separate political administrations for the Army, the Navy, the Air Force and PVO in April 1955. These constituted a link between the MPA and its control organizations in the services which were under Zhukov's control. In addition to that Zhukov allegedly prohibited direct contacts between the MPA and the CPSU Central Committee. *Zampolits* were abolished on company level, those on battalion level moved up to that of the regiment, and their general powers to interfere with officers' activities severely curtailed. Criticism of officers was also restricted, as was the general level of political activity; for example, officers could now substitute combat training for political education. The study of ideology and Party History was made a voluntary activity. Criticism/self-criticism sessions were also strongly curtailed; indeed Zhukov's measures were designed to exempt a commander's professional decisions from Party criticisms.[19] The Military Councils were radically changed; appointments to the council were no longer to be made on the basis of a Central Committee decision, but rather by the Minister of Defence. At the same time the places on the committee reserved for regular Party members were abolished.[20] All this shows Zhukov's drive to restore the principle of *edinonachalie* (one-man command) in the military, eliminate political interference in military affairs and thus achieve a large degree of professional autonomy for the armed forces.

At the Party Conference of the armed forces in December 1955 in preparation for the 20th CPSU Congress the work of the political administration came under severe attack, with Marshal V. I. Chuikov (then commander of the Kiev military district) being exceptional in refraining from such attacks. An indication of the reduced status of political officers was that the main reports of the military districts were not given by them (as was usual), but rather by the commanders themselves.[21]

The Congress itself was nothing less than a triumph for Zhukov. No officials from the political administration were elected to the Central Committee; the new head of the political administration, Zheltov, was omitted from the Central Committee altogether. The standing of the military establishment itself was improved; after the Congress full members of the Central Committee included Konev, Malinovskii, Moskalenko, Sokolovskii, Vasilevskii and Zhukov (Malinovskii and Moskalenko were new CC members); Bagramian, Biriuzov, Budennii, Chuikov, Eremenko, Garbatov, Gorshkov, Grechko, Luchinskii, Nedelin, Timoshenko and Zhigarev were Candidate Members.[22] During his Secret Speech denouncing Stalin's crimes, Khrushchev heaped praise upon Zhukov, and his enhanced standing became manifest when he was made a Candidate Member of the Presidium, the first time that a professional military man had reached such a high position in the Party. The 20th Congress marked an intensification of Zhukov's campaign for professional autonomy for the military. In 1957 he reached the peak of his power when he helped Khrushchev to defeat the Anti-Party Group's bid to remove him in June. As a result, Zhukov became a full member of the Presidium. Soon, he attempted to widen his influence from the military to the political realm. As Garthoff put it:

> in the months from June to October, 1957, Zhukov spoke with authority not only on military strategy in the specific sense of doctrine and plans . . . but also on strategic implications of other policies. In short, since military and political strategy must be integrated, Zhukov wanted to do some of the integrating.[23]

The Party leadership became rather alarmed about Zhukov's growing power and independence. As Khrushchev's memoirs record:

> [Zhukov] assumed so much power that it began to worry the leadership. One by one the other members of the Presidium started coming up to me and expressing their concern. They asked me whether I could see, as they could, that Zhukov was striving to seize control − that we were heading for a military coup d'etat. We received information that Zhukov was indeed voicing Bonapartist

aspirations in his conversations with military commanders. We couldn't let Zhukov stage a South American-style military take-over in our country.[24]

By a rather elaborate conspiracy planned by Khrushchev in alliance with other political and military leaders Zhukov was ousted from his post as Minister of Defence, the Presidium and the Central Committee in October 1957 for developing a personality cult and attempting to dismantle Party leadership and control over the armed forces.

The Stalingrad Group

Central to any understanding of Party-military relations during the Khrushchev period must be the special relationship between Khrushchev and a number of military commanders called *the Stalingrad group* by Roman Kolkowicz in his incisive analysis of party-military relations in the Soviet Union.[25] These relationships were formed during World War II when Khrushchev was based in the Ukraine as political supervisor of the Southwestern Theatre and later the Stalingrad Front. In this capacity he was involved with many military operations, culminating in the battle of Stalingrad which constituted one of the important turning-points of the war. The military commanders Khrushchev was working with experienced two important sources of frustration in the course of the war (apart from any defeats at the hands of the Germans). One was the lack of authority of the commanders, which required consultation with the political supervisors who were often better informed about military plans. The other was the frequent intervention of the *Stavka* in command decisions:

> *the Stavka* [frequently] rejected correct decisions of Theatre Commands; it gave directives to the fronts over the heads of the commanders-in-chief of the Theatres, did not take into consideration their opinions, and, moreover, during the first period of the war, abolished, created, and again abolished Theatre Commands. Consequently, this important strategic command level became transformed into a sort of information center and did not become a superior instrument . . . of rapid operational command.[26]

Khrushchev, instead of being Stalin's man in the field, usually sided with the commanders and attempted to mediate in any conflict. He was often successful in sorting out difficulties between certain commanders and the *Stavka*, for example. As a result, he forged relationships with many military commanders which later proved to be of great value to him.

The second irritant that was to affect the post-Stalin political situation appeared in the form of Zhukov who arrived at the Stalingrad Front as a representative of the Stavka. The resultant changes in the field command and the military deployments created bad feelings. These were exacerbated by Zhukov's rude arrogance and the bad treatment he accorded his commanders, which involved frequent sharp criticism and dismissals. Although Khrushchev was generally unable to override Zhukov's decision even by direct appeals to Stalin himself, he appeared at least to take the side of other commanders against Zhukov. The feelings against Zhukov deepened when Stalin and Zhukov claimed the credit for the victory at Stalingrad. All this was exacerbated by conflicts about involvement in the battle for Berlin.

The Stalingrad group therefore consisted of a number of high-ranking military officers who remained loyal to Khrushchev for a long time after the war.[27]

As Khrushchev came into conflict with the military after the fall of Zhukov, the Stalingrad group divided into two factions, one of which remained strongly loyal to Khrushchev, whereas the other saw its primary loyalty to the military establishment. This division appears to have started in the war years already and became more pronounced as Party-military relations worsened. The most prominent members of the faction loyal to Khrushchev were Biriuzov, Chuikov and Moskalenko; those of the other faction Malinovskii, Zakharov, Krylov and Grechko.

The war-time conflicts in the military between the Zhukovites and the Stalingrad group remained suppressed in the immediate post-war period, but re-emerged when Zhukov became Minister of Defence and found their most visible expression in the claims and counter-claims about Zhukov's importance during the Great Patriotic War, the relative importance of the battle for Moscow versus the battle for Stalingrad etc. Although Khrushchev entered an alliance of convenience with Zhukov, he soon began to promote his supporters in the military. Of sixteen very high-level promotions following the ouster of Malenkov, thirteen involved members of the Stalingrad Group. Six of these were promotions to the rank of Marshal of the Soviet Union; all six were close Khrushchev associates. Zhukov did, of course, still have associates in key positions; First Deputy Minister Vasilevskii and Chief of the General Staff Sokolovskii belonged to the Zhukov fraction; so did Nedelin and Gorbatov. The rise of the Stalingrad group, however, was unmistakable; of the twenty military officers who were members or candidate members of the Central Committee after the 20th CPSU Congress in 1956 ten belonged to the Stalingrad group, and only five to the Zhukov faction. Members of the Stalingrad group also were promoted to major commands: Biriuzov became commander of the PVO Strany; Malinovskii Commander-in-Chief of the Ground Forces and Kazakov commander of the Southern Force Group.[28] It is important to emphasize that the rivalries and personal animosities between the Zhukov faction and the Stalingrad group were very severe; Konev and Zhukov, in particular, were arch-enemies, as is indicated by Konev's venomous outbursts against Zhukov following the latter's ouster from the Ministry of Defence. As a result there was little opposition from the military to the removal of Zhukov.

Military reforms after Zhukov: 1957–1960

The removal of Zhukov accompanied an attempt by the Party to reinstitute its controls in the military. This was apparent from the resolution on the improvement of Party-political work in the Soviet Army and Navy passed by the October plenum of the Central Committee. The first concrete measure was the statute on the Military Councils passed by the Central Committee in April 1958. The Military Councils were to be no longer subordinate to the military commanders, but became collective bodies in practice controlled by loyal Party functionaries. Their formal responsibility was not merely to the Ministry of Defence, but also to the Central Committee, the CPSU and the Government. Binding resolutions were to be adopted by majority votes; the members of Military Councils had to be confirmed by the Central Committee.[29] In August 1958 the composition of the Military Councils at the district and army group levels was fixed by the Central Committee in such a way that party representatives outnumbered the professional military and would thus retain control.

The rôle of the MPA was considerably enhanced; it was to be the central authority for all Party activities in the military; its status as a section of the Central Committee was emphasized and its dependence on the Ministry of Defence reduced. The rôle of the MPA in the administration of Military Councils and the selection of their members was also increased. The deputy directors of the MPA also became members of the Military Councils of the branches of the armed forces.

Political indoctrination and political education also received a significant boost by means of the *Statute on the Political Organs in the Soviet Army and Navy* which strengthened considerably the rôle of the political organs and removed the restraints imposed upon them during Zhukov's time. Furthermore it had become extremely important for commanders to be Party Members, as changes in the *Instructions to the Party Organizations in the Soviet Army and Navy* in April 1958 implied a great reduction in the authority of commanders who were not Party members, thus promoting increased attention to political matters by the commanders themselves.[30] Nonetheless, the principle of *edinonachalie* had become all but defunct, and criticism/self-criticism was reintroduced into the military sphere.

The military reforms resulted in a virtual state of war between the professional military and the political officers. The latter saw Zhukov's downfall and the reforms as an invitation to indulge in a vindictive campaign of settling scores in what Kolkowicz has called a 'campaign of intimidation, blackmail, dismissals and other coercive devices'.[31] Thus political officers used every available opportunity to replace commanders with their own people. The general effect was a dramatic decline of morale and discipline.

By the summer of 1958 the military began to reassert itself and the first signs of a widening rift between the political control organs and the professional military appeared. *Krasnaia Zvezda*, for example, representing the view of the professional military, reported various incidents where commanders had been treated rather rudely by their political 'assistants'.[32] Other articles and even a book (signed for publication in November 1958) warned of the damage done by interference with the professional work of commanders, of the burden of unnecessary political work and frequent inspections by political officials.[33] The deterioration of military discipline and the problems caused by the political organs was officially recognized by Malinovskii in *Krasnaia Zvezda* on 1 November 1958. He demanded that political organs should cease those activities which damaged the military and took a strong line of the need for *edinonachalie*, exhorting the political organs to strengthen the authority of the commander so that he could carry out his professional tasks.

The strong reaction by the professional military forced some modification of the reforms. On 20 January 1959 the Political Departments at military academies, research institutes and the Ministry of

Defence, which were responsible to the MPA, were transformed into Party Committees which were allegedly more democratic, but given the continued indirect influence of the MPA in the Party Committees these changes cannot be considered to have been substantial. At the 21st Congress of the CPSU in February 1959, the political organs were curbed, in particular in as much as they had interfered with the training and combat readiness of troops. Nonetheless the policies of collectivist decision-making and of egalitarianism (breaking down the barriers between ranks) continued to be pursued.

More radical changes were in the offing, however, as a result of Khrushchev's determination to modernize the military. This would mean making available to the military more modern equipment and large amounts of new weapons; it also meant, however, the modernization of Soviet strategic doctrine with a principal emphasis on nuclear weapons (in particular strategic missiles) accompanied by a depreciation of the Ground Forces. Large standing armies were considered to be expensive and to have lost much of their significance in the age of nuclear weapons. Khrushchev was also aware that the traditional values of the professional military which he was trying to combat were most strongly represented in the Ground Forces. The main driving force of Khrushchev's attempts to reform the military and reduce the rôle of the Ground Forces lay in the difficulties of the economy; a reduction in the Ground Forces would both ease the burden of the defence budget and at the same time release manpower for the economy which was suffering an acute manpower shortage. However, the conflict over the rôle of the Ground Forces did not start in earnest until a year later. Meanwhile the military were enjoying a respite in the pressure from the Party while some of the equipment modernization was carried out. As a result, relations between the Communist Party and the professional military enjoyed a brief period of tranquillity until the beginning of 1960.

Renewed Conflict: 1960–1963

The implementation of Khrushchev's planned reforms was announced on 14 January 1960 in his speech at the Fourth Session of the Supreme Soviet of the USSR. In the context of a discourse on Soviet proposals for general and complete disarmament, he set out to give yet further proof of benign Soviet intentions by announcing a reduction of the Soviet armed forces by 1.2 million men to a level of 2,423,000. He then raised the question as to whether such cuts would endanger Soviet security and invite 'aggressive forces' to unleash a war against the Soviet Union and the other Socialist countries'.[34] His reply was:

> Our state has at its disposal powerful rocket equipment. The air force and military navy have lost their previous importance in view of the modern development of military technology. This kind of military equipment is not being reduced, but replaced. The air force will be replaced by rocket equipment almost completely. We have now reduced it sharply and will probably reduce it further, and even discontinue the manufacture of bomber planes and other out-of-date technical equipment. In the navy, the submarine fleet assumes great importance while surface ships can no longer play the part they once did. Our armed forces have been transferred to a considerable extent to rocket and nuclear arms . . . The reduction of the numerical strength of the Army will not prevent us from maintaining the defence capability of the country on the required level. We will continue to have at our disposal all necessary means to defend our country, and the opponent will be well aware of this, and if he does not know it, we will warn him and draw his attention to it and declare openly: When we reduced the numerical strength of our Armed forces, we do not reduce their firepower; quite to the contrary, it will be qualitatively multiplied.[35]

Khrushchev estimated the force reductions to yield savings of 16–17 billion roubles per annum.

It is important to emphasize that Khrushchev's proposals amounted to nothing less than a sweeping revision of Soviet strategic doctrine. The importance of strategic nuclear forces was such, in Khrushchev's view, that conventional forces largely lost their significance, in particular the ground forces, to such an extent that the gradual transformation of the regular professional army into a territorial militia similar to that which existed in the early years of the Soviet Union was now again under consideration:

> Looking into the future one can predict that we can have military units formed on the territorial principle. Their personnel will be trained in military matters without an interruption of production, and, when necessary, equipment will make it possible to concentrate troops at the required place on our territory.[36]

There were signs even at this session of the Supreme Soviet that the members of the Stalingrad Group were not all willing to follow Khrushchev far down this route. Thus Minister of Defence R. Ia.

Malinovskii, while speaking in favour of the troop reduction as a 'quite sound and timely measure'[37] and furthermore asserting that the Soviet Union had a 'sufficient' number of nuclear weapons, he did strike a distinctively different note from Khrushchev:

> The rocket troops of our armed forces are undoubtedly the main type of armed forces. However, we understand that it is not possible to solve all tasks of war by one type of troop. Therefore, proceeding from the premise that the successful carrying out of military actions in a modern war are only possible on the basis of a unified use of all means of armed fighting and the combining of the efforts of all types of armed forces, we are retaining at a definite strength and in relevant sound proportions all types of our armed forces whose military operations, as far as their organization and their means of action are concerned, will resemble what took place in the past war.[38]

Malinovskii thus, while not opposing Khrushchev's immediate policies, clearly contradicted his more general objectives and central aspects of Khrushchev's new strategic doctrine.

Military opposition grew in the aftermath of Khrushchev's announcement. The troop reduction proposals were an obvious target, because of their general implications for the status of the Ground Forces, but also because the 250,000 officers released faced quite a bleak future, having been shifted from a privileged position in society to being virtual non-persons. In April 1960 Chief of the General Staff Marshal Sokolovskii and the First Deputy Minister of Defence and Commander in Chief of the Warsaw Pact Forces Marshal Konev were dismissed from their posts for their opposition to the troop reductions. (Sokolovskii, one of the surviving members of the Zhukov group, was replaced by Matvei Zakharov, a member of the Stalingrad Group.)

In the months after Khrushchev's speech to the Supreme Soviet, the threatening nature of Khrushchev's policies, as seen from the perspective of the military, became clear, as Kolkowicz has pointed out:

> A vast majority in the military was beginning to see in Khrushchev's policies toward the armed forces a major threat to many of their traditional prerogatives, interests and objectives. With each new regulation, statute, and decree it became clearer that Khrushchev envisaged, ultimately, a severely truncated military organization, shot through with a network of political organs and divided between the strategic forces, to be given preferential treatment, and the conventional forces in a greatly reduced role. This vision

included an officer corps divested of meaningful professional authority, in which commanders were at best primus inter pares in
their own commands, dependent on collective decision-making
bodies and subject to harassment from the Komsomol at the bottom,
the MPA and Political Departments at the top, and civilian Party
apparatchiks on the outside.[39]

Opposition within the military to other aspects of Khrushchev's
defence and foreign policy gained some impetus as a result of the U2
affair in May 1960. By undermining Khrushchev's policy of détente
with the West, by proving that the United States was acting in a
hostile and belligerent fashion, his economic and military policies
which had resulted in the troop reductions could be attacked.

Marshal Malinovskii chose this particular moment to break ranks
with Khrushchev to some (limited) extent and mount a defence of the
interests of the military. While Khrushchev insisted that the U2 affair
was no reason to increase military spending, or reverse the planned
troop reductions (indeed, he threatened further reductions in the
future),[40] Malinovskii attacked Khrushchev's line at a Conference of
Communist brigades at the end of May:

> History teaches us that one should not trust the words of the
> imperialists, sweet as they may be. The latest lesson of Camp David
> is too clear to allow us to forget history. No, we do not believe the
> imperialists. We are convinced that they are only waiting for a
> favourable opportunity to attack the Soviet Union and the other
> socialist countries, and the only thing that stops them is the risk of
> the total destruction of imperialism.[41]

A hostile international environment, however, was the traditional
rationale for maintaining and increasing defence allocations.

In December 1960 the head of the MPA, Marshal Golikov, complained that the Party's instructions about reforms were being
ignored by some commanders and political workers. He also noted
with alarm indications of apathy and a deterioration in discipline.
Another article by Colonels E. Tarasov and S. Il'ni in *Kommunist
Vooruzhennykh Sil* made the same point.[42] The deterioration was one
manifestation of the attempt by military officers to frustrate the
implementation of Khrushchev's egalitarian reforms in the military
(which had had to be abandoned in 1958 due to military opposition
but had been resumed in 1960). Military resistance, while stopping
short of direct disobedience, involved open criticism of political
functionaries who were not from the professional military,
obstruction of the performance of their tasks, neglect of political

indoctrination and spreading a general atmosphere of inertia and indiscipline.[43]

In November 1960 Lieutenant General S. Krasil'nkov published a critique of Khrushchev's strategic doctrine, thus confirming the unhappiness in the military with the Khrushchev line. Krasil'nkov criticized the view of a future war as:

> a push-button war, which could be conducted without mass arm-ies . . . In the new war, massive multimillion armies would without a doubt be participating, which would require large reserves of commanding personnel and vast contingents of soldiers.[44]

As a result, while accepting that rocket forces were becoming the most important element of the Soviet military, this did not imply that one could minimize the Ground Forces.

The deterioration in the international situation in 1961 and the American military build-up no doubt served to strengthen the military opponents of Khrushchev's defence policy. Thus the doub-ling of the planned production rate of solid-fuel ICBMs and the acceleration of the Polaris programme announced by President Kennedy in January 1961 made a considerable impact on the debates about Soviet defence planning. The plans published by the Kennedy Administration on 28 March 1961 envisaged the deployment of 126 Atlas ICBMs, 464 Polaris SLBMs and 600 Minuteman ICBMs. If our reconstruction of Soviet plans at the time is anywhere near correct (not to speak of actual deployments), then this must have been very alarming from a purely military standpoint. Khrushchev's strategy of countering the US bomber threat by generating the image of a Soviet Union surging ahead into the missile age had triggered off a counter-reaction in the United States that threatened to deepen Soviet vulnerabilities. Thus the Soviet military could perceive them-selves to be at the losing end of an 'action-reaction' process triggered by a leadership that was unwilling to match the stakes of the adversary. This was reinforced by a tense international situation. On 17 April the abortive Bay of Pigs invasion took place, which was interpreted as proof of belligerent intentions by the imperialists. Khrushchev's failure to obtain any concessions from President Kennedy at the Vienna summit meeting in June and, in particular, the inability to pressure the West into concessions with regard to Berlin contributed to Khrushchev's forced retreat. Thus, on 21 June, Khrushchev now echoed the Malinovskii line that while rocket weapons continued to be the prime means of defence, the strengthening of the defence of the Soviet Union depends on the perfecting of all branches of forces of our armed forces. [45]

After a consultation with military leaders on 4–6 July, Khrushchev announced on 8 July an increase in defence allocations of 3,144 million roubles, thus raising the total defence budget of 1961 to 12,399 million roubles. At the same time the troop reductions were being suspended (the terms of those on military service who were to be released at the end of August were extended). These measures, while also serving as a means to exert additional pressure on the West with regard to Berlin, were clearly a major concession to the military opposition.

It is significant to observe that the additional increases in the defence budget of $3.5 billion announced by the Kennedy Administration on 25 July 1961, which were earmarked almost exclusively for conventional forces, came after Khrushchev announced increases in the Soviet military budget. The pressure for such increases in the Soviet Union was generated by the internal disputes about military doctrine and the nature of the Soviet force posture and was not a reaction to these actions by the Kennedy Administration. At first glance Kennedy's actions may appear to be a response to the announcements made by Khrushchev. While there may be an element of 'reaction', and while the tense situation of the Berlin crisis was clearly preoccupying the administration, these developments were also part of a more long-term plan to develop capabilities for a shift away from massive retaliation to *flexible response*. A careful look at the events reveals that what appears as a classic example of an 'action-reaction' cycle is a more complex phenomenon, and the actions of the other side were only one of a range of inputs into policymaking.

Every aspect of Khrushchev's policies appeared to be under threat. Instead of a policy of détente, domestic pressure for a foreign-policy success resulted in very aggressive approach to relations with the West. As Carl A. Linden has pointed out:

> In sum, Khrushchev's erratic behaviour during the summer of 1961, stoking the Cold War one day and dampening it down the next, was more a sign of weakness than of strength. He was not in so secure a position that he could pursue a single and consistent course; he could not ignore the powerful pressures and cross pressures of the internal politics of the Soviet ruling group.[46]

Among the cross pressures was a very heated debate about the priorities in resource allocation and, in particular, about the rôle of heavy industries and Khrushchev's 'revolution' in agriculture launched in January 1961 as well as his support for the increased production of consumer goods. The intensity of the debate, as well as the fact that most of Khrushchev's programme was not adopted by the Plenum in January, indicates that the opposition was gaining strength and that Khrushchev's control over policy was weakening substantially. Indeed, during 1961 the view of Khrushchev's opponents appeared to prevail in economic policy. As we have seen in chapter 3, the resumption of nuclear testing was forced upon Khrushchev by his opponents in the Presidium with the support of the military leadership.

The climax of the power struggles of 1961 came at the 22nd CPSU Congress in October. An indication of the strong position of the military can be seen in the fact that 330 officers were elected to the Congress, the highest number ever, of which 305 had voting rights. Moreover, 31 of these were elected as members of the Central Committee, the highest number by 1961. Michael MccGwire has given the following interpretation of the events at the 22nd Congress:

> In January 1960, Khrushchev announced the result of what appears to have been a thoroughgoing defence review, which included the formation of the Strategic Rocket Force, its designation as the primary arm of the nation's defence, a substantial reorganisation of military research and development, and the cutting back of conventional ground forces. Given Khrushchev's faith in nuclear missiles and his belief that nuclear war would be suicidal, the new policy could only indicate a shift in emphasis towards the Western concept of nuclear deterrence and away from the traditional reliance on balanced forces and a war-fighting capability. But by October 1961 the shift had been reversed and at the 22nd Party Congress, Marshal Malinovsky's speech clearly indicated a return to the traditional military values.[47]

A close study of Malinovskii's speech, however, does not entirely support MccGwire's conclusion. It is true that Malinovskii restated the revisions of Khrushchev's strategic doctrine which he had already enunciated in earlier speeches. Nonetheless, many important aspects of Khrushchev's strategic doctrine were reaffirmed. For example, Malinovskii emphasized:

the significance of the initial period of war;
that the most important task of the Soviet armed forces consisted
    in preparing for the contingency of a surprise nuclear attack;
that any armed conflict would inevitably escalate into a general
    nuclear war.

Furthermore, despite references to the continued need for mass armies and the continued development of all branches of the armed forces, the sheer amount of space devoted to nuclear rockets and their capabilities gives his speech an almost Khrushchevian character.

For example, Malinovskii praised the quality (i.e. accuracy) and the combat-readiness of Soviet rockets:

> Now our rocket troops are completely in a high state of combat-readiness. They are always ready for employment and capable of fulfilling their tasks successfully. I can add that in 1961 the practical missile tests in the rocket units under combat conditions yielded convincing results: More than 90 per cent of all firings of medium-range rockets were evaluated as 'excellent' and 'good'. As far as intercontinental rockets are concerned however, they fulfilled all their tasks only with 'excellent' and 'good' [results]. It may appear strange, but rockets hit their targets more accurately over long distances than over short distances.[48]

This statement was patently untrue, from what is now known about the accuracies of Soviet missiles and the technical difficulties encountered with the SS-6.[49] Malinovskii must have exaggerated Soviet missile capabilities deliberately. The notion that he was following in Khrushchev's footsteps in this regard and thereby quite consciously supporting Khrushchev's views on strategic arms policy is indicated by the following statement:

> I can tell you, that the scale of the production of rocket weapons has grown during the last years to such an extent that our supply of rockets of various types and for various purposes is not merely sufficient, but richly abundant.[50]

This can hardly be interpreted as a call for the increased production of nuclear missiles. MccGwire's attempt to trace a decisive shift in Soviet strategic arms policy to 1961 and Malinovskii's speech in particular finds little support in the speech itself. Thus Malinovskii emphatically supported Khrushchev's troop reductions (at least as far as they had been implemented) and justified them by the modernization programme of the armed forces, in particular the introduction of missile technology into all branches of the armed forces, and the subsequent increase in firepower achieved despite the decrease in manpower. (He also explained that the reductions affected in particular the administration and the service organizations of the armed forces, rather than combat personnel.)

Thus it appears that a fundamental compromise had been reached between Khrushchev and Malinovskii. The concessions extracted by the Defence Minister included the general recognition that all branches of the armed forces were still of importance in modern war, that multi-million man armies were still required, and that a suspension of the troop reductions and an increase in the 1961 budgetary allocations of the military were necessary. In return, Malinovskii offered emphatic support to many of the general themes of Khrushchev's defence policy that still remained.[51]

The result of the 22nd Party Congress was some sort of stalemate; Khrushchev had regained part of the authority he had lost, but his opposition was by no means defeated. There were signs that the compromise with Malinovskii continued during 1962.[52] Roman Kolkowicz has discerned the existence of three major groupings in the military in the early Sixties. He calls those who favoured the line developed by Khrushchev in January 1960 the 'radicals', and those following more traditional lines of military thought in strong opposition to Khrushchev's military doctrine the 'conservatives'. Then there is the Malinovskii line, whose adherents are called 'the moderates' by Kolkowicz, and who accepted the compromise with Khrushchev's strategic doctrines outlined in Malinovskii's speech.

As Kolkowicz has noted, the most notable feature of the debates in 1962 consisted in the silence of the 'radicals' like S. Kozlov, P. Sidorov and N. Sushko, who had strongly supported Khrushchev in articles in military journals in 1961. This is a further indication of a compromise between the 'radicals' and the 'moderates'. It was the 'moderates', in turn, who carried on the debates with the 'conservatives'.[53]

Another debate which continued at the same time was that about political control between the Ministry of Defence and the Main Political Administration. Malinovskii raised the issues during his speech to the 22nd Party Congress:

> Our Soviet officer – this is the representative of the Party and Government in the army and navy, this is the commander with single command, and his order is law for subordinates. At the same time, he is also the solicitous educator of his subordinates and the champion of the ideas of the party. It is significant that the proportion of all communists and komsomols among officers, generals, and admirals constitute almost 90 per cent . . .
>
> . . .A very important role in strengthening the army and navy was played by the resolutions, adopted in 1957 by the October Plenum of the CC CPSU, which laid down measures for intensifying the leadership by the Party of the Armed Forces and for a radical improvement in party-political work. As a result of the

October Plenum and subsequent resolutions of the CC CPSU, the Leninist principle of the leadership of the Armed Forces was completely restored, the role of the political organs and party organizations in the troops was raised, the connection of the army with the people was strengthened, and party-political work with personnel was significantly improved.[54]

Malinovskii appeared to differ with Marshal Golikov, the head of the MPA, on two crucial issues. One is that of *edinonachalie*; Golikov insisted that one-man command should be on a Party basis. Whereas Malinovskii stated that the order of the commander 'is law for subordinates', Golikov's view was that

> one-man command requires from every commander a party and state approach to entrusted affairs, the skill firmly and consistently to implement in action the policy of the Communist Party, basing himself in all his work on party organizations and on the forces of the community.[55]

The other, as Michael Deane has pointed out, is that Golikov claimed that the October 1957 Plenum had served to

> enhance the role and authority of party organizations, political organs and military councils . . . to raise the role of the community and so to intensify party authority in all aspects of the life of troops.[56]

Golikov also praised the appointment of political officers to command positions. Malinovskii, on the other hand, was eloquently silent about the appointment of political officers to command positions and the authority of party-political organs and merely asserted that party-political work had been improved.

Although Malinovskii did not attack the MPA or the political control organs directly at this point, it appears to be beyond doubt the Ministry of Defence quietly supported the post-Congress opposition to the political reforms of the military. Thus an attack on political workers and on the failure to strengthen *edinonachalie* and the commanders' authority was published in *Kommunist Vooruzhennykh Sil* in February 1962,[57] while in the same month a three-part series in *Krasnaia Zvezda* emphasized the importance of Party leadership over the armed forces. The notion that the Ministry of Defence was supportive of the attacks on the political control organizations is indicated by an article published in March 1962 which originated from the MPA reporting 'serious deficiencies' in the central apparatus of the defence ministry. These allegedly included the discouragement of *kritika/samokritika*, the obstruction of Party functionaries in carrying out their duties with regard to indoctrination and imposing Party control within the Ministry, and serious breaches of discipline.[58]

The seriousness of the situation was underlined by the intervention of the Central Committee in April 1962, which instructed the MPA to hold a meeting of the top political functionaries in the military; they were to discuss steps to improving Party control in the military. The meeting resulted in serious criticism of military officers, which is not surprising given the 'guerilla tactics' current among officers directed against the political personnel.

In May 1962, Marshal F. I. Golikov was replaced as head of the MPA by A. A. Epishev. This move has been subject to conflicting interpretation by Western analysts. Roman Kolkowicz presents the following view:

> A close associate of Khrushchev, with a long career in the security organs and a deep involvement in political control activities, Epishev was clearly the man to break the officer corps' resistance, and his appointment suggested that a showdown was imminent.[59]

Michael J. Deane, however, has argued, on the basis of a detailed analysis of Epishev's career, that it is unlikely that Epishev was a Khrushchev protegé and it appears more likely that his main supporter in the Presidium was Suslov.[60] If this interpretation is correct, it would support Robert Slusser's contention that Epishev's appointment was part of the factional struggles against Khrushchev.[61] Suslov was involved in several disputes with Khrushchev at the time, one of which was an ideological debate with Khrushchev's protegé Ilichev; another concerned the increase of agricultural allocations which Suslov opposed.[62]

What we must explain, however, is not only the choice of Golikov's replacement, but the reason for his removal in the first place. That this was due to disagreements over policy is indicated by the fact that in April 1962 other changes were made in high-level military command positions: Marshal Konev was removed as Commander of the Soviet forces in Germany (a move connected with the situation in Berlin)[63] and S. S. Biriuzov replaced Moskalenko as Commander of the Strategic Rocket Forces.[64] Michel Tatu has suggested that these changes may have been related to the decision to place medium-range nuclear missiles in Cuba. Thus Tatu presents the following reconstruction:

in April 1962, contemplating the futility of all previous efforts to obtain a settlement on Berlin, Khrushchev devised a new means of pressure on the United States – the shipment of nuclear missiles to Cuba. The matter may have been discussed at the formal Party Presidium meeting held on the occasion of the Supreme Soviet session between April 22 and 25, and this may have heightened the difficulties of that agitated period. It is safe to assume that Moskalenko opposed the plan, and Golikov probably did too, hence their resignation . . .[65]

Tatu also mentions that Khrushchev received the Cuban Minister for Public Works, Cienfuegos on 28 April and saw the Cuban Ambassador in Moscow on 5 May. The suggestion is that at these occasions preliminary soundings of the idea of placing the missiles on Cuba may have been made.[66]

Tatu's reconstruction stands in complete contradiction to the account in Khrushchev's memoirs:

It was during my visit to Bulgaria that I had the idea of installing missiles with nuclear warheads in Cuba without letting the United States find out they were there until it was too late to do anything about them . . . I didn't tell anyone what I was thinking. I kept my mental agony to myself. But all the while the idea of putting missiles in Cuba was ripening inside my mind. After I returned to Moscow from Bulgaria I continued to think about the possibility. Finally we convened a meeting and I said I had some thoughts to air on the subject of Cuba . . . I presented my idea in the context of the counter-revolutionary invasion which Castro had just resisted.[67]

However, Khrushchev's visit to Bulgaria took place on 21 May 1962. While it is unlikely that the perceived threat to Cuba was the only motive underlying the emplacement of the missiles (as is discussed elsewhere), there is no evidence that would lead us to doubt Khrushchev's account about the timing of the decision.

Given that Moskalenko was Commander of the SRF, the branch of the armed forces most directly involved in the Cuban missile venture, it is suggestive, to follow Tatu's hypothesis, that his removal was due to disagreements with Khrushchev over the Cuban plans. Nonetheless, if Khrushchev's account about the timing of the decision is correct, then Tatu's hypothesis must be false.

Contrary to Roman Kolkowicz's view, who classes Moskalenko as a faithful Khrushchev ally,[68] Khrushchev's memoirs paint a different picture. While praising him as 'devoted to the defense of our country . . . energetic, and hard-driving',[69] he also described him as having a 'violent temper', being 'mentally unbalanced', accused him of a 'lack of principles' and claimed that 'he'd do dirt to anyone as long as he felt there was something in it for him'.[70] Furthermore, Khrushchev believed that Moskalenko had criticized the civilian leadership of the Soviet Union in private conversations with Zhukov and, on the whole, seems to have thought Moskalenko highly unreliable, despite their apparently closer relationship during the war.[71]

If we cannot connect Moskalenko's removal directly to the Cuban missile venture, it is likely that Moskalenko played an active part in the bitter debates about economic priorities during that time. In the context of the first Kennedy budget and the defence procurement plans it involved, the emerging 'missile gap' favouring the United States, as well as the international tension of the Berlin crisis, with Soviet military doctrine firmly based on its alleged nuclear strategic power, the unreliability of first-generation Soviet ICBMs, it is likely that Moskalenko will have argued strongly (if behind closed doors) in favour of a large increase in spending on the SRF, thus getting involved in a head-on conflict with Khrushchev and possibly providing part of the inspiration for the Cuban missile venture even though this idea came after his removal.

At first sight one might interpret the changes in the military leadership in April 1962 as a 'reshuffle' designed to enhance Khrushchev's authority.[72] Close analysis shows, however, that the changes were not necessarily related. In the case of Konev, it arose directly out of a diplomatic agreement with the United States.[73] Moskalenko was replaced by a close Khrushchev ally, thus indicating disagreement with Khrushchev over strategic arms policy. In May 1962, Epishev was appointed to succeed Golikov as head of the MPA. The meeting in April 1962, which the MPA convened at the direction of the Central Committee, was a clear indication that Party leaders were not satisfied with the degree of Party control over the military. This constituted the fundamental reason for Golikov's removal. Epishev was appointed to restore this control, but this does not answer the question, as Michael Deane points out, on whose behalf Party control was to be restored. The analysis provided by Deane and Slusser suggests that it was not on Khrushchev's behalf, but on that of his opponents in the Presidium, notably Suslov.[74]

In the immediate period following Epishev's appointment, there were attempts from all sides to be conciliatory. The second issue in May 1962 of the MPA journal *Kommunist Vooruzhennykh Sil* carried an article by Colonel General N. Lomov, the main thrust of which was that Soviet military doctrine is formulated in a co-operative venture between the Party and the military. In this view, the Central Committee exercised leadership and control over the formation of military doctrine, but at the same time a substantial contribution in this effort is made by military officers. The advantage of Soviet military doctrine, as compared to bourgeois military doctrine, resided precisely in the unity of view between the civilian and the military leadership. Lomov's main thrust therefore, was without doubt the reconciliation of differences between the Party and the military leadership.[75]

The following issue of *Kommunist Vooruzhennykh Sil* carried an article by Malinovskii which sharply criticized the political instruction in the armed forces. What is notable about this article, however, is the fact that it attacked shortcomings among the political officers and the professional military commanders alike. It cannot, therefore, be interpreted as an attack against the political control organs as such; indeed, the evenhandedness of the criticism can be interpreted to imply a more conciliatory stance towards the MPA as such.[76] Likewise, Epishev appeared to take Malinovskii's concerns about the failure of the political functionaries to care for the actual well-being of the troops seriously when he convened an all-army conference to address these issues.[77]

The truce, however, was short-lived. The MPA under Epishev soon returned to the attack of political short-comings in the military; one particular issue which again played a central rôle was that of *edinonachalie* on a party basis.[78] Epishev instituted new review procedures and controls, and engaged in strong public criticism of the military academies. It thus became clear that Epishev was taking the task to which he had been appointed (i.e. to tighten Party control of the military) very seriously. In August, the MPA published a report which constituted a severe and wide-ranging indictment of the military hierarchy and the administrative apparatus of the General Staff and the Ministry of Defence. The charges were, as usual, resistance to the MPA, to *kritika/samokritika* and the neglect of political (i.e. ideological) education.[79]

In October 1962 there was another conference of MPA officials from all branches of the armed forces. Top leaders from the professional military, including Malinovskii, Zakharov, Moskalenko,

Sokolovskii and Timoshenko also attended. Malinovskii's speech at the conference constituted a fierce attack on the political functionaries. His main thrust appeared to be that the present political functionaries lacked the proper education needed to carry out their task (in particular, technical knowledge relating to modern combat and weapons). The criticism of young people entering the armed forces by political functionaries was blamed for the low morale and the resulting disciplinary problems in the armed forces. He also attacked the use of *kritika/samokritika*, describing it as a 'sharp weapon' which needed to be used judiciously.[80] Epishev, for his part, reaffirmed the need for *kritika/samokritika* to overcome distortions and the Party-basis of one-man-command in a long article on party-military relations in *Kommunist Vooruzhennykh Sil*.

The renewal of conflict between the Party organs and the professional military coincided with internal disputes about the Cuban missile crisis. The official party line, enunciated by A. N. Kosygin in a speech in early November,[81] was to praise Khrushchev's actions and describe the outcome of the crisis as being based on 'mutual concessions'. Kosygin hinted, however, at the existence of opposition to those 'concessions'. Later in the same month Marshal Chuikov emphasized the leadership of the Party in military affairs in an interview published in *Krasnaia Zvezda*; at the same time he criticized the suggestion that 'diplomacy sometimes successfully wrecks the results of our military successes', a thinly disguised attack on military opposition to the agreement that ended the Cuban missile crisis.[82] The fact that this dispute persisted for some time is indicated by Khrushchev's speech on 12 December when he once again felt compelled to defend the agreement with regard to Cuba.[83]

The Cuban missile crisis thus exacerbated the already growing Party-military conflict. Those who were concerned about Party control, or who were Khrushchev supporters, generally accepted the 'mutual concessions' interpretation, while another group opposed the concessions as capitulation to the United States. The situation is rather difficult to reconstruct because one can detect not only the rift between the Party control organs and the professional military, but also splits within the professional military itself. One particular forum for this dispute was provided by publications to commemorate the twentieth anniversary of the battle of Stalingrad. Some gave credit to the military leadership, while others emphasized the important rôle of the Party leadership and Khrushchev in particular.

Articles by Marshals Rotmistrov, Voronov and Kazakov fell into the first of these two categories, whereas those by Marshals Biriuzov, Chuikov and Eremenko were in the latter.[84] Malinovskii apparently avoided taking sides in this debate and gave credit to everyone, including even Marshal Zhukov.

It is very clear that the failure of the Cuban missile adventure was a serious blow to Khrushchev's prestige and, in the aftermath, opposition to Khrushchev's policies and leadership was gaining ground in every area. This was evident in the re-stalinization in early 1963, the shifts in economic policy forced on Khrushchev (his consumer programme had to be shelved for an indefinite period in favour of heavy industry and defence allocations), the shifts in foreign policy (in particular a new conciliatory disposition towards China), as well as in the decline of Kosygin and the strengthening of the positions of Kozlov and Suslov. In the military sphere it led to the *development of an independent line* by the MPA. What this means is that while Epishev was still fighting the battle to strengthen Party control in the armed forces, he advocated policies which were more along traditional military lines and opposed to Khrushchev's views. Affirming the need to develop 'all branches of the armed forces and all types of troops', he also reaffirmed the need for mass armies:

> The practice of contemporary wars testifies to the fact that the reasoning of some theoreticians on the necessity of renunciation of the creation of mass armies and on the replacement of men by technology has turned out to be groundless. The popular masses with weapon in hand in a field of battle and the popular masses at the rear, where are created the material means for conducting the armed struggle, are the decisive force, determining the course and outcome of contemporary wars. With the increasing role and significance of technology in contemporary war is also increasing the role and importance of the popular masses and the role of mass armies.[85]

Meanwhile Khrushchev himself, in a speech in February 1963, still emphasized his reliance on nuclear rockets as the most important means to defeat the enemy in a world war. He furthermore expressed the view that if the imperialists were to unleash a new war it would end in failure 'on the very first day'.[86] The implication seemed to be that there would be no need for larger armies than presently in existence. However, Khrushchev was forced to concede the need to increase defence appropriations; yet another indication of how little control over policy Khrushchev was enjoying in this particular period.[87]

A sharp public challenge to Khrushchev came from none other than the Minister of Defence himself, Marshal Malinovskii. In an article published in *Pravda* on 2 February 1963 to commemorate the victory at Stalingrad, he systematically attacked Khrushchev's claim to a key rôle in planning the counter-offensive which resulted in the German defeat. He also identified none other than Zhukov as being involved in the planning and execution of the operation.

The articles published to commemorate Stalingrad showed up a stark division in the Stalingrad group. Among Khrushchev's supporters were Marshals Biriuzov, Chuikov and Eremenko who ascribed to Khrushchev a central rôle in the conception and planning of the counter-offensive. Marshals Rotmistrov, Voronov and Kazakov, on the other hand, omitted any mention of Khrushchev and emphasized the rôle of various military leaders, notably Malinovskii, who then quite bluntly and directly attacked the 'myth' of Khrushchev's military achievements.[88]

The period from November 1962 to mid-March 1963 was, therefore, a very crucial period, in which Khrushchev had little control over policy and where those Party leaders (e.g. Suslov and Kozlov) who favoured policies more in line with the views of the traditionalists in the professional military had the upper hand. The result was not only an increase in defence expenditure, but also, as will be discussed in greater detail in chapter 7, a reorganization of the defence industry, associated with plans of increased investment including the increased production of missiles.

By late March, however, it was becoming evident that Khrushchev was reasserting his control. Chief of the General Staff Matvei Zakharov, apparently a leading figure of the opposition to Khrushchev in the aftermath of the Cuban crisis, was removed from his post, to be replaced by a still loyal Khrushchevite (also from the Stalingrad group), S. S. Biriuzov on 28 March.[89] Another military leader more favourable to Khrushchev, Krylov, succeeded Biriuzov as Chief of the Strategic Rocket Forces. The question raises itself why Malinovskii remained in his post. The most likely answer is that the Defence Minister, who now was clearly identified with Khrushchev's opponents, had acquired powerful political protection.[90]

Khrushchev's position was strengthened by the fact that Frol Kozlov, his chief protagonist, suffered a stroke on 10 April 1963 and thus effectively ceased to be a threat (even though he lived until 30 January 1965). Towards the end of April there were indications that Suslov was also suffering a decline in political power.[91] As a result, the MPA no longer felt able to pursue its independent line and MPA spokesmen no longer gave support to the mass armies concept, but rather tailored their positions to be more compatible with Khrushchev's views.

The effect of these political power struggles on Party-military relations was somewhat paradoxical. A Party plenum convened by the Central Committee in June initiated renewed intense conflict between the professional military and the MPA, this time centring around the issue of ideological education. The main protagonists were Epishev and Malinovskii; Malinovskii's central theme was the need to overcome

> the alienation of propaganda and theoretical studies from the concrete task, from life, and from our practical work.[92]

Malinovskii blamed the MPA for the deficiencies of political education. But, at the same time, the Defence Minister was careful to express support for the Party and Khrushchev in particular, to whom he referred as 'Supreme Commander in Chief' (a reference which occurred only rarely). By December 1963, Khrushchev appeared ready to continue the implementation of his policies in the economic and military sphere.

The Soviet military and the fall of Khrushchev

Despite Khrushchev's political recovery, opposition to his policies among the professional military continued unabated, as is indicated by an article published in October 1963 in *Voennaia Mysl'*:

> although with rocket-nuclear armament the significance of the first blow in the outcome of the entire war is increasing immeasurably and the concept of 'first blow' in contemporary warfare differs radically from such a concept in past wars, nevertheless it should be pointed out that even with present-day military technology and weapons it is hardly possible to count on winning a world war with one blow. Even now, complete victory is won by difficult and strenuous fighting.[93]

Amazingly, the author managed to quote Khrushchev himself in support of a strategic doctrine which was actually, as we have seen, contrary to Khrushchev's views:

> At the fourth session of the USSR Supreme Soviet N. S. Khrushchev stated: 'But would it really be possible for the attacking side, even if we assumed for a moment that it succeeded in delivering a surprise

attack, to knock out of action all at once the reserves of nuclear weapons and all rocket equipment installations on the territory of the nation subjected to attack? Of course not. The state being subjected to a surprise attack, if, of course, the question concerns a sufficiently large state, will always have the capability of properly repulsing the aggressor.' And this means that, acknowledging the tremendous significance of the first rocket-nuclear blow and not denying the possibility of a short-lived war, we must be ready in the event that a decisive armed struggle 'can be dragged out and require the prolonged and maximum efforts of all forces of the army and the entire country'. He concluded that therefore a great quantity of troops would be required.

In such a manner, the resoluteness of the political objectives of a war, its coalition character, huge losses of military personnel, broad spatial range, and the factors of manoeuvrability, difficult and persistence, as we see, inevitably lead to the formation of mass, multi-million armies.[94]

The author stated furthermore that for victory, enemy armed forces must be routed and enemy territory occupied (key strategic areas). Main forces would consist of ground forces and operational tactical rocket troops. All branches must be well-equipped, and large mass armies would clearly be necessary. He quoted Maxwell Taylor in support of the need for mass armies. The clearest contradiction of Khrushchev's strategic doctrine consisted in the refutation of the view that modern weapons allowed troop reductions. Quite to the contrary, the author maintained that *modern* troops will require more troops for back-up:

we are forced to concern ourselves in good time about the creation of reserves who are trained in accordance with the demands of modern warfare.[95]

In the same issue, Maj. Gen. Kruchinin reaffirmed the argument:

the final victory in a war against a strong, unfriendly coalition is possible only as a result of the combined efforts of all branches of the armed forces . . .[96]

He also stressed the need for strategic reserves.

Nonetheless, Khrushchev resumed his endeavours to reduce military spending and manpower to shift resources to other sectors of the community. He was helped in this by a general relaxation of East–West tensions in the aftermath of the Cuban missile crisis, which had a very sobering effect both in the Soviet Union and the United States, resulting in a breakthrough in the negotiations leading to the Partial Test Ban Treaty. There was a manpower reduction of 300,000 and, in December 1963, a cut in official military expenditures by 600 million roubles was announced; this represented a decline from 16.1 per cent of the 1963 budget to 14.6 per cent of the budget in 1964.[97] Further manpower cuts were also announced.

Not surprisingly, Khrushchev met with great opposition from the military. The mildest reaction, coming from a spokesman from the MPA, emphasized the importance of the Ground Forces, but recognized the primary rôle of the SRF and saw the Ground Forces as supplementary.[98] Other articles, such as that by Prof. N. A. Lomov published in *Krasnaia Zvezda* in January, unashamedly defended the need for mass armies and asserted the possibility of a prolonged war. The most significant opposition came from Ground Forces Commander Chuikov, up to now a loyal Khrushchev supporter, who asserted in an article in *Izvestiia* in December 1963 that victory

> can be achieved only by means of the joint actions of all types of armed forces

and thus

> in modern conditions the ground forces continued to be not only a mandatory but also a most integral part of the armed forces.[99]

Chuikov's defence of the Ground Forces was by no means premature, since in 1964 they were abolished as a separate service with its own high-command structure (and thus Marshal Chuikov was removed from his post), and instead were to be administered by the General Staff.[100]

The perceived weakness in Soviet military posture, as starkly demonstrated by the Cuban fiasco, and the resumption of policies which the military believed had been defeated in 1961 and which would contribute nothing to correcting the deficiences finally created a consensus among the military against Khrushchev and his policies. There is no evidence that the military in any way participated in preparing Khrushchev's ouster in October 1964. But it is clear that Khrushchev could expect no support from the military to avert it, either.

Defence policy under the new collective leadership

The new leadership took over in the Kremlin in 1964 having rejected not so much any specific policies but rather Khrushchev's style of leadership and the institutional conflicts and havoc that it generated.

Khrushchev's foreign policy, for example, was considered to have been a failure, but not necessarily because of its specific content; rather his bombastic and adventurous style, followed by inevitable and at times humiliating retreats, such as at Suez, Berlin and, most of all, Cuba, was rejected as a dangerous form of gambling where Khrushchev had frequently overreached himself, seeking objectives he did not have the means to obtain.[101] This analysis had a direct bearing on military policy, since Khrushchev's failure to translate Soviet military might into political gain could at least in part be attributed to Soviet strategic inferiority.

The result was that the new leadership was in agreement about its rejection of Khrushchevism, but there was no consensus about the policies to be pursued instead. Indeed, a coherent set of policies took a considerable time to emerge and the central policy disputes of the Khrushchev era resurfaced at various stages in the subsequent years.

In the foreign-policy arena, the new collective leadership initially adopted a conciliatory attitude towards the United States; as regards military policy there was no consensus in the Politburo on increased military allocations or a shift from a minimum deterrence stance, as became evident when Kosygin announced on 9 December 1964 that military expenditures in 1965 would amount to 12.8 billion roubles, which was a reduction of 0.5 billion roubles compared to Khrushchev's 1964 military budget.

The professional military, on the other hand, was unashamedly advocating a hard line designed to promote a shift away from Khrushchevian policies. Thus Malinovskii made a speech in which he adopted a more hostile attitude towards the United States; an indication of a difference of emphasis between the Party leadership and the professional military may be that *Pravda* deleted Malinovskii's remarks from its report of the speech.[102] One important success for Malinovskii was the reappointment of Matvei Zakharov as Chief of the General Staff after Biriuzov died in an airplane crash in October 1964.

The first two years of the Brezhnev–Kosygin–Podgornii regime were a time in which the entire defence establishment was reorganized and issues of military strategy and the Soviet force posture were subject to a general review and internal debate. After the reorganization of the defence industries in March 1965, there was public controversy between Nikolai Podgornii, then Party Secretary in charge of personnel, and Mikhail Suslov, who was responsible for ideological questions and foreign policy in the Party Secretariat. In a

speech on 21 May 1965, Podgornii appeared to endorse the controversial ideas of the economist Yevsei Liberman, who was the
leading voice of a number of intellectuals favouring liberal reforms in
the Soviet economic system, and who had enjoyed Khrushchev's
backing. Podgornii strongly endorsed a profit-earning capacity in
industrial and agricultural production, consistent with the view he
had expressed during the Khrushchev period. What Podgornii was
saying amounted by implication to a call for reducing military
expenditures:

> There was a time when the Soviet people consciously accepted
> material restrictions for the sake of the priority development of
> heavy industry and the strengthening of our defence capacity. That
> was fully justified . . . But now collective wealth is multiplying year
> by year, while conditions are emerging that make it easier to satisfy
> the workers' ever-growing domestic and cultural needs.[103]

Suslov attacked these ideas directly during a speech given in Sofia on
2 June 1965:

> At a time when the imperialist powers are pursuing the arms race
> and unleashing military aggression first in one and then in another
> region of the world, our Party and our Government have to
> maintain the country's defence at the highest level and improve it
> constantly . . . All these naturally demand considerable material
> sacrifices from the Soviet people and the appropriation of a major
> part of the national revenue for defence.[104]

According to Tatu, Suslov represented a pro-military faction in the
Politburo, and from the veiled allusions in his speech it appears that
the military and their supporters were using the American involvement in Vietnam and the intervention in the Dominican Republic as
a justification for demanding a greater allocation of resources.

The professional military began to press its demands more seriously in the spring of 1965. Marshal Zakharov issued a strong attack
on Khrushchev's policies, which amounted to saying that amateurs
(i.e. politicians) should not meddle in military affairs which were the
province of professionals. Sokolovskii also emphasized the need for
military expertise in military planning.[105] The top military leadership
also became increasingly vocal in promoting its views on military
policy. Thus Chuikov warned of the increasing stocks of thermonuclear weapons amassed by the imperialist powers, implying the
need for the Soviet Union to increase its own capabilities.[106] The
commander of the SRF, Marshal Krylov, affirmed that final victory is
only possible

as the result of combined actions of all arms of the armed forces.[107]

The Vietnam war served as argument for the military to demand the build-up of capabilities which would allow the Soviet armed forces to exercise their liberating rôle against imperialist aggression. On 18 March Colonel I. Larionov rebutted the argument that a single nuclear rocket strike would be sufficient to defeat an aggressor or that a future war would necessarily be of short duration and argued both for a 'united effort' of all branches of the armed forces and a military build-up.[108] Sokolovskii and Cherednichenko added their contribution to these arguments, as well as Marshal Rotmistrov, who argued in *Kommunist*:

> The aggressiveness of imperialism compels the Communist Party and the whole of the Soviet people to continuously raise the military power of our homeland, to develop the national economy, and to strengthen all other areas of state organization of the USSR in order to increase its defence capacity.[109]

In his view, the Soviet State had to proceed from the assumption that the imperialist states were preparing for a Third World War.[110] In the same context, he also made his views on Party-military relations clear; thus he spoke of

> the strengthening of one-man command as the most important principle of military organization.[111]

Perhaps the clearest exponents of the two sides of the debate on the rôle of war as an instrument of policy in the age of nuclear weapons and the issue of minimum deterrence were Major-General Nikolai Talenskii and Lieutenant-Colonel E. I. Rybkin.[112]

As we have mentioned in chapter 3, Rybkin was at that time attached to the Main Political Administration of the Soviet Army and Navy. His central argument was that victory in a nuclear war was not impossible and depended not merely on the character of the weapons employed, but also on the more general correlation of forces.[113] Rybkin, furthermore, was more willing than other Soviet military writers to consider a large variety of future war scenarios, including limited wars and even limited nuclear wars.[114]

As we have already mentioned, Nikolai Talenskii, the former editor of *Voennaia Mysl'* and a prominent military historian, was then associated with the arms-control community centred around the Academy of Sciences, providing an influential connection between the Disarmament Committee of the Academy and the Ministry of

Defence, and had been a regular participant in the *Pugwash* meetings. He expounded the view that in nuclear war it was no longer possible to ensure the survival of the societies which were at war with one another. The implication was that nuclear war could not serve as an acceptable instrument of policy. Talenskii's article provided support at the right time to the Podgornii faction in the Politburo. Ghebhardt has analysed the political background to this controversy in the following terms:

> The argument between Talensky and Rybkin appears more as an argument between two spokesmen for two bureaucracies: Talensky on behalf of the arms control group clustered around the Academy of Science and disarmament section of the Foreign Ministry, and Rybkin for the MPA . . . As the Politburo in 1965 was split on the priorities for the national economy, it is possible that Talensky and Rybkin represented the views of the two competing factions within the high political body.[115]

John Erickson has analysed the debate with and within the military in the following manner:

> There were, in fact, two arguments going on more or less at the same time – a form of dialogue with the leadership about what was needed to secure the credibility of the Soviet 'deterrent' and also a dispute within the military which ran on the familiar lines of inter-service rivalry – the proponents of increased conventional/ general purpose forces, the advocates of an offensive strategy backed with the appropriate weapons and those who wished to implement an effective strategic defensive force . . .[116]

It is not so clear what Brezhnev's position was while the political infighting grew between the Suslov and the Podgornii group. Between March and June 1965 Brezhnev made no public statement about defence matters at all; perhaps he was just waiting to see how the situation would develop. It did not take very long before the military and its supporters appeared to gain the upper hand, and Podgornii was appointed Chairman of the Presidium of the Supreme Soviet, thus gaining a more prestigious, but politically less influential position.

That the military and its political allies had won an important victory was confirmed by a speech given by Brezhnev at the beginning of July 1965:

> history has taught us that the stronger our armed forces are, the more watchful we are, the stronger the peace of our frontiers . . . We have learnt that well.[117]

Brezhnev's statement was backed up by a 5 per cent increase in military allocation in December 1965. The result of the internal Party debate and the consistent lobbying effort of the professional military was that the long-standing dispute about the nature of the Soviet force posture and the share of the resources allocated to heavy industry and the military was at least partially resolved in favour of heavy industry, a determined build-up of strategic nuclear forces and an all-round build-up of military strength.

The professional military and the MPA in the post-Khrushchev period

Despite the reassertion of the professional military under the collective leadership, the conflict between the former and the MPA continued after Khrushchev's ouster. Epishev retained his position as head of the MPA. The issue of *edinonachalie* continued to be a focus of the debate. Western analysts usually distinguish between those representatives from the professional military, who take the strengthening of one-man command to mean the exclusion of interference from political functionaries in command decisions, and the MPA representatives who call for 'strengthening one-man command on a Party basis' (*edinonachalie na partiinoi osnove*), according to Deane

> a euphemism for saying that the commander must be more dependent on the political worker.[118]

As becomes clear from an article published by Epishev in October 1962, this meant virtually the opposite of one-man command, making command subject to the influence of political organs on the basis of the principle of *kritika/samokritika*.[119]

However, in the course of time the debate became more confused when even those who strongly supported the literal interpretation of one-man command (and rejected the MPA interpretation) also began to use the phrase 'one-man command on a Party basis', such as, for example, Malinovskii in an article in *Krasnaia Zvezda* on 5 July 1963.[120] In the September 1964 issue of *Voennaia Mysl'* Major Gen. Justice I. Pobezhshimov and Col. Justice P. Romanov addressed the issue in an article entitled 'Organizational and Legal Principles of the Structure of the Armed Forces'.[121]

> Centralisation of leadership, one-man command and military discipline are the basic organizational-legal principle of Soviet military structure.[122]

One of the most important principles in the structure of the USSR Armed Forces, as stated in the CPSU Program, is one-man command. From an organizational and legal standpoint, this means the concentration of all leadership functions in one person (commander or chief); these functions are related to command, political supervision, drill, administration and supply, as well as control of the activities of the subordinates. One-man command also involves the establishment of responsibility of a single person (commander or chief) for all aspects of life and activities in a military unit or soedinenie (establishment or institution), together with personal responsibility of officials for individual aspects of life and activities in a military unit or soedinenie (establishment or institution).[123]

The task of legal control of Soviet military structure is to continue strengthening the principle of one-man command and to provide the most favourable conditions for a commander or chief to perform his leadership functions and to develop his organizational abilities. For this purpose, the legal norm has established rules confirming this principle and favouring its consistent application, i.e. *the compulsory nature of orders issued by commanders or chiefs*; the strict order of subordination of officials (functionaries); the conformity between the extent of rights and obligations of officials and the nature of their functions; personal responsibility of all servicemen and officials for the tasks entrusted to them, and encouragement of reasonable initiative aimed at the best possible implementation of orders.[124]

... A commander, like any supervisor must not only teach the masses, but must learn from them. Naturally, *the commander always retains the right to make the final decision*.[125] [Emphases added].

This article thus clearly sides with the professional military in their stricter interpretation of *edinonachalie*; on the other hand they also assert that one-man command 'should exist on a Party basis'.[126]

Thus this formulation of 'one-man command' had acquired the status of orthodoxy (even though it was interpreted quite differently by different authors), and was officially endorsed by Brezhnev himself:

One-man command in the Soviet army is built on a party basis. This means that the commander must in his work constantly rely upon party and komsomol organizations and make use in full measure of their mobilizing forces and authority and their creative activity for raising the combat readiness of units and ships. Party-political work is an important inherent part of the activity of the Soviet officer.[127]

However, in the first years of the collective leadership (1964–68), while the rhetoric of the MPA became generally accepted as official policy, the substance of the issue was settled in favour of the professional military. The authority of the commander was increased and recognized in the manner explained by Major Gen. Justice I. Pobezhshimov and Col. Justice P. Romanov (as cited above) and there was increased emphasis on military professionalism. At the same time the military (and, in particular, the Minister of Defence, Malinovskii and, after his death in 1967, his successor Marshal Grechko) clearly accepted and emphasized the principle of Party dominance and the need for political education.[128]

The period 1964–67 was marked by a convergence of interests between the MPA and the professional military. Thus the MPA, in common with the professional military, lobbied hard for the recognition of the seriousness of the imperialist threat, the need for greater military spending, the development of all branches of the armed forces, more substantial aid of national liberation movements in the Third World and the need to increase vigilance and combat readiness – issues about which there were uncertainty and substantial differences of view in the Party leadership. At the same time there was a reduced emphasis on ideological work and technical training was frequently given precedence. As a result, the MPA came under severe criticism leading to a Central Committee decree on Party-political work in the armed forces in January 1967, which listed the shortcomings in the Party-political work in the armed forces and decreed their correction by the MPA.

The death of Malinovskii on 31 March 1967 reopened the debate about Party control. At issue was the question of whether or not a civilian should now be appointed as Minister of Defence – the obvious candidate being Dmitri F. Ustinov – to strengthen Party control over the military. This would also allow the containment of demands from the professional military for increased resources and the redirection of budgetary allocations to consumer spending.[129] In the factional debate within the Party leadership the supporters of the appointment of a professional military Defence Minister were eventually successful. The appointment of Marshal A. A. Grechko marked the emergence of a more hard-line foreign policy and an increased emphasis on the dangers of the imperialist threat and greater budgetary allocations for defence. MPA support for these hard-line policies was particularly evidenced by Epishev's opposition to the reforms in Czechoslovakia and his support for the military intervention in 1968.[130]

After the events in Czechoslovakia, conflicts between the MPA and the professional military briefly re-emerged. In late 1968 the MPA launched a campaign on ideological training, strongly criticizing the deficiencies of ideological work in troop training.[131] In early 1969 the debate on *edinonachalie* was reopened; the MPA once again strongly advocated 'one-man command on a Party basis' and demanded that the rôle of the Party organs be strengthened, while professional military authors, in particular Defence Minister Grechko and (even more forcefully) SRF Commander Krylov emphasized the rôle of the Commander.[132] In May 1969 there was a brief but intense debate between Chief of the General Staff Zakharov and Epishev on the issue of technical versus ideological training.[133] However, these debates soon came to a halt. As the political leadership was engaged in entering talks with the United States on the limitation of strategic arms, resulting in a less hostile attitude towards the United States, the threat to military interests brought intra-military disputes to an end and MPA and the professional military united in their opposition to the political leadership's arms-control policies.

The military and SALT

On 27 June 1968 Foreign Minister Andrei A. Gromyko announced in a report to the Supreme Soviet:

> One of the unexplored fields of disarmament is the search for agreement on reciprocal limitations and subsequent reduction of strategic means of delivery of nuclear weapons – offensive and defensive, including anti-ballistic missiles. The Soviet Government is prepared for an exchange of opinions on this problem, too.[134]

In a Soviet government memorandum of 1 July 1968 it was stated that the implementation of such measures would contribute to a reduction in the threat of nuclear war.[135] The existence of disagreements on arms control was alluded to by Gromyko in his speech when he criticized

> those good-for-nothing theoreticians who try to attack us, as do all the opponents of disarmament, saying that disarmament is an illusion, we answer: in taking such a position you join ranks with the most extreme imperialist reactionaries, weakening the front of the struggle against them.[136]

Colonel Rybkin seemed to fall into this category when he wrote in *Kommunist Vooruzhennykh Sil* in September 1968:

> One cannot agree that disarmament can be realized as the result of a quiet discussion of this acute and complex problem by representatives of the opposing social systems. Disarmament cannot be the result of some kind of utopian 'tranquilization' of the class, political conflict in the international arena. On the contrary, it can be achieved only as a result of the extremely active pressure on their own governments of the revolutionary forces in the imperialist countries, in combination with the flexible and principled policy of the socialist camp. Any other imagined way to the achievement of disarmament is illusory.[137]

Military opposition to strategic arms limitations was also manifest when statements about such negotiations in Foreign Minister Gromyko's speech at the United Nations on 3 October 1968 were omitted in the report of the speech in *Krasnaia Zvezda*, a time-honoured method for conducting debates among the Soviet foreign policy elite.

A serious commitment to Soviet participation in SALT negotiations was made in June 1968, but the process was delayed by the invasion of Czechoslovakia. In confidential exchanges in the autumn of 1968 before the negotiations got under way, there was agreement that the objective should be a 'stable mutual strategic deterrence', recognizing an 'integral interrelationship' between offensive systems and strategic defence,[138] thus rejecting the Talenskii view that ABMs had no effect on strategic stability.[139]

Military concern about SALT was evidenced by the fact that during the entire period of the SALT I negotiations, from 1969 to 1972, there was virtually no comment whatsoever on SALT in the Soviet military press.[140] The opponents of arms control promoted their case indirectly. One emphasis in military writings was to stress the aggressive intent of the United States and thus cast doubt on the sincerity of their interest in arms control and détente. In mid-1969 Epishev, for example, declared that

> the ruling circles of the imperialist states are feverishly preparing a new world war . . .[141]

The second issue in May 1969 of *Kommunist Vooruzhennykh Sil* contained another strident attack, alleging that

> in their striving to block the road to revolutionary renewal and to liquidate socialist countries by means of war, the imperialists are beginning to prepare for any adventure.[142]

Even more forceful was an article published in the same journal in July:

In all stages of its heroic history, the Communist Party of our country has considered work for the education of hatred of imperialism as one of the chief tasks. The significance of it in contemporary conditions has increased even more. This is caused first of all by aggravation of internal tension and by the increased war danger being stirred up by aggressive actions of the imperialists headed by the USA . . . It is absolutely clear that the new war being prepared for by the imperialists will be aimed against the Soviet and the other socialist countries. The aggressors openly announce their crazy plans to abolish the socialist countries by means of war. All of this makes it necessary to intensify the education of Soviet troops in a spirit of high vigilance and class hatred for the imperialist aggressors and on this basis support the constant combat readiness of our armed forces.[143]

One Soviet commentator in *Izvestiia* cast doubt on American sincerity with regard to arms control:

Official Washington has given out not a few statements in order to convince American and world society of its interest in these negotiations. However the facts speak otherwise. The closer comes the time for the beginning of negotiations in Vienna, the more feverish becomes the activity of the Pentagon. The American military hasten to carry out the creation of new types of strategic weapons.[144]

In the same vein an editorial in the MPA journal stated:

From time to time the leaders of the capitalist states declare their aspiration to put an end to the arms race. However these fair words are paradoxically accompanied by concrete plans for the creation of ever more new military weapons.[145]

The internal Soviet debate about SALT was, however, not just a debate between the military and the civilian leadership, but also involved the arms control experts in the civilian research institutes which, although their work is far from an official enunciation of the Soviet foreign policy, does have a discernible influence on the policy-making process.[146]

In the publications of the civilian experts one can discern a definite perspective on East–West relations and arms control which differs substantially from that of the military and its supporters. Thus, for example, the 'ruling circles' of the United States are not seen as uniformly hostile and aggressive. Instead, elaborating a distinction already made by Khrushchev and academics of his period, they see American ruling circles as being divided between the hard-line imperialists, in league with the military-industrial complex, and those 'sober minded realists' who have recognized the need to reach agreement with the Soviet Union on a wide range of issues, including strategic arms limitations. In this view, it is not just the American working class which opposes the arms race, but even elements of the ruling elite of the United States.[147] As G. A. Arbatov has pointed out:

> All this forces the rulers of America to consider the problem of a so-called 'national re-orientation', that is, in the interests of the USA, changing policy in order to devote greater means and resources to the resolution of acute internal problems. That demands also a certain change in foreign policy, a certain lessening of tension, the reduction of expenditures on the arms race and military adventures.[148]

In this view, the 'sober minded' element in the American ruling elite recognizes that a continuation of the arms race cannot serve American interests. It engenders public opposition, damages the American economy in the pursuit of an entirely illusory objective (i.e. superiority over the Soviet Union). The main assumption underlying this analysis is the achievement of strategic parity by the Soviet Union, which is seen as an irreversible fact. The reduced relative power of the United States (the shift in the correlation of forces) is the principal reason why, in this view, the United States may be prepared to negotiate seriously on arms control:

> There exists in the United States among opponents of the arms race the conviction that 'strategic superiority' loses all meaning under modern conditions, since its political utilization in peacetime and even more its realization in the eventuality of war are ruled out. Blackmail with the aid of military force in political actions does not now promise success, since accumulated military might cannot be used without a guarantee of strategic superiority.[149]

The following arguments are used to justify the view that arms control is both necessary and possible:

> Further change in the relationship of forces in the world arena to the advantage of peace, democracy and socialism in essence deprives the aggressive circles of imperialism of any hopes for the resolution of the historic conflict between the two opposed social systems by military means, makes the arms race senseless. The very emergence of weapons of great destructive power is fraught with disastrous consequences for all humanity (including, it goes without saying, a potential aggressor) . . . The already accumulated experience of cooperation in the international arena of states with different social systems testifies in favour of the possibility of carrying out [arms control].[150]

As Samuel B. Payne has pointed out, the Party leadership accepted the SALT I accords for the same reasons that had been advanced by the proponents of strategic arms limitations:

> Ideas that had previously been aired in *SShA* and *Mirovaia ekenomika i mezhdunarodnye otnosheniia* now appeared in Brezhnev's speeches and in authoritative editorials in *Pravda, Izvestia,* and *Kommunist* . . . Brezhnev and other Soviet leaders defended strategic arms limitation as a means to avoid this costly, dangerous, and profitless new round. They also said that the SALT I agreements had secured American acceptance of Soviet equality and that they would allow the resources that might have been spent on armaments to be devoted to other ends.[151]

However, the advocates of strategic arms limitation did not have it all their own way. The military leaders, who were forced by the political leadership to accept SALT, took an important part in the process. The military was needed by the political leadership, of course, because it required the military's expertise. Although the Soviet Union followed the American example and appointed a civilian as chief negotiator, First Deputy Chief of the General Staff Nikolai V. Ogarkov (among other military experts) devoted considerable time to the SALT negotiations as second-ranking member of the Soviet delegation. The objectives of the military were to ensure that the agreements would not result in any military disadvantage to the Soviet Union (and, if possible, in some advantage); to allow the maximum possible leeway for strengthening Soviet strategic forces; to prevent the development and deployment of an extensive BMD system by the United States; and to prevent on-site inspection (basing verification instead on national technical means) or any other framework in which Soviet military secrets would be revealed. The pursuit of these objectives resulted in some success. The military did influence the entire process very substantially, and SALT I did not end the quantitative and qualitative improvement of American and Soviet strategic force deployments.

The endeavour of the political leadership to co-opt the military leadership into the process of arms control and détente proved only partially successful. At the 24th Party Congress in 1971, there was again a marked difference between the appraisals of the international situation as presented by Brezhnev and Defence Minister Grechko. While Brezhnev stressed the need for improvement in Soviet–American relations to consolidate peace, Grechko forcefully emphasized the American threat:

> The preparations of the imperialists of the USA for aggression have never ended and are today proceeding at an unflagging speed. They

have encircled the socialist states by aggressive military-political blocs, have enmeshed the world with a barbed wire of military bases, are continuously building up and perfecting the means of war, and from year to year increasing allocations for military purposes . . . [the Soviet Union] has been forced to make the necessary defence arrangements and support its peaceful policy by a reinforcement of defence capability and an increase in the defence potential of the armed forces and their combat readiness.[152]

As a result of the SALT process, the MPA and the professional military closed ranks against the threat from the political leadership. Despite its partial acceptance of strategic arms limitation and its cooperation with the political leadership in achieving the agreements, SALT did not result in reducing military demands for increased allocations to heavy industry, for increases in the military budget and the strengthening of the armed forces. As the MPA sided with the professional military, the political leadership was ultimately forced to take steps to reassert control. It is in this light that the public announcement of the creation of the *Sovet Oborony* and the appointment of a civilian, D. F. Ustinov, to the position of Minister of Defence must be seen.[153]

Implications for strategic arms policy

The military policies pursued by Malenkov and later by Khrushchev were clearly in opposition to the institutional interests of the military. Malenkov was unable to defeat the opposition to his position of developing a minimum deterrence, and the military allied itself with Khrushchev to bring about his downfall. At first, Khrushchev had to tolerate a great deal of autonomy within the military, but from 1957 onwards attempted to reassert control over the military by way of promoting members of the Stalingrad group to top positions – thus pursuing a 'divide and rule' policy *vis-à-vis* the military leadership – and strengthening political control over the armed forces at all levels through the MPA.

Khrushchev's essential purpose was to ensure that the Party leadership retained the prerogative of defining military doctrine and policy, while at the same time countering the strong tendencies towards an apolitical professionalism within the military which served to reduce political control by the Communist Party and encouraged the perception of institutional interests which in many respects were contrary to the policies he was pursuing. The resulting conflicts within the military leadership (in particular interservice rivalry) and between the professional military and the functionaries of the MPA served Khrushchev's purposes for a time. But the deep resentment against the perceived interference of the Party political organs with the work and authority of military commanders, in interaction with intra-Party disputes gradually diminished Khrushchev's control over military policy. His policies of reliance on strategic nuclear weapons (which existed only in small numbers), downgrading and reducing traditional forces (in particular the Ground Forces) and his attempts to reduce resources allocated to the military and defence industries in general became particular targets for his opponents. Thus his former supporters from the Stalingrad group began to turn against him.

The period of 1961–62 was marked by a compromise between Malinovskii and Khrushchev, whereby Malinovskii supported Khrushchev on strategic arms policy (and supported what remained of the 'strategic bluff') in return for halting troop reductions, increases in defence allocations and some revision of Khrushchev's military doctrine. While Khrushchev was clearly under pressure about increasing Soviet military strength, the only indication of substantial pressure to close the gap between public claims and actual deployments of strategic nuclear forces consisted in pressure to resume nuclear testing in 1961, which had important political as well as military reasons. The lack of apparent pressure can be partially explained by the public stance of Soviet superiority in this field. Still, the lack of even subtle evidence of pressure on Khrushchev in this area is surprising. The reason undoubtedly lies in the fact that the military leaders opposed Khrushchev's emphasis on nuclear missiles and were exerting pressure to maintain and build up other branches of the Armed Forces. A more convincing strategic force posture would undoubtedly have strengthened Khrushchev's hand with regard to the military. *The priorities set by the interaction of institutions in the bureaucratic politics of the Soviet decision-making process were thus capable of suppressing an 'action-reation' cycle of which the initial signs could be discerned at various points in 1961.* Since he was not prepared to allocate sufficient resources to achieve this, he attempted a cheap solution to the problem of deploying medium-range missiles in Cuba. This venture and its failure marks another turning point in Khrushchev's relationship with the professional military. Malinovskii now opposed Khrushchev more openly and aligned himself with Khrushchev's opponents in the Party. In the period November 1962–March 1963 Khrushchev's grip on Soviet decision-making was slipping to the point where he nearly had to resign. During this time, decisions were made about the production of third-generation ICBMs which, although later modified by Khrushchev, nevertheless were the result of the assertion by the military leadership of its institutional power. It acted in collusion with other interests in the Soviet Union against the leader of the Party and the Government in the implementation of strategic arms policy. In this way the foundation for the policy of the post-Khrushchev era was laid.

Khrushchev, however, recovered substantially in late March 1963 to such an extent that he felt strong enough to resume the pursuit of his previous policies, including reducing troops (and abolishing the separate command structure of the Ground Forces), reducing the defence budget and shifting resources away from heavy industry. By early 1964 the leadership of the professional military was more unified in opposition to Khrushchev than ever before. As a result, the military acquiesced in Khrushchev's ouster in October 1964.

Under the collective post-Khrushchev leadership, the dispute about the nature of the Soviet force posture and the share of resources allocated to heavy industry and the military were eventually partially resolved in favour of heavy industry and an all-round build-up of conventional and nuclear strategic forces. Not only were objections by the military to the 'one-sided' aspects of Khrushchev's military doctrine thus taken into account, but the military leadership acquired a relatively free hand in the formulation and implementation of military doctrine with regard to force structure decisions (i.e. the military-technical side of military doctrine), while the political leadership contented itself with general political pronouncements (the political side of military doctrine). Although the military was not actively involved in Khrushchev's ouster, its passive support nevertheless had the result of reversing what the military leadership interpreted as the encroachment of the political leadership in its affairs and area of professional expertise and a substantial enhancement in the institutional power of the military.

The changes in military policy thus instituted resulted in the impressive build-up of the Soviet strategic forces documented elsewhere. The post-Khrushchev era saw increased co-operation between the professional military and the MPA in support of military interests vis-à-vis the Party leadership. The threat to military interests perceived in détente and arms control resulted in a suspension of conflicts between the MPA and the professional military. SALT became the focus of a reassertion of political control over strategic arms policy but, at the same time, gave the military leadership an opportunity for direct interaction with the Party leadership in the shaping of arms-control policy. This analysis indicates how institutional conflicts within the military and between the military and Party leadership influenced the evolution of Soviet strategic arms policy.

Part II

Soviet Decision-Making in Strategic Arms Policy

6   The development of strategic bombers in the Soviet Union

Introduction to Part II

Soviet strategic arms policy was the product of a complex political process. In the post-Stalin era, the Soviet leadership was faced with the task of redefining its own rôle in the structure of Soviet society, the direction of economic and social development as well as the rôle and position of the Soviet Union in the international environment. In terms of the latter, the rôle of Soviet strategic power was of critical significance. The previous chapters have analysed, in general terms, the various influences which shaped Soviet strategic arms policy. The inconsistencies and contradictions in Soviet security policy during the period under study and the general trends in the emerging strategic force posture can thus be explained in a more satisfactory manner.

The preceding chapters have focussed primarily on the general lines of policy, the political process and the manifestations of institutional interests which shaped them and Soviet military thought in general. We have not discussed in any detail specific decisions on the deployment of particular systems of the Soviet strategic arsenal. It is the objective of this section to apply the framework of the general analysis to seek answers to more specific questions about the various components that made up the Soviet strategic force posture in and beyond the Khrushchev period.

Weapons-procurement decisions are not only guided by certain policy objectives and the resulting mission requirements, but also are subject to the constraints of resources and technical capabilities. The case studies which follow endeavour to apply what is known about the Soviet weapons acquisition process to specific weapons systems or classes of systems. This will involve an analysis of how the political pressures manifested themselves in particular ways, but will also require a study of the more technical issues such as the technological constraints, the formulation of mission requirements and the development cycle which can yield clues about crucial decision periods, as well as explain why certain systems were procured and deployed in certain numbers, whereas others were discarded or only deployed on a small scale.

The first case study is that of the strategic bomber. As has already been pointed out, the main feature of the Soviet strategic bomber programme that requires explanation is the decision not to proceed with the development and deployment of a large bomber force. The second is a more detailed study of ICBM development and deployment, focussing in particular on the SS-6, the SS-9 and the SS-11. The third study concerns itself with the Soviet perspective on strategic defence, a detailed analysis of the Moscow ABM system and the decision to forgo a nationwide ballistic missile defence. The fourth case is that of the Soviet military space programme, where the political dimension of the Soviet space programme, the internal debates about its direction and the technical aspects of Soviet space capabilities are discussed. These case studies will allow us not merely to understand the general picture of the evolution of the Soviet strategic force posture arising out of the empirical data given in chapter 1, but also to arrive at a more detailed understanding of how and why many of the critical decisions in Soviet strategic arms procurement were made.

The Soviet strategic bomber programme after World War II

At the end of World War II, the Soviet Union was a formidable military power. As the possession of nuclear weapons became a critical factor of military power, the same applied to their means of delivery – then strategic bombers. The first Soviet heavy bomber capable of carrying out nuclear missions was the Tu-4 (codenamed *Bull* in the West). The first three Tu-4s were presented at the 1947 Air Day, but the first deliveries of TU-4s to the Long-range Aviation Force (*Dal'niia Aviatsiia*, formed in 1946) took place in 1949. Until the end of production in 1954 around 1,200 Tu-4s were built.

The Tu-4 was not an effective delivery vehicle for strategic nuclear strikes on the continental United States since it lacked the range for a two-way mission (even if one does not take into account having to cope with air defence) and the Soviets did not at the time possess a capability for in-flight refuelling. The four-turbojet strategic bomber developed by Miasishchev (called Mya-4 or *Bison*) was, according to Khrushchev,[1] not ready before Stalin's death and made its first public appearance at the May Day parade in 1954. The specified range for the strategic bomber project was 16,000 km, but the Mya-4 had a range of only 9,000 km and this fell short of the requirements of a strategic bomber of intercontinental range.[2]

The Tu-16 *Badger* was a medium-range bomber which became the workhorse of the long-range air fleet in the European theatre. The difficulties with the *Bison*, however, appear to have prompted the Soviets to work on mid-air refuelling for the *Badger* to extend its range. In May 1955, another plane was spotted by Western observers; codenamed the *Bear*, it was a long-range bomber developed by the Tupolev design bureau (designated the Tu-20). The *Bear* did apparently have the range for two-way missions to the continental United States, but its subsonic speed made it vulnerable to air defence.

By 1960 the Soviet Union had deployed 100 Mya-4s and 60 Tu-20s; by 1969 this had risen to 110 and 90 respectively (with about half the Bisons now being used as tankers for in-flight refuelling). The number declined somewhat in the following years with some of the Bisons being taken out of service. Given the technical limitations of the Mya-4 and the Tu-20 (in particular the latter's vulnerability to air defence), the conclusion is inescapable that *at no time in the period under consideration did the Soviet Union deploy a substantial strategic bomber force that could play a significant rôle in an attack on the continental United States.*

The development of the medium-range strike force of the Long-range Aviation was far more impressive. In 1955 the Soviet Union had 1,296 bombers for use in the European theatre, including 400 Tu-4s and 600 Tu-16s; the Soviet Union was estimated to have a total stockpile of 324 nuclear warheads. Most of the bombers were thus assigned to conventional missions.

Why did the Soviet Union fail to deploy a strategic bomber force comparable to the SAC of the United States? To answer this question, we shall consider the following main influences on Soviet policymaking: (i) the constraints imposed by the limitations of Soviet technology; (ii) strategic doctrine; (iii) political factors.

(i) The constraints imposed by technological limitations

At the end of World War II, Soviet military power was faced with a range of considerable technological challenges with the emergence of jet engines, rocket propulsion and nuclear fission. The Tu-4 was essentially a copy of the US B-29. In August and November 1944 three B-29s landed on Soviet territory after bombing missions over Japan and were never returned to the United States. Two of the aircraft were dismantled by the Tupolev design bureau which had been given the task of producing a Soviet equivalent. The technological difficulties which the Soviet engineers faced in keeping up with American developments in jet technology and the construction of adequate delivery vehicles for strategic nuclear weapons is illustrated by a passage in Khrushchev's memoirs:

> Stalin wanted a strategic bomber which could reach the United States and return to the USSR. This was one of the toughest problems facing our designers. Stalin ordered Tupolev to build a plane capable of bombing the territory of the USA. Tupolev refused, explaining that the limits of contemporary technology made such a task simply impossible to fulfil . . . He knew such a plane was impossible, and he told Stalin so. After that, Stalin started to rely on Miasishchev instead of Tupolev.[3]

The next candidate for a Soviet strategic bomber of intercontinental range was the *Bison* developed by Miasishchev. Its first public appearance at the May Day parade in 1954 sparked off the 'bomber gap' controversy in the United States. Khrushchev describes the various problems associated with the Mya-4:

> The plane failed to satisfy our requirements. It could reach the United States but it couldn't come back . . . there were other problems with the Mya-4. We weren't sure it could fly through dense anti-aircraft fire. Nor did it perform well in its flight tests. A number of test pilots were killed . . . In the end, we decided to scrap the whole project because it was costing us too much money and contributing nothing to our security.[4]

Although Khrushchev's account undoubtedly reflects some of his feelings, it is nonetheless clear that he exaggerates the situation in important respects. Whatever reservations Tupolev may have had in the early Fifties with regard to the technical feasibility of building a bomber of intercontinental range, the Tupolev design bureau continued working in this field and developed the Tu-20 by 1955. The Tu-95, which entered service in 1965, is also considered to have been designed as a strategic bomber, although in the end it failed to satisfy the range requirements.[5] It is also not true that the Mya-4 was entirely scrapped. The Mya-4 continued to be deployed as a naval reconnaissance and tanker aircraft as well as a strategic bomber until well after Khrushchev's fall.[6] Miasishchev produced a second design, the Mya-50, which also failed to live up to its requirements. Its use was confined to research and development projects. Khrushchev closed down the design bureau and turned the production facilities over to helicopter production.

It is quite evident, therefore, that the Soviet Union had great difficulties in mastering the various technologies required to produce a modern supersonic bomber of intercontinental range. Samples obtained by Western intelligence showed that the heat resilience of Soviet metals had been overestimated.[7] A principal problem was the development of sufficient thrust. The Tu-20 was a turboprop described in the literature in 1959 already as 'becoming obsolescent',[8] it was claimed that the four-jet Bison 'will soon be replaced by a supersonic bomber' but this did not happen.

On the surface it seems, therefore, that there was no large-scale deployment of strategic bombers because the Soviet Union lacked the technological capability to produce them. Although this was a very important factor, it is not a sufficient explanation given that the only other alternative, the ICBM, presented even greater technological difficulties. The time frame within which the Soviet Union could have developed a respectable rival to the B-52 would have been expected to be no greater than that of achieving the mastery of a new technology – that of the ICBM – and with considerably greater certainty of success. Not to attempt to match the US bomber force was evidently a political decision taken by the Krushchev leadership which requires further explanation.

(ii) Strategic bombing and Soviet military doctrine

The experience of World War II would, one would imagine, have provided a strong impetus to the re-evaluation of the rôle of airpower in general and strategic bombing in particular. There is evidence that Stalin himself took great interest in strategic bombing.[9] Some evidence that strategic air missions were assuming greater importance in Soviet military thought emerged in 1946 when Major General of Aviation Tatarchenko pointed out that besides the traditional operational tactical tasks of aviation

> there must also exist strategic aviation. It would appear that contemporary air forces are capable of deciding not only tactical, but also operational and strategic tasks, which no arm other than

> aviation can fulfil . . . in future engagements the place of application of the main force will be not so much the front as the rear of the enemy.[10]

The significance of strategic operations was also recognized in other articles, written by such prominent officers as Marshal of Aviation Skripko and General Staff Officer Major General Korkodinov.[11] Soon, however, the freedom to explore new developments in military thought was restricted and adherence to Stalinist military doctrine, which confined the rôle of air forces almost exclusively to the support of ground forces, became mandatory. The integration of strategic bombing into Soviet military thought thus did not occur until after Stalin's death in 1953, but this should not be interpreted as meaning that there was no interest in long-range bombing capabilities. According to Khrushchev, Stalin himself ordered the development of intercontinental bombers. After the death of Stalin the Soviet military began to explore more directly the consequences of nuclear weapons for military strategy and thus also that of long-range bombing missions. However, the parameters of the discussion were very different from the rôle of strategic bombing as conceived in the West.[12] In the military literature during the 1950s the following central features of the Soviet military evaluation of the rôle strategic bombing in the post-war age can be discerned:

(1) In the words of Minister of Defence Marshal Zhukov:

> air power and nuclear weapons by themselves cannot determine the outcome of an armed conflict.[13]

Therefore

> in the postwar construction of the armed forces we are proceeding from the fact that victory in future war will be achieved only by the combined efforts of all arms of the armed forces and on the basis of their coordinated employment in war.[14]

(2) The theory of 'strategic bombing' which developed in Western military thought saw its primary function in the destruction of the economic base and the morale of the enemy population, with counterforce operations being of subsidiary importance.[15] The devastating effect of nuclear weapons was designed to produce a rapid victory, inspired by the example of the bombing of Hiroshima and Nagasaki. The Soviet view in the 1950s saw as the main mission of the Soviet armed forces in a general nuclear war the destruction of the enemy's military capabilities. In this context the mission of

long-range aviation would therefore be to destroy the British Bomber Command and the capabilities of the US Strategic Air Command. Attacks against population and industrial centres were seen as a complimentary and not the primary rôle of strategic bombing.[16] *Voennaia Mysl'* in 1955 expressed the view that

> the defeat of the enemy will be achieved above all by means of the annihilation of his armed forces.[17]

If the emphasis on deploying Soviet long-range bomber assets in the European theatre was in part dictated by technological limitations, it nonetheless fitted in well with Soviet perceptions about the rôle of strategic bombing. Since military operations were most likely to occur in the European theatre, and the greatest perceived threat emanated from US forward-based bombers in Europe, a strong deployment of nuclear and conventional bombers by the Soviet Union made sense. This does not mean that no significance was attached to attacks against SAC bases in the United States or other targets in North America. The failure to build up a substantial intercontinental bomber force cannot be explained on the basis of Soviet military strategy alone. It was essentially a political decision in the second half of the Fifties not to engage in a major effort to develop and deploy strategic bombers of intercontinental range on a large scale. In the Sixties, after this decision had been made, the military literature echoed the view which gave priority to missiles over long-range bombers, particularly as the vulnerability of bombers to air defence had considerably increased. Thus we find in the Sokolovskii volume:

> Today, the Air Force is a special situation. In recent years, there has been keen competition between the bomber, the missile and air defense weapons. In this competition, air defense weapons have gained a great advantage over bomber aviation. [Long-range bombers, whose flight it is practically impossible to conceal, given the modern radar reconnaissance resources, have become especially vulnerable.][18]

Furthermore,

> modern PVO has become almost insurmountable for bomber aircraft. Consequently, its role in war has changed . . .[19]

The first edition of Sokolovskii did, however, concede the possibility that stand-off missiles would considerably increase the combat potential of the long-range missile since the missiles could be fired from outside the air-defence zone.[20] In the second edition, however, it was asserted that even the use of air-to-surface missiles could not restore the 'lost importance' of the long-range bomber as a strategic delivery system.[21] It is evident, therefore, that during the Khrushchev period the long-range bomber was not considered as an important delivery vehicle for strategic missions against the United States, and thus only a token number were deployed after production ceased in 1962.

(iii) The demise of the strategic bomber: a political decision

Khrushchev's initial attitude to strategic bombers resembled that which can later be discerned with respect to ICBMs. While the development of Soviet military power clearly implied the need to develop a capability to strike at targets in the United States, Khrushchev was happy to develop a token force and maximize its political potential while awaiting technological developments without making the considerable resources available that would be required for a serious and determined 'crash programme' to overcome the American lead. Although the 'bomber gap' episode which, as has been indicated in chapter 3, was given much impetus by the mistaken interpretation of the events during an airshow, was a successful 'strategic bluff' in the Khrushchevian manner, the strategic bomber did not become the main symbol of Soviet military might. The advent of the ICBM in 1957 opened up new opportunities for Khrushchev: as a weapon based on new technical principles which had not yet been deployed in large numbers by the United States, the Soviet Union could exploit its apparent technological lead to political advantage to offset the not easily disputable quantitative American advantage in strategic bombers. At the same time, the setting up of a new military service (the Strategic Rocket Forces) allowed Khrushchev to strengthen his control over the military by weakening the position of the established services, notably the Ground Forces, but also the Air Force (VVS). In his speech to the Supreme Soviet in January 1960 Khrushchev went as far as to say, as was pointed out in chapter 5, that military aviation was being replaced by missile technology. He went on to say that:

> We have already sharply reduced, and will probably continue to reduce or even halt the production of bombers and other obsolete technology.[22]

Like so many statements in Khrushchev's speech, it outlined a basic principle of his policy with a great deal of hyperbole. It is true, however, that strategic bomber production virtually ceased. The existing bomber force was maintained at improved operational capability, with the development of in-flight refuelling techniques and stand-off air-to-surface missiles; while not being an effective 'leg' of a strategic 'triad', it nonetheless caused the United States to expend a great deal on air defence. The decision not to proceed with the build-up of a strategic bomber force was well in line with the general thrust of Khrushchev's efforts to curtail military expenditure across the board and denigrate the rôle of the traditional services, using the arrival of a new technological development, the ICBM, as his justification.

Conclusion

Soviet strategic bomber deployment evidently is contrary to the behaviour predicted by the arms-race paradigm. Soviet military doctrine in the early years after Stalin, while defining a definite rôle for the long-range bomber, is consistent with the emphasis on theatre deployments. The limitations of Soviet technology, which made the development of a modern long-range bomber a difficult and expensive task, exacerbated by improvements in air defence, played an important rôle in the force posture adopted. In the final analysis the political priorities of Khrushchev, which were partly driven by his economic agenda, resulted in the renunciation of a large-scale deployment of long-range bombers and the emphasis on missiles of intercontinental range as the principal delivery vehicle for nuclear weapons.

7   Soviet ICBM deployment:
two case studies

While the primary purpose of strategic nuclear forces may be political, a force posture is generally designed on the basis of military objectives. The military capabilities of ICBMs are evidently a function of their technical characteristics, i.e. their payload, range and accuracy as well as other factors such as their vulnerability to a pre-emptive strike, the time they require to be launched etc. In theory one would assume that the technical characteristics of missiles are based on certain mission requirements. It might, therefore, be possible to draw certain conclusions about Soviet nuclear strategy and even political objectives on the basis of the types and numbers of missiles deployed. However, the long development cycle of missiles (of the order of a decade) may mean that by the time designs have reached the stage of prototype testing the mission objectives on which they were originally based no longer apply. Furthermore, the difficulties involved in mastering such advanced technologies meant that only a limited number of useful designs for ICBM were available and that their characteristics may not have exactly fulfilled the mission requirements. This chapter looks at some of the principal elements of the Soviet ICBM force in the sixties in some detail to investigate how these factors interacted in particular cases and what conclusions we can draw about Soviet strategic arms policy in general.

The decision not to deploy the SS-6

Karl Spielmann has attempted an institutional analysis to explain the Soviet decision not to deploy their first-generation ICBM, the SS-6.

The commonly given explanations revolve around the technical difficulties encountered with the SS-6. It used a highly unstable propellant which could not be stored, which made launching difficult, and furthermore needed ground stations for guidance. Its guidance system was also subject to disruption by electronic interference. Spielmann expresses his view, however, that this may not be sufficient to explain the lack of deployment.

The Strategic Rocket Forces were not set up until 1959. Spielmann argues that therefore there may have been no strong organizational proponent for the ICBM[1] in the services. He contrasts this with the medium-range ballistic missiles.[2]

No doubt there was some confusion about how strategic missiles would fit into the established programmes and operations of military services, but it seems difficult to argue that the SS-6 failed for lack of support of an ICBM. Quite to the contrary, Soviet ICBM capability had become the linchpin of Khrushchev's military and foreign policy, and there must have been very strong reasons in favour of deployment, even if institutional support was lacking.

Spielmann seems to be more on the right track when he suggests possible competition between the Korolev and Iangel design bureaux. The Iangel bureau had been responsible for the successful MRBM, the SS-4, and had begun work on an ICBM in 1954. Spielmann discusses the possibility that there may have been a lobby for increased investment in MRBMs as opposed to ICBMs, but rejects this on the grounds that the design bureaux working on MRBMs were also involved with work on the ICBMs.[3] Given the technical difficulties of the SS-6, however, the Soviet leadership may have been convinced that the Iangel design looked promising and that it was worth waiting with a larger deployment until it was ready. The Iangel SS-7 missile was indeed deployed in the early Sixties, while Korolev produced a second-generation missile himself. Again, he was not very successful in his competition with Iangel and only small numbers of his SS-8 were deployed.[4]

Korolev's reputation, therefore, seems to derive largely from the success of the SS-6 as a launch vehicle for Soviet space satellites. Indeed, there is some evidence that Korolev himself had little interest in ICBM development and was more interested in devoting himself to the development of space flight.[5] Most of his work did indeed find its primary application in that area.

Spielmann then goes on to consider defence-industrial interests. The Ministry of General Machine-building, which is now responsible for the production of ballistic missiles, was not established until 1965. Spielmann speculated that the tardiness in establishing the Ministry of General Machine-building suggests that resistance on the part of existing defense-industrial ministries may have been encountered.[6]

He suggests that for a large-scale SS-6 programme perhaps a separate ministry might have been considered, to the detriment of the interests of other ministries, in particular the Ministry of Aviation Industry.[7]

Spielmann's hypothesis is implausible, for a number of reasons. There was, after all, in the late Fifties and early Sixties a fairly large-scale missile programme, including a modest ICBM production, and if a separate ministry was a possibility at this stage then there was a sufficiently large-scale production of missiles to justify it. The creation of the Ministry of General Machine-building is perhaps more indicative of events in 1965 than the Khrushchev period, when a great deal of confusion was introduced into the organizational structure of the bureaucracy in any case.

The most plausible argument to explain the SS-6 decision thus remains its failure to perform adequately. The competition between design bureaux, with the more promising Iangel design already in the pipeline, was presumably also an important factor. Given that while Khrushchev was eager to promote the strategic nuclear rocket as the most important part of Soviet military force, but was nonetheless willing to make only limited resources available for their development and production, the decision not to deploy the first-generation ICBM in large numbers becomes comprehensible.[8]

The deployment of the SS-9 and SS-11

Deployment of the SS-9 began in 1966 and continued at a regular rate until 1970 (see chapter 1). Some analysts believe that at some time in 1963 a decision was made to commence a general expansion of Soviet strategic capability[9] or even to achieve parity with the United States. The conviction with which this view has been reiterated is not matched with any concrete evidence, however. The most one gets are some vague references to lead times.[10]

The first test flight of the SS-9 was reported in July 1964,[11] a few months before Khrushchev was ousted in October. By the end of 1964 42 hardened silos for the SS-9 had been discovered by US intelligence.[12]

These observations do support the view that some decision with regard to SS-9 deployment was taken in 1963, but the nature of this decision is unclear. The first modification of the SS-9 tested in July 1964 apparently revealed some problems because no SS-9 became operational until 1966 and the first SS-9s deployed were of modification 2.[13] Meanwhile a total of 108 silos were being made ready. In 1966, 72 missiles were deployed, and deployment continued at a constant rate of 42 missiles per year, levelling off at a number of about 280 SS-9s. The data thus do not necessarily imply that under Khrushchev there was a decision to abandon minimum deterrence and make a determined attempt to achieve parity with the United States, but would be equally compatible with the interpretation that the SS-9 was intended as a modernization of the existing force of second-generation missiles. It is likely that the extent of SS-9 deployment had not been decided under Khrushchev. Given that there must have been some question mark over the performance of the SS-9 during his time, it appears that 1964/65 was the critical point of decision-making – i.e. after Khrushchev's ouster from office.

There is some evidence that in the aftermath of the Cuban missile crisis, early in 1963, the conflict between Khrushchev and the military reached a high point. In March the long-standing efforts by Khrushchev's opponents to reverse his policies of decentralization reached their climax at a time when Khrushchev was politically weak. This becomes apparent from the drastic organizational changes that were announced on 13 March which involved nothing less than

> a mass-promotion of all the top officials in the defence industry, the heavy industry lobby and other 'steel-eaters' against whom Khrushchev had been fighting ever since 1960.[14]

The central element of the announcement of 13 March concerned the creation of a *Supreme Sovnarkhoz* at the apex of the administrative structure, to eliminate the disputes and rivalries among Gosplan, the federal Sovnarkhoz and the many other federal agencies created by Khrushchev's reforms in 1957. It is clear that Khrushchev was diametrically opposed to the idea of a Supreme Sovnarkhoz and the decision of 13 March therefore constituted a significant political defeat, another step in the relentless efforts to reverse his programme of decentralization.[15]

What is significant for our study is the remarkable fact that the person entrusted with the management of the Supreme Sovnarkhoz was none other than D. F. Ustinov, who was thus promoted to First

Deputy Chairman of the Council of Ministers. In this way what Vernon V. Aspaturian has called the emerging military-industrial apparatus coalition[16] gained important influence in the state administration. Frol Kozlov, the leader of Khrushchev's opposition and no doubt the driving force behind the changes announced on 13 March, seems to have had close links with Ustinov. These probably date back as far as the time, from 1936 to 1944, when Kozlov was involved with organizing the war industry in Izhvesk from where Ustinov was consistently elected deputy to the Supreme Soviet. Those that were promoted in the course of the reorganization of 13 March were either allies of the defence industry or people well known for their opposition to Khrushchev.[17] L. V. Smirnov, Chairman of the State Committee for Defence Technology, became Deputy Premier. Smirnov's position was taken over by his deputy S. A. Zverev, thereby gaining the rank of Minister. The most significant aspect of the organizational changes lay in the direct attachment of the State Committees for defence technology, aeronautics, electronics, atomic energy and medium-machine building etc. to the Supreme Sovnarkhoz under Ustinov. Thus Ustinov maintained direct control over the defence industry, and the changes amounted to a major promotion of the entire industry and its chiefs.

As a consequence of Kozlov's illness in April 1963 Khrushchev made a substantial political recovery and, although he did not reverse the changes made in March, he managed to reassert some of his control over the system. He made the following comments about the appointment of Ustinov:

> Comrade Ustinov, who was responsible for the defense industry, has now been appointed Chairman of the Supreme Council of the National Economy. He knows where, what and how things are in the defense industry too. Therefore we shall hope that he establishes better order in this matter as well. It is interesting to note how widely astray the capitalist press has gone. When Comrade Ustinov was approved as Chairman of the Supreme Council of the National Economy (they had long ago sniffed out that he was engaged in defense industry matters), this press drew the conclusion that the Soviet Union had taken the course of militarization of the country. They announced: 'Ustinov has been made head of the Supreme Council of the National Economy; it follows that the Soviet Union will now make only missiles.' What nonsense! We appointed Comrade Ustinov simply because he is well qualified for the post.[18]

Michel Tatu's interpretation of this speech, probably correct, is that Khrushchev was using the foreign press as a 'stalking-horse' to upbraid the armament producers and Ustinov in particular.[19] Then follows a clear warning that it was out of the question that 'the Soviet Union will now make only missiles'. Khrushchev also made a direct reference to Smirnov which was less than flattering:

> Comrade Smirnov has been appointed in Ustinov's place. He is younger than comrade Ustinov and we can prod him just as successfully as we have prodded comrade Ustinov, who used to be answerable for the defence industry.[20]

A clear indication that Khrushchev was determined to keep Ustinov under control was the appointment of a 'first deputy to the head of the Sovnarkhoz on 9 May 1963, a chemist by the name of S. M. Tikhomirov.[21]

It is therefore apparent that the defence industry and the proponents of a build-up in the Soviet force posture gained influence in early 1963. If the above interpretation of Khrushchev's remarks is correct, this also involved plans to invest more in the production of missiles. It is therefore likely that some plans for the production and deployment of third-generation missiles were made at that time. Resources were made available for the production of prototypes and the construction of silos. It may be that Khrushchev's political comeback reimposed some limitations in the plans for missile production, and the deployment programme which emerged in 1964 was therefore comparatively modest. In summary, we can trace some aspects of the decision to produce and deploy SS-9 missiles back to 1963. However, the deployment pattern which emerged in 1966 and the Soviet force posture of the late Sixties was probably not determined until after the fall of Khrushchev.

The new leadership took over in the Kremlin in 1964 having rejected many central aspects of Khrushchev's foreign, military and economic policies. His foreign policy was considered to have been a failure. His bombastic and adventurous style, followed by inevitable and, at times, humiliating retreats, such as at Suez, Berlin and, most of all Cuba, was rejected as a dangerous form of gambling where Khrushchev had frequently overreached himself, seeking objectives which he did not have the means to obtain.[22] The military leadership had, of course, been well aware of the glaring discrepancies between Khrushchev's claims with regard to Soviet strategic nuclear forces and the reality – his failure to translate Soviet military might into political gain could at least in part be attributed to Soviet strategic inferiority.[23] These views were reinforced by an increase in international tension with the escalation of the American involvement in Vietnam and the intervention in the Dominican Republic. It appeared to the Kremlin that the United States was exploiting its strategic superiority in the pursuit of a more adventurous foreign policy than would otherwise be the case.[24] Thus Leonid I. Brezhnev and others endorsed the already growing conviction that the Soviet Union should increase its strategic effort to catch up with the United States.

The other area in which Khrushchev's policies were sharply criticized was that of the organization of the bureaucracy. His decentralization programme was generally considered to be a failure, leading to a cumbersome bureaucracy and a confused decision-making process, quite apart from all the various institutional interests that were affected. The abolition of the Sovnarkhoz and the recentralization of the bureaucracy was therefore a high priority for the new leadership. This also involved the defence industries, which were reorganized in March 1965. Dmitri Ustinov was moved from the Council of Ministers to head the Central Committee Secretariat responsible for defence production, presumably a further promotion since he also became a candidate member of the Politburo. Ustinov thus remained at the very top of the defence industry establishment, and his place in the Council of Ministers was taken by Leonid V. Smirnov, who was later identified as head of the VPK. The year 1965 also saw the creation of the Ministry of General Machine-building exclusively concerned with the production of ballistic missiles, another strong indication of the new emphasis placed on increasing strategic strength by the deployment of ICBMs.

During the early years of the Brezhnev regime the dispute about the nature of the Soviet force posture and the share of resources allocated to heavy industry and the military was at least partially resolved in favour of heavy industry and an all-round build-up of conventional and nuclear strategic forces.[25] However, given the absence of separate Ground Forces command and the difficulties the PVO was encountering with its ballistic missile defence systems,[26] it appears that the navy and the Strategic Rocket Forces were able to get the upper hand in the inter-service rivalry for modernization and budgetary priorities.[27]

Another aspect of the reorganization of the defence establishment appears to have been an increase in the importance of the General Staff in the weapons procurement process.[28] Immediately after Khrushchev's fall, Marshal Biriuzov, the Chief of the General Staff, was killed in an aircraft accident, and M. V. Zakharov, who had been removed from his post as Chief of the General Staff in 1963 because he demanded a more balanced development of all military forces, was reinstated. This was a significant move, since Zakharov was clearly allied with Khrushchev's military critics. In the subsequent internal debates about ABM deployment, Zakharov turned out to be a significant supporter of the build-up of Soviet ICBM forces, as opposed to missile defence.[29]

In this general context, we can summarize the important decision with regard to the deployment of the SS-9 and SS-11 missiles as follows.

The Iangel and Chelomei design bureaux began work on the missiles in the 1950s. Presumably at this stage there was no very specific mission requirement for the SS-9, given that neither the Soviet nor the American ICBM force were yet in existence. The work continued for a number of years merely as an effort to develop a technically more advanced ICBM. In the late Sixties there was much speculation about the SS-9 as a possible counterforce weapon, given its enormous throw-weight[30] (it initially carried a 20-megaton warhead), but it seems unlikely that it was originally designed for this rôle. Early Soviet nuclear-weapons development indicated a predisposition to the development of high-yield warheads. The SS-6 had a 5-megaton warhead; the SS-7 in its first two modifications carried a 3-megaton warhead and the SS-8 likewise; the third modification of the SS–7, which became operational in 1963, had a 6-MT warhead. The first third-generation ICBM, the SS-9, carried a warhead in the 20-MT range. In September 1961 a nuclear test series included the detonation of a 57-MT warhead and the testing of a triggering device for a much larger warhead still, perhaps in the region of 100 MT. The Proton space booster tested in 1965 which, in the view of Robert Berman and John Baker, was part of an ICBM development programme that never came to fruition could have carried warheads of very high yields.[31]

The notion of deploying high-yield nuclear weapons fits in very well with Khrushchev's general scheme of substituting quantity of military forces with weapons of increased firepower. Warheads of large yield could be pictured as the kind of 'terror weapons' which were useful to Khrushchev's exaggerated pictures of Soviet military power. In his colourful threats Khrushchev seemed to advance a concept of area devastation by high-yield nuclear weapons that portrayed them as some sort of 'doomsday weapon'; he declared that six hydrogen bombs would be enough to annihilate the British Isles, while nine would destroy France.[32]

Hyperbole apart, warheads of high megatonnage designed to achieve area devastation appeared to be a cost-effective use of resources, given that the same target set could be covered by fewer missiles; the availability of fissionable material was a significant constraint on the Soviet nuclear weapons programme at the time.[33] There are indications in the Soviet military literature that large yield was perceived as a means of compensating for lack of accuracy.[34] The command and control centres, the administrative and economic complexes that were to be targeted, covered large areas but were soft targets. The Atlas and Titan missiles sites were also relatively soft and deployed on concentrated sites; the same is true for Strategic Air Command (SAC) bomber bases.[35] An operational plan involving large-scale area devastation with high-yield nuclear warheads thus made some sense in the conditions of the late Fifties and early Sixties (while at the same time corresponding to the available technical capabilities). The early tendency towards large missiles was also significantly dictated by the technical difficulties the Soviets encountered in building small warheads.[36]

As the Minuteman missile started to be deployed in hardened silos, the SS-9 was not accurate enough as a counter-force weapon, except to attack the soft Minuteman control centres. The testing of warheads for the SS-9 and SS-11 missiles most probably took place under the auspices of the Ministry of Medium-machine Building in 1961–62.[37] The decision to make funds available for the construction of prototypes and silos with the view to at least limited deployment of the SS-9 was most likely made in early 1963, when the advocates of building up Soviet military strength were in a strong political position. The choice of the SS-9 may have been influenced at this point by the simple fact that it was the most advanced third-generation ICBM available.[38] Khrushchev apparently had some interest in the fractional orbital bombardment system (FOBS), which was the kind of spectacular weapon that fitted in well with his boastful announcements about Soviet military capabilities designed to support his foreign-policy ventures. Development of the system began during his time, and it was based on the SS-9. This may be another reason why the SS-9 found support.[39] It must be emphasized that the deployment of a third-generation system was absolutely vital from the military point of view, since the first and second generation systems used non-storable fuels. The implication was that they could be alert only for very short periods of time which, as has already been discussed,[40] drastically reduced the strategic options open to Soviet decision-makers. When the decision was made to go for strategic parity with the United States, the SS-9 became an important component of the Soviet strategic arsenal; as we have seen in chapter 2, the main rôle in countering the large number of US Minuteman missiles was given, however, to the SS-11.

According to Robert P. Berman and John C. Baker, the original intention behind the development of the SS-11 was

> To provide a land-based missile system that could be used to target the enemy's naval task forces at various ranges. At that time, nuclear-armed carrier-based aircraft were a main component of the American strategic strike force, and the Soviet navy was trying to extend its defensive perimeter against these Western attack carriers.[41]

Berman and Baker support their interpretation with the following arguments:

V. N. Chelomei's design bureau had, until its work on the SS-11, specialized exclusively on naval missiles;
the initial version of the SS-11 was small in size, had a small payload and a relatively short range, thus differing substantially from the characteristics of other Soviet ICBMs;
its first test flights coincided with the first tests of the Soviet ocean reconnaissance satellite system.

Although it is not clear to what extent deployment decisions were made under Khrushchev, since the first test flight did not take place until after his fall, it seems safe to assume that he gave some support to Chelomei's work, judging from the remarks in his memoirs and the fact that his son was one of the engineers working with Chelomei.[42]

If Berman's and Baker's interpretation is correct, then there must have been a complete change in the mission objectives of the SS-11 some time in 1965. Thomas Wolfe, taking into account the time needed for launching site construction, concludes that the production and deployment decisions with regard to the SS-11 were taken shortly after the advent of the new regime.[43] Deployment of both the SS-9 and SS-11 began in 1966. As the data indicate, the SS-11 became the main instrument for redressing the quantitative imbalance which up to then favoured the United States, and was thus deployed in very large numbers, reaching 720 in 1970, by which time the deployment of the solid-fuelled, mobile SS-13 had begun (a missile even smaller than the SS-11). The SS-13 was not deployed in very large numbers, since solid-fuelled missiles require a more sophisticated guidance system than was available at the time. The reason for the choice of the SS-11 seems clear: it was a small missile compared to the SS-9, carrying a warhead of about 1 megaton, and could thus be more easily produced and deployed on a large scale. The SS-9 was deployed, as we have already pointed out, at a constant rate of 49 missiles per year, levelling off at a total of about 280 missiles.

Conclusion

The detailed study of the pattern of Soviet strategic arms deployment shows that although the external environment and the rôle of the Soviet Union as a world power are fundamental driving forces of its security policy in general and its strategic arms policy in particular, they are not sufficient to explain them. Other factors, principally rooted in domestic policy, played a substantial part. Thus, Khrushchev's priorities for the Soviet economy and industry were a substantial factor in his efforts to reduce defence expenditure and achieve strategic military power 'on the cheap'.

The foregoing analysis indicates that a study of the weapons-acquisition process itself can contribute to our understanding of the details of strategic arms deployment. One important aspect consists in the development of ICBM technology and the technical constraints imposed upon military planning. Examples of such constraints are the problems of engine design, warhead design, the difficulty of developing storable fuels and solid fuels in particular, the problems in perfecting inertial guidance systems with gas bearings which would allow the guidance systems to be permanently turned on and, at a later stage, difficulties in the development of multiple-warhead technology. Another aspect is that of mission requirements. These obviously changed in the course of missile development, as the nature of the targets was not apparent when missile design began in the 1950s. The analysis presented above and in chapter 3 has shown, however, how mission requirements can contribute to understanding the choice of missiles with particular characteristics.

A more general, theoretical issue is the question of whether there is a 'military-industrial complex' in the Soviet Union and to what extent its institutional interests influenced decisions in strategic arms policy. We have shown in this chapter (and presented additional evidence in other chapters) how a coalition of politicians, industrial interests and the military attempted to change the direction of industrial policy in such a manner as to favour the requirements of increased military spending and weapons procurement, including greater efforts to build up strategic nuclear weapons. Under Khrushchev this tendency was largely suppressed, although it did at times manage to gain the upper hand, particularly in 1961 and early 1963. These institutional disputes continued in the post-Khrushchev period, resulting eventually in a partial victory for the proponents of greater investment in the defence industries. The 'military industrial complex' model therefore contributes substantially to the explanation of the contradictions of strategic arms policy in the Khrushchev period and is seen as an important factor in promoting the arms build-up after the fall of Khrushchev.

8   Soviet strategic nuclear power at sea

At the end of World War II the Soviet Union embarked on a
twenty-year construction programme to build up the Soviet Navy
which included plans to build 1,200 submarines, a large number of
surface ships and naval aircraft. The principal threat perceived at the
time was that of a Western seaborne invasion. By 1954, Soviet threat
perceptions had changed substantially. Their principal focus was
now an American strategic nuclear attack. The naval element consisted of nuclear strikes from aircraft based on American carriers.
The new strategic environment had two major consequences: The
first of these was a fundamental reorientation of naval strategy and a
drastic cutback (amounting to about 60 per cent of annual production
tonnage) in the naval construction programme, preparing the navy to
face the new threat while at the same time releasing resources for the
civilian economy. The second consequence was that the delivery of
nuclear warheads to the continental United States could become a
central mission for the Soviet Navy.[1]

The first sea-based capability for nuclear attack developed by the
Soviet Union was a nuclear warhead on a torpedo based on a
diesel-powered submarine which could theoretically be exploded on
the approaches to the Eastern seaboard of the United States, for
example. A ballistic missile was test-launched from a Zulu class
submarine in September 1955. The Zulu class, of which the first
submarine was delivered in 1952, was the first generation of Soviet
submarines with a strategic nuclear mission. Four different classes of
submarines were being developed in the 1950s:

1 The diesel-powered Foxtrot which carried torpedoes.
2 The diesel-powered Golf which carried ballistic missiles.
3 The nuclear-powered attack submarine November, armed with
   torpedoes.

4 The nuclear-powered Hotel designed to carry three ballistic missiles.[2]

The principal naval strategic missile deployed by the Soviet Union in the 1950s was the SS-N-4 developed by the Iangel bureau with a range of 350 nautical miles. It could only reach US territory if deployed relatively close to the American coast. Furthermore, it could only be fired if the submarine surfaced first. The design of the Zulu was modified to carry two SS-N-4s. The first Golf with three SS-N-4s became operational in 1958. The Hotel I began operation in 1959.[3]

The early Soviet programme to develop a submarine-based strategic nuclear force was, like the strategic bomber programme, part of a drive to obtain a capability to strike at the American homeland but, as a result of the decision to concentrate efforts on the land-based ICBM programme in 1957–58, the submarine-based programme was significantly curtailed.[4]

An important factor in this decision was the technical inadequacy of the submarine-based systems. The nuclear reactors were very noisy and easy to detect. The short range of the SS-N-4s meant that they had to penetrate US anti-submarine warfare (ASW) systems. The surface launch procedure increased their vulnerability even further. Another factor was the greater priority given to defence against the American carrier-based nuclear-armed strike aircraft which could now operate from a very long range; it was considered that nuclear-powered submarines were increasingly required for this purpose.

The creation by the United States of a large sea-based force consisting of *Polaris* submarines and the growing ICBM deployment by both sides gave sea-based systems a new strategic significance. Whereas land-based missiles were, in principle, vulnerable to a pre-emptive strike, a large-scale deployment of sea-based missiles represented a strategic reserve which ensured a second-strike capability even in the event of a massive and successful first strike on the land-based missiles and aircraft.[5]

Consistent with the basic theme of the shift in Soviet military doctrine announced by Khrushchev in January 1960 was the notion that the conventional elements of the navy, such as surface ships, were 'outmoded'. The principal element of the navy would be the nuclear submarine. The major warship construction programme of the navy was much reduced and, in contrast to Western concepts of 'sea control', the Soviet navy during the Khrushchev period based itself on the concept of 'sea denial', i.e. denying control of the sea to others and concentrating on homeland defence. Despite the rhetorical emphasis on the most modern component of sea-based forces, in particular SSBNs, there was no determined effort to develop a substantial force of sea-based nuclear missiles capable of a large-scale strike on the United States.[6]

A renewed emphasis on the development of a substantial strategic nuclear capability based at sea can be seen from 1961, in response to the announcement by President Kennedy of an accelerated increase to build and deploy *Polaris* SSBNs. In 1963 the Golf II and the Hotel I became operational, armed with SS-N-5 missiles that had a range of 750 nautical miles – a small improvement over the SS-N-5. Forward deployment of Hotel class submarines equipped with SS-N-5s began in 1965.[7]

The shift in Soviet military policy after the fall of Khrushchev, which manifested itself in the emphasis on an all-round strengthening of Soviet military power, including a determined effort to match American strategic nuclear forces, also resulted in a change of emphases in the importance of naval missions. Whereas previously the threat of Western carrier strike forces and amphibious attack had been given priority, now the rôle of providing a sea-based strategic nuclear force was described as the primary mission of the navy.[8] Thus Admiral Gorshkov declared at the 23rd Congress of the CPSU:

> Nuclear powered submarines equipped with ballistic missiles have now become the main force of the Navy.[9]

The priority of creating a substantial SSBN force to provide a strategic reserve and an adequate response to the American SSBN force is confirmed by the fact that from the time of Gorshkov's statement more than 40 per cent of naval construction efforts were devoted to SSBNs.[10] Nevertheless it is interesting to observe that in the period of 1965–70 the Soviet navy was increasingly deployed outside its traditional areas of the Arctic, Baltic and Black Seas and the Seas of Okhotsk and Japan, with the establishment of a significant operational presence in the Indian Ocean and the Caribbean. This indicates that the restrictions which Khrushchev imposed on the navy were not accepted by its leaders – indeed Gorshkov's views on the need of a global presence were well known, and that the 'all round' build-up of military forces not only applied to the ground forces, but also to the navy.[11]

The programme decided on in 1961 and accelerated in 1965 came to fruition in 1968 with the deployment of the third generation of SLBMs. While constituting an important improvement in Soviet SSBN capabilities, it must be emphasized that the SS-N-6 deployed on Golf IV and Yankee I submarines in 1968 was not a missile of strategic range such as the American *Polaris* missile – according to Western experts, by 1970 the Soviets had deployed not more than 41 SLBMs in a strategic mode.[12]

There appears, therefore, to be some discrepancy between the actual size of the force deployed (a total of 341, counting all SS-N-4, SS-N-5 and SS-N-6) and its capability to strike at the continental United States. There are several possible explanations for this. One is that the SLBM force constituted a reserve force, kept in the safety of home waters, to be forward deployed when needed. Given their lack of accuracy, they were not very suitable instruments for a co-ordinated attack on the United States in any event. The move towards forward deployment of some SSBNs can be seen in conjunction with the continuous extension of out-of-area patrols of the Soviet navy in general as outlined above, beginning in 1966 (with submarine patrols in the open seas starting in 1964). The first regular patrols by Yankee SSBNs along the Atlantic coast began in 1969. It is also likely that SLBMs were targeted at Europe to provide an additional medium-range capability in the Central European theatre or against European naval bases. Furthermore there have also been statements which indicate that SLBMs were intended not only to attack targets on land but also at sea, thus fulfilling a more traditional rôle for naval forces.

In summary, the pattern of decision-making with regard to the development of the Soviet SSBN force bears some resemblance to other aspects of strategic arms policy. Khrushchev used the emphasis on nuclear weapons to drastically reduce expenditure on the navy in order to be able to advance his domestic economic objectives. The American *Polaris* induced a reconsideration of the strategic function of a submarine-based nuclear force and the Yankee SSBN programme was given much greater priority. It was not until after the fall of Khrushchev that a sustained programme to develop a sea-based nuclear force which could adequately fulfil the function of strategic reserve was undertaken and given sufficient resources.[13]

It came to fruition with the fourth generation SS-N-8s which first became operational in 1973. It represented a quantum jump forward in Soviet SLBM development. It had a range of 4,200 nautical miles (greater than any American SLBM then deployed), was the first

Soviet SLBM to use stellar inertial guidance and was deployed on the Hotel III and the new Delta I and Delta II submarines. It was now possible for the Soviet Union to maintain a strategic reserve strike-force that could inflict substantial damage on the continental United States from a much safer position closer to home waters. However, even though the range of Soviet SLBMs was now in fact greater than that of American SLBMs, the gap in technical capabilities between the Soviet Union and the United States was still greater with regard to SLBMs than ICBMs. The Soviet SLBM programme slowly continued in its development and, by 1978, the SS-N-18 was ready for deployment on the Delta III submarine, a modern, liquid-fuelled missile with three MIRVed warheads (later increased to seven) of 0.2 megaton and a range of 3,200 nautical miles.[14] By 1980 the Soviet Union had deployed 522 SLBMs in a strategic mode. This represented less than 20 per cent of all strategic warheads deployed by the Soviet Union, whereas the United States had then more than 50 per cent of all its warheads deployed on SLBMs. A number of explanations have been advanced for this fundamental asymmetry in the strategic force postures. First of all, there is a greater naval tradition in the United States, whereas the Soviet Union is more a continental power and has only recently emerged as a global sea power. It is also evident that the Soviets had great difficulties in mastering the technologies required for submarine basing. There is a great asymmetry in submarine vulnerability – whereas Soviet submarines are quite vulnerable to the extensive US ASW network (although this is insufficient to eliminate the Soviet SLBM force from the strategic equation entirely) given that Soviet submarines are relatively noisy and the Soviets do not have the technical capabilities to locate and track the missile-carrying US submarines on station at any period of time. The peace-time deployment rate for Soviet submarines is very low (of the order of 15 per cent of submarines are on station at any given time, compared with 55 per cent of the US submarines).[15] It is also known that the Soviets are concerned about the command and control problems posed by submarines, including the dangers of unauthorized launch. Although the Soviet Union now is in possession of a substantial sea-based strategic nuclear force, the primary emphasis on land-based ICBMs is likely to endure.

9 Strategic defence

The origins of ballistic missile defence in the Soviet Union

Defence of the homeland against attack from the air is the domain of the branch of the military services known as PVO-S (*Protivovozdush-naia oborona strany* – anti-air defence of the country). The PVO became a separate major component of the armed forces in 1955 after a substantial reorganization of the air-defence system. Marshal S. S. Biriuzov was appointed its commander.

The effort of the 1950s to develop an effective system of defence against air attack had two main components. The first consisted of a programme to provide capable interceptor fighters. This began with the MIG-15. In 1955 the MIG-19 became operational and by the early Sixties had become the mainstay of the PVO inventory of interceptors. In 1955 the all-weather YAK-25 was introduced, the YAK-28 in 1962 and the supersonic SU-9 in 1959.

The second component of this programme was the development of surface-to-air missiles to defend the Soviet Union against the threat from the growing American intercontinental bomber force. The technology of surface-to-air missiles apparently became available to the Soviet Union in 1952.[1] Deployment of the first missiles began in 1956 around Moscow. The SAM-1 (Western designation) was not deployed elsewhere, presumably due to deficiencies in performance.[2] The SAM-2 became available in 1958. It was a high-altitude missile which was responsible for the spectacular success in downing the U-2 spyplane, an event which had a significant influence on East–West relations at the time.[3] The SAM-2 was widely deployed throughout the Soviet Union and Eastern Europe, and was later used in North Vietnam to defend against American bombing missions.[4]

The next logical step, entirely consistent with the defensive tradition represented by the PVO, was to develop a defence against the threat from American ICBMs which began to emerge in the late Fifties. When the Soviet leadership learnt of an American missile test in the summer of 1953, seven Marshals of the Soviet Union, led by Chief of the General Staff V. D. Sokolovskii, sent a letter to the Central Committee of the CPSU requesting that the creation of an anti-missile system be examined. Despite considerable scepticism about the feasibility of ballistic missile defence from the scientific community, a scientific team led by Grigorii Kisunko was given the task of studying the problem of defence against missiles. By 1956 the decision was made that the results of this research were sufficiently encouraging to build a test range. A military construction team headed by Colonel A. Gubenko began its work in the desert of Betpak-Dana on 8 July 1956. These developments were not known in the West. However, in 1957 there were already indications that the Soviet Union was contemplating the deployment of an anti-ballistic missile system.[5] US intelligence observed one or two large radar systems which, judging by their size and location, appeared not to be connected with the air-defence system. The suggestion that the Russians might be experimenting with ballistic missile defence was based on comparisons with the kinds of radars that were being studied for a possible American ABM development.[6]

In 1958, the air-defence command was reorganized in anticipation of ABM deployment. The command split into the PSO (*protivo-samoletnaia oborona* – anti-aircraft defence) and the PRO (*protivo-raketnaia oborona* – anti-rocket defence).[7] The military literature of the late Fifties and early Sixties indicates a very high level of interest in ballistic missile defence.[8] By 1960, it appears, the development of an operational ABM system had assumed some degree of importance for the Soviet leadership. On 4 March 1961 a test was conducted in which a ballistic missile (an SS-4) was successfully destroyed by a surface-to-air missile with a conventional (high-explosive fragmentation) warhead. In the same year Khrushchev explained in an interview with C. L. Sulzberger that the Soviet leadership was

> very satisfied with the work of the scientists and engineers who produced the means of combatting such rockets [ICBMS].[9]

At the 22nd CPSU Congress Defence Minister Marshal Malinovskii declared:

> Especially I have to report that the problem of destroying missiles in flight has been successfully solved.[10]

Then a few months before the Cuban missile crisis, in July 1962, Khrushchev made his famous remark about 'missiles which could hit a fly in outer space'.[11]

All this optimism was accompanied by the deployment of the SAM-5 missile, code-named *Griffon* by Western intelligence, around Leningrad in 1962.[12] A. O. Ghebhardt has pointed out that the bold claims with regard to Soviet ballistic missile defence capabilities were an integral part of the general propaganda campaign pursued by Khrushchev to give an exaggerated impression in the West of Soviet military capabilities, particularly with regard to nuclear missiles.[13] However, in 1963 deployment of the Leningrad ABM system came to a halt, most likely due to its poor technical performance. It was dismantled in 1964. This did not appear to dampen official enthusiasm for ballistic missile defence, given that another ABM system was under development.

Ghebhardt has argued that the PVO, and Marshal Biriuzov in particular, made use of the successful and impressive demonstration of its capabilities in the U-2 incident in 1962 to press Khrushchev and Malinovskii for support to proceed with the ABM programme.[14] In his conflict with elements of the Soviet military leadership which objected strongly to Khrushchev's 'one-sided' reliance on ICBMs and the dismantling of the Ground Force command, resulting in the ouster of Chuikov and Chief of the General Staff Zakharov, Khrushchev relied heavily on the support of the Commander of the Strategic Rocket Forces Nedelin and the PVO commander Biriuzov. Presumably some support for the ABM programme was thus obtained. Biriuzov became Chief of the General Staff in March 1963 to replace Zakharov.

At the PVO, Biriuzov's place was taken by Marshal V. Sudets, a man of less influence that Biriuzov. While this may be interpreted as a decrease in the influence and importance of the PVO, it must be remembered that with Biriuzov the PVO now had an important supporter in the General Staff, a very crucial position. There were certainly indications that Biriuzov continued to defend the case for strategic defence. Thus he stated in November 1963:

> The Armed Forces of the Soviet Union possess anti-missile weapons capable of intercepting missiles in the air. This circumstance permits our country to be defended against an enemy rocket attack.[15]

Marshal Sudets made the following claims with regard to Soviet BMD capabilities immediately on his appointment:

> The combat capabilities of the weapons of these (PVO) forces permit the destruction of practically all means of air-space attack, at maximum range, high and low altitudes, and supersonic speeds.[16]

He also claimed that, in contrast to the achievements of Soviet scientists who had created the means to combat rockets:

> The air defence of the USA is helpless against ballistic missiles – the main weapon of a nuclear attack from the air.[17]

Given the close relationship between Biriuzov and Khrushchev, it is likely that the ABM programme continued to enjoy support right up to late 1964, when, with the ouster of Khrushchev and the death of Biriuzov in an aircrash, the PVO no longer continued to enjoy the same degree of political support as before.[18]

The political and strategic issues facing the Khrushchev regime

Like all other aspects of strategic arms policy, ABM development and deployment decisions under Khrushchev took place in the context of internal strategic debates, domestic power struggles and a confused and at times contradictory foreign policy. For Khrushchev, ABM deployment had a number of advantages. In the pursuit of translating a (largely non-existent) strategic nuclear capability into political gains, a ballistic missile defence capability would have served to at least create the impression of substantially downgrading US offensive capabilities and thus reducing American options for retaliation against Soviet actions, for example, in Berlin. It would thus have increased the extent to which the Soviet strategic bluff could be pushed. Even a rudimentary ABM system, therefore, could be incorporated into the general Soviet strategy of seeking foreign-policy advances supported by exaggerated strategic claims and thus be an important asset.

In Khrushchev's domestic conflicts with the military, ballistic missile defence also seemed to offer advantages, since it served to emphasize the importance of modern rocket technology over conventional warfare. In addition, Khrushchev's supporters in the military, as we have already pointed out, had a vested interest in the ABM programme.

On the other hand, there were a number of disadvantages. ABM development and deployment demanded additional resources, and the technical difficulties of an adequate strategic defence system were such that serious pursuit of such a programme would have imposed an unacceptable burden on the Soviet economy, particularly given Khrushchev's other budgetary priorities. Increased ICBM deployment would have promised to be a much cheaper way of achieving the same effect on the overall strategic balance. All this would have been true even if the effectiveness of large-scale ABM deployment against a massive US ICBM attack could have been proven, but this was far from being the case. Hence there seemed to be a definite limit to the political advantage obtainable from ballistic-missile defence deployment while, on the other hand, it might threaten to trigger a strong US reaction and a massive build-up of American ICBMs.[19]

The policy which emerged from these considerations resembles somewhat Khrushchev's approach to ICBM development. There was general support for a modest ABM programme, about which there was a great deal of boasting, as witnessed by the famous remark about the missile which could hit 'a fly in outer space'. On the other hand, resources for the determined development of a ballistic-missile defence system that might even be half-way effective were not made available.[20]

In terms of strategic doctrine, strategic defence would have logically fitted in much better with the thinking of Khrushchev's opponents, as John R. Thomas explained:

> [large-scale ABM deployment] . . . would accord with Soviet strategic views which assume that even general nuclear war might result in a protracted conflict. This would be won by the side with the greatest capability of surviving the initial nuclear missile blows. A relatively effective ABM system, combined with other measures such as civil defense, might increase such survival to a meaningful level.[21]

Similarly John Erickson has argued that Khrushchev's 'one-sided' emphasis on offensive strategic forces

> played havoc with military ideas about the relationship between 'deterrence' and 'defence'.[22]

It is interesting then to observe that while in terms of the logic of strategic doctrine Thomas and Erickson are quite correct, this does not coincide with the positions actually defended by Soviet strategists in the strategic debate of the period.

The primacy of strategic, offensive missile forces was clearly affirmed in both editions of the Sokolovskii work *Voennaia Strategiia*:

> One must recognize that the present instrumentalities of nuclear attack are undoubtedly superior to the instrumentalities of defence against them.[23]

In the interpretation of Thomas Wolfe, the sum total of the discussion of the 'offence-versus-defence' question in the Sokolovskii work 'amounted to saying that a good offense is the best defense'.[24] The protection of the Soviet Union against nuclear attack will, therefore, according to the authors of *Voennaia Strategiia*,

> be achieved primarily by destroying the enemy's nuclear weapons where they are based.[25]

With regard to BMD, the first edition which appeared in 1962 stated with some scepticism that

> ballistic missiles are still practically invulnerable to existing means of air defence.[26]

This passage was significantly omitted from the second edition published in October 1963 and the future possibility of an effective ABM system was described with some optimism:

> The great effectiveness of modern PVO resources permits a successful solution to the difficult and important task – the complete destruction of all enemy planes and missiles, preventing them from reaching the targets marked for destruction. The crux of the matter lies in making skilful use of the great potential of modern means of antiaircraft and antimissile defense.[27]

Nevertheless, the general attitude with regard to the relationship between offence and defence appeared to remain unchanged; the statements in the Sokolovskii volume on ballistic-missile defence bear the hallmark of bureaucratic compromise.

While the second edition of *Voennaia Strategiia* was clearly less critical of Soviet ABM development than the first,[28] elsewhere a great deal of criticism was directed against reliance on strategic defence from other sections of the military. Thus the Chief of Staff of the Ground Forces Colonel S. Shtemenko wrote:

> The striking power and range of modern weapons puts the question of strategic defence in a different light than formerly. Our contemporary military doctrine flows from the decisiveness of the goals in war. The combat potential of modern armed forces manifests itself to the greatest degree in the offence, not in the defence. Therefore, Soviet military doctrine regards the strategic

defence as an unacceptable form of strategic operations in a modern war.[29]

The Ground Forces were, of course, under considerable pressure and were abolished as a separate service in 1964. Shtemenko's attack on the PVO and the ABM effort was supported by other Ground Forces officers in the military journals, thus indicating that a full-fledged organizational struggle was taking place, in which the PVO was one of the central targets (one reason being, quite possibly, that it was more vulnerable to such pressure than the SRF).[30] Opposition to ballistic-missile defence was not confined, however, to the Ground Forces. In November 1963, the Commander-in-Chief of the Strategic Rocket Forces, whose service would be an obvious beneficiary of an increased emphasis on offensive rather than defensive missile systems, declared:

> [The Pentagon] is directing special efforts to secure the necessary conditions for the employment of strategic means of attack. Therefore to support quantitative and qualitative superiority over the adversary in this field is one of the most important tasks of the organization of the armed forces in the modern era ... Existing systems of anti-aircraft and anti-missile defence cannot repulse nuclear missile strikes.[31]

The case of ballistic-missile defence is, therefore, a good example of the interaction between the formulation of military strategy and institutional interests. Those sections of the military which would have been expected to be strong supporters of the ABM effort from the point of view of the logic of their doctrinal views opposed it for reasons of institutional interests. This trend could be observed even more distinctly in the post-Khrushchev era.

Soviet efforts at ballistic missile defence and civil defence fitted well into the trend of strategic thinking which emphasized the development of a war-fighting capability, which required what John Erickson has called a 'defensive–offensive mix' of forces,[32] in contrast to Khrushchev's emphasis on deterrence,

> founded in the belief that war with the United States was unlikely, that if it came such a war would be an apocalyptic and unwinnable catastrophe and under these circumstances there was only a diminishing place for large conventional forces.[33]

However, two factors influenced Khrushchev's opponents to take precisely the opposite view with regard to the ABM programme than expected on the basis of this analysis. The first was the technical difficulties of the ABM system. It was not clear that greater allocation of resources would in fact produce an effective ballistic missile defence, while a return for greater investment in ICBM production seemed assured.[34] Secondly, the institutional interests of other military services, in particular the Ground Forces and the Strategic Rocket Forces, conflicted strongly with a substantially increased allocation of resources for the development of strategic defence.

The strategic debate after the fall Khrushchev

The new ABM intended for deployment around Moscow, code-named *Galosh* (by NATO), was shown on the Red Square three weeks after the fall of Khrushchev, on 7 November 1964. The argument in favour of the development and deployment of a strategic defence system was advanced in October 1964 by Major-General Nikolai Talenskii, a prominent military historian in the Soviet Academy of Sciences, in the journal *International Affairs*:

> Thus, *anti-missile systems are defensive weapons in the full sense of the word*: by their technical nature they go into action when the rockets of the attacking side take to their flight paths, that is when the act of aggression has started. The advantage of antimissile systems in the political and international law context is that their use is caused by an act of aggression, and they will simply not work unless an aggressor's rocket makes its appearance in flight over a given area. There will be no difficulty at all in deciding who is the aggressor and who is the attacked.[35]

Talenskii rejected the argument that the ABM could be destabilizing or a threat to mutual deterrence. Rather,

> from the standpoint of strategy, powerful deterrent forces, and an effective anti-missile defence system, when taken together, substantially increase the stability of mutual deterrence . . .[36]

He did, however, concede that if one side could not keep up with the other in the development of ABM technology and the deployment of such systems, it might decide to pursue an increased deployment of offensive weapons instead, thus giving renewed impetus to the arms race. His response to this possibility was:

> There is one reasonable alternative to a race in anti-missile systems, and it is the early implementation of general and complete disarmament.[37]

Talenskii, as we have already pointed out, was then associated with the arms-control community centred around the Academy of

Sciences.[38] A. O. Ghebhardt writes about another group of academics which at this time became interested in the research of laser systems which could be deployed in defence against ballistic missiles.[39] Ghebhardt states that

> It seems probable that achievement of progress in this field by a group of scientists who were originally assigned to perform this task, attracted attention and support from an important segment of decision-makers which presumably included some military leaders, Politburo members and Khrushchev himself.[40]

There was a significant voice in the Soviet scientific community at the time, however, which was highly critical of the entire ABM effort. These criticisms were succinctly advanced in a book by N. P. Shibayev, which contained a thorough analysis of the principal difficulties inherent in ABM technology and which are still central to the whole strategic defence debate today,[41] in particular the problems associated with the recognition, tracking and successful elimination of incoming missiles, as well as the various counter-measures that can be taken against a ballistic-missile defence system. It appears, therefore, that there were a number of scientists who were extremely doubtful about the feasibility of an effective ballistic-missile defence and on purely technical grounds recommended a concentration of resources on ICBMs.

These views found some support also in the military. Thus an article appeared in *Voennaia Mysl'* in August 1964 which consisted of a very detailed and highly critical discussion of the American Nike Zeus ABM system. It concludes:

> In the opinion of many foreign specialists who have soberly evaluated the level of development of various projects, an effective means of combatting ballistic rockets has not yet been developed in the capitalist world.[42]

Although this article discusses the ABM issue entirely in terms of the American programme, it seems a safe conclusion that the arguments were clearly directed at the Soviet programme which was encountering the same kinds of difficulties.

The first two years of the Brezhnev–Kosygin–Podgornii regime were a time in which the entire defence establishment was reorganized and issues of military strategy and the Soviet force posture were subject to a general review and internal debate. After the reorganization of the defence industries in March 1965, there was public controversy between Nikolai Podgornii, then Party Secretary in charge of personnel, and Mikhail Suslov, who was responsible for ideological questions and foreign policy in the Party Secretariat. This controversy, which is discussed in greater detail in chapter 5, related to economic priorities in general and defence expenditure in particular. As has been pointed out in chapters 4 and 5, this debate was eventually partially resolved in favour of the protagonists of higher military spending. This became clear as the result of a speech by Brezhnev in July 1965. Brezhnev also made a direct reference to ABMs, making it clear that the Politburo might support a programme which could be shown to be effective and properly managed.[43]

As we have already seen, the political infighting in 1965 was accompanied by a considerable debate about the rôle of war as an instrument of policy in the age of nuclear weapons. The two most prominent protagonists of this debate were Major-General Nikolai Talenskii and Lieutenant-Colonel E. I. Rybkin.[44]

Talenskii argued that nuclear war could not serve as an acceptable instrument of policy since it was no longer possible to ensure the survival of the societies which were at war with one another. His article provided support at the right time to the Podgornii faction in the Politburo.[45] With regard to ballistic missile defence, both groups supported it in principle. We have already seen that Talenskii was a strong supporter of the ABM programme. The support given by Rybkin and other representatives of the military establishment was more qualified, emphasizing also the need of strong offensive capabilities.[46] There was again indirect criticism voiced in *Voennaia Mysl'* in an article published in September 1965 by V. Aleksandrov on 'The Search for a Solution to the Problems of Antimissile Defense in the US'. The arguments deployed by Aleksandrov uncannily foreshadow the discussions in the 1980s about the American *Strategic Defence Initiative* in their analysis of the problems of early warning, tracking guidance, distinction between warheads and decoys, other counter-measures such as dummy warheads with interference transmitters, giving missiles a reflective surface (effective against laser weapons) to the point of dividing the flight-path of a missile into three phases (boost phase, mid-course and terminal phase). Aleksandrov proposes the following reasons why the United States had not so far deployed an ABM system:

> there are many reasons: the imperfection and insufficient effect-
> iveness of the systems which have been studied (technical reasons),
> the extremely high cost of deployment and the relatively small
> political advantages over the enemy which would be achieved by

the very costly wide or even partial deployment of a system of limited effectiveness.[47]

It is clear that Aleksandrov supported building up the SRF as opposed to BMD:

> In every phase of this work *it has been shown that the development and perfection of offensive means are more promising, cheaper and simpler.* In the opinion of Herzfeld there theoretically is no antimissile defense which cannot be overcome by an enemy.[48] [Emphasis added]

After describing the various possible countermeasures developed in the United States Aleksandrov concludes:

> Thus, the development of means of overcoming an anti-missile defense has, in the view of the US, outstripped the development of antimissile defense systems.[49]

The article, despite the fact that it concerns itself exclusively with American research in ballistic missile defence, unmistakably addresses the issues relating to the Soviet ABM debate. Furthermore, in its emphasis on *American* countermeasures to BMD it is evidently directed at Soviet BMD efforts.

It is clear that by 1966 the ABM programme was given a significantly reduced priority. Public statements by representatives of the military establishment indicate a more realistic assessment of what an ABM system, pursued within present technological capabilities and a realistic investment of resources, could and could not do. Thus Malinovskii stated during his speech at the 23rd CPSU Congress:

> Highly effective new anti-aircraft missile systems and complexes of interceptor planes have been developed and adopted by the armed forces. Our anti-aircraft resources ensure the reliable destruction of any enemy planes and *many* missiles.[50] [Emphasis added]

Note the distinction between anti-aircraft capabilities and anti-missile defence. A very similar statement was made by Chief of the General Staff Zakharov.[51] This may have indicated a shift in resources from the PRO to the PSO branch of the PVO, due to the increasing need for anti-aircraft missiles in Vietnam and the decision to invest in the large-scale Tallinn anti-aircraft system. The shift towards the PSO may have been due to a greater confidence in the ability to deal with the bomber threat, a conclusion that seems to be suggested by the absolute claims made for the anti-aircraft capabilities as opposed to the more qualified claims regarding ballistic missile defence. One of the crucial factors was most likely the disappointing technical performance of the *Galosh* system. Furthermore, since in 1966 there was already considerable momentum for the dramatic build-up of the ICBM force, this most likely resulted in less resources being made available for ballistic missile defence. The failure of the Commander-in-Chief of the PVO Marshal Sudets to be re-elected to the Central Committee in April 1966, followed by his retirement in July (when he was succeeded by Army General Batitskii) may also have been related to a reduced emphasis on ABMs.[52]

More direct, even though still by no means explicit opposition to the ABM came from another interesting and influential source, described by Ghebhardt as a 'powerful alliance of high-ranking Soviet officers and spokesmen for some of the East European armed forces'.[53] Their main emphasis was the primacy of the offence over the defence, which is not surprising, since the defence of Hungary and East Germany depended on Soviet troops and offensive nuclear weapons, whereas the ABM would merely serve to defend the Soviet Union. Army General Pavel F. Kurochkin, Commander of the Frunze Military Academy declared in an interview published in East Berlin in October 1966:

> The strategic missile units now represent the foundation of the Soviet Army. No rocket defense system could save the aggressor from these fearful weapons.[54]

This campaign which Ghebhardt refers to had started with East German Defence Minister General Heinz Hoffmann's speech at the twelfth plenary session of the Central Committee of the SED, in which he stated:

> The means of cosmic defence, missile defence and air defence guarantee already today the destruction of any airplane and many types of rockets of the potential aggressor . . . all these new strategic weapon systems . . . are capable of overcoming the defence of the opponent and reach the designated targets.[55]

In a similar vein Lieutenant-Colonel P. M. Derevianko emphasized in a speech broadcast on Radio Moscow in Hungarian that

> the strategic rocket troops and nuclear rocket equipped submarines have become *the principal means* for bridling the aggressors.[56] [Emphasis added]

Marshal Chuikov, who at this stage was responsible for Civil Defence, joined in:

> The USSR Armed Forces are always ready to repel an attack of the aggressor. But there is no full guarantee that some of the enemy's weapons of mass destruction will not reach their targets.[57]

The institutional interests reflected in this statement are not hard to discern.

It is interesting to note that the dividing lines in the controversy about BMD in 1966 coincided to some extent with those in the more general debate about economic priorities and the allocation of resources. Thus Kosygin, who favoured increased investment in consumer production and a liberalization of the economy, came out in support of continuing the deployment of the Galosh system. Similarly Talenskii, who argued in support of the ABM development, opposed the build-up of strategic forces. The opponents of the ABM, however, were in favour of increased military spending and the build-up of ICBM and SLBM forces. Indeed, as we have seen, the commander of the Strategic Rocket Forces, N. I. Krylov, had argued in favour of superiority in offensive forces. The proponents of a build-up of strategic offensive forces were supported by Chief of the General Staff Zakharov and had the backing of a faction in the Politburo led by Suslov. For example, while Kosygin emphasized in his speech to the 23rd Party Congress the need to improve the lot of the ordinary worker,[58] Zakharov in his report to the Armed Forces about the Congress emphasized the need for increased investment in heavy industry:

> we are speaking primarily of the development in the field of machine building. It plays a vitally important role in the technological re-equipping of our economy, raising the productivity of labour, and providing the Army and Navy with the most modern equipment.[59]

Zakharov became one of the principal supporters of the build-up of strategic ICBM and naval forces, whereas according to Ghebhardt

> during his seven years' tenure as Chief of the General Staff, from 1964 to September 1971, not a single word of praise was heard from him in regard to ABM.[60]

The decline of strategic defence and the ABM Treaty

The debate continued well into 1967, when it became part of the emerging SALT process. In January 1967 President Johnson asked Llewellyn E. Thompson, who was returning to Moscow for a second term as Ambassador, to explore the possibility of negotiations to limit ABM deployment. The response by Thompson's counterpart Dobrynin indicated Soviet interest in such negotiations provided that offensive forces were also included. In a public speech, however, Kosygin seemed to pour cold water on the idea of limiting ballistic missile defence deployments:

> It seems to me that the system that warns of an attack is not a factor in the arms race. On the contrary, it is a factor that reduces the possibility of the destruction of people. That is why I think it is a mistake to look at this question the way some people do. According to some theories that are gaining ground in the world, the question is posed in the following way: Which is cheaper, to destroy man, that is, to have an offensive weapon that destroys people, cities, entire states, or to have a weapon that prevents such destruction? . . . The anti-missile system probably costs more than an offensive weapon. But these questions are unrelated.[61]

Kosygin's apparent rebuff to Johnson may well have been intended also for a domestic audience, because in January an article by Malinovskii was published in *Kommunist* in which the primacy of offensive forces was affirmed:

> first priority is being given to the strategic missile forces and atomic missile launching submarine forces which are the principal means of deterring the aggressor and decisively defeating him in war.[62]

The debate, therefore, was still in progress. It is important to point out, however, that while Kosygin's statements clearly appear to echo the kinds of arguments advanced by General Talenskii, the position of the Soviet leadership, including Kosygin, was not that there should be no limitations on ABMs, but rather that such limitations could only be accepted in a general framework that also limited offensive weapons. This is the clear implication of what Kosygin said at a Western news conference in 1967:

> As regards an anti-missile system, our position is well known. We believe that the discussions should center not on merely the problem of an anti-missile defense system. Because, after all, the anti-missile system is not a weapon of aggression, of attack; it is a defensive system. And we feel therefore that what should be considered is the entire complex of armaments and disarmament questions . . . Because otherwise, if – instead of building and deploying an anti-ballistic missile system – the money is used to build up offensive missile systems, mankind will not stand to gain anything. It will, on the contrary, face a still greater menace and will

come still closer to war. And we therefore are in favor of considering the whole range of questions relating to arms and disarmament, and we're ready to discuss that question – the general question of disarmament.[63]

Kosygin's objective thus was quite clearly to gain support for negotiations on the limitations of offensive nuclear weapons, and he was holding out against an ABM-only treaty for this reason. His remarks were directed both at a foreign and a domestic Soviet audience, where the notion of Strategic Arms Limitations Agreements had by no means won universal acceptance.

In the Soviet Union, the discussion continued. Although no-one directly questioned that ABMs should be deployed, the primacy of offensive forces, coupled with pointed statements that Soviet BMD was not capable of destroying all in-coming enemy missiles in the event of war,[64] was supported by such prominent military leaders as Defence Minister Malinovskii, Marshal Grechko, then Commander-in-Chief of the Warsaw Pact and soon to become Defence Minister, M. Zakharov and Chuikov.[65] There were, of course, still strong supporters of the ABM programme, most notably General Pavel F. Batitskii, the new Commander-in-Chief of the PVO, who claimed that the *Galosh* system would be able to defend the Soviet Union in the event of an enemy attack.[66]

For a time, the *Galosh* programme continued under its own momentum. The first launch positions were installed by 1967, and it appeared that the Moscow system would on completion involve about 100 launch positions. In late 1968 the work on the Moscow system came to a complete halt, however, having been about two-thirds completed.

It is clear that already in 1967 the PVO, and the ABM programme in particular, experienced a continuous erosion of support in the Soviet military.[67] This was because the realization that the *Galosh* system would not provide a satisfactory defence against an American ICBM attack and, indeed, a general disillusionment with regard to the system's capabilities. The radars constituted a particular problem. For the initial detection of a missile attack the PVO relied on Hen House phased radars and a combination of Dog and Cat House phased array battle management systems. The actual task of missile interception was to be performed by the mechanically scanning Try Add engagement radars. In case of a large-scale attack these systems were completely inadequate, because of the slowness of the Try Add systems and the data processing for the Dog and Cat House radars.

All of the radar systems were highly vulnerable to nuclear blasts and electromagnetic pulses.[68]

Another reason for disillusionment may have been the realization that the American Nike-X system was in fact superior to the Soviet ABM. This would create an interesting paradox for Soviet military writers, since their attacks on Soviet BMD were often formulated in terms of a critique of US systems. Nonetheless, some evidence of respect for American capabilities and, more importantly, future plans can be found in the expert literature.[69] However, there is no evidence that Soviet military experts considered the development of an effective ballistic missile defence by the United States a likely contingency. They appear to have been more impressed by the improvements in offensive capabilities. The development of MIRVed missiles further diminished the credibility of effective ballistic missile defence; in particular the development of decoys and penetration aids must have been a source of concern to the Soviet military planners given that the *Galosh* was an exoatmospheric missile, while a combination of exoatmospheric and hypersonic endoatmospheric missiles (such as the American *Spartan* and *Sprint* systems) would have provided a more realistic chance of an effective terminal defence system. An indication that these problems were exercising the minds of the Soviet military could be found in an article by Major General I. I. Anureev which contained an analytical model of the correlation of forces. The probability co-efficient for overcoming anti-air defence was given as 0.7 (assuming a kill-ratio of 30 per cent), while the probability for overcoming anti-missile defences was assumed to be 1. Although Anureev described the given values as purely hypothetical, some conclusion about what these values were likely to be would seem to be warranted. Of symbolic significance was the fact that for the first time since 1963 the November military parade in 1968 did not feature any ABMs (nor did any subsequent parades).[70] Anureev's 1971 book contains a diagrammatic representation of an interception of a MIRVed RV by an American ABM system. Anureev does, however, point out the vulnerability of radar systems to nuclear strikes and maintains that it will not be possible in practice to defend them. Radar stations, he maintains, can be blinded by nuclear detonations at great height.[71]

As becomes clear from Kosygin's statements, the debate with regard to strategic defence in 1967 and 1968 concerned both the issue of the allocation of resources and, as the other side of the coin, the question of SALT negotiations with the United States. The ABM critics in the military were strongly opposed to SALT. As we have seen in chapter 5, Colonel Rybkin, for example, wrote critically of arms-control negotiations.[72] Military opposition to strategic arms limitations manifested itself mostly, however, by almost complete silence about SALT in the military press.[73]

A serious commitment to Soviet participation in SALT negotiations was made in June 1968, but the process was delayed by the invasion of Czechoslovakia. In confidential exchanges in the autumn of 1968 before the negotiations got under way, there was agreement that the objective should be a 'stable mutual strategic deterrence', recognizing an 'integral interrelationship' between offensive systems and strategic defence, thus rejecting the Talenskii view that ABMs had no effect on strategic stability.[74]

Raymond Garthoff, executive officer of the US delegation to the SALT talks from 1969 to 1973, has described the initial presentation by the head of the Soviet delegation on the ABM issue in the following terms:

> In one of the first formal SALT meetings, in November 1969, Deputy Minister Vladimir Semenov, the head of the Soviet delegation, set forth the Soviet position on ABM limitation. He acknowledged indirectly the change in Soviet views by saying that, although initially it had seemed that ABM would serve humane goals and that the only problem seemed to be a technical one, it was later found that ABM systems could stimulate the arms race and could be destabilizing by casting doubts on the inevitability of effective retaliation by missile forces of the side attacked. In view of the strategic defensive–offensive interrelationship, ABM deployment could be strategically destabilizing.[75]

By 1970 the arms-control experts in the Soviet Union appear to have come out strongly in opposition to ABM, which is not surprising given that Soviet arms-control policy had evolved in this direction. The literature of the arms-control community contains some of the direct discussions of the link between offence and defence, and ABM and MIRV:

> The next round of the arms race will be marked by . . . the wide development of work on weapons systems – above all anti-rockets defenses (ABMs) and separable, individually targeted warheads (MIRVs). This threatens to create, in the opinion of experts on strategic matters, a very 'destabilizing' momentum. Speaking more simply, the threat of a thermonuclear war is increasing.[76]

While *Galosh* deployment came to a halt in late 1968, a high level of research in ballistic-missile defence continued and work on the uncompleted Moscow site started again in 1971. However, the Soviet leadership came to the conclusion that it was more advantageous to negotiate an agreement whereby further Soviet BMD deployment would be given up and thus prevent the deployment of the technologically superior American ABM system, than to extend the *Galosh* system throughout the Soviet Union. In signing the ABM Treaty in 1972, the Soviet Union accepted a mutual ceiling of 200 ABM launchers, which was reduced to 100 in a further agreement in June 1974, thus bringing to a conclusion the Soviet debate about ballistic-missile defence for the time being.

Conclusion

Soviet interest in ballistic-missile defence started as a response to the developing American offensive missile threat. The technical difficulties in developing an effective system of BMD meant that offensive strategic forces soon became predominant. Nevertheless support for BMD survived for a number of reasons – the Soviet predilection for 'overinsurance', exploiting all possibilities, because BMD was another suitable element in Khrushchev's propaganda campaigns, and furthermore the issue of ABM became important in Khrushchev's exploitation of inter-service rivalry to maintain his control over the military.

In the post-Khrushchev period the ABM programme eventually was curtailed. Political disputes about economic and industrial policy became associated with inter-service rivalry in which the PVO and its political supporters (most notably Kosygin) had to give way to the determination of the General Staff to achieve parity with the United States in offensive strategic nuclear forces given the technical limitations of Soviet BMD, particularly in the face of the development of MIRVed ICBMs.

From 1974 onwards the issue of ballistic defence remained off the arms control agenda until President Reagan launched his Strategic Defence Initiative (SDI) in 1983. The Soviet attitude to strategic defence was an important issue in the Western debates about SDI. Many of those who supported SDI as a response to Soviet efforts in the field of ballistic-missile defence expressed the conviction that the Soviet Union merely signed the ABM Treaty to forestall American BMD at a time when the United States had a technological advantage, that Soviet support for the ABM Treaty did not signal a definite renunciation of strategic defence and the acceptance of mutual vulnerability and that the Soviets have been engaged in a major effort to develop new BMD capabilities for a long time. In this view, the Soviets are seeking a major enhancement of the nuclear war-fighting capabilities which might accrue from a substantial national ballistic missile defence system if the technological level of development is such as to make deployment advantageous. Part of the argument in this debate hinges on the interpretation of Soviet motivations in first developing strategic defences and then accepting the limitations on ballistic missile defence in the ABM Treaty.

After the signing of the ABM Treaty, discussion of ballistic missile defence virtually disappeared from the open military press. The journal of the air-defence troops confined its attention to anti-aircraft defence, even though the operation of the Moscow ABM continued under the aegis of the PVO. The only body of evidence that yields any clues about Soviet thinking lies in the observed development and deployment of systems. Whereas the United States dismantled all their ABM launchers of the Safeguard system, the Soviet Union maintained the Moscow system and engaged in a long-term development programme to upgrade it. This finally came to fruition in 1980 when the capabilities of the system were substantially improved within the limits of the ABM Treaty limitations. Thirty-two of the old *Galosh* launchers were dismantled and new missiles deployed, increasing their number to the permitted ceiling of 100. The new deployments consisted of a modernized version of the *Galosh* and the SH-08 (*Gazelle*). The *Gazelle* is a high-acceleration endoatmospheric missile and thus represents a substantial step forward in overcoming the limitations of a system based only on exoatmospheric missiles. Another important component of the modernization programme has been the construction of the new Pill Box Large Phased Array Radar system at Pushkino which makes the simultaneous interception of a number of incoming missiles a more realistic prospect. A realistic assessment of the capabilities of the modernized Soviet ABM system around Moscow (referred to as ABM-3-X) is that it essentially raises the technology to the standard of the US Safeguard system and provides a limited capability against hostile missile launches. Thus the system can be expected to perform well against the very limited Chinese strategic missiles. American, and even French and British strategic forces are easily capable of saturating and penetrating the Moscow defences. The radar system is an obviously vulnerable point – one direct hit or high-altitude nuclear detonations generating a large electromagnetic pulse can disable the entire system. The British Chevaline warhead for the *Polaris* system was specifically designed to overcome Moscow defences. The continuation of the Moscow ABM system indicates some interest in providing protection of the national capital but there has been no determined attempt to upgrade this protection to a high level. It bears all the hallmarks of an existing programme continuing under its own momentum, rather than a shift in the rôle of strategic missile defence.

10 The military uses of space

The origins of the space race

The advances in rocket technology made during the course of World War II (particularly by Germany) promised not only a revolution in the nature of warfare (which came about by the nearly simultaneous development of long-range missiles and nuclear weapons), but also the possibility of the realization of a very old dream of mankind, namely the exploration of outer space. Thus both military imperatives as well as the possibility of astounding scientific endeavours provided impetus for the rocket programme. Furthermore, even space technology as opposed to ICBM technology had a very significant military potential. During the last year of Stalin's life, Soviet scientists were confronted with a number of pressures and opportunities. On the purely scientific front, there was the invitation to participate in the International Geophysical Year. The final proposal for the IGY envisaged an 18-month period of geophysical observations (to be carried out from 1 July 1957 to 31 December 1958), also involving observations from satellites. From the military perspective, there was the clear imperative to improve rocket technology for the development of ICBMs. But the potential value of satellites in orbit for reconnaissance purposes or as weapon platforms was also clearly recognized. According to Nicholas Daniloff, the year 1954 was a crucial turning-point, because in that year the RD-107 and the RD-108 rocket engines, which were later used to launch Sputnik and the SS-6 ICBM reached the final stage of their development.[1] In 1954 a space flight commission was established in the Academy of Sciences.[2] This fact and the clear intention to proceed with the development of an artificial satellite did not become known until it was made public in a relatively obscure article in the evening newspaper *Vechernaia Moskva* on 16 April 1955. Another important fact that emerged from this article was that scientific and military efforts were being coordinated with regard to the satellite programme. Although the launching of Sputnik on 4 October 1957 was a great surprise to the general public in the West, experts were clearly aware of the developments leading up to it. In 1955 already the CIA had presented evidence to the National Security Council about Soviet efforts to launch an artificial satellite. Announcements in the Soviet press that Soviet scientists had theoretically solved the problem of putting an artificial satellite in orbit (together with the frequencies on which *Sputnik* would broadcast) in mid-1957 and about the successful testing of intercontinental rockets can, with hindsight, be seen to have provided clear pointers as to what was coming.[3]

There is clear evidence that there was a conscious effort by the Soviet Union to beat the United States in an undeclared 'race' to be the first in space.[4] But the space 'race' as such did not really start until after the launch of Sputnik and as a result of the reaction to this event in the United States. The launch of Sputnik was followed by a number of other dramatic Soviet achievements in space, two of which were the sending of the first living creature into space and also the conducting of the first manned orbital flight. In the United States, it was President John F. Kennedy who made surpassing Soviet achievements in space a priority, thus picking up the Soviet challenge to the space race.

The political significance of the space programme

For the Soviet Union (and also for Khrushchev himself) the space programme promised a number of substantial political benefits. The most immediate exploitation of the Sputnik flight occurred with regard to ICBM development claims. Note, for example, Khrushchev's statement in an interview with James Reston of the *New York Times*:

> When we announced the successful testing of an intercontinental rocket, some U.S. statesmen did not believe us: the Soviet Union, you see, was saying it had something it did not really have. Now that we have successfully launched an earth satellite, only technically ignorant people can doubt this. The U.S.A. has no intercontinental ballistic rocket, otherwise it would also have easily launched a satellite of its own. We can launch satellites because we have a carrier for them – namely, the ballistic rocket.[5]

Khrushchev's statements continued to link the achievements of the Soviet space programme with Soviet strategic rocket capabilities. When a half-ton Sputnik II was launched a month after Sputnik I,

Khrushchev was quick to point out that the weight to be carried by Soviet missiles could still be substantially increased.[6] The launch of the first lunar probe produced the following comment:

> If the Soviet Union knows how to send a rocket over hundreds of thousands of kilometers into the cosmos, it can send powerful missiles to any spot in the world without fail.[7]

Just before Khrushchev visited the United States in the autumn of 1959 Luna II was launched. Khrushchev made his view of the significance of this event clear by presenting President Eisenhower with a replica of the emblem transported to the moon by Luna II. The successful Soviet mission served to enhance Khrushchev's prestige during his visit.

Again, in 1961, Khrushchev stated that the rockets which put Gagarin and Titov into orbit could be used to project 100-megaton warheads to any place in the world. In March 1962 the Vostok flights were cited as evidence for Khrushchev's claims of the accuracy of the new 'global rocket' which allegedly could hit the United States from any direction.[8] Arnold L. Horelick has pointed out that Khrushchev used the Soviet successes in space as evidence not only of Soviet capabilities, but also of the quantity of Soviet ICBMs.[9]

The Soviet leadership under Khrushchev certainly recognized the potential of the space programme as a focus of national unity and pride. It was presented as peaceful in nature and as conducive to the promotion of peace.

Soviet achievements in space were also used as diplomatic tools in relations with neutral and Third World countries, and Soviet astronauts were frequently sent on tours to promote the image of the Soviet Union.

Obviously the space programme was useful as a propaganda tool not only abroad, but also at home. Achievements in space which demonstrated Soviet missile capability bolstered Khrushchev's arguments for reliance on the strategic missile as the major factor in Soviet security.

Another crucial area in which Khrushchev's foreign and domestic goals coincided was that of economic development. He challenged the United States to an economic competition, claiming the ability to outproduce and overtake the US by the year 1970. The advancement of the Soviet economy, particularly in the sectors of consumer goods, the chemical industry and agriculture were central to Khrushchev's domestic policies. They were also declared to be the focus of competition with the capitalist system and, in the near future, would irrevocably prove the superiority of communism. In this way the space programme could serve as a tool to reinforce Soviet ideology at home as well as demonstrating its superiority abroad. Thus in May 1962, for example, Khrushchev boasted in his familiar fashion:

> Those who have tried to liquidate trade between the capitalist countries and the Soviet Union sat down in a puddle, while we took ourselves into the cosmos and we continue to have priority in the exploration of space.[10]

The military significance of the space programme

For quite some time, the existence of a military dimension to the space programme was not admitted by the Soviet Union, with the exception of the use of rockets to deliver nuclear warheads. As Herbert L. Sawyer has pointed out, in 1961, statements appeared for the first time urging its *creation*.[11] Before considering these statements, however, it is important to point out that there were indications of direct military implications of the Soviet space programme prior to 1961.

Satellite reconnaissance

One Soviet preoccupation was no doubt with reconnaissance satellites. This potential application was already clearly perceived by military planners in 1953.[12] In 1962 the Soviet Union launched five photoreconnaissance satellites – in April, July, September, October and November.[13]

Nonetheless, despite its own work in the development of satellite surveillance, the Soviet Union was initially hostile to the American use of reconnaissance satellites, following its frustrations over the overflights of Soviet territory by U-2 spyplanes which it was unable to stop until May 1960 when a U-2 was shot down over Sverdlovsk. During the Paris summit in May 1960 with President Eisenhower, which was aborted as a consequence of the U-2 incident, Khrushchev condemned the Americans for sending spy planes over Soviet territory when de Gaulle pointed out that a Soviet satellite had recently passed over France and most likely taken photographs. According to Eisenhower's memoirs,

> Khrushchev broke in to say that he was talking about airplanes, not about satellites. He said any nation in the world who wanted to photograph Soviet areas by satellite was completely free to do so.[14]

As Paul Stares has pointed out, this was probably an unguarded moment, since just a month later Khrushchev warned that spy satellites could also be 'paralysed', and soon a Soviet campaign began condemning 'American espionage from space' combined with a diplomatic attempt to have reconnaissance satellites banned by the United Nations. Typical of the official Soviet attitude at the time, for example, was the article by B. Alexandrov in *Krasnaia Zvezda* on 23 July, which asserted that:

> whatever altitude spies fly at, they remain spies; the flight of a spy satellite over foreign territory is an aggressive act.[15]

For the United States, however, particularly in the light of the 'missile gap' controversy at the end of the Eisenhower administration, the need for reliable information about Soviet ICBM capabilities had reached paramount importance and, by the autumn of 1960, photore-connaissance satellites were beginning to yield some hopeful results. The Soviet diplomatic offensive to ban reconnaissance satellites began with a proposal at the meeting of the Legal Subcommittee of the UN Outer Space Committee in June 1962. It stated very directly:

> The use of artificial satellites for the collection of intelligence information in the territory of foreign states is incompatible with the objectives of mankind in its conquest of outer space.[16]

A Soviet text on space law published in the same year went even further by claiming:

> The right of a state to destroy a satellite spy and in general every space device whatsoever interfering with the security of this state is indisputable.[17]

The formal American response to the Soviet Draft Proposal was given in a speech by Ambassador Gore to the First Committee of the United Nations on 3 December 1962. In it Gore affirmed that outer space should be used for peaceful purposes, but did not exclude military activities in space:

> There is, in any event, no workable dividing line between military and non-military uses of space. One of the consequences of these factors is that any nation may use space satellites for such purposes as observation and information gathering. Observation from space is consistent with international law, just as is observation from the high seas.[18]

This view was categorically opposed by Soviet Representative Moro-zov who replied with regard to satellite reconnaissance:

> The object to which such illegal surveillance is directed constitutes a secret guarded by a Sovereign State, and regardless of the means by which such an operation is carried out, it is in all cases an intrusion into something guarded by a Sovereign State in conformity with its sovereign prerogative.[19]

When the Legal Subcommittee reconvened in April 1963, the Soviets reaffirmed their position. However, as the Kosmos programme was now beginning to show results, the Soviet position began to change. In July it was revealed that Khrushchev had offered to show Soviet satellite photos to Paul Henri Spaak, the Belgian Foreign Minister. Further claims for the possession of a satellite reconnaissance capability were made in 1963, when the editor of *Izvestiia*, Khrushchev's son-in-law Aleksei Adzhubei, referring to a picture of Moscow taken by an American satellite, claimed that the Soviet Union could publish such a picture of New York taken by one of their own satellites. Khrushchev made a similar claim to US Senator William Benton when the latter was on a visit to Moscow in 1964.[20]

Confirmation that Soviet opposition to reconnaissance from space was now abating came when the new Soviet delegate to the UN Outer Space Committee desisted from the customary condemnation of spy satellites in a speech on 9 September 1963.[21] An important rôle was no doubt played by the Test Ban Negotiations, where satellite surveillance offered a solution to the verification problems which had dogged the negotiations for such a long time. Given the Soviet dislike of on-site inspections, 'national technical means' (i.e. mainly reconnaissance satellites) became for the Soviet Union the principal acceptable means of the verification of arms-control agreements; as a result, official Soviet opposition to satellite reconnaissance came to an end.[22]

Space weapons

The actual development of a space-based weapons system was also part of the Soviet space programme. The possibility of basing nuclear weapons in space was referred to by Khrushchev at a Kremlin reception on the occasion of Titov's successful space flight of 9 August 1961. Khrushchev boasted that unlike the United States, the Soviet Union had bombs 'stronger than 100 megatons'. Then he commented:

> We placed Gagarin and Titov in space and we can replace them with other loads that can be directed to any place on earth.[23]

Khrushchev again referred to the possibility of sending 'other payloads' than the two astronauts into space in December 1961. Although in the United States the prevailing consensus was that satellites would be less useful for launching nuclear weapons than ICBMs, Khrushchev's boast were taken seriously. Furthermore, on 16 March 1962 Khrushchev announced the successful test of what was called a 'global rocket', which in 1963 was described in a Soviet publication as having achieved 'cosmic velocity', i.e. the velocity to achieve an earth orbit. The distinction between this 'global rocket' and ICBMs was further elaborated in an article in *Krasnaia Zvezda* by Major General of the Artillery I. Baryshev entitled *Chto takoe protivo-kosmicheskaia oborona* ('What is Anti-Space Defence') on 2 September 1962, in which he stated clearly that anti-missile defences would be ineffective against a 'global rocket'.[24] This claim had also been made by V. Siniagin in the military journal *Kommunist Vooruzhennykh Sil:*

> Now our scientists and engineers have created a global rocket. It can fly around the globe in any direction and inflict a strike on any given point. This weapon is irresistible; it is invulnerable to anti-missile defence.[25]

Biriuzov, Commander-in-Chief of the Soviet Rocket Forces, declared in a Radio Broadcast in February 1963:

> It has now become possible at a command from earth to launch missiles from satellites at any desired time and at any point in the satellite trajectory.[26]

How much the existence of such a weapon as the 'global rocket' was simply taken for granted by Soviet military writers becomes apparent in an article published in February 1963 by General-Colonel S. Shtemenko where the global rocket is casually included in a list of other Soviet strategic weapons systems:

> Global intercontinental and medium-range rockets are able to deliver to their target nuclear charges of large calibre . . . in the Soviet Union, as is known, nuclear munitions have been created equivalent to the power of 20, 30, 50 and 100 million tons of TNT.[27]

Ironically such weapons systems did not actually become operational and were never tested during the first half of the Sixties; nonetheless Soviet claims did have an effect on American thinking (despite McNamara's scepticism regarding the utility of satellites as platforms for launching nuclear weapons) and added impetus to the development of an anti-satellite capability in the United States.[28]

The Soviet initiatives on the banning of photoreconnaissance satellites in the United Nations again brought the issue of also banning nuclear weapons in space on to the arms-control agenda. At the Eighteen Nation Disarmament Conference in Geneva, the United States and the Soviet Union both maintained the position that disarmament in space depended on the acceptance of an overall General and Complete Disarmament package. The main fear of the Americans was that arms control in space would affect satellite reconnaissance; a proposal in Geneva by the Canadian Secretary of State for Foreign Affairs Howard Green for a separate ban of weapons of mass destruction in space, however, sparked off a policy review in Washington. The result of the American internal debate was that the United States was willing to negotiate a separate ban on weapons of mass destruction in space without the requirement of inspection or verification.[29]

In conversations with Soviet officials after the Cuban missile crisis, American officials made it clear that they were not only renewing a proposal made in 1957 which sought to ban all objects travelling through space for military purposes (including ICBMs), but also were concerning themselves with weapons stationed in space, and that they were not insisting on inspection as part of an agreement. At this time, the Soviet Union had come to agree that satellite reconnaissance was permissible; it thus became clear that American and Soviet views on the military use of space were converging. On 19 September 1963 Soviet Foreign Minister Gromyko said in a speech to the United Nations General Assembly:

> the Soviet Government deems it necessary to reach agreement with the United States Government to ban the placing into orbit of objects with nuclear weapons on board. We are aware that the United States Government also takes a positive view of the solution to this question. We assume also that an exchange of views on the banning of the placing into orbit of nuclear weapons will be continued between the Governments of the USSR and the U.S. on a bilateral basis.[30]

The result was the approval by the United States and the USSR of UN General Assembly Resolution 1884 (XVIII) (which had been proposed by the Mexican Government) which called on all states not to place in orbit or station in space 'nuclear weapons or any other kinds of weapons of mass destruction'.[31]

Despite the fact that both sides had therefore agreed to forgo the development of space weapons, the 'global rocket' (later known as

Fractional Orbital Bombardment System or FOBS) programme continued, although it clearly did not constitute a high priority for the
Soviet Union. The 'orbital rocket' made its first appearance in the
May Day parade of 1965, i.e. after Khrushchev's fall. This may
suggest that the FOBS programme was revived in line with the
general effort to redress the perceived imbalance in offensive missile
forces *vis-à-vis* the United States. The missile which provided the
booster for the system was designated SS-10 'Scrag' by Western
analysts. Since such a weapon was potentially in contravention of the
1963 UN Resolution, the United States discreetly raised the question
of this 'orbital rocket' with Soviet representatives. The Johnson
Administration was satisfied with the Soviet explanation that 'orbital' simply meant 'intercontinental'.[32]

The SS-10 was never deployed,[33] and instead the SS-9 was used as
the booster for FOBS. The system, which was tested on 17 September
and 2 November 1966, enabled a high megaton warhead to fly on a
depressed trajectory (thereby reducing its flight-time), or else extend
its flight-path to a partial orbit around the earth, passing over the
South Pole and approaching the United States from the South. In this
way it could outflank ground-based early warning radars and reduce
American early warning time. It was also a system, as Khrushchev
had boasted in the early Sixties, which (having unlimited range since
the warhead was projected into a low-earth orbit) could be targeted
on any point of the globe.

US Defence Secretary McNamara was not particularly perturbed by
FOBS, the existence of which was revealed by him on 3 November
1967. Although he acknowledged that it would reduce the warning
time for Strategic Air Command bomber bases (a purpose which may
have been uppermost in the designers of FOBS as the first plans were
made in the 1950s), it was clear to him that FOBS could not do
anything that could not also be done (and perhaps done better with
technical improvements) by ICBMs. When the United States
deployed early warning satellites in 1968, FOBS seems to have lost its
raison d'être. Presumably as a result of this, only 18 FOBS launchers
were ever deployed (at the space launch centre in Tyuratam).[34]

Anti-space defence

The possibility of putting satellites into orbit, either for purposes of
reconnaissance or for stationing weapons on them raised the question of how to defend against satellites at an early stage both for the

Soviet Union and the United States. In the United States the concern over Soviet satellite reconnaissance was not widespread and, in any event, was short-lived, whereas, as we have pointed out, US satellite reconnaissance was more central to Soviet concerns until 1963. The possibility of using satellites as platforms for nuclear weapons was an important motivating factor for the development of anti-satellite systems both in the US and the Soviet Union.

References to space weapons and anti-space defence began to appear in the Soviet military press in 1961/62 (of particular significance perhaps was the article by General Baryshev in September 1962).[35] As with the former, the references to the latter were far in advance of any operational systems. The first two editions of *Voennaia Strategiia* more cautiously described the problem of anti-space defence as being at the study stage; the second edition commented:

> It is still early to predict what line will be taken in the solution of this new problem, but as surely as an offensive weapon is created a defensive one will be too . . .[36]

The existence of a Soviet anti-space defence programme was announced by Defence Minister Marshal Malinovskii in February 1963 when he stated that Soviet armed forces had been given

> the extremely important rôle of combatting an aggressor's modern means of nuclear attack and his attempt to reconnoitre our country from the air and from space.[37]

In 1964, a new branch of the PVO was set up to deal with anti-space defence, called *Protivo Kosmicheskaia Oborona* (PKO).[38] However, the first experiments related to the development of an anti-satellite capability did not occur until 1967. The launch of Kosmos 185, which was first sent into a low orbit and was then manoeuvred into a high orbit, is generally interpreted as a test of manoeuvrability associated with the subsequent satellite interceptor programme.[39] On 27 October 1967, Kosmos 186 was launched by means of a Soyuz booster (i.e. SS-9 modification 3, also designated F-1 m by Charles Sheldon of the Congressional Research Service);[40] on 30 October it executed a rendezvous – a docking manoeuvre with Kosmos 188 launched on the same day of the manoeuvre. A similar experiment was carried out with Kosmos 212 and 213. The first attempt to test a full anti-satellite capability was probably the launch of Kosmos 217 on 24 April 1968. The orbital parameters announced in a Tass statement were similar to those of Kosmos 185, but it failed to achieve its predicted orbit and instead only debris in a considerably lower orbit was detected. It appears that the satellite exploded when it began to make orbital manoeuvres, indicating a possible fault in the 'm' stage of the F-1 booster.

Another attempt was made six months later. On 19 October 1968, Kosmos 248 was launched into an orbit similar to the one previously announced for Kosmos 217. The following day Kosmos 249 was put into an eccentric orbit that matched the orbital plane and apogee of Kosmos 248. The two satellites came extremely close to each other, when suddenly, after the flypast, Kosmos 249 exploded. This was obviously intended, since a TASS statement declared after the event that 'the scientific investigations under the programme have been carried out'.[41] A similar test was carried out in November 1968 when Kosmos 252 was sent up to pass close by Kosmos 248 and exploded. Again TASS confirmed that the objectives of the launch had been achieved. It appeared somewhat strange that the satellites which were sent up to intercept were also the ones that exploded, with no damage being done to the other satellite. The explosion appeared quite clearly to have been caused by a self-detonation mechanism (given that no perturbations occurred in the orbit of Kosmos 248 which would have been caused by, for example, missiles being directed at the other satellites) and Kosmos 248 was just a passive target. The conclusion drawn by Western analysts is that the Soviet Union was testing the ability to approach and inspect a target satellite in orbit. This would result in an anti-satellite capability, even though the destruction of target satellites as such was not actually tested.

There were no more ASAT tests for two years, although two tests could have been associated with the ASAT programme: Kosmos 291, launched on 6 August 1969, exhibited orbital characteristics similar to the other target satellites, and Kosmos 316 could be interpreted as another test of manoeuvrability.[42] There were three satellite interceptor tests in 1970. The target satellite, Kosmos 373, was launched on 20 October; the interceptors Kosmos 374 and 375 (launched three and ten days later respectively) self-destructed after the intercept in line with the previous tests.

The pattern of tests changed considerably from 1971 onwards. A target satellite (Kosmos 394) was launched from Pletsetsk (and not from Tyuratam as before) on a booster based on the SS-5 missile (with an additional stage) designated C-1 on 9 February 1971. On 25 February the interceptor, Kosmos 397, was launched from Tyuratam with an F-1 m booster. The interceptors were able to match the orbits and orbital velocities of their targets much more closely than before, thus allowing a much slower flyby, as would be required for not merely an ASAT, but also for a possible satellite inspection capability, such as might be required for arms control verification purposes.

By the end of the 1960s, therefore, the Soviet Union had acquired a limited anti-satellite capability that could threaten important American satellites.

The controversy about the military space programme in the Soviet Union

The Soviet leadership under Khrushchev was engaged, as we have seen in previous chapters, in fierce political struggles and ideological controversies spanning the whole range of issues involving foreign policy, military doctrine, civil-military relations, the Soviet force posture and thus the allocation of resources. It would have therefore been rather surprising if there had not been any controversy about the military space programme. An analysis of the Soviet military and scientific press from 1961 to 1963 carried out by Herbert L. Sawyer has indeed revealed unmistakable indications of such a controversy.[43] Sawyer has identified three distinct protagonists in this debate: the traditionalists, who were rather suspicious of Khrushchev's reliance on new and modern weapons (such as nuclear rockets) and were seeking to preserve the strength and rôle of more traditional armed forces and military doctrines; the modernists, consisting of technically well-educated officers who were seeking to develop the most modern technology (missiles, cybernetics and computers, space systems) for military purposes and, in the middle, Khrushchev himself who, on the one hand, was doing battle with the traditionalists but, on the other hand, was not willing to provide the kind of resources that the modernists were seeking to develop new technologies for military purposes.

First signs of impatience with the existing military space programme were revealed in an article by B. Aleksandrov which appeared in *Krasnaia Zvezda* on 23 July 1961 as part of the campaign against satellite reconnaissance. Aleksandrov did not merely attack the United States, however, but also clearly implied the need for Soviet countermeasures, saying that the Soviet Union could not ignore American satellite espionage.[44] A similar message was contained in a less propagandist article by V. Liutii, published in *Voenno-istoricheskii zhurnal* in August 1961. Liutii highlighted the

American military space programme, in particular the effort to develop an anti-satellite capability, as well as alleged American plans to station missiles on satellites, and stated very clearly that the Soviet Union could not ignore these developments and was therefore forced to divert some resources from the strategic rocket programme to the development of new kinds of weapons.[45]

Khrushchev was under a great deal of pressure from the military at the time and had already been forced to postpone some of the planned force reductions and increase defence expenditures. As a result, he was quite anxious to stem the demand for yet further increases of military expenditure in whatever area. In a speech broadcast on radio and television he proclaimed that

> The resources already allocated are sufficient. Our missile technology is progressing satisfactorily, therefore additional resources are not necessary. We are paying the necessary attention to other types of military technology also.[46]

Support for the Khrushchev line came in an article in *Krasnaia Zvezda* by Mikhail Makoveev which asserted that the progress of the Soviet space programme was satisfactory. More direct support (and clear opposition to the military space lobby) came in an economic journal in November 1961. N. Varvarev criticized the United States for placing too much importance on the military significance of outer space and, using an example from World War II where, in his view, narrow overemphasis by the German General Guderian of the importance of the tank resulted in defeat, he claimed that the Americans would suffer similar problems. The article clearly emphasized the high costs of space exploration and argued in favour of international cooperation to avoid duplication of efforts.[47] That this was very close to the Khrushchev line is evident from the emphasis on the resources necessary for the space programme, thus coinciding with Khrushchev's central preoccupation, and Khrushchev's statement after the flight of John Glenn in February 1962 in which he proposed Soviet–American cooperation in space, without this time the usual precondition of the acceptance of general and complete disarmament.[48]

As a result, the United States worked out a set of proposals for US–Soviet cooperation in space exploration which the Soviet Union received on 7 March. Khrushchev responded on 21 March with counter-proposals about cooperation with regard to geodetic, communications and meteorological satellites (which had also been part of the American proposal). While he now added the qualification that the degree of cooperation could only be *limited* until 'General and Complete Disarmament' had been realized, this still constituted a visible departure from the previous Soviet position. It is evident that those in the Soviet military establishment who favoured an increased military space effort were concerned about Khrushchev's remarks (despite the fact that there was no contradiction in principle between US–Soviet cooperation in space exploration and an increased Soviet military space effort).[49]

This is evident in the writings of one of the most ardent supporters of the military space programme, V. Larionov, author of an article which appeared in *Krasnaia Zvezda* on 18 March 1962, which described the American space programme as being primarily military in nature. In a further contribution on 21 March 1962, Larionov asserted the strategic significance of space without the usual attribution to American strategists. He furthermore emphasized that the Soviet Union could not ignore the 'feverish' American military efforts in space and directly called for the Soviet Union to pay continuous attention to the newest developments in military technology (i.e. the space programme).[50] H. L. Sawyer has commented:

> What does strike a discordant note . . . is that Larionov should choose just this moment to attack publicly the American program. It was hardly a propitious moment, when discussions on cooperation were being carried out at the highest possible level, to assert that the Americans were 'crawling out of their skins' in the interests of accelerating the arms race.[51]

In Sawyer's view, Larionov's influence can also be seen in the first edition of V. D. Sokolovskii's *Voennaia Strategiia* which was published in the summer of 1962. As Lawrence Freedman has pointed out:

> Despite the balanced judgement on Western weaponry elsewhere in the book, *Military Strategy* contained a detailed, but exaggerated and distorted study of United States military and space programmes, including a chart purporting to provide a 15-year time table for the 'launching of space weapons'. This attention suggests a desire to urge corresponding exertions on a sceptical Soviet Leadership.[52]

Indeed, it was asserted that the United States was planning a surprise nuclear attack on the Soviet Union from space, and therefore the study of the military uses of space would be imperative, since the imperialists must not be allowed to achieve superiority over the

Soviet Union in this area. Since Larionov was one of the editors of *Voennaia Strategiia* and had a particular interest in this subject, it is not unreasonable to suppose that he influenced the treatment of this particular subject.

Another two contributions by Larionov (with co-author Vaneev) appeared in *Krasnaia Zvezda* on 30 June and 3 July 1962. They were not principally concerned with the space programme as such, but were intended to more generally support what H. L. Sawyer has called the 'scientific-technological elite' in the military. The authors emphasized, in particular, the need for development in the field of cybernetics and computer technology, which they saw as vital for strategic military planning in general and military space operations in particular. Larionov and Vaneev left their readers in no doubt about the importance they attached to increased resources to advance military technology, particularly the development of computers and space technology. Further support for the need of new technology, particularly space technology, in response to American military preparations was expressed in an article in *Krasnaia Zvezda* by Rudenko.[53]

In reaction to Khrushchev's offer to President Kennedy in March 1962 to engage in cooperation with the United States in the exploration of space and the ensuing negotiations which began in May 1962 the Soviet military space lobby continued to warn against the American space programme, implying that the Americans could not be trusted to engage in such cooperation with the Soviet Union in good faith.[54] I. I. Anureev went as far as to say in *Kommunist Vooruzhennykh Sil* (August 1962)[55] that the United States had rejected Khrushchev's March offer, which was, of course, not true. He cited American high-altitude explosions as evidence for the militaristic objectives of the US space programme. Anureev asserted the superiority of Soviet space technology, including its 'invulnerable global rocket', but warned at the same time that

> We must take measures in order to increase our combat readiness, including the capability of defence against an attack from space.[56]

In the same month A. A. Blagonravov, who was the Soviet negotiator with the Americans following the March exchanges, asserted the new Khrushchev line in the magazine *Ogonek* which appeared in the same month as the Anureev article. Thus he declared:

> Although only general and complete disarmament will make unlimited cooperation in space possible, we do not reject partial measures now, if for no other reason than the costs involved.[57]

The military space lobby, however, was not convinced by assurances that the Soviet space programme was proceeding at the appropriate pace and was able to cope with any threat, nor did it want to accept the notion of cooperation with the United States, the purpose of which was to reduce the Soviet resources necessary for space exploration; thus the debate continued in 1963.[58] Meanwhile the negotiations between Blagonravov and Dryden proceeded, resulting in a Memorandum of Understanding which was accepted by Blagonravov on behalf of the Soviet Union on 1 August 1963.

Neither the MoU nor the discussions in the United Nations about the banning of weapons of mass destruction in space had any effect on the military space lobby. On 30 August 1963 the second edition of *Voennaia Strategiia* was signed to the press. It repeated the warnings of the first edition about American military space plans, and added new ones, the most notable being a report on an article by Walter Dornberger in *Aviation Week*, which had been published in September 1961 and advocated an intensified US military space programme, including the placing of hundreds of bombardment satellites in orbit in order to enable a surprise attack on the Soviet Union. The second edition also paid very considerable attention to the military potential of the moon.[59]

Another lengthy contribution emphasizing the military aspects of the American space programme by Aleksandrov appeared in the September 1964 issue of *Voennaia Mysl'*, just as the opposition forces against Khrushchev (including the military) were gathering momentum. The article was entitled 'Problems of Space Defense and Means of Solving Them' and summarized its argument in this way:

> One purpose of the extensive research and investigation of outer space for military purposes being conducted in the US is to launch a great number of various military devices into space. Presently the most important of these devices are all kinds of reconnaissance and navigation satellites. Work is also being conducted on different types of space communications systems which carry nuclear and rocket weapons, manned space ships, and space stations for military purposes.[60]

The article discussed at some length the United States inspector satellite system SAINT. Aleksandrov concluded that 'an effective space defense system has not yet been developed abroad',[61] but despite this conclusion his detailed analysis of American achievement and potential developments allows no other interpretation than that the United States was in the process of developing an ASAT system and that the Soviet Union would be required to respond in some way. For example:

> The use of lasers in antimissile and space defense is considered possible in principle, but not practical at the present level of technology. However, in spite of this pessimistic evaluation, intensive work is being done to perfect lasers with the intention of developing future ray weapons.[62]

Despite this critical evaluation of the US capabilities, he states:

> The use of laser weapons on the Saint-2 manned space interceptor and in anti-rocket and space defence space stations *is considered most probable*. [emphasis added][63]

The question of the institutional interests of the military space lobby is a rather intriguing one. There is no doubt that the PKO was part of the PVO and under the command of the Commander-in-Chief.[64] On the other hand, the space programme (including interceptor satellites) and thus the actual means of space defence, as well as the 'global rocket' were under the command of the Strategic Rocket Forces.[65] It is therefore not very clear what function the PKO may actually have had. Furthermore, some of the prominent military authors who were strong advocates of countermeasures against the American military space programme were at the same time also *opponents of ABM deployment*; among these are B. Aleksandrov, S. Shtemenko and I. Anureev. Aleksandrov was a vigorous proponent of anti-space defence, but also wrote a very incisive analysis of the US ABM systems which led him to the conclusion that the technical difficulties and possible countermeasures were such that the offence would have the advantage.[66] Shtemenko, an unashamed proponent of the applications of modern science to military programmes, rejected strategic defence, but strongly emphasized the decisive rôle of reconnaissance in a nuclear war, thus indirectly advocating aspects of a military space programme.[67] Anureev, as we have seen, called for countermeasures against the US military space programme.[68] At the same time, he appeared to be sceptical about the efficacy of strategic defence.[69] It seems therefore that at least some members of the military space lobby were, in their advocacy of anti-space defence, promoting the case of the strategic rocket forces rather than that of the PVO which became the service officially responsible for anti-space defence.

The question thus is raised: if the main components of the military space programme, including anti-satellite weapons, were in the hands of the SRF, what was the function of the PKO? One possible answer is that Galosh ABM (with a range of 322 km) may have been used in an anti-satellite capacity. If this supposition is correct, it was probably deployed at the Saryshagan ABM range in Central Asia. However, it is not known whether the Galosh was ever deployed for this purpose.[70] Furthermore, it is most likely that the PKO concerned itself with advanced weapons research, including lasers and, at a later stage, particle beam weapons.[71]

In attempting to assess the success or failure of the military space lobby, one approach used by Sawyer is an analysis of the frequency of space launches. This shows a slow-down of the programme in 1963 and an acceleration in 1964 and 1965. The number of Kosmos launches more than doubled in 1964 and doubled again in 1965. The Luna programme saw only one launch in the years 1960–63, but if the Elektron launches are correctly interpreted as part of the programme it also accelerated in 1964.

Less emphasis appears to have been given to the manned programme after 1963.[72] There has been some controversy in the West as to whether there was a 'race' to send a manned spaceship to the moon or not. As James Oberg has argued, the manned spaceflight programme appears to have been severely affected by the unexpected death of Korolev as the result of an operation in 1966. There are many indications that the Soviets were interested in a manned moon landing, but the programme experienced severe technical difficulties. Part of the evidence assembled by Oberg includes cosmonaut training programmes which appear to have a useful purpose only in connection with a moon landing; the attempted development of a large booster with a throwweight far in excess of that needed for other aspects of the space programme; orbital rendezvous procedures the only discernible purpose of which would be a moon flight using a large rocket assembled in a near-Earth orbit; and tests of equipment to support manned moon explorations. Various prominent Soviet cosmonauts claimed in the mid-Sixties that the Soviet Union would be first in landing a manned spacecraft on the moon. Also the *Encyclopedia of Spacecraft* published in 1969 asserted that the Zond space craft, widely used for unmanned missions, was in fact designed to carry a pilot.[73] The manned moon flight programmes apparently centred around a one-man version of the Soyuz-Zond system. Korolev's death appears to have seriously affected the schedule; tests in 1967 of the booster and spacecraft experienced grave difficulties. The first manned spaceflight after Korolev's death ended in disaster. Not until September 1968 was there a successful unmanned flight around the moon. Soviet hopes to be the first to land a man on the moon were finally defeated when a large booster exploded during a test in June 1969 (apparently followed by further tests ending in explosions).[74]

Thus Sawyer concluded about the success of the military space lobby:

> the lobby's efforts were not sufficient to forestall the decreased activity of 1963, but . . . its efforts in that year were rewarded with at least marginal success in 1964 and even more so in 1965, except for the absence of manned launches until 1967.[75]

Given the results of our analysis of the strategic missile programme, which shows that in March 1963 Krushchev's opponents who favoured increased resources for military industries and services (including the SRF) won at least a temporary victory with the recentralization of the defence industries, it is possible that the increased activity in the Soviet space programme was the result of the events of 1963.

The booster for FOBS and the ASAT programme did not become available until 1966, when the first SS-9 missiles were deployed. The SS-6, which was the basis of the booster for the preceding Kosmos flights, was most probably technically inadequate for the purposes of the ASAT programme. The technical difficulties of the Soyuz programme, as well as possibly the preoccupation with the moon programme, meant that the ASAT programme required another type of booster, the SS-9 being the most obvious candidate. In the wake of Khrushchev's ouster military programmes across the whole spectrum of the services received more resources, and the military space lobby was to some extent successful in obtaining support for the development of the 'global rocket' and an ASAT programme. However, as Stephen Meyer has pointed out:

> The ASAT programme seems to have been pursued at a leisurely pace, one that is not characteristic of the Soviet military's priority programmes.[76]

The same is true for the FOBS programme, in this case because new developments in radar technology and satellite observation obviated any military rationale for the system. In the case of the ASAT programme, the first priority of the SRF was to catch up with the American superiority in ICBM deployment, thus limiting the resources available.

The military space lobby certainly kept up the pressure after the fall of Khrushchev and continued to argue both for the development of Soviet military space systems (e.g. reconnaissance and navigation satellites) and for 'anti-space defence' as the ASAT development was soon going to enter the testing stage. Thus B. Aleksandrov and A. Yur'yev published an article on 'Air and Space Reconnaissance in Armed Conflict' in *Voennaia Mysl'* in October 1965 which was a detailed technical discussion of air and satellite reconnaissance methods *and their necessity*.[77] Col. A. Krasnov wrote in *Voennaia Mysl'* in April 1966

> At the present stage of development of space vehicles, combat with space reconnaissance of the enemy assumes the highest importance. The presence on satellites of various kinds of reconnaissance equipment enables the discovery of various objects, including those which have been concealed with artificial camouflage . . . therefore combat with reconnaissance space vehicles or neutralization of their operation already is not a problem for the distant future, but assumes pressing importance at the present time.[78]

In August 1966 Engr. Lt. Col. Yu. Subarov, writing on 'Communications Through Space: Opportunities and Prospects', advocated a global communications system by satellite.[79] The need for space defence was underlined in a contribution by Col. S. Vol'nov on 'Space and Electronics Warfare' published a month later:

> Foreign specialists think that because of the development of military space equipment, the necessity will arise to create defensive space systems, and specifically, interceptor satellites whose basic purpose will be to detect and destroy enemy military satellites that are in orbit. For these interceptor satellites, the possibility is under consideration to develop radio reconnaissance equipment which will ensure measurement of the operating frequency ranges and radiation power of radio-electronic equipment on board enemy satellites. The United States has been working on this project since 1960.[80]
>
> . . . Available data indicates that 'Ferret' satellites are being used to conduct radio and radio-technical reconnaissance and, specifically, for reconnaissance against air defence (PVO) radar stations, systems for guiding missile flights, and also to intercept and record information transmitted over radio communication links.[81]
>
> . . . US military specialists are coming to the conclusion that radio countermeasure means will be used in space in order to carry out the following fundamental radio warfare missions: neutralize ground and space facilities used by the enemy to destroy artificial satellites . . . neutralize interference by various ground radio-

electronic means . . . against facilities on board of artificial satellites and neutralize interference by military space installations against ground facilities . . .[82] According to the US estimate, highly favourable conditions exist for using active and passive interference in the 'space-surface' and 'space-space' links in the struggle against military space equipment.[83]

Despite all these arguments, the Soviet leadership did indicate some measure of interest in limiting the emerging arms race in space, a concern shared by the United States, by concluding the Outer Space Treaty which was agreed to in the UN General Assembly on 19 December 1966, signed by the Soviet Union and the United States on 27 January 1967 and acquired legal force on 10 October 1967. The Treaty was a further development of the UN General Assembly Resolutions 1884 (XVIII) and 1962 (XVIII). Article IV of the Treaty states:

> States Parties to the Treaty undertake not to place in orbit around the earth any objects carrying nuclear weapons or any other kinds of weapons of mass destruction, install such weapons on celestial bodies, or station such weapons in outer space in any other manner.
>
> The Moon and any other celestial bodies shall be used by all States Parties to the Treaty exclusively for peaceful purposes. The establishment of military bases, installations, and fortifications, the testing of any type of weapons and the conduct of military maneuvers on celestial bodies shall be forbidden . . .[84]

Article IX dealt with the issue of the interference with space activities of other nations:

> If a State Party to the Treaty has reason to believe that an activity or an experiment planned by it or its nationals in outer space . . . would cause potentially harmful interference with the activities of other State Parties in the peaceful exploration and use of outer space, it shall undertake appropriate international consultations before proceeding with any such activities or experiment. A State Party may also 'request consultation' if it believes that such an activity or experiment is about to happen.[85]

As Paul Stares has pointed out, it could be argued that

> the treaty represented nothing more than an agreement to desist from activities which neither side had any intention of doing anyway.[86]

This would assume that FOBS was not properly an 'orbital weapon' and thus not prohibited by the Treaty. More importantly, anti-satellite systems were not prohibited.[87] In the light of the Outer Space Treaty, one military commentator felt obliged to emphasize the continued military nature of the US space programme. Thus the planned Manned Orbital Laboratory was described by Engr. Col. A. Vasilev as

the basis for the conquest of outer space for military purposes.[88]

Vasilev described the virtues of manned space stations for reconnaissance, early warning, detection and identification of spacecraft as well as the service and repair of unmanned space craft. He also referred to military communications systems using satellites as being 'in the stage of experimentation and practical evaluation'.[89] The issue of ASAT was central to Vasilev's article:

Development of inspector satellites in the US is in the scientific research phase. The preparatory phase of the development of such satellites involves the systematic launching of Gemini-type space craft for the purpose of working on rendez-vous in outer space, approach and docking. During the current year the Americans completed five launchings of such space craft (Gemini -8, -9, -10, -11 and -12).[90]

Vasilev then went on to establish the military nature of the Gemini launches and concluded:

The examples provided show that the American command continues to devote great attention to the development of supporting space systems of armament.[91]

Then he contrasted the Soviet attitude to space exploration with that of the United States:

Up to this time some have attempted to look upon space as a sort of undeveloped jungle and hoped that the law of the jungle – might makes right – would prevail there. The [outer space] treaty forces the reflection of and review of such views. The achievements of science and the study of outer space should be used in the interests of peace.[92]

Despite this affirmation of the Outer Space Treaty, both the warnings about US intentions and the technical possibilities inherent in new developments make Vasilev's contribution into an indirect, but nonetheless forceful plea for the development of anti-space defence systems and manned space stations (the article is particularly eloquent about the virtues of the latter).

Conclusion

The development of space technology offered substantial political and military strategic benefits to the Soviet leadership. While

Khrushchev sought to exploit these as much as possible, at the same time the space programme also became a victim of the economic and budgetary pressures arising out of his domestic priorities; paradoxically, while on the one hand the existence of a Soviet military space programme was denied, on the other hand capabilities were claimed which existed only in the planning stage (if at all). As a result, some prominent military representatives advocated that increased resources should be made available to the military space effort; their efforts were only moderately successful (and also had to compete with the moon programme).

The attitude of the Soviet leadership to 'anti-space defence' appears to have been marked by considerable ambivalence. Initially, the need to deny the Americans a satellite reconnaissance capability appeared to play a central rôle. There was also a fear that the United States might develop and deploy space-based weapons. As these fears receded and satellite reconnaissance came to be accepted it was nonetheless clear that in war-time the capability to interfere with American reconnaissance and navigation satellites could be extremely useful. The result was the development and deployment of a relatively crude ASAT system of limited effectiveness against certain types of US satellites.[93]

The Strategic Defence Initiative announced by President Ronald Reagan in 1983 put the issue of the military use of space back on the international agenda. At the centre of this programme was research into 'exotic BMD technologies'. Particular attention was paid to Soviet research into lasers, particle beams, space platforms and anti-satellite systems. President Reagan's Assistant Secretary of Defence Richard Perle justified the need for the Strategic Defence Initiative on the basis of Soviet advances in these areas. There is no question that research and development of lasers is being intensively pursued in the Soviet Union, for a whole range of different applications. There has been some discussion of the use of laser systems for BMD purposes in the Soviet literature. The Department of Defence claimed in 1986 that two ground-based laser installations had been built at Saryshagan (a launching site for ASAT), possibly intended to provide a capability to blind the sensors of US satellites. The ground testing of a small hydrogen-fluoride high-energy laser and preparations to launch the device on air-borne platforms has been observed, but the only experimental air-craft was destroyed in a fire in 1986, resulting in a severe setback for the programme. The evidence available so far indicates, however, that the state of the art in Soviet laser technology is not in advance of that in the United States, and no systems have been developed with a definite capability for a rôle in strategic defence. The final area of concern is the military space programme. As a result of a dedicated application of resources over a long period of time, the Soviet Union has developed unmanned space-lifting capabilities and space platforms which far exceed operational US capabilities. The Soviets have also accumulated much experience in manned orbital space stations and keeping people in space for a long period of time. Nevertheless, it is clear that from a purely technological point of view, the United States is well able to match the Soviet Union, which relies on the adaptation of relatively crude technology. The Soviet space shuttle, for example, has yet to become fully operational. The Soviet ASAT system has remained at a level where only a small proportion of American satellites are within the range of this system (i.e. low-orbit satellites), and to destroy even all of those would take at least a week. American ASAT capabilities (miniature homing vehicles, i.e. missiles based on F-15 fighter aircraft), although they have not as yet been deployed, are potentially much more effective and capable.

The Soviet Union expressed grave concern about the Strategic Defence Initiative. It was concerned about becoming involved in a new technological arms race that would prove devastating to the Soviet economy and would seriously undermine its strategic position. Furthermore, the Strategic Defence Initiative was considered to be in breach of the ABM Treaty. If X-ray lasers were to be deployed in space with the purpose of destroying ballistic missiles in mid-course, as envisaged in one of the programmes pursued under SDI, it would also be in breach of the Outer Space Treaty because an X-ray laser has to be powered by a nuclear explosion, thus contravening the prohibition against stationing weapons of mass destruction in space. Under the Bush administration, the Strategic Defence Initiative has lost much of its political salience and continues as a research programme without any political commitment to future deployment. There is a good prospect that the existing agreements to limit the military use of space may remain intact for a considerable time in the future.

11   Conclusion

The 'military superiority model'

The understanding of Soviet strategic arms policy arrived at in this study differs significantly from that prevalent at the time. The dominant model during Khrushchev's time was the 'national leadership model', that of a totalitarian leadership in pursuit of global dominance. In this view, Soviet military policy was motivated by the purposeful pursuit of absolute military superiority. The analysis of Soviet foreign-policy objectives in the post-Stalin era substantially contradicts this model. The general foreign-policy line pursued by Khrushchev, the development of Soviet doctrine on the use of war as a political instrument and the actual strategic arms policy pursued are all fundamentally inconsistent with it. Some of the tactics of intimidation used by the Khrushchev leadership, however, imply the opposite since they could only succeed if the West believed the claims made for Soviet strategic power.

The inconsistencies in Soviet foreign policy were at least partly the result of substantial differences within the Soviet leadership about foreign-policy objectives. The general line of seeking détente and peaceful coexistence and shifting the East–West competition away from the military sphere was, despite some of Khrushchev's tactics, the dominant influence on his strategic arms policy. However, some of Khrushchev's opponents were closer to the Chinese leadership in their interpretation of Soviet ideology and its implications for foreign-policy objectives and therefore were pushing for a more active foreign policy and a more hostile stance towards the West supported by Soviet military power. These objectives were more in line with the 'military superiority model'. The conflict over foreign-policy objectives mirrored the more general conflicts over de-stalinization and domestic policies and the direction that the Soviet Union should take in social and economic policies.

The post-Khrushchev foreign policy also does not fit the 'military superiority model'. However, military power was the main basis for the Soviet claim to superpower status. A sustained build-up of Soviet strategic power is consistent with this observation. The decision to accept the codification of parity through arms control, however, was a political decision, based on a political rationale, which the military leadership has to be persuaded to accept. It was part of a larger framework of foreign policy which was directed at achieving a political accommodation with the United States and a partial resolution of the East–West confrontation in Europe based on the ratification of the territorial status quo.

The 'action-reaction model'

The second major model for explaining Soviet strategic arms policy is the 'action-reaction' model. It is evident that the US strategic threat constituted a major impetus to Soviet strategic arms policy. An initial response to the US bomber threat was the rebuilding and strengthening of Soviet air defences. Nonetheless, the Soviet response took unexpected forms. There was no sustained effort to match the United States in strategic bombers, even though this option was technologically less demanding than the pursuit of an ICBM capability and would therefore have fitted in more logically with the general pattern of Soviet responses to American weapons deployments.

While, as was pointed out in the introduction, there are some classic examples which illustrate the 'action-reaction' model, it is very limited in explaining strategic arms policy. The early Soviet ICBM programme was conceived prior to the existence of an American ICBM capability. Likewise initial Soviet efforts to develop ballistic missile defence precedes US ICBM testing and deployment. While most of the major programmes under discussion in this study were initiated before the nature of the US strategic missile threat had become clear, the pattern of US weapons deployment nevertheless provided an important stimulus. One such period was the announcement of the defence programme of the Kennedy Administration in 1961. It became clear that the United States was going to engage in a major deployment of ICBMs and SLBMs. In this environment, the Soviet military partially reasserted its influence on military doctrine, forcing Khrushchev to withdraw his manpower and budgetary cuts. However, the pressure on Khrushchev from the military was primarily with regard to non-nuclear forces. The need for the military to defend its institutional interests partially suppressed the 'action–reaction' process. There was no discernible military pressure for a crash programme to strengthen Soviet ICBM capabilities. The sustained Soviet effort to achieve strategic parity with the United States, however, can be traced back to this point, although Khrushchev in subsequent years provided a moderating influence, and the shape of the Soviet strategic arms build-up was not determined until some time later. The Cuban missile crisis provided a stimulus to Soviet strategic arms policy of a different nature. It demonstrated that bluff and interim solutions were no substitute for countering American strategic capabilities. Military reaction to the Cuban missile crisis reached its height in early 1963. This appears to have been another critical decision period in which the Soviet strategic arms build-up – in particular the SS-9 and SS-11 programmes – received renewed impetus, only to be moderated by Khrushchev as he regained greater political control within a month. Other political stimuli which fed into the Soviet decision-making process were US military involvements in the Dominican Republic and Vietnam, which raised defence expenditures beyond a tacit limit agreed with the Soviet leadership and served as an illustration for the exploitation of US strategic power in limited conflicts.

The development of MIRV technology is a frequently cited example of the 'action-reaction' phenomenon, often in connection with the Soviet acceptance of the ABM Treaty. Although it is true that Soviet military planners were acutely aware of the significance of MIRV technology, the technological difficulties with the Moscow ABM system and the need to constrain US BMD played an important part. It is significant, however, that the Soviets made no determined effort to have MIRV technology banned in SALT I, despite the danger that US capabilities would be vastly enhanced even with SALT as a result of MIRV. Evidently the Soviet Union did not want to accept the banning of MIRV testing which would have prevented it from developing the technology itself. This reflects an important principle, namely that the acceptance of strategic parity in the Soviet perspective did not imply the end of the arms race or strategic arms policy. While, contrary to the opinions of some Western analysts, the Soviets did not envisage an escape from the predicament of 'mutual assured destruction' by acquiring a credible first-strike capability, the continued modernization of its arsenal and the need to respond to developing Western capabilities was fully understood. The 'action-reaction model' is therefore more suited to the explanation of military policies after SALT I, because the continuation of an 'arms race' after the achievement and recognition of strategic parity does require an explanation.

The Soviet military-industrial complex

The study of Soviet defence industries is important, because the weapons-acquisition process itself has an impact on some of the details of strategic arms deployment. One important aspect is the development of ICBM technology and the technical constraints imposed upon military planning. A study of the development cycle will give clues about crucial decision periods. Another aspect was that of mission requirements. These obviously changed in the course of missile development, as the nature of the targets was not apparent when missile design began in the 1950s.

The interaction of institutions, as postulated in the 'military-industrial complex model', has an important rôle in the understanding of how decision-making on strategic arms policy in the Soviet Union took place. A loose coalition of politicians, industrial interests and the military attempted to change the direction of industrial policy in such a manner as to favour the requirements of increased military spending and weapons procurement, including greater efforts to build up strategic nuclear weapons. Under Khrushchev this tendency was largely suppressed, although it did at times manage to gain the upper hand, particularly in 1961 and early 1963. The influence of Khrushchev fits into the mirror image of 'interest group models' which can be described as the 'national leadership model'. It is evident that the 'one-sided' emphasis on strategic nuclear missiles was a preference imposed by Khrushchev on the military. The best characterization of the Khrushchev period would be that of an alternation of the influence of interest groups and the national leadership. The policies initiated in 1959/60 thus were clearly the result of the 'national leadership', whereas the interest groups and the military-industrial complex asserted itself in 1961 and late 1962/63. The period of mid-1963 until Khrushchev's ouster was again dominated by the 'national leadership', while Khrushchev's fall represents the final defeat of the 'national leadership'. The post-Khrushchev leadership could not impose its priorities in the same manner; consequently institutional disputes continued in the post-Khrushchev period, resulting eventually in a partial victory for the proponents of greater investment in the defence industries ratified by the national leadership. The 'military-industrial complex' model therefore contributes substantially to the explanation of the contradictions of strategic arms policy in the Khrushchev period and is seen as an important factor in promoting the arms build-up after the fall of Khrushchev. The boundaries defining the institutional alliances shifted, however, and the acceptance of détente and strategic arms limitation marks a partial defeat of the most militant elements in the Soviet leadership.

Implications

The policies of Stalin's successors must be understood as attempts to come to terms with the Stalinist heritage. Two central elements of this are the claim of the Soviet Union to world power status as leader of the socialist camp and the centrally planned domestic economy. The military confrontation between the Soviet Union and the United States was a consequence of the political conflict referred to as the Cold War. There was a consensus in the Soviet leadership that in order to maintain its position the Soviet Union had to embark on the process of building up an enormous military machine involving the development of weapons systems based on new technological principles, such as thermonuclear weapons, jet engines and ballistic missiles. Although the scientific, engineering and industrial potential existed in the Soviet Union to create such a massive military-industrial complex, nevertheless the centrally planned command economy was very inefficient and industrial production was not as advanced as in Western countries. The creation of its enormous military potential consumed resources on a large scale and exacerbated the existing very severe difficulties in the civilian economy. The Soviet Union therefore found itself at a considerable disadvantage by comparison with its principal competitor, the United States, in terms of the capability to compete both militarily and in the provision of consumer goods for its own population. To put it simply, the dilemma of having to choose between 'guns and butter' was a very real one for the Soviet Union, because the Soviet economy was unable to provide both in a satisfactory manner.

Those Western evaluations of Soviet policies that are based on the assumption that the primary explanations for Soviet behaviour are to be found in Soviet relations within the international system, be it in terms of a general Soviet strategy to achieve global domination, or the interaction between the main protagonists according to a principle of action and reaction, such as would be implied by certain realist interpretations of international relations, fail to explain the consequences of the attempts by Soviet leaders to resolve this fundamental dilemma. David Easton's systems theory of international relations defines political interactions, as distinct from other kinds of interaction, as being principally oriented toward the 'authoritative allocation of values for a society'.[1] The values of Soviet society are defined by Marxism-Leninism as interpreted by the Communist Party, which meant Stalin until March 1953. Malenkov's and Khrushchev's policies can be understood as an attempt to redefine the basic values of Soviet society in order to pursue policies that they believed would resolve the dilemmas that the Soviet Union faced. The internal political conflicts can be interpreted as arising from resistance to such a redefinition and adherence to values closer to those inherited from the Stalin period. The bureaucratic policy model finds application in so far as one can show that this resistance was in some measure due to vested interests which had established themselves on the basis of the old value system. The development of the doctrine of 'peaceful co-existence' and the emphasis on economic and political rather than military competition with the West can be seen as part of the system of values Khrushchev was advocating which affected both domestic and foreign policy. The rôle of the Soviet Union in the international system can be accommodated within this approach. Despite the official adherence to the goal of 'world socialism' in which the Soviet Union would play a leading rôle, there were evidently deep differences about how the Soviet Union should adapt to the international environment. During the period under discussion it was not self-evident that the Soviet Union was forced to follow one or the other; their distinction lay primarily in the consequences for Soviet society.

The dilemmas which Khrushchev faced are fundamentally the same as those that were confronted by the Gorbachev leadership. From a realist perspective, one could see the primary source of *New Thinking* in the adaptation to an environment where the Soviet Union is no longer capable of playing a global rôle and must reduce its international rôle. On the basis of a detailed study of the domestic context of Soviet foreign policy in the post-Stalin era, a very good case can be made for the primacy of domestic policy priorities. This is not to deny that the position of the Soviet Union in the international system and its interaction with other powers is significant, but it is rather to affirm that Soviet relations with other countries have to a great extent been formulated on the basis of their effect on the domestic political environment. Similarly, it can be argued that New Political Thinking is primarily a response to the systemic domestic crisis of the Soviet Union. The primary focus of Western analysis is usually the economic situation. There is no doubt that the Soviet economy has faced a dramatic decline which has reached crisis proportions. The steady decline in growth rates since the 1950s, the consistent underfulfilment of production targets, the under-mechanization and labour shortage, the extraordinary degree of wastage in the centrally planned economy, the lack of infrastructure and the poor performance of agriculture are all part of the dismal story. More important even than the economic problems, however, have been the sociological factors. The increasing alienation from the regime of all strata of the population, but in particular the middle class and intelligentsia, which find themselves stifled and deprived of economic and non-material rewards, is the dominant feature of a social and political system, as Seweryn Bialer would put it, 'in an advanced state of political breakdown'. The reassertion of national-ism in various parts of the Soviet Union, presenting, as some observers have put it, various centres of potentially violent conflict on its territory, is merely the most visible manifestation of the process of political and social disintegration. Gorbachev's pro-gramme of economic and political reform was ultimately not able to progress unless he could persuade the military to cooperate. Indeed, it was vital for him to gain control over the defence agenda, because military policy played a key part in his endeavours to create a new international climate and in the restructuring of the economy at home. The resolution of the internal and external political problems facing the Soviet leadership required a degree of institutional and organizational change so far-reaching that nothing less than a fundamental reinterpretation of the meaning of Marxism-Leninism could legitimize it. In its foreign-policy dimension the ideological shift involved the assumption that a genuine and enduring relaxa-tion of tension in East–West relations and a significant restraint in the arms competition is an important prerequisite for the success of the policy of domestic perestroika. The driving force behind the new thinking was the perception that in the long term the competition with the United States for military power on the basis of a weak economy is unsustainable. For Gorbachev, new political thinking had become the ideological handle to change the fundamental values of the Soviet political system and achieve the institutional change required by perestroika.[2]

Does this analysis have any implications for policy-makers? The most intriguing question which it poses is whether the arms race might in fact have been avoided, or halted at a very much lower level of strategic forces than those that are deployed today. It is clear that the answer hinges very much on the interpretation of Khrushchev, since in the post-Khrushchev period US ICBM deployments were already too far advanced. At first sight one would have to come to a rather pessimistic conclusion since although the shape of the arms build-up was largely decided after Khrushchev the major programmes were clearly initiated under Khrushchev and there is little doubt that some deployment of third-generation missiles would have taken place even if Khrushchev had remained in power. Some of the general directions of Khrushchev's policies do, however, suggest the possible existence of a period of opportunity. His commitment to reduce the rôle and power of the military, to redirect economic resources to agriculture and consumer-goods production, and to engage in a political process of relaxing tensions with the West while directing competition away from the military into the sphere of economic and political life all were in principle conducive to constraining the arms race. US strategic bomber capabilities (and their forward deployment), the deployment of American IRBMs in Europe and the strategic missile programme of the Kennedy Administration resulted in a substantial margin of US nuclear superiority and a threat scenario which gave a powerful impetus against the reliance on a minimum deterrent. It is important to stress that not all the information which formed the basis of this study was available to Western policymakers at the time. Nonetheless, it provides a good argument for the case that the nature of the strategic confrontation and East–West relations in general might have been very different if Soviet policy had been made in a different external environment.

Notes

1 Introduction

1. Among the standard literature on Soviet military policy during the Khrushchev period, the most substantial discussions on Soviet strategic arms policy can be found in the following works: Lincoln P. Bloomfield, Walter C. Clemens and Franklyn Griffiths, *Khrushchev and the Arms Race*, Cambridge: M.I.T. Press 1966; Thomas Wolfe, *Soviet Power and Europe 1945–1970*, Baltimore: Johns Hopkins Press 1970; Arnold L. Horelick and Myron Rush, *Strategic Power and Soviet Foreign Policy*, Chicago: University of Chicago Press 1966. Some recent studies, which include work on the Khrushchev period, are: David Holloway, *The Soviet Union and the Arms Race*, New Haven: Yale University Press 1984; Robbin F. Laird and Dale R. Herspring, *The Soviet Union and Strategic Arms*, Boulder: Westview Press 1984; Robert P. Berman and John C. Baker, *Soviet Strategic Forces*, Washington: The Brookings Institution 1982; Michael MccGwire, *Military Objectives in Soviet Foreign Policy*, Washington: The Brookings Institution 1987.
2. Horelick and Rush, *Strategic Power*.
3. Thomas Wolfe, *Soviet Strategy at the Crossroads*, London: Oxford University Press 1964.
4. Roman Kolkowicz, *The Soviet Military and the Communist Party*, Princeton: Princeton University Press 1967.
5. A good example is Joseph D. Douglass and Amoretta M. Hoeber, *Soviet Strategy for Nuclear War*, Stanford: Hoover Institution Press 1979.
6. A. A. Gromyko, *Pamiatnoe*, Moscow: Izdatel'stvo politicheskoi literatury 1988 (2 vols.).
7. V. S. Golubvich, *Marshal Malinovskii*, Kiev: Izdatel'stvo politicheskoi literatury Ukrainy 1988. Only the last chapter is concerned with Malinovskii's post-war career.
8. Fyodor Burlatsky, 'Why Khrushchev Failed', *Encounter*, vol. 70, no. 5, May 1988.
9. Based on conversations with Prof. David Holloway, Stanford University in April 1989.
10. Mikhail Gorbachev, *Perestroika i novoe myshlenie*, Moscow: Politizdat

1987; for an exposition of the *new thinking* and its relation to Soviet ideology, see Stephen Shenfield, *The Nuclear Predicament*, London: Routledge, Kegan & Paul for the Royal Institute of International Affairs 1987.

11. A good example is the article by V. V. Zhurkin, S. A. Karaganov, A. V. Kortunov, 'O razumnoi dostatochnosti', *S Sh A*, no. 12, 1987, pp. 11–21, where the entire history of arms control in the post-war era is interpreted as a historical evolution towards 'reasonable sufficiency'. This could be described as the replacement of the old ideological concepts in the framework of which world events were explained, whether such explanations were adequate or not, by the new concepts.

12. Carl A. Linden, *Khrushchev and the Soviet Leadership: 1957–1964*, Baltimore: Johns Hopkins Press 1966.

13. Michel Tatu, *Power in the Kremlin*, London: Collins 1969.

14. Robert M. Slusser, *The Berlin Crisis of 1961*, Baltimore: Johns Hopkins University Press 1973.

15. Bloomfield, Clemens and Griffiths, *Arms Race*; Edgar Bottome, *The Balance of Terror: A Guide to the Arms Race*, Boston: Beacon Press 1971; Hedley Bull, *The Control of the Arms Race*, London: Weidenfeld & Nicolson 1961; Colin Gray, *The Soviet-American Arms Race*, Farnborough: Saxon House 1976; Holloway, *Soviet Union*; Herbert York, *Race to Oblivion: A Participant's View of the Arms Race*, New York: Simon & Schuster 1971; Thomas C. Schelling, *The Strategy of Conflict*, New York: Oxford University Press 1960; Thomas C. Schelling, 'Managing the Arms Race', in Henry A. Kissinger (ed.), *Problems of National Strategy*, New York: Praeger 1965, pp. 361–75.

16. Lawrence Freedman, *US Intelligence and the Soviet Strategic Threat*, London: Macmillan 1986, p. 67; for a detailed analysis of the 'bomber gap', see John Prados, *The Soviet Estimate*, Princeton: Princeton University Press 1986, chapter 4. The 'asymmetric nature' of the Soviet response to US bomber superiority in the late Fifties is used by Zhurkin, Karaganov, Kortunov, *S Sh A*, pp. 16 f. as an example of the advantages of not following action-reaction type arms-racing behaviour. Their analysis is flawed in that it overestimates the significance of this for the achievement of strategic nuclear parity with the United States.

17. Freedman, *US Intelligence*, p. 101.

18. Daniel Yergin, *Shattered Peace*, Harmondsworth: Penguin 1977, p. 11.

19. See Douglass and Hoeber, *Soviet Strategy*; also Richard Pipes, 'Why the Soviet Union Thinks It Could Fight and Win a Nuclear War', *Commentary*, vol. 64, no. 1, July 1977, pp. 21–34; Richard Pipes, 'Soviet Strategic Doctrine: Another View', *Strategic Review*, Fall 1982, pp. 52–57.

20. Graham T. Allison, *Essence of Decision*, Boston: Little Brown and Company 1971, p. 33.

21. Allison, *Essence*, p. 35.

22. A good example is the reaction of some Western defence experts to the INF agreement. See Gerhard Wettig, 'Comments on the Paper of Lawrence Freedman', in Murray Feshbach (ed.), *National Security Issues of the USSR*,

Dordrecht: Martinus Nijhoff Publishers 1987, pp. 91–97; Wettig evidently could not make up his mind whether the Soviets would prefer an INF
agreement or not. In either case it would be based, in his view, on hostile
intentions. Another example is Lothar Rühl, formerly Head of the
Planning Staff of the Ministry of Defence in Bonn. His recently published
book on INF constitutes a detailed argument on why the SS-20
deployment was particularly threatening, and why it represented a
particularly offensive action by the Soviet Union. In television interviews since the INF agreement, Rühl has stated that all the targets
previously covered by SS-20 missiles can be covered by other Soviet
missiles and that militarily the INF agreement does not affect Soviet
military options. See Lothar Rühl, *Mittelstreckenwaffen in Europa: Ihre
Bedeutung in Strategie, Rüstungskontrolle und Bündnispolitik*, Baden-Baden:
Nomos Verlagsgesellschaft 1987.

23. Allison, *Essence*; for critical analysis see Lawrence Freedman, 'Logic,
    Politics and the Foreign Policy Process: A Critique of the Bureaucratic
    Politics Model', *International Affairs*, vol. 52, no. 3, July 1976, pp. 434–49;
    Nicholas J. Wheeler, *The Roles Played by the British Chiefs of Staff
    Committee in the Evolution of Britain's Nuclear Weapon Planning and
    Policy-Making, 1945–55*, Ph.D. Thesis, University of Southampton 1988,
    chapter 1; James E. Dougherty and Robert L. Pfaltzgraff, Jr, *Contending
    Theories of International Relations*, New York: Harper & Row 1981,
    pp. 468–510.
24. The caveat of Allison's critics must be accepted in the sense that the
    institutional interests often embodied different views about Soviet
    national security interests and the best means to safeguard them; see
    Freedman, *International Affairs*.
25. Robert S. McNamara, 'The Dynamics of Nuclear Strategy', *Department of
    State Bulletin*, LVII (9) October 1967, quoted from Lawrence Freedman,
    The Evolution of Nuclear Strategy, London: Macmillan 1981, p. 254.
26. Freedman, *Evolution*, p. 254.
27. Michael MccGwire, 'The Rationale for the Development of Soviet Sea
    Power', in John Baylis and Gerald Segal (eds.), *Soviet Strategy*, London:
    Croom Helm 1981, pp. 210–54, particularly p. 216.
28. Desmond Ball, *Politics and Force Levels*, Los Angeles: University of
    California Press 1980.
29. For a detailed analysis of the institutional conflicts which produced the
    decision to deploy a 'thin' area defence against a Chinese ICBM threat,
    see John Newhouse, *Cold Dawn: The Story of Salt*, New York: Holt,
    Rinehart & Winston 1973, pp. 150–57; see also Freedman, *Evolution*,
    p. 336.
30. For an exposition of this point of view, see Alva Myrdal, *The Game of
    Disarmament: How the United States and Russia Run the Arms Race*,
    Manchester: Manchester University Press 1977.
31. For explanations of Soviet strategic arms policy based on the particular
    interests and ideas of the national leader, see Matthew Gallagher and

Karl Spielmann, *Soviet Decision-Making for Defense*, New York: Praeger 1972. See also Stephen M. Meyer, 'What Do We Know and What Do We Understand', in Jiri Valenta and William Potter (eds.), *Soviet Decisionmaking for National Security*, London: Allen & Unwin 1984, pp. 255-97.

32. See, for example, Wolfe, *Soviet Strategy*; Wolfe, *Soviet Power and Europe*; Holloway, *Soviet Union*; Raymond L. Garthoff, *Soviet Military Policy*, London: Faber & Faber 1966; Roman Kolkowicz, *Communist Party*; John Erickson, *Soviet Military Power*, London: RUSI 1971; a notable exception is Bloomfield et al., *Arms Race*, but they recognize Kozlov's rôle only in 1963; the rôle of Kozlov and his allies in Soviet defence and foreign policymaking is analysed in Linden, *Soviet Leadership*; Slusser, *Berlin Crisis*; Tatu, *Power*.

2 Decision-making in the Soviet Union

1. Note that the description of Soviet decision-making institutions is given entirely in the past tense, regardless of the connection to present-day institutions, given the fundamental changes which have occurred recently. The attempt by the anti-party group to oust Khrushchev is interesting from the constitutional point of view, since Khrushchev saved himself by insisting on the entire Central Committee being allowed to vote on this issue and in this unique case the CC outvoted the Party Presidium. (Khrushchev's demand was supported, of course, by Marshal Zhukov and his forces.) Cf. Roy A. Medevedev and Zhores Medvedev, *Khrushchev*, Oxford: Oxford University Press 1977, pp. 76–79. The Government was of course strongly represented in the Politburo.

2. Arthur J. Alexander, *Decision-Making in Soviet Weapons Procurement*, Adelphi Paper no. 147/48, London: IISS 1978, p. 6.

3. Alexander, *Decision-Making* p. 8. Alexander discusses favourably the argument by Jerry F. Hough that by allowing the specialized government complexes autonomy in policy and by giving nearly all these groups incremental budget increases each year, Brezhnev avoids the anger that Khrushchev's 'voluntarist' and 'subjective' intervention provoked in Party and government circles. Although the Party formally retains control of the defining of goals, and has even strengthened its hold on the various control mechanisms, the trend towards 'scientific' decision-making based on specialized knowledge has informally shifted policy formation to the specialized complexes. (Alexander, *Decision-Making*, p. 10).

4. Nikita S. Khrushchev, *Khrushchev Remembers*, edited and translated by Strobe Talbott, vol. 2, London: André Deutsch 1974, pp. 35–37. Khrushchev's involvement in the Soviet space programme has also been described in Leonid Vladimirov, *The Russian Space Bluff*, New York: Dial Press 1971.

5. Iu. P. Petrov, *Partiinoe stroitel'stvo v Sovetskoi Armii i Flote, 1918–1961*,

Moscow: Voenizdat 1961, p. 462. Quoted in English translation from Alexander, *Decision-Making*, p. 15.

6. See Holloway, *Soviet Union and the Arms Race*, p. 109, Raymond Garthoff claims that the Defence Council has existed at least since 1964. See Raymond L. Garthoff, 'The Soviet Military and SALT', in Jiri Valenta and William Potter (eds.), *Soviet Decisionmaking for National Security*, London: George Allen & Unwin 1984, pp. 136–61, p. 144.

7. Edward L. Warner, *The Military in Contemporary Soviet Politics: An Institutional Analysis*, New York: Praeger 1977, chapter 2; Alexander, *Decision-Making*, p. 15; Garthoff, 'Soviet Military and SALT', pp. 144 f.

8. Holloway, *Soviet Union*, p. 110.

9. Alexander, *Decision-Making*, p. 15.

10. Ibid., pp. 15 f.

11. Ibid.

12. Alexander, *Decision-Making*, p. 11. For a detailed description of the CC Secretariat see Jerry F. Hough and Merle Fainsod, *How the Soviet Union Is Governed*, Cambridge: Harvard University Press 1979, chapter 11.

13. Hough and Fainsod, *How the Soviet Union is Governed*, p. 411.

14. This is the view of Alexander, *Decision-Making*, p. 11 f. An elaborate but entirely hypothetical discussion of how differences of view between the various ministries might arise is given in Karl F. Spielmann, 'Defense Industrialists in the USSR', *Problems of Communism*, Sept.–Oct. 1976, pp. 52–69.

The difficulty with such an analysis of institutional interests lies in the basic lack of real hard information. It is rare that one can make even educated guesses, as Spielmann's elaborate hypothetical schemes vividly demonstrate. For a discussion of this problem see Stephen M. Meyer, 'What Do We Know and What Do We Understand', in Valenta and Potter, *Soviet Decisionmaking*, pp. 255–97.

15. Kolkowicz, *Communist Party*; Malcolm Mackintosh, 'The Soviet Military – Influence on Foreign Policy', *Problems of Communism*, Sept.– Oct. 1976, pp. 1–12; William E. Odom, 'The Party Connection', *Problems of Communism*, Sept.–Oct. 1976, pp. 12–16.

16. Alexander, *Decision-Making*, p. 17.

17. Ellen Jones, 'Defense R&D Policymaking in the USSR', in Valenta and Potter, *Soviet Decisionmaking*, pp. 116–35, p. 125.

18. Alexander, *Decision-Making*, p. 18, speculates that Marshal Iakubovskii, Chief of the Warsaw Pact Forces, was too senior and powerful to be relegated to third place. About the historical rôle of the General Staff and the gradual enhancement of its position since the mid-Sixties, see Thomas Wolfe, 'The Soviet General Staff', *Problems of Communism*, Jan.–Feb. 1979, pp. 51–54; Kenneth Currie, 'Soviet General Staff's New Role', *Problems of Communism*, March–April 1984, pp. 32–40.

19. Viktor G. Kulikov, *Pravda*, 13 November 1974; translation in Currie, 'General Staff's New Role', p. 35.

20. Currie, 'General Staff's New Role', p. 32.

21. Currie, 'General Staff's New Role', p. 31; Garthoff, 'Soviet Military and SALT'.
22. Alexander, *Decision-Making*, p. 18.
23. Alexander O. Ghebhardt, *Implications for Organizational Bureaucratic Policy Models for Soviet ABM Decisionmaking*, unpublished Ph.D. Dissertation, Political Science, Columbia University, 1975, p. 66.
24. The five services of the armed forces are the Strategic Rocket Forces, the National Air Defence Troops (PVO-S), the Air Forces (VVS), the Navy and the Ground Forces.
25. Alexander, *Decision-Making*, p. 19; it was not rare for inferior products to be rejected.
26. David Holloway, 'Technology and Political Decision in Soviet Armaments Policy', *Journal of Peace Research*, vol. 11, no. 4, 1974, pp. 257–80; p. 260
27. Hannes Adomeit and Mikhail Agursky, *The Soviet Military-Industrial Complex and Its Internal Mechanism*, mimeographed, p. 13; Alexander, *Decision-Making*, p. 22; Spielmann, 'Defense Industrialists', p. 54; Vernon V. Aspaturian, 'The Soviet Military-Industrial Complex – Does It Exist?', *Journal of International Affairs*, vol. 26, no. 1, 1972, pp. 1–28; pp. 14 f.
28. Brezhnev at the 24th CPSU Congress, *Pravda*, 31 March 1971, p. 1, quoted in translation from Adomeit and Agursky, *Soviet Military-Industrial Complex*, p. 14.
29. Ibid.
30. Ibid., p. 15.
31. Ibid., p. 16.
32. Ibid., p. 23.
33. *Khrushchev Remembers*, vol. 2, p. 42.
34. The system would, for example inhibit the formulation of proposals which could upset the institutional balance of power, e.g. by inducing a shift of resources from one sector to another. In the 1960s, it was realized that the existing system was inhibiting technological innovation and much emphasis was put on finding ways of developing methods of organization and weapons systems which are *new in principle*. Cf. Alexander, *Decision-Making*, p. 38.

3 Strategic nuclear power and foreign-policy objectives

1. Yergin, *Shattered Peace*, p. 11.
2. Gar Alperovitz, *Atomic Diplomacy*, Harmondsworth: Penguin 1985.
3. Yergin, *Shattered Peace*.
4. Raymond L. Garthoff, *Soviet Military Policy*, London: Faber & Faber 1966, p. 11.
5. Alois Rilkin, *Weltrevolution oder Koexistenz?*, Zürich: SAD 1969, p. 23.
6. Rilkin, *Weltrevolution*, pp. 23–25; Freedman, *Evolution* pp. 148 ff.; Frederic S. Burin, 'The Communist Doctrine of the Inevitability of War', *American Political Science Review*, vol. 57, no. 2, June 1963, pp. 334–54.

7. Rilkin, *Weltrevolution*, p. 24; V. Pechorkin, 'The Problem of Preventing War', *International Affairs* (Moscow), no. 9, September 1960, pp. 3–6.
8. Pechorkin, 'Preventing War', p. 4.
9. Quoted from Garthoff, *Soviet Military Policy*, p. 74; for an earlier exposition of Lenin's views, see Vladimir I. Lenin, *The Military Programme of the Proletarian Revolution*. Collected Works, vol. 23, London: Lawrence & Wishart, 1964, pp. 677–93; for discussion see Margot Light, *The Soviet Theory of International Relations*, Brighton: Wheatsheaf 1988.
10. Rilkin, *Weltrevolution*, cites A. A. Gromyko, *Die Friedliche Koexistenz*, East Berlin 1963, pp. 33 f. and p. 266. See also the references in note 6.
11. Quoted from Garthoff, *Soviet Military Policy*, p. 75.
12. Quoted in translation from Garthoff, *Soviet Military Policy*, p. 69; original *Izvestiia* editorial, 22 January 1929.
13. E.A. Korovin (ed.), *Mezhdunarodnoe pravo*, Moscow: Izdatelstsvo Iuridicheskoi Literatury, cited from Margot Light, *The Soviet Theory of International Relations*, Brighton: Wheatsheaf Books 1988, p. 216.
14. M. Gus, 'General'naia liniia sovetskoi vneshnei politiki', *Zvezda* (Leningrad), no. 11, November 1953, pp. 106–25. The significance of this article was first pointed out by Herbert S. Dinerstein, *War and the Soviet Union*, New York: Praeger 1962.
15. V. Kruzhkov, 'V. I. Lenin – korifei revoliutsionoi nauki', *Kommunist*, no. 1, 1954, pp. 15–33; see pp. 21 and 22.
16. *Krasnaia Zvezda*, 6 January 1954, cited in Dinerstein, *War and the Soviet Union*, p. 68.
17. Colonel A. Piatkin, 'Some Questions of the Marxist-Leninist Science of War', *Voennaia Mysl'*, no. 3, March 1954, p. 16; cited in Dinerstein, *War and the Soviet Union*, pp. 68 f.
18. *Kommunist* (Erevan), 12 March 1954; cited in Dinerstein, *War and the Soviet Union*, pp. 71 f.
19. Mikoian, cited from Dinerstein, ibid.
20. Dinerstein, *War and the Soviet Union*, pp. 76 f.
21. See Light, *Soviet Theory of International Relations*, pp. 28 f.
22. See Rilkin, *Weltrevolution*, p. 27.
23. Garthoff, *War and the Soviet Union*, p. 96; Linden, *Soviet Leadership: 1957–1964*, pp. 213–15; Robert M. Slusser, *Berlin Crisis*, and the numerous references therein.
24. Pechorkin, 'Preventing War', p. 4.
25. Quoted from David Floyd, *Mao Against Khrushchev*, London: Pall Mall Press 1964, pp. 94 f.; original article in *Kommunist*, no. 13, 1960.
26. N. S. Chruschtschow, *Für dauerhaften Frieden und Koexistenz*, Berlin (East) 1959, pp. 124 f.
27. See Rilkin, *Weltrevolution*, p. 42 and sources cited therein.
28. Rilkin, *Weltrevolution*, p. 67.
29. D. A. Volkogonov et al. (eds.), *Voina i Armiia*, Moscow: Voenizdat 1977,

pp. 354 f.; for discussion see Holloway, *Soviet Union*, New Haven: Yale University Press 1984, pp. 81 f.

30. V. D. Sokolovskiy (ed.), *Soviet Military Strategy*, English language edition edited by Harriet Fast Scott, New York: Crane, Russal & Company Inc. 1968, p. 173.

31. Quoted from Sokolovskiy, *Soviet Military Strategy*, p. 173.

32. Sokolovskiy, *Soviet Military Strategy*, p. 15.

33. N. Talensky, 'The Late War: Some Reflections', *International Affairs* (Moscow), no. 5, May 1965, pp. 12–18; p. 15.

34. Affirmation of the continued validity of the Clausewitz dictum was affirmed, for example, in a book review in *Voenno-Istoricheskii Zhurnal*, no. 4, April 1972, pp. 105–10, and an article on 'Theory, Politics, Ideology on the Essence of War', *Krasnaia Zvezda*, 24 January 1967. See Robert L. Arnett, 'Soviet Attitudes Towards Nuclear War: Do They Really Think They Can Win?', in Baylis and Segal, *Soviet Strategy*, pp. 55–74.

35. For expressions of this viewpoint see Richard Pipes, 'Why the Soviet Union Thinks It Could Fight and Win a Nuclear War', *Commentary*, vol. 64, no. 1, July 1977, pp. 21–34; Richard Pipes, 'Soviet Strategic Doctrine: Another View', *Strategic Review*, Fall 1982, pp. 52–57; Douglass and Hoeber, *Soviet Strategy*; Jean-Francois Revel, *How Democracies Perish*, London: Weidenfeld & Nicolson 1985.

36. Pipes, 'Why the Soviet Union Thinks', pp. 30, 34.

37. E. I. Rybkin, 'O sushchnosti mirovoi raketno-iadernoi voiny', *Kommunist vooruzhennykh sil*, no. 17, September 1965, pp. 50–56; this quotation in translation from William R. Kintner and Harriet Fast Scott, *The Nuclear Revolution in Soviet Military Affairs*, Norman: University of Oklahoma Press 1968, p. 109. Rybkin reiterated this view in a later article in which he berated the well-known journalist A. Bovin for holding views similar to those of Talenskii. While reaffirming the connection between politics and war in the nuclear age, he also stated, 'the most important conclusion of the Communist Party set forth in its programme, that such a [nuclear] war "cannot and must not serve as a means of solving international disputes". Thus, we are not speaking of the "abolition" of the class political essence of war with the use of nuclear weapons, but of the introduction of a new element into the essence of war, which makes such a war an unfeasible means of policy.' E. Rybkin, Leninskaia Kontseptsiia voiny i sovremennost', *Kommunist Vooruzhennykh Sil*, no. 20, October 1973, pp. 21–28.

38. *War and the Army*, p. 28. This point is also made in an article by Colonel T. Kondratkov, 'War as Continuation of Policy', *Soviet Military Review*, February 1974, pp. 19–21, where he states, 'the deep interconnection between politics and war has not lost its significance in the "nuclear age", it has merely assumed a more complex form . . . Considering the essence of a possible nuclear war, Marxist-Leninists do not confuse it with another question, close to but not identical with it – concerning the admissibility or inadmissibility of nuclear war as a means of politics.

They resolutely condemn this war, considering it the greatest crime against humanity' (pp. 20 f.).

39. Quoted from J. Malcolm Mackintosh, *Strategy and Tactics of Soviet Foreign Policy*, London: Oxford University Press 1962, p. 188.

40. Mackintosh, *Strategy and Tactics*, p. 190.

41. Freedman, *US Intelligence*, p. 66; Prados, *The Soviet Estimate*, Princeton: Princeton University Press 1986, chapter 4; Horelick and Rush, *Strategic Power*, pp. 27–28.

42. *Pravda*, 11 October 1957, quoted in translation from Horelick and Rush, *Strategic Power*, p. 43.

43. *Pravda*, 29 November 1957; for discussion see Horelick and Rush, *Strategic Power*, pp. 44 f.

44. *Pravda*, 5 February 1959, quoted in translation from Horelick and Rush, *Strategic Power*, p. 51.

45. *Pravda*, 18 November 1959, p. 1.

46. Freedman, *US Intelligence*, p. 71.

47. Horelick and Rush, *Strategic Power*, p. 82.

48. N. S. Khrushchev, *Stroitel'stvo kommunizma v SSSR i razvitie sal'skogo khoziaistva*, vol. V. Moscow: Gospolitizdat 1963, p. 128; quoted in translation from Horelick and Rush, *Strategic Power*, pp. 81. f.

49. This speech is discussed in some detail in chapter 8.

50. Alfred L. Monks and Kenyon N. Griffin, 'Soviet Strategic Claims, 1964–1979', *Orbis*, vol. 16, no. 2, Summer 1972, pp. 520–44.

51. N. Talensky, 'On the Character of Modern Warfare', *International Affairs* (Moscow), no. 10, October 1960, pp. 23–27.

52. 'Vystuplenie N. S. Khrushcheva na sobranii v Avstro-sovetskom obshchestve', *Pravda*, 4 July 1960, pp. 1–3; p. 2.

53. *Pravda*, 15 January 1960, quoted in translation from Horelick and Rush, *Strategic Power*, p. 78.

54. Horelick and Rush, *Strategic Power*, pp. 79 f.

55. *Pravda*, 13 March 1954.

56. For a more detailed analysis see Hans Wassmund, *Kontinuität im Wandel*, Köln: Böhlau-Verlag 1974, pp. 75 ff.

57. Dinerstein, *War and the Soviet Union*, p. 147.

58. For an analysis of the Hungarian Crisis in the context of Soviet policy towards Eastern Europe, see Jörg K. Hoensch, *Sowjetische Osteuropa Politik 1945–1975*, Düsseldorf: Droste Verlag 1977, chapter 5. For the wider political context, see Wassmund, *Wandel*, chapter 3.

59. Quoted in translation from Angela Stent, *From Embargo to Ostpolitik*, Cambridge: Cambridge University Press 1981, p. 71.

60. Nikita S. Khrushchev, *Khrushchev Remembers*, edited and translated by Strobe Talbott, vol. 1, London: André Deutsch 1974, p. 453.

61. Linden, *Soviet Leadership*, p. 82; Wassmund, *Wandel*, p. 110; Stent, *Embargo to Ostpolitik*.

62. John Dornberg, *Brezhnev: The Masks of Power*, London: André Deutsch 1974, p. 149.

63. Slusser, *Berlin Crisis*, p. 214.
64. The reason for the fall of the U-2 plane has never been satisfactorily determined. Khrushchev obviously was eager to create the impression that the SAM 2 downed the plane at high altitude. The good condition of the remains of the U-2 that were displayed in Gorky Park encourage some doubt on this issue. The evidence is reviewed in Michael R. Beschloss, *Mayday*, London: Faber & Faber 1986, pp. 355–82.
65. Dornberg, *Brezhnev*, p. 160.
66. A. McGehee Harvey, *Life*, 18 December 1970. Prof. Carl A. Linden drew this article to the author's attention.
67. *Khrushchev Remembers*, vol. 2, pp. 449–61. This account is strangely ignored by Michael Beschloss when he speculates on the reason why Khrushchev untypically used a typed statement, even though he is aware of the memoirs. See Beschloss, *Mayday*, p. 276.
68. For a more detailed analysis of the political context, see Tatu, *Power in the Kremlin*, pp. 53–122.
69. See *Khrushchev Remembers*, vol. 2, p. 450. Khrushchev claims that the inclusion of Malinovksii in the delegation was his idea. For alternative hypotheses, see Beschloss, *Mayday*, p. 275; Stent, *Embargo to Ostpolitik*, p. 74; Jack M. Schick, *The Berlin Crisis, 1958–1962*, Philadelphia: University of Pennsylvania Press 1971, pp. 108–26. Schick takes the view that Malinovskii forced the break-up of the summit.
70. Quoted in translation from Beschloss, *Mayday*, p. 305.
71. Beschloss, *Mayday*, p. 305.
72. Evidence for military pressure to this effect is provided by Linden, *Soviet Leadership*, p. 115. Slusser, *Berlin Crisis*, chapter 7, shows that the decision to abandon the moratorium was taken in Khrushchev's absence.
73. See *Khrushchev Remembers*, vol. 1, p. 454.
74. See *Khrushchev Remembers*, vol. 1, p. 455.
75. Horelick and Rush, *Strategic Power*, p. 124.
76. Slusser, *Berlin Crisis*, p. 95.
77. Slusser, *Berlin Crisis*, chapter 5.
78. Interview 23 June 1959, in *Life*, 8 July 1959; quoted from Horelick and Rush, *Strategic Power*, p. 120.
79. See Slusser, *Berlin Crisis*, p. 165.
80. D. C. Watt, *Survey of International Affairs 1961*, London: Oxford University Press 1965, p. 256; for discussion see Slusser, *Berlin Crisis*, p. 168.
81. Slusser, *Berlin Crisis*, p. 178.
82. Linden, *Soviet Leadership*, p. 152.
83. Raymond L. Garthoff, *Reflections on the Cuban Missile Crisis*, Washington: Brookings Institution 1987, p. 12.
84. For a careful statement of this view, which is not necessarily in conflict with the point made here, see Freedman, *Evolution*, p. 361.
85. See the account in Elie Abel, *The Missile Crisis*, New York: Lippincott 1966.

86. Garthoff, *Cuban Missile Crisis*, pp. 59 f. For a collection of official Soviet statements during and after the Cuban Missile Crisis, see Ronald R. Pope (ed.), *Soviet Views on the Cuban Missile Crisis*, Washington: University Press of America 1982.

87. See, for example, Horlick and Rush, *Strategic Power*, p. 180; Mike Bowker and Phil Williams, *Superpower Detente: A Reappraisal*, London: SAGE Publications for the RIIA 1988, pp. 21–22; Edward Crankshaw, *Khrushchev*, London: Collins 1966, pp. 280–81.

88. For more detailed analysis, see Robin Ranger, *Arms and Politics 1958–1978*, Toronto: Macmillan 1979. For a Soviet study on nuclear disarmament from the post-war period to SALT, see A. Y. Yefremov, *Nuclear Disarmament*, Moscow: Progress Publishers 1979.

89. Arkady N. Shevchenko, *Breaking with Moscow*, London: Jonathan Cape 1985, pp. 101 f.

90. For more detail, see Bloomfield, Clemens and Griffiths, *Arms Race*, p. 186.

91. For more detailed analysis, see Linden, *Soviet Leadership*, pp. 174–201 and Tatu, *Power*, chapters 4–6.

92. The misunderstanding consisted in the belief of the Soviet negotiator V. V. Kuznetsov that the American negotiator, Ambassador Arthur Dean, had stated that two to four on-site inspections per year on Soviet territory would be sufficient. In the light of this, the American insistence on a minimum of eight to ten such inspections made it appear that the United States was going back on its word. For more detailed discussion see Glenn T. Seaborg, *Kennedy, Khrushchev and the Test Ban*, Berkeley: University of California Press 1981, pp. 178–81.

93. Seaborg, *Test Ban*, p. 185.

94. Bloomfeld, Clemens and Griffiths, *Arms Race*, p. 188.

95. It is important to recognize that the hot-line agreement was not a consequence of the shift in Soviet foreign policy initiated by Khrushchev in April 1963; rather the hot-line agreement can be seen as a direct consequence of the Cuban Missile Crisis. The Soviet Union had indicated an interest in a direct phone link in July 1962; at that time President Kennedy opposed the idea. The technical communication problems during the crisis convinced him that a direct teletype link would be desirable. Soviet agreement to the American proposal came on 5 April 1963, a time when Khrushchev's influence was at a very low point. See Tatu, *Power*, pp. 336–40 and Seaborg, *Test Ban*, pp. 206 f.

96. From the *Report of the Central Committee of the CPSU to the Twenty-Third Congress*, Moscow: Novosti Press Agency Publishing House 1966, quoted from Jonathan Steele, *The Limits of Soviet Power*, Harmondsworth: Penguin 1984, p. 23.

97. Raymond L. Garthoff, 'The Soviet Military and SALT', pp. 154–84.

98. Holloway, *Soviet Union*, pp. 86–90. For a statement of the official Soviet position on collective security in Europe, see Y. Nalin and A.

Nikolayev, *The Soviet Union and European Security*, Moscow: Progress Publishers 1973.

99. Hans J. Morgenthau, *Politics Among Nations*, New York: Knopf 1967; Robert Gilpin, *War and Change in World Politics*, Cambridge: Cambridge University Press 1980; J. David Singer, *A General Systems Taxonomy for Political Science*, New York: General Learning Press 1971; David Easton, *A Framework for Political Analysis*, Englewood Cliff: Prentice-Hall 1965; Ekkehardt Krippendorf, 'Ist Außenpolitik Außenpolitik?', *Politische Vierteljahres-Schrift*, vol. 4, 1963. pp. 243–65; Peter Gourevitch, 'The Second Image Reversed: The International Sources of Domestic Policies', *International Organization*, vol. 32, no. 4, Autumn 1978, pp. 881–911; Graham T. Allison, *Essence of Decision*, Boston: Little Brown and Company 1971. For discussion see Thomas Risse-Kappen, *Die Krise der Sicherheitspolitik*, München: Christian Kaiser Verlag 1988, Section A.
100. For a more detailed analysis of the rôle of 'power' in realist thinking, see Richard Little, 'Structuralism and Neo-Realism', in Margot Light and A. J. R. Groom (eds.), *International Relations. A Handbook of Current Theory*, London: Pinter 1985, pp. 74–89.
101. Easton, *Political Analysis*, p. 50.
102. Marie Mendras, 'Policy Outside and Politics Inside', in Archie Brown (ed.), *Political Leadership in the Soviet Union*, Macmillan: London 1989, pp. 127–62, especially pp. 135–47.

4 Soviet military doctrine and policy

1. Army General S. Ivanov, 'Soviet Military Doctrine and Strategy', *Voennaia Mysl'*, no. 5, May 1969, pp. 40–51; this quotation from pp. 44 f.
2. I. S. Baz', S. N. Kozlov, P. A. Sidorov and M. V. Smirnov, *O Sovetskoi Voennoi Nauke*, Moscow: Voenizdat 1964, p. 379.
3. Baz' et al., *O Sovetskoi Voennoi Nauke*, p. 383.
4. Ivanov, 'Soviet Military Doctrine', p. 46.
5. Ivanov, 'Soviet Military Doctrine', p. 40.
6. Baz' et al., *O Sovetskoi Voennoi Nauke*, p. 385.
7. Andrei A. Grechko, *Vooruzhenyie Sily Sovetskogo Gosudarstva*, Moscow: Voenizdat 1975, pp. 340–41; Harriet Fast Scott and William F. Scott (eds.), *The Soviet Art of War*, Boulder: Westview Press 1982, p. 5.
8. S. N. Kozlov (ed.), *Spravochnik Ofitsera*, Moscow: Voenizdat 1971, p. 68. Quoted in English translation from Scott and Scott, *Soviet Art of War*, p. 7.
9. V.D. Sokolovskiy, *Soviet Military Strategy*, pp. 7 f. (This quotation appeared first in the 2nd edition.).
10. Grechko, *Vooruzhenyie Sily*, p. 335; quoted in English translation from Scott and Scott, *Soviet Art of War*, p. 8.
11. Sokolovskiy, *Soviet Military Strategy*, pp. 8 f. (This quotation first appeared in the 2nd edition.).
12. General Colonel Nikolai A. Lomov, 'Vliianie sovetskoi voennoi dokriny

na razvitie voennogo iskusstva', *Kommunist Vooruzhennykh Sil*, no. 21, November 1965, pp. 15–24; this quotation from pp. 16 f.

13. See Kozlov, *Spravochnik Ofitsera*; Baz' et al., *O Sovetskoi Voennoi Nauke*, pp. 210–14; see also Scott and Scott, *The Soviet Art of War*, p. 11.

14. See Raymond L. Garthoff, *The Soviet Image of Future War*, Washington: Public Affairs Press 1959, p. 24; original source: I. V. Stalin, *O Veliko Otechestvennoi voine Sovetskogo Soiuza*, Moscow: Gospolitzdat 1947, pp. 43–44.

15. H. S. Dinerstein, *War and the Soviet Union*, New York: Frederick A. Praeger 1962, p. 6.

16. Quoted from Garthoff, *Soviet Image*, p. 25.

17. Maj. Gen. Nikolai Talenskii, 'On the Question of the Character of the Laws of Military Science', *Voennaia Mysl'*, no. 9, September 1953, pp. 31–38; an abbreviated translation of this article has been reprinted in Scott and Scott, *Soviet Art of War*, Boulder: Westview Press 1982, pp. 127–31; see also Talenskii, 'The Permanently Operating Factors of War', *Bol'shaia Sovetskaia Entsiklopediia*, 2nd edition, vol. 34, 1955, p. 257.

18. Laird and Herspring, *Strategic Arms*, Boulder: Westview Press 1984, p. 11; the erroneous view that the military doctrine expounded in the Special Collection' was essentially the same as that announced by Khrushchev in 1960 is found in, for example, David Holloway, *Soviet Union*, p. 38 and the Editor's introduction to Harriet Fast Scott's edition of V.D. Sokolovskiy, *Soviet Military Strategy*, p. xx.

19. Talenskii, quoted from Scott and Scott, *Soviet Art of War*, p. 128.

20. Talenskii, quoted from Scott and Scott, *Soviet Art of War*, p. 129.

21. Dinerstein, *War and the Soviet Union*, p. 46.

22. Talenskii, quoted from Scott and Scott, *Soviet Art of War*, p. 130.

23. Scott and Scott, *Soviet Art of War*, p. 124.

24. 'On the Question of the Character of the Laws of Military Science', *Voennaia Mysl'*, no. 11, November 1954, pp. 33 f.; quoted from Dinerstein, *War and the Soviet Union*, p. 59.

25. Dinerstein, *War and the Soviet Union*, p. 61.

26. Ibid., p. 60.

27. Ibid., p. 61.

28. S. Kozlov, 'The Development of Soviet Military Science After World War II', *Voennaia Mysl'*, no. 2, February 1964, pp. 28–49, p. 37.

29. Quoted from Garthoff, *Soviet Image*, p. 61.

30. Colonel I. Nenakhov, *Voennaia Mysl'*, no. 10, October 1953; quoted in English translation from Garthoff, *Soviet Image*, p. 61.

31. Nenakhov, quoted from Garthoff, *Soviet Image*, p. 61.

32. Garthoff, *Soviet Image*, p. 62.

33. Army General V. G. Kulikov (ed.), *Akademiia General'nogo Shtaba*, Moscow: Voenizdat 1976, p. 129; Holloway, *Soviet Union*, p. 36.

34. P. A. Rotmistrov, 'O roli vnezapnosti v sovremennoi voine', *Voennaia Mysl'*, no. 2, February 1955, pp. 14–25; quoted in English translation from Garthoff, *Soviet Image*, pp. 64 f. On the question of Zhukov's rôle

in the publication of this article, see William F. Scott and Harriet Fast Scott, *The Armed Forces of the USSR*, Boulder: Westview 1979, p. 40.

35. Quoted from Dinerstein, *War and the Soviet Union*, p. 187. Lawrence Freedman has commented on Rotmistrov's assertion that the Soviet army and navy possesses everything to implement a strategy of pre-emption. 'These statements were only true if the author was thinking of counter-value rather than counter-force nuclear attacks, or of attacks involving conventional forces.' See Freedman, *Evolution*, London: Macmillan 1981, p. 150. As will be argued later, Rotmistrov's and like assertions by Soviet military writers were not true, but were merely designed to provide a reassurance that the Soviet military was able to defend the Soviet Union adequately (no matter what the real objective situation was).

36. Editorial, 'On Some Questions of Military Science', *Voennaia Mysl'*, no. 3, March 1955; quoted from Dinerstein, *War and the Soviet Union*, p. 189.

37. Editorial, 'The World-Historical Victory of the Soviet People', *Voennaia Mysl'*, no. 5, May 1955; quoted in English translation from Dinerstein, *War and the Soviet Union*, p. 190.

38. Lieutenant General B. S. Shatilov, 'An Important and Noble Theme', *Literaturnaia Gazeta*, 28 May, 1955; quoted in English translation from Dinerstein, *War and the Soviet Union*, p. 191.

39. Berman and Baker, *Soviet Strategic Forces*, p. 41.

40. *Pravda*, 13 March 1954, p. 2.

41. N. S. Khrushchev, *Report of the Central Committee to the 20th Congress of the CPSU*, London: Soviet News Booklet 1956, p. 28; quoted from Holloway, *Soviet Union*, p. 32.

42. Scott and Scott, *Armed Forces*, Boulder: Westview Press 1979, p. 41.

43. Scott and Scott, Ibid.; Douglass and Hoeber, *Soviet Strategy*, Stanford: Hoover Institution Press 1979, p. 4.

44. Rotmistrov, 'O roli vnezapnosti', p. 74; as noted above some of these assertions may have been made with the purpose of providing reassurance that the Soviet Armed Forces were capable of defending the Soviet Union adequately.

45. P. A. Rotmistrov, 'Surprise in the History of Wars', *Voennyi Vestnik*, no. 11, November 1955, p. 94; quoted in English translation from Garthoff, *Soviet Image*, p. 74.

46. Garthoff, *Soviet Image*, p. 32.

47. Colonel V. Gorynin, Colonel P. Derevianko, Colonel V. Seregin, 'Inadequacies in a Book on an Important Subject', *Krasnaia Zvezda*, 19 February 1957, quoted in English translation from Dinerstein, *War and the Soviet Union*, p. 52.

48. Ibid.

49. Colonel N. Baz', 'V. I. Lenin on the Basic Factors Determining the Course and Outcome of War', *Krasnaia Zvezda*, 19 February 1957, quoted in English translation from Dinerstein, *War and the Soviet Union*, p. 53.

50. Garthoff, *Soviet Image*, pp. 32–36.

51. Quoted in English translation from Garthoff, *Soviet Image*, p. 36.

52. Quoted in translation from Curt Gasteyger (ed.), *Strategie und Abrüstungspolitik der Sowjetunion*, Frankfurt: Alfred Metzner Verlag 1964, where Lomov's article is reprinted in its entirety, p. 109. Original source: N. Lomov, 'O sovetskoi voennoi doktrine', *Kommunist Vooruzhennykh Sil*, no. 10, 1962, pp. 11–21.
53. Quoted from Garthoff, *Soviet Image*, p. 37.
54. Colonel A. Piatkin, *Voennaia Mysl'*, no. 3, March 1954, p. 21; quoted in English translation from Garthoff, *Soviet Image*, p. 38.
55. Major General G. Pokrovskii in *Marksizm leninizm o voine, armii i voennoi nauke*; quoted in English translation from Garthoff, *Soviet Image*, p. 38.
56. Marshal G. Zhukov, *Krasnaia Zvezda*, 4 February 1957; quoted in English translation from Garthoff, *Soviet Image*, p. 43.
57. Marshal of the Army Pavel A. Rotmistrov, 'On Modern Soviet Military Art and Its Characteristic Features', *Voennaia Mysl'*, no. 2, February 1958; reprinted in abbreviated form in English translation in Scott and Scott, *Soviet Art of War*, pp. 137–45; this quotation from pp. 138 f.
58. Rotmistrov, in Scott and Scott, *Soviet Art of War*, p. 140.
59. Scott and Scott, *Soviet Art of War*, p. 141.
60. Ibid., p. 142.
61. Ibid., p. 143.
62. Ibid., p. 144.
63. Ibid., p. 145.
64. Ivanov, 'Soviet Military Doctrine', p. 44.
65. Personal interview with Notra Trulock at the Rand Corporation, Santa Monica, May 1988 and Michael MccGwire, Washington D.C., May 1988.
66. *Pravda*, 15 January 1960, pp. 1–5.
67. We have used the English edition of Sokolovskii (where the editor's name is spelt Sokolovskiy) edited by Harriet Fast Scott, in which those passages which only appeared in the second or third editions have been marked. We shall indicate in the notes which edition particular quotations have been taken from.
68. Sokolovskiy, *Soviet Strategy* (1st edition), p. 209.
69. Ibid., p. 201.
70. Ibid., p. 193.
71. Ibid., p. 204.
72. Ibid., p. 202.
73. Lomov, in Gasteyger, *Strategie*, p. 114.
74. Major General I. Zav'ialov, Major General V. Kolechitskii, Major General M. Cherednichenko and Colonel V. Larionov in *Krasnaia Zvezda*, 2 November 1963; this article was a response to Western comments on the Sokolovskii volume and explicitly and strongly denied that the Soviet Union was thinking in terms of preemption. For comments, see Wolfe, *Soviet Strategy*, p. 66. Marshal Malinovskii in his 1962 pamphlet accuses (with direct reference to the Cuban missile

crisis) the United States of harbouring plans for 'preventive war' and contrasts this with Soviet position of retaliation. See Marshal Malinovskii, *Bditel'no Stoiat' na Strazhe Mira*, Moscow: Voenizdat 1962, Introduction.

75. Quoted in translation from Gasteyger, *Strategie*, p. 132; for comment see Edward L. Warner, *The Military in Soviet Politics*, p. 151.
76. Sokolovskiy, *Soviet Strategy* (1st edition), p. 210.
77. Wolfe, *Soviet Strategy*, p. 67.
78. Sokolovskiy, *Soviet Strategy* (1st edition), p. 210.
79. Malinovskii, *Bditelno*, p. 23. (Quoted from an unpublished English translation available at the Soviet Studies Centre, Royal Military Academy, Sandhurst.)
80. Wolfe, *Soviet Strategy*, p. 67.
81. For an analysis of Soviet risk-taking and crisis behaviour, see Garthoff, *Soviet Military Policy*, p. 192; Hannes Adomeit, 'Soviet Risk Taking and Crisis Behaviour', in Baylis and Segal, *Soviet Strategy*, pp. 185–209.
82. On early warning systems and warning times, see Curtis Peebles, *Battle for Space*, Poole: Blandford Press 1983, p. 37; on restraints on launching times due to the fuel systems, see Berman and Baker, *Soviet Strategic Forces*, p. 86; this quotation from Berman and Baker, p. 88. The difficulties described by Berman and Baker were also referred to in the third edition of the Sokolovskii volume, '*The chief factor* hampering an earlier attainment of high combat readiness in previous types of rockets was the time required for it to attain momentum and go over to the gyroscope system of missile guidance. The limited operational capability of the gyroscopes did not allow keeping them engaged during the entire time the missile was on combat alert. Sokolovskiy, *Soviet Strategy*, p. 79 (3rd edition) [Emphasis added]. For more technical details, see Donald MacKenzie, 'The Soviet Union and Strategic Missile Guidance', *International Security*, vol. 13, no. 2, Fall 1988, pp. 5–54. MacKenzie's research indicates that a primary reason for the delay in the development of solid fuel missiles by the Soviet Union resides in the higher requirements imposed on the guidance systems by the uneven burning of solid rocket fuel.
83. Sokolovskiy, *Soviet Strategy* (1st edition), p. 209.
84. MccGwire, *Military Objectives*, p. 483.
85. Erickson, *Soviet Military Power*, pp. 44 f.; for the discussion in the United States about the 'first strike' potential of the SS-9 see Freedman, *US Intelligence*, chapters 6–8.
86. Berman and Baker, *Soviet Strategic Forces*, pp. 116–24.
87. Marshal V. D. Sokolovskii and General Major M. I. Cherednichenko, 'O sovremennoi voennoi strategii', *Kommunist Vooruzhennykh Sil*, no. 7, April 1966, pp. 59–66; p. 65.
88 Sokolovskiy, *Soviet Strategy*, (3rd edition), p. 280.
89. V. I. Varfolomeyev and M. I. Kopytov, *Design and Testing of Ballistic Missiles – USSR*, translated by the Joint Publications Research Service,

JPRS–51810, Washington, D.C.: 1970. See Douglass and Hoeber, *Soviet Strategy*, pp. 48 f. for a discussion of this material.

90. Holloway, *Soviet Union*, p. 57; Raymond L. Garthoff, 'Mutual Deterrence and Strategic Arms Limitation in Soviet Policy', *International Security*, Summer 1978, pp. 114–33.

91. Marshal of the Soviet Union N. Krylov, 'The Nuclear-Missile Shield of the Soviet State', *Voennaia Mysl'*, no. 11, November 1967, pp. 13–21, p. 18.

92. MccGwire, *Military Objectives*, p. 27.

93. General Colonel Nikolai A. Lomov, 'The Influence of Soviet Military Doctrine on the Development of Military Art', reprinted in translation in Kintner and Fast Scott, *Nuclear Revolution*, pp. 154–69; originally from *Kommunist Vooruzhennykh Sil*, no. 21, November 1965.

94. Marshal P. Rotmistrov, *Krasnaia Zvezda*, 29 December 1964.

95. Lt. Col. E. I. Rybkin, 'A Critique of the Book *On Peace and War*', *Voennaia Mysl'*, no. 7, July 1966, pp. 78–85, p. 83.

96. MccGwire, *Military Objectives*, p. 28.

97. Kai Uwe von Hassel, Organizing Western Defense: The Search for Consensus', *Foreign Affairs*, vol. 43, no. 2, January 1965. pp. 209–16; Denis Healey, 'NATO, Britain and Soviet Military Policy', *Orbis*, vol. 13, no. 1, Spring 1969, pp. 48–58.

98. Sokolovskiy, *Soviet Military Strategy*, p. 71. (This quotation appeared only in the third edition.). Although the Soviet military was aware the Americans wanted to raise the nuclear threshold as much as possible, they did not see in the early Seventies any serious efforts to provide the military means to implement such a strategy on the part of NATO and therefore had to conclude that the British/German version of 'flexible response' was the more likely one to be valid in the event of war. This point was made to the author in a discussion with Notra Trulock. Trulock has learnt from lecture materials obtained from the General Staff Academy that in the mid-Seventies Soviet officers were taught to expect that nuclear weapons would first be used by NATO troops in the event of war in Central Europe. An exposition of the Voroshilov lecture materials was given by Trulock at a seminar at the RAND Corporation, Santa Monica, on 25 May 1988. One of the Voroshilov lectures was recently published in English: I. E. Shavrov, 'Principles and Content of Military Strategy', *Journal of Soviet Military Studies*, vol. 1, no. 1, April 1988, pp. 29–53.

99. Yuri Nepodayev, 'On the Nuclear Threshold in NATO Strategy', *Voennaia Mysl'*, no. 6, June 1966, pp. 77–79.

100. Major General N. Vasendin and Colonel N. Kuznetsov, 'Modern Warfare and Surprise Attack', *Voennaia Mysl'*, no. 6, 1968, 69, p. 45.

101. General Major Vasiliy I. Zemskov, 'Characteristic Features of Modern War and Possible Methods of Conducting Them', *Voennaia Mysl'*, no. 7, 1969; excerpts reprinted in translation in Scott and Scott, *The Soviet Art of War*, pp. 211–15; this quotation from p. 211.

102. See Nepodayev, 'Nuclear Threshold'.
103. Krylov, 'Missile Shield'.
104. General Major S. V. Shtrik, 'The Encirclement and Destruction of the Enemy During Combat Operations Not Involving the Use of Nuclear Weapons', *Voennaia Mysl'*, no. 1, 1968; excerpts reprinted in translation in Scott and Scott, *Soviet Art of War*, pp. 202–5.
105. Chief of the General Staff Matvey V. Zakharov, 'The Development of Soviet Military Science', from M. V. Zakharov (ed.), *50 Let Vooruzhennykh Sil SSSR*, pp. 522–25; excerpts reprinted in translation in Scott and Scott, *Soviet Art of War*, pp. 178–81.
106. Ivanov, 'Soviet Military Doctrine', p. 48.
107. Ivanov.
108. Ibid.
109. Ibid., p. 49.
110. Ivanov, Ibid.
111. Ibid.
112. For an authoritative, more traditional formulation of military doctrine see A. A. Grechko, 'On Guard Over Peace and Socialism', *Kommunist*, February 1970, quoted in translation from Scott and Scott, *Soviet Art of War*, p. 208. See also the sources cited in notes 12–16. For a spirited defence of the nuclear revolution in Soviet military affairs, see Lt. Colonel V. Bondarenko, 'Sovremennaia revoliutsiia v voennom dele i boevaia gotovnost' Vooruzhennykh Sil', *Kommunist Vooruzhennykh Sil*, no. 24, December 1968, pp. 22–29.
113. Talenskii, in Scott and Scott, *Soviet Art of War*, p. 127.
114. Captain V. Kulakov, 'Problems of Military-Technical Superiority', *Voennaia Mysl'*, no. 1, January 1964, pp. 1–14.
115. *Pravda*, 28 February 1963, quoted in English translation from Wolfe, *Soviet Strategy*, p. 80.
116. Malinovskii in Gasteyger, *Strategie*, p. 130.
117. Kulakov, Ibid.
118. Sokolovskiy, *Soviet Strategy*, p. 211 (1st edition); the issue of war as an instrument of policy (or as the 'continuation of politics') will be discussed in another chapter.
119. Sokolovskiy, *Soviet Strategy*, p. 209 (2nd edition).
120. E. I. Rybkin, 'O sushchnosti', p. 56.
121. Colonel V. Bondarenko, 'Voenno-tekhnicheskoe prevokhodstvo – vazhneishii faktor nadezhnoi oborony strany', *Kommunist Vooruzhennykh Sil*, no. 17, September 1966, pp. 7–14.
122. Bondarenko, 'Voenno-tekhnicheskoe prevokhodstvo', p. 6.
123. Bondarenko's other publications indicate that he is a defender of the 'nuclear revolution in military affairs' and the Khrushchevian tendency to substitute nuclear firepower of quantitative superiority; whether this is a reference to MIRVs is not clear. See Lt. Colonel V. Bondarenko, 'Sovremennaia revoliutsiia v voennom dele i boevaia gotovnost' Vooruzhennykh Sil', *Kommunist Vooruzhennykh Sil*, no. 24, December 1968, pp. 22–9.

124. See Pipes, 'Why the Soviet Union Thinks', Pipes, 'Soviet Strategic Doctrine'; Douglass and Hoeber, *Soviet Strategy*.

125. It is clearly stated in Rybkin, 'O sushchnosti', for example, that all efforts should be made not to permit the unleashing of war. The formulation in Ivanov, 'Soviet Military Doctrine', p. 48, 'a new world war, if the aggressors succeed in unleashing it', is quite standard in Soviet military writings.

126. One exception to this rule is cited by Garthoff. At a meeting in Yalta in 1974 in the context of SALT negotiations Brezhnev and Grechko (supported by other military experts) presented the Americans (including Henry Kissinger) with a picture of overwhelming US superiority. See Raymond L. Garthoff, 'The Soviet Military and SALT', p. 179.

127. MccGwire, *Military Objectives*, p. 51.

128. MccGwire, *Military Objectives*.

129. For evidence that the SS-11 was not accurate enough to have a significant hard target kill capability, see Berman and Baker, *Soviet Strategic Forces*, p. 124; for the debate in the United States about the SS-11 as a first-strike weapon, see Freedman, *US Intelligence*, chapter 9.

130. Zemskov, 'Characteristic Features of Modern War', p. 213.

131. Thomas W. Wolfe, *The SALT Experience*, Cambridge, MA: Ballinger Publishing Corporation 1979, pp. 131–33 for a discussion of this point.

132. Berman and Baker, *Soviet Strategic Forces*, p. 138.

133. The attitude of the military towards SALT is discussed in Chapter 5 on Party-military relations.

134. Thomas Wolfe cites a Soviet radio commentator from a round-table discussion on Radio Moscow on 28 June 1972: '[Senator Jackson and others] claim that the Moscow accords are an advantage to the Soviet Union, that they supposedly place American in an unequal situation . . . [because] the Soviet Union is allowed a few more land-based ICBMs and missile-launching submarines. [The SALT accords] . . . do not give one or the other state military superiority. In setting the number of ICBMs and submarines, they take into careful consideration the geographic position of both countries and some factors . . . Senator Jackson . . . forgets one very important detail – namely life itself has forced Washington to recognize the military parity of the Soviet Union.' Wolfe, *The SALT Experience*.

    Wolfe states that 'In none of the voluminous Soviet commentary on SALT I was there any suggestion that the agreements were tilted in Soviet favour' (p. 19).

135. Garthoff, 'Soviet Military and SALT', p. 175.

136. Krylov, *Missile Shield*.

137. Ivanov, 'Soviet Military Doctrine'.

138. Zemskov, 'Characteristic Features of Modern War'.

139. On disagreements about SALT, see chapter 5 on Party–military relations.

140. Lieutenant Colonel T. Kondratkov, 'Limited War of Imperialist Aggression', *Kommunist Vooruzhennykh Sil*, no. 8, April 1969, pp. 24–31; this

quotation from unpublished English translation available at the Soviet Studies Centre, Royal Military Academy, Sandhurst, p. 2.

141. See William T. Lee and Richard F. Staar, *Soviet Military Policy Since World War II*, Stanford: Hoover Institution Press 1986, p. 63; MccGwire, *Military Objectives*, pp. 359 f. for more detail. A detailed examination of these assertions goes beyond the scope of the present study.

5 Party–military relations and strategic arms policy

1. Kolkowicz, *Communist Party*, pp. 112 f.
2. Dinerstein, *War and the Soviet Union*, chapters 4 and 5.
3. *Pravda*, 13 March 1954, p. 2.
4. *Pravda*, 12 March 1954, quoted in translation from Dinerstein, *War and the Soviet Union*, p. 103.
5. *Izvestiia*, 11 March 1954, quoted in translation from Dinerstein, *War and the Soviet Union*, p. 104.
6. Colonel I. N. Nenakhov, 'The Policy of the Communist Party in Strengthening the Active Defence of the Soviet State', *Voennaia Mysl'*, no. 10, October 1953, pp. 3–18, p. 8. Quoted from Kolkowicz, *Communist Party*, p. 109.
7. Kozlov, 'Soviet Military Science', p. 31. It should be pointed out that Kozlov is generally regarded as a Khrushchev supporter.
8. Kozlov, 'Soviet Military Science', p. 32.
9. Kozlov, 'Soviet Military Science', p. 35.
10. Kozlov, 'Soviet Military Science', p. 39.
11. Talenskii, 'Laws of Military Science', Talenskii, 'The Permanently Operating Factors of War'; for discussion and analysis see Dinerstein, *War and the Soviet Union*, and Raymond L. Garthoff, *Soviet Image*. The course of this debate is analysed in more detail in chapter 4.
12. See Dinerstein, *War and the Soviet Union*, pp. 41. f. and chapter 4.
13. Rotmistrov, 'O roli vnezapnosti'; for discussion see Kolkowicz, *Communist Party*, p. 119.
14. Editorial in *Voennaia Mysl'*, no. 3, March 1955.
15. Dinerstein, *War and the Soviet Military*, p. 52.
16. Kozlov, *Soviet Military Doctrine*, p. 45.
17. Garthoff, *Soviet Military Policy*, p. 49.
18. Yu. Petrov, *Partiinoe stroitel'stvo v Sovetskoi Armii i Flote, 1918–1961* Moscow: Voenizdat 1961, p. 454.

   In 1955 the MPA's name was changed from 'Main Political Administration of the Army and Navy' to simply 'Main Political Administration'. This was reversed in 1958, as Yosef Avidar points out, 'In April 1958 the Central Committee changed the name of the MPA, in the cadre of "improvements in Party-Political activity" consequent on the October 1957 Plenary Resolutions. The change was no mere formality but expressed the reversal in the hierarchy of organisation. From then on it was not the "MPA of the Ministry of Defence", but the "MPA of the

Army and Navy". In fact the MPA was now turned into an institution parallel to or alongside the Ministry of Defence, not part of it, responsible to the Central Committee. The Minister of Defence *and the MPA Head* now signed all instructions on questions of Party-political action in the Army and Navy.' Yosef Avidar, *The Party and the Army in the Soviet Union*, London: Frank Cass & Co. 1983, p. 206.

19. Michael J. Deane, *Political Control of the Soviet Armed Forces*, London: Macdonald and Jane's Publishers Ltd 1977, p. 59.

20. See Kolkowicz, *Communist Party*, p. 126; Kolkowicz refers to A. M. Larkov and N. T. Filippov, *Edinonachalie v Sovetskikh Vooruzhennykh Silakh*, Moscow: Voenizdat 1960, p. 16.

21. Deane, *Political Control*, p. 61.

22. Garthoff, *Soviet Military Policy*, p. 51; Deane, *Political Control*, p. 60.

23. Garthoff, *Soviet Military Policy*, p. 53.

24. *Khrushchev Remembers*, vol. 2, p. 14.

25. Kolkowicz, *Communist Party*.

26. Maj. Gen. N. Pavlenko, 'Letopis' surovykh ispytanii i pervykh pobed sovetskogo naroda v Veliko Otechestvennoi voine', *Voenno-istoricheskii zhurnal*, no. 11, November 1961, pp. 93–103, p. 102; English translation quoted from Kolkowicz, *Communist Party*, p. 229.

27. Kolkowicz counts the following among the Stalingrad group: I. K. Bagramian, P. F. Batitskii, P. I. Batov, S. S. Biriuzov, V. I. Chuikov, A. A. Epishev, A. I. Eremenko, I. I. Fediuninskii, K. N. Galitskii, A. L. Getman, F. I. Golikov, A. A. Grechko, I. I. Iakubovskii, M. I. Kazakov, G. I. Khetagurov, I. S. Konev, P. K. Koshevoi, N. I. Krylov, D. D. Leliushenko, I. I. Liudnikov, R. Ia. Malinovskii, N. R. Mironov, K. S. Moskalenko, I. G. Pavlovskii, V. A. Pen'kovskii, I. A. Pliev, M. M. Popov, S. I. Rudenko, N. S. Skripko, A. T. Stuchenko, V. A. Sudets, M. V. Zakharov.

28. Kolkowicz, *Communist Party*, p. 249.

29. See Petrov, *Partiinoe stroitel'stvo*, pp. 469–71 f.; for discussion see Kolkowicz, *Communist Party*, p. 139 f.

30. Kolkowicz, *Communist Party*, p. 141.

31. Kolkowicz, *Communist Party*, p. 142.

32. *Krasnaia Zvezda*, 9 August 1958; for discussion see Kolkowicz, *Communist Party*, p. 145.

33. *O samostoiatel'nosti i initsiative ofitserov flota*, Moscow: Voenizdat 1959, cited in Kolkowicz, *Communist Party*, p. 145.f.

34. N. S. Khrushchev, *O vneshenii politike Sovetskogo Soiuza, 1960 god*, Moscow: Gospolitizdat 1961, p. 36.

35. N. S. Khrushchev, quoted from *Izvestiia*, 15 January 1960, p. 4.

36. Khrushchev, ibid. For comment see Deane, *Political Control*, p. 71.

37. *Izvestiia*, 16 January 1960, p. 2.

38. *Izvestiia*, 16 January 1960, p. 2. See also Deane, *Political Control*, p. 71.

39. Kolkowicz, *Communist Party*, p. 157; Kolkowicz states that for the time being Khrushchev still had the support of the top layer of the military

and thus could risk alienating the middle and lower echelons' (ibid.). Although there were no direct attacks against Khrushchev, nonetheless Kolkowicz's statement cannot be accepted without severe qualifications. Indeed, as is shown below, Malinovskii himself soon became active against Khrushchev. For Malinovskii's rôle at the abortive Paris Summit, see Beschloss, *Mayday*, p. 275; a useful analysis of the effect of the manpower cuts on Party-military relations is given in Matthew P. Gallagher 'Military Manpower: A Case Study', *Problems of Communism*, vol. 13, no. 3, May–June 1964, pp. 53–62.

40. See Tatu, *Power*, p. 76.

41. *Pravda*, 31 May 1960, p. 3. Malinovskii's speech constitutes a long diatribe to the effect that Khrushchev had been wrong to trust Eisenhower (although Khrushchev's rôle is implied rather than referred to explicitly), and that the U2 incident and Eisenhower's refusal to apologize at the Paris Summit prove this. He furthermore stated that as Minister of Defence he would give the order to attack the bases from which American planes that violated Soviet airspace came.

42. Colonels E. Tarasov and S. Il'ni, 'Vsemerno sovershenstvovat' rabotu partiinykh komitetov akademii', *Kommunist Vooruzhennykh Sil*, no. 5, December 1960, pp. 36–42.

43. Kolkowicz, *Communist Party*, p. 165.

44. General S. Krasil'nikov, 'O kharaktere sovremennoi voiny', *Krasnaia Zvezda*, 18 November 1960, pp. 2–3, p. 3.

45. *Pravda*, 22 June 1961. Cited in translation from Deane, *Political Control*, p. 76; see also Slusser, *Berlin Crisis*, p. 18.

46. Linden, *Soviet Leadership*, p. 116.

47. MccGwire, 'Rationale for Soviet Seapower', *Soviet Strategy*, London: Croom Helm 1981, pp. 210–54, p. 216. Recently MccGwire appears to have changed his views somewhat, and his interpretation of Malinovskii's attitude and relationship with Khrushchev at the time of the 22nd Party Congress now seems to be closer to the one advanced here; see MccGwire, *Military Objectives*, p. 25.

48. *Pravda*, 25 October 1961, pp. 4–5; p. 4.

49. See Berman and Baker, *Soviet Strategic Forces*, pp. 104 f.

50. See note 41 above.

51. This view is now also held by Michael MccGwire. Thus MccGwire writes: 'By July 1961 a compromise was apparently made on this aspect of the debate. An agreement was reached that while strategic nuclear strikes would be decisive, a war could only be won through the combined operations of all arms. The reduction in the size of the armed forces was halted, and Minister of Defense Marshal Rodion Malinovskiy announced the revised policy at the Twenty-second Party Congress', MccGwire, *Military Objectives*, p. 25. Linden discusses these debates in the context of Khrushchev's economic policies; see Linden, *Soviet Military Leadership*, chapter 7.

52. Malinovskii, 'Programma KPSS i voprosy ukrepleniia Vooruzhen-
    nykh Sil SSSR', *Kommunist*, no. 7, May 1962, pp. 11–12.
53. The 'radical' viewpoint was expressed, for example, by Colonel P. Sido-
    rov, 'Neustanno krepit' oboronosposobnost' strany' *Kommunist Vooruz-
    hennykh Sil*, no. 12, June 1961, pp. 59–65; Colonels N. Sushko, S.
    Tiushkevich and G. Fedorov, 'Razvitie marksistsko-leninskogo uche-
    niia o voine v sovremennykh usloviiakh', *Kommunist Vooruzhennykh Sil*,
    no. 18, September 1961, pp. 19–29. In the summer of 1962 *Voennaia
    Strategiia* edited by Marshal Sokolovskii was published and thus
    became a major focus of the debate. The general consensus in the West
    is that the Sokolovskii volume represented mostly the perspective of the
    'moderates' (including Malinovksii), thus becoming the object of attack
    for the 'radicals' and the 'conservatives' (see Wolfe, *Soviet Strategy*, and
    also Kolkowicz, *Communist Party*, pp. 163 f.). For other important
    contributions to the debate, see Malinovskii, *Kommunist*; Malinovskii,
    Bditel'no (some Western observers believe that this pamphlet repre-
    sented a collective rather than Malinovskii's personal viewpoint; see
    Deane, *Political Control*, p. 103 and Wolfe, *Soviet Strategy*, pp. 93 f.);
    Colonel General N. Lomov, 'O sovetskoi voennoi doktrine', *Kommunist
    Vooruzhennykh Sil*, no. 10, May 1962, pp. 11–21; the review of *Voennaia
    Strategiia* by P. Kurochkin in *Krasnaia Zvezda*, 22 September 1962 (an
    English translation of the article by Kurochkin is reprinted in the Rand
    Corporation translation of *Voennaia Strategiia*, V. D. Sokolovskii (ed.),
    Soviet Military Strategy, translated and introduced by Herbert S. Diner-
    stein, Leon Gouré and Thomas W. Wolfe, Englewood Cliffs: Prentice
    Hall 1963, pp. 523–29) and the article by Marshal p. Rotmistrov, *Izvestiia*,
    20 October 1962.
    The divisions discerned in the early Sixties superseded the political
    allegiances which could be discerned in the Fifties, such as the
    Stalingrad group.
54. *Pravda*, 25 October 1961, p. 5.
55. Golikov, *Pravda*, 30 October 1961, p. 3; see also Deane, *Political Control*,
    p. 80.
56. Golikov, *Pravda*.
57. Unsigned article in *Kommunist Vooruzhennykh Sil*, no. 3, February 1962,
    p. 37.
58. 'O robote partiinogo komiteta i partorganizatsii shtaba i upravleniia
    tyla Ministerstva oborony SSSR', *Kommunist Vooruzhennykh Sil*, no. 5,
    March 1962., pp. 55–57.
59. Kolkowicz, *Communist Party*, p. 167; Wolfe seems to take a similar view
    – see Wolfe, *Soviet Strategy*, pp. 142 f.
60. Deane, *Political Control*, pp. 86–93.
61. Robert M. Slusser, 'America, China and the Hydra-Headed Opposition:
    The Dynamics of Soviet Foreign Policy', in Peter H. Juviler and Henry
    W. Morton (eds.), *Soviet Policy-Making: Studies of Communism in Tran-
    sition*, New York: Praeger 1967, p. 217.

62. Linden, *Soviet Leadership*, pp. 134–38; Tatu, *Power*, pp. 200–4, 208–11, 214–17; Deane, *Political Control*, p. 92.

63. Konev's appointment in 1961 to be Commander of the Soviet Forces in Germany was, in Khrushchev's words, 'just an "administrative" appointment to demonstrate to the West that we regarded the situation [in Berlin] as seriously as they [the Americans] did . . . The fact that Konev spent most of his time in Moscow proves that we weren't expecting the confrontation to escalate into a full-scale military conflict' (*Khrushchev Remembers*, vol. 1). Konev had been passed over for the position of defence Minister when Zhukov was dismissed in 1957. Khrushchev, who then favoured Malinovskii, explains the reason in his memoirs: 'Konev made us very uneasy. We were afraid his attitude toward the government and the Party leadership was similar to Zhukov's' (*Khrushchev Remembers*, vol. 2, p. 17). Konev retired from his position of Commander of the Warsaw Pact Forces in April 1960 at the same time as Sokolovskii went into retirement (according to Khrushchev both Marshals retired due to ill health, see *Khrushchev Remembers*, vol. 2, p. 17) most likely because they refused to endorse Khrushchev's military doctrine and in particular the troop cuts. As part of the resolution of the Berlin crisis, General Lucius Clay, who had been appointed by Kennedy to command Western forces in Berlin during the crisis, and Konev were withdrawn in a reciprocal arrangement.

64. Moskalenko became Chief Inspector in the Ministry of Defence.

65. Tatu, *Power*, p. 238.

66. Ibid., p. 234.

67. *Khrushchev Remembers*, vol. 1, pp. 493 f.

68. Kolkowicz, *Communist Party*, p. 265.

69. *Khrushchev Remembers*, vol. 2, p. 15.

70. Khrushchev, ibid.

71. Thus we read in Khrushchev's memoirs: 'I was especially struck by Moskalenko's lack of principles when we were discussing with the inner circle of the leadership what to do about the putsch which Zhukov was organizing. Suddenly Moskalenko came out with an impassioned denunciation of Zhukov, spewing out all kinds of accusations against him. [Here there is an interruption in the narrative, but from what follows it appears that Zhukov, on hearing Moskalenko's accusations against him, revealed that Moskalenko himself had criticized the civilian leadership in private conversation with Zhukov – and perhaps that Moskalenko had toyed with the idea of joining the putsch.] I believe that what Zhukov told us about Moskalenko was true' (*Khrushchev Remembers*, vol. 2, pp. 15 f.).

72. John Erickson, 'The "Military Factor" in Soviet Policy', *International Affairs*, vol. 39, no. 2, April 1963, pp. 214–26; p. 220.

73. See note 67.

74. Deane, *Political Control*, p. 93; Slusser, *Dynamics of Soviet Foreign Policy*, p. 217.

75. Lomov, 'O Sovetskoi voennoi doktrine'; for more detailed discussion, see Deane, *Political Control*, pp. 95 f.

76. This is the view of Deane, *Political Control*, p. 98; R. Ia. Malinovskii, 'Nasuschchnye voprosy vospitaniia lichnogo sostava Vooruzhennykh Sil SSSR', *Kommunist Vooruzhennykh Sil*, no. 11, June 1962, pp. 3–15.

77. Deane, *Political Control*, p. 98.

78. Colonel M. Timofeechev, 'Edinonachalie – vazhneishii printsip stroitel'stva sovetskikh vooryzhennykh sil', *Kommunist Vooruzhennykh Sil*, no. 12, June 1962, pp. 44–56; see also A. A. Epishev, 'Tverdo provodit' v zhizn' politiku partii v Vooruzhennykh Silakh', *Kommunist Vooruzhennykh Sil*, no. 19, October 1962, pp. 2–15.

79. 'O rabote partkoma i partiinykh organizatsii shtaba i upravelnii Sukhoputnykh voisk', *Kommunist Vooruzhennykh Sil*, no. 15, August 1962, pp. 38–41.

80. R. Ia. Malinovskii, *Krasnaia Zvezda*, 25 October 1962, p. 3. For comment, see Kolkowicz, *Communist Party*, p. 170 and Deane, *Political Control*, p. 100. This took place in the middle of the Cuban missile crisis. Malinovskii briefly referred to American aggressive plans against Cuba in his speech, but made no direct reference to the missile crisis. Interestingly, however, he put great emphasis on the possession by the Soviet Union of 50–60 megaton weapons.

81. *Pravda*, 7 November 1962.

82. V. I. Chuikov, 'Osnova osnov voennogo stroitel'stva', *Krasnaia Zvezda*, 17 November 1962, pp. 3–4. This is a direct quotation from Lenin. Chuikov interprets it as a response to errors by Stalin and thus not applicable in the post-Stalin era.

Malinovskii stated in the pamphlet *Bditel'no stoiat' na strazhe mira* that 'having given a stern warning to the American aggressors and taken measures to increase the battle readiness of the Armed Forces, the Soviet government and its head, Comrade N. S. Khrushchev, by their sage proposals showed the way to a reasonable compromise'.

Having thus supported Khrushchev's interpretation of the Cuban missile crisis, Malinovskii then went on to argue that 'Our answer to any provocations of the imperialist aggressors must be the strengthened defensive power of the Soviet Union . . . Consequently, real reasons exist that force the Soviet Government and the Communist Party to strengthen the Armed Forces' (quoted from the English translation of the Joint Publications Research Service, no. 39 127, p. 12).

83. N. S. Khrushchev, *The Present International Situation and the Foreign Policy of the Soviet Union*, New York: Crosscurrents Press 1963, p. 17; cited in Deane, *Political Control*, p. 103.

84. See Deane, *Political Control*, pp. 104 f.

85. General of the Army A. A. Epishev, 'O vozrastaiushchei roli KPSS v rukovodstve Vooruzhennymi Silami', *Voprosy istorii KPSS*, no. 2, February 1963, pp. 3–14, p. 10.

86. *Pravda*, 28 February 1963.

87. One notable aspect of this debate is that Epishev and Malinovskii surprisingly gave some degree of recognition to the disgraced Marshal Zhukov, as if to enlist his authority in the cause of those opposing Khrushchev's military policies. See Epishev, 'O roli KPSS', p. 7 and Malinovskii, *Pravda*, 1 February 1963. For comment see Deane, *Political Control*, p. 108.
88. Marshal P. Rotmistrov, *Krasnaia Zvezda*, 16 January 1963; Marshal N. N. Voronov, *Pravda*, 31 January 1963; Marshal V. I. Kazakov, *Izvestiia*, 1 February 1963; Marshal S. S. Biriuzov, 'Velikaia bitva na Volge', *Politicheskoe samoobrazovanie*, no. 2, 1963, pp. 33–41; Marshal V. I. Chuikov, *Izvestiia*, 2 February 1963; Marshal A. I. Eremenko, *Pravda*, 27 January 1963. For discussion see Kolkowicz, *Communist Party*, pp. 210–14.
89. *Krasnaia Zvezda*, 28 March 1963.
90. Herbert L. Sawyer, *The Soviet Space Controversy, 1961–1963*, unpublished Ph.D. Dissertation, Fletcher School of Law and Diplomacy, Massachusetts, May 1969, p. 233.
91. Tatu, for example, points out that 'on the day when Khrushchev delivered his speech, the members of the Presidium were seated together with him at the official table as usual, except for two of them who, as though by way of punishment, were relegated to the back with the alternates and the Secretaries. These were Poliansky and Suslov. For Poliansky, a "junior" member, this happened once or twice later, but for someone in Suslov's position it was quite unheard of' (Tatu, *Power*, p. 346). Tatu bases his analysis on a photograph published in *Pravda* on 25 April 1963.
92. R. Ia. Malinovskii, 'Za novyi moshchnyi pod"em ideologicheskoi raboty', *Krasnaia Zvezda*, 5 July 1963, pp. 2–3.
93. Col. A. Iovlev, 'On Mass Armies in Modern War', *Voennaia Mysl'*, no. 10, October 1963, pp. 1–12, p. 8.
94. Iovlev, 'On Mass Armies'.
95. Ibid., p. 11.
96. Maj. Gen. V. Kruchinin, 'Contemporary Strategic Theory on the Goals and Missions of Armed Conflict', *Voennaia Mysl'*, no. 10, October 1963, pp. 13–24, p. 13.
97. Even if much of the military expenditure is hidden, the nominal 'military budget' is of great psychological and political importance.
98. Colonel p. Derevianko, 'Nekotorye osobennosti sovremennoi revoliutsii v voennom dele', *Kommunist Vooruzhennykh Sil*, no. 1, January 1964, pp. 15–25.
99. Marshal V. I. Chuikov, 'Sovremennye sukhopotnye voiska', *Izvestiia*, 22 December 1963, p. 5.
100. *Krasnaia Zvezda*, 28 August 1964.
101. John Dornberg, *Brezhnev*, chapter 12; Medvedev and Medvedev, *Khrushchev*, chapter 15.
102. See Deane, *Political Control*, p. 137.
103. *Pravda*, 22 May 1965; see also Tatu, *Power*, p. 498.

104. *Pravda*, 5 June 1965, p. 3.
105. Erickson, *Soviet Military Power*, p. 8.
106. V. I. Chuikov, *Komsomolskaia Pravda*, 23 February 1964.
107. Interview with N. I. Krylov, *Trud*, 21 February 1965, p. 1.
108. *Krasnaia Zvezda*, 18 March 1965, cited in Deane, *Political Control*, p. 145.
109. See the articles cited in Deane, *Political Control*, pp. 145 f.; see also Marshal P. Rotmistrov, 'Rukovodstvo partii – istochnik moguchshestvo sovetskoi Armii i Flota', *Kommunist*, no. 4, March 1965, pp. 15–24; p. 23.
110. Ibid.
111. Ibid., p. 24.
112. Talensky, 'The Late War', p. 15, Rybkin, 'O sushchnosti'. Rybkin presented the substance of his article also in a lecture the text of which was distributed by the Frunze Central Club of the Soviet Army 'to help propagandists' (cf. Kintner and Fast Scott, *Nuclear Revolution*, p. 340. For another condemnation of Talenskii's views and support for Rybkin's see the article by Colonel I. A. Grudinin, *Krasnaia Zvezda*, 12 July 1966. For a discussion of this debate see Freedman, *Evolution*, p. 269; Erickson, *Soviet Military Power*, pp. 8–10. The standard text on the different views of 'militarists' and 'arms controllers' in the Soviet Union in the 1960s is Samuel B. Payne, *The Soviet Union and SALT*, Cambridge: MIT Press 1980.
113. Rybkin, 'O sushchnosti', p. 56.
114. Rybkin, 'A Critique'.
115. Alexander O. Ghebhardt, *Soviet ABM Decisionmaking*, p. 69.
116. Erickson, *Soviet Military Power*, p. 9.
117. L. I. Brezhnev, 'Speech to Soviet Officers', Radio Moscow Domestic Service in Russian, 3 July 1965; quoted from Ghebhardt, *Soviet ABM Decisionmaking*, p. 60.
118. Deane, *Political Control*, p. 77.
119. Epishev, 'Tverdo provodit'', p. 9.
120. R. Ia. Malinovskii, 'Za novyi moshchnyi pod"em ideologicheskoi raboty', *Krasnaia Zvezda*, 5 July 1963, pp. 2–3; p. 3.
121. Major Gen. Justice I. Pobezhimov and Col. Justice P. Romanov 'Organizational and Legal Principles of the Structure of the Armed Forces', *Voennaia Mysl'*, no. 9, September 1964, pp. 12–25.
122. Ibid., p. 17.
123. Ibid., p. 18.
124. Ibid., p. 19.
125. Ibid.
126. Ibid., p. 20.
127. *Pravda*, 4 July 1965, pp. 1–2; p. 2.
128. See M. Timofeechev, 'Vazhneishii printsip sovetskogo voennogo stroitel'stva', *Kommunist Vooruzhennkykh Sil'*, no. 4, February 1969, pp. 12–19; S.A. Tiushkevicha, N. Ia. Syshko and Ia. S. Dziuby (eds.), *Marksizm – leninism o voine i armii*, Moscow: Voenizdat 1968,

pp. 218–21; Marshal A. A. Grechko, 'V. I. Lenin i stroitel'stvo Sovetskikh vooruzhennykh sil', *Kommunist*, no. 3, February 1969, pp. 15–26.

129. Deane, *Political Control*, p. 171.
130. Ibid., chapter 6.
131. E. Bugayev, 'Istoricheskoe znachenie opyta KPSS v stroitel'stve sotsializma i kommunizma', *Kommunist Vooruzhennykh Sil*, no. 1, January 1969, pp. 17–26; I. Gusakovskii, 'Zabota partii o podgotovke i vospitanii voennykh kadrov', *Kommunist Vooruzhennykh Sil*, no. 1, January 1969, pp. 27–33; V. Kotov, 'Partiino-politicheskaia rabota v voiskakh nariadakh', *Kommunist Vooruzhennykh Sil*, no. 1, January 1969, pp. 44–48; *Kommunist Vooruzhennykh Sil*, 'Ideologicheskaia rabota partiinykh organisatsii', no. 4, February 1969, pp. 3–8.
132. Grechko, 'Sovetskykh Vooruzhennykh Sil', p. 17; Krylov, *Krasnaia Zvezda*, 20 February 1969.
133. Marshal M. V. Zakharov, *Partiinaia Zhizn'*, no. 9, May 1969, p. 11, cited in Deane, *Political Control*, p. 201; A. Epishev, 'Leninism – osnova vospitaniia sovetskikh voinov', *Kommunist*, no. 6, April 1969, pp. 60–71; A. Epishev, 'Politicheskim organam sovetskoi armii i voenno-morskogo flota – piat'desiat let', *Kommunist Vooruzhennykh Sil*, no. 7, April 1969, pp. 9–22.
134. Yefremov, *Nuclear Disarmament*, pp. 159 f.
135. Ibid., p. 160.
136. A. A. Gromyko, 'O mezhdunarodnom polozhenii i vneshnei politike Sovetskogo Soiuza', *Pravda*, 28 June 1968. English translation quoted from Samuel P. Payne, *The Soviet Union and SALT*, Massachusetts: MIT Press 1980, p. 65.
137. E. I. Rybkin, 'Kritika burzhuaznykh kontseptsii voiny i mira', *Kommunist vooruzhennykh sil*, no. 18, September 1968, pp. 87–90, p. 90.
138. See Raymond L. Garthoff, 'BMD and East–West Relations', in Ashton B. Carter and David N. Schwartz (eds.), *Ballistic Missile Defense*.
139. *Krasnaia Zvezda*, 4 October 1968; for comment see Payne, *SALT* p. 64, and Garthoff, *Ballistic Missile Defense*, p. 300.
140. See Payne, *SALT*, p. 64; for a discussion of the military's participation in SALT see Raymond L. Garthoff, 'Soviet Military and SALT'.
141. A. A. Epishev, 'Leninism', p. 68.
142. Colonel S. Lukonin and Lieutenant Colonel N. Tarasenko, 'V. I. Lenin ob oboronoi funktsii sotsialisticheskogo gosudarstva', *Kommunist Vooruzhennykh Sil*, no. 10, May 1969, pp. 18–25; quoted in English translation from Deane, *Political Control*, p. 211.
143. Lieutenant Colonel B. Demin, 'Nenavisit' k vragu – neot"emlemaia storona patriotizma sovetskikh voinov', *Kommunist Vooruzhennykh Sil*, no. 13, July 1969, pp. 25–32, p. 29; quoted in English translation from Deane, *Political Control*, pp. 211 f.
144. Iu. Barsukov, 'Oposnoe reshenie', *Izvestiia*, 12 March 1970, p. 2; quoted in English translation from Payne, *SALT*, p. 35.

145. 'Za uglubenie razriadki, protiv provoiskov reaktsii', *Kommunist Vooruzhennykh Sil*, no. 1, January 1979, cited from Payne, *SALT*.

146. Among the most important of these are the Soviet Academy of Sciences, the Institute of World Economy and International Relations IMEMO (which publishes the journal *MEMO*) and the Institute of the USA and Canada ISKAN (which publishes the journal S Sh A). For a general analysis about the influence of the research institutes on Soviet policy-making, see Payne, *SALT*, especially chapters 1 and 8; see also Pat Litherland, *Gorbachev and Arms Control: Civilian Experts and Soviet Policy*, Peace Research Report Number 12, Bradford: School of Peace Studies 1986, chapters 1–3.

147. B. Strel'nikov, 'Iadernyi kot v meshke', *Pravda*, 10 June 1969, p. 5; G. A. Arbatov, 'Amerikanskii imperializm i novye real'nosti mira', *Pravda*, 4 May 1971, p. 4; for a discussion of the conflict within the American ruling circles about arms control see Yefremov, *Nuclear Disarmament*, p. 160.

148. G. A. Arbatov, 'Sila politika realizma', *Izvestiia*, 22 June 1972, p. 4. For discussion see Payne, *SALT*, pp. 38 f.

149. V. V. Larionov, 'Strategicheskie debaty', *S Sh A*, no. 3, March 1970, p. 29, cited from Payne, 'SALT', p. 21.

150. A. Svetlov, 'Razoruzhenie – nasushchnaia zadacha bor'by za mir', *MEIMO*, no. 7, July 1976, pp. 3–16, p. 7.

151. Payne, *SALT*, p. 76.

152. Grechko's speech in *XXIV s?ezd Kommunisticheskoi parti Sovetskogo Soiuza: Stenograficheskii otchet*, 1, p. 346, quoted in English translation from Deane, *Political Control*, p. 224.

153. See Deane, *Political Control*, pp. 270–73.

6 The development of strategic bombers in the Soviet Union

1. *Khrushchev Remembers*, vol. 2, p. 39.

2. Alexander Boyd, *The Soviet Air Forces Since 1918*, London: Macdonald and Jane's 1977, p. 223; see also *Khrushchev Remembers*, vol. 2.

3. Khrushchev, *Khrushchev Remembers*, vol. 2, p. 39.

4. Ibid.

5. Stephen M. Meyer, *Soviet Theatre Nuclear Forces, Part II: Capabilities and Implications*, Adelphi Paper no. 188, London: IISS 1984, p. 54.

6. See Boyd, *Soviet Air Forces*, p. 223.

7. Prados, *The Soviet Estimate*, Princeton, NJ: Princeton University Press 1982, p. 46.

8. Asher Lee (ed.), *The Soviet Air and Rocket Forces*, London: Weidenfeld & Nicolson 1959, caption for a photograph opposite p. 121.

9. Raymond L. Garthoff, *How Russia Makes War*, London: George Allen & Unwin Ltd 1954, p. 348.

10. Ye. Tatarchenko, 'Some Problems of the Development of Air Power', *Vestnik Vozdushnogo Flota*, no. 5–6, May–June 1946, pp. 60 and 64, quoted

in English Translation from Raymond L. Garthoff, *Soviet Strategy in the Nuclear Age*, London: Atlantic Books 1958, p. 171.

11. Garthoff, in *Nuclear Age*, p. 192, cites the following sources: P. Korkodinov, 'Operational Art of the Red Army', *Morskoi sbornik*, no. 6, June 1946, p. 11; N. Skripko, 'Long Range Aviation', *Krasnaia Zvezda*, 11 August 1946.

12. Garthoff, in *Nuclear Age*, p. 192, cites the following sources: N. Denisov, *Boevaia slava sovetskoi aviatsii*, 1953, p. 67; I. Maryganov, *Peredovoi kharakter sovetskoi voennoi nauki*, 1953, p. 32.

13. Marshal G. Zhukov, *Pravda*, 20 February 1956, quoted from Garthoff, *Nuclear Age*, p. 180.

14. Marshal G. Zhukov, *Krasnaia Zvezda*, 23 March 1957, quoted from Garthoff, *Nuclear Age*, p. 180.

15. Freedman, *Evolution*, pp. 6–9; for a Soviet critic of American reliance on strategic bombing see V. Khlopov, *Voennaia Mysl'*, no. 1, January 1954, pp. 83–84, cited in Garthoff, *Nuclear Age*, p. 194.

16. Garthoff, *Nuclear Age*, pp. 181 f.

17. Editorial, *Voennaia Mysl'*, no. 4, April 1955, pp. 21–22; quoted from Garthoff, *Soviet Strategy*, p. 183.

18. Sokolovskiy, *Soviet Military Strategy*, p. 252 (the text in brackets first appeared in the 2nd edition).

19. Sokolovskiy, *Soviet Military Strategy*, p. 200.

20. This analysis is based on Wolfe, *Soviet Strategy*, p. 178.

21. Sokolovskiy, *Soviet Military Strategy*, p. 253.

22. Nikita S. Khrushchev, 'Razoruzhenie – put' k uprocheniiu mira i obespecheniiu druzhby mezhdu narodami', *Pravda*, 15 January 1960, pp. 1–5; p. 3.

7 Soviet ICBM deployment: two case studies

1. Karl Spielmann, *Analyzing Soviet Strategic Arms Decisions*, Boulder: Westview Press 1978, p. 117.

2. Soviet missile development was initially supervised by personnel from the artillery branch of the Ground Forces. Spielmann, *Soviet Strategic Arms Decisions*, p. 177.

3. Spielmann, *Soviet Strategic Arms Decisions*, p. 118.

4. Nonetheless, Korolev was chief designer of Soviet missiles until his death in 1966, when his erstwhile collaborator Iangel took over his position. Cf. Berman and Baker, *Soviet Strategic Forces*, pp. 78 f.

5. James Oberg, *Red Star in Orbit*, New York 1981.

6. Spielmann, *Soviet Strategic Arms Decisions*, p. 120.

7. Ibid., p. 120.

8. For an interesting article in the Soviet military press which explains the basic principles of an ICBM, see N. Shchapov, 'Chto takoe mezhkontinental'naia ballisticheskaia raketa?', *Voenni Vestnik*, no. 9, 1957, p. 60. The article states that ICBMs can be located anywhere and launch-sites

easily camouflaged. They can reach any point on the earth. The article describes the accuracy of ICBMs as 10–20 km. For more detailed technical discussion see T. M. Mel'kumov, 'Nekotorye problemy raketnoi tekhniki', *Vestnik Vozdushnogo Flota*, no. 2, 1958, pp. 79–89; M. N. Nikolaev, *Snriad protiv snariada*, Moscow: Voenizdat 1961.

9. Warner, *The Military in Soviet Politics*, p. 190; see also the analysis in Thomas W. Wolfe, *Soviet Power and Europe*.
10. David Holloway, *Soviet Union*, p. 44.
11. Freedman, *US Intelligence*, p. 107.
12. Ibid.
13. Berman and Baker, *Soviet Strategic Power*, pp. 104 f.
14. Tatu, *Power*, p. 329.
15. Ibid., p. 328.
16. Vernon V. Aspaturian, 'The Soviet Military-Industrial Complex', p. 16.
17. Hannes Adomeit, *Soviet Risk-Taking and Crisis Behavior*, London: George Allen and Unwin 1982, p. 269; Tatu, *Power*, p. 331.
18. *Pravda*, 26 April 1963; translation from Aspaturian, 'Military-Industrial Complex', p. 16.
19. Tatu, *Power*, pp. 343 f.
20. Tatu, *Power*, p. 344; for a discussion of the significance of these events, see also Aspaturian, 'Military-Industrial Complex', pp. 15–17.
21. Tatu, *Power*, p. 345.
22. Medvedev and Medvedev, *Khrushchev*, chapter 15; Dornberg, *Brezhnev* chapter 12.
23. The meaning for strategic superiority or inferiority and its implications for foreign policy are somewhat debatable. This issue is discussed in some detail in chapter 3.
24. Freedman, *US Intelligence*, p. 110.
25. Erickson, *Soviet Military Power*, pp. 9–11, 41 ff.
26. A separate Ground Forces command was not reinstituted until 1967. The Ground Forces were not absorbed into another service, but administered by the General Staff after their high command structure was abolished by Khrushchev in August 1964. See Warner, *Military in Soviet Politics*, p. 30.
27. Alexander O. Ghebhardt, *Soviet ABM Decisionmaking*, p. 86.
28. The rôle of the General Staff in the weapons procurement process under Khrushchev was illuminated by an interesting incident during the Berlin crisis in 1961 when Khrushchev called for a build-up of tank forces. This sparked off a controversy in the General Staff over resource allocation. It was thought that too much money had been made available for tank troops, thus depriving other services of planned budgetary allocations. Alexander, *Soviet ABM Decisionmaking*, p. 17. For information the evolution of the rôle of the General Staff, see the references in note 18.
29. Ghebhardt, *ibid*. Zakharov's rôle in the reorganization of the military establishment after Khrushchev's fall is also described in Erickson, *Soviet Military Power*, pp. 9–11.

30. This possibility was raised in the late 60s with the advent of multiple warheads. Cf. Freedman, *US Intelligence*, pp. 132 ff.; Erickson, *Soviet Military Power*, pp. 42 ff. A quantitative analysis of the SS-9 as a potential first-strike weapon is given in Berman and Baker, *Soviet Strategic Forces*, p. 138.

31. Berman and Baker, *Soviet Strategic Forces*, pp. 113–15.

32. See Slusser, *Berlin Crisis*, p. 44.

33. Michael MccGwire presents the following argument in favour of large warheads in conditions where availability of fissile material is a constraint, 'The requirement for fissionable material increases by some root of the yield, which compensates for the blast effect increasing in proportion to the two-thirds roots of the yield' (MccGwire, *Military Objectives*, p. 481).

    The counter-argument might be that such large warheads were not necessarily a military requirement and that distributing the fissile material over a larger number of warheads would increase the number of targets that could be covered. See note 36 for a further development of this argument.

34. B. T. Surikov, *Boevoe primenenie raket*, Moscow: Voenizdat 1965, pp. 58–66.

35. For a detailed analysis of the basing of Atlas, Titan and Minuteman missiles (with regard to the latter, which had not been deployed when the article was written, underground silo deployment was projected), see R. G. Tumkovskii, 'Bazirovanie raketnykh chastei VVS SShA', *Vestnik Vozdushnogo Flota*, no. 12, 1959, pp. 86–89; see also G. Nazarov and V. I. Mikhailov, *Razvitie tekhniki puska raket*, Moscow: Voenizdat 1976, pp. 123–32.

36. An increase in explosive force will multiply four-fold in the vertical compared with the horizontal direction. Increasing the yield of the warheads beyond a certain size therefore results in diminishing returns. The concept of 'area devastation' such as apparently understood by Khrushchev is partly a misunderstanding of the technology of nuclear explosions. The technical difficulties the Soviets experienced in constructing small warheads was pointed out to the author in a conversation with Prof. Kosta Tipsis. However, this is not sufficient to account for proceeding with the SS-9 as the mod. 3 of the SS-7 had a warhead of increased yield over its predecessor, thus indicating a deliberate policy choice.

37. Berman and Baker, *Soviet Strategic Forces*, p. 80.

38. As Warner has pointed out, 'The SS-9 appears to be the product of the heavy missile design tradition noted earlier . . . The decision to proceed with the deployment of this system may also have been influenced simply by the availability of the system for prompt deployment without reference to its possible employment.' Warner, *Military in Soviet Politics*, pp. 190 f.

39. Berman and Baker believe that 'this system was probably a response to

the late 1950s problem of neutralizing the prospective U.S. B-52 inter-continental-range bombers'. Berman and Baker, *Soviet Strategic Forces*, p. 118.

40. See chapter 4.
41. Berman and Baker, *Soviet Strategic Forces*, p. 121.
42. Berman and Baker, *Soviet Strategic Forces*, p. 79; *Khrushchev Remembers*, vol. 2, p. 43; Berman and Baker state that 'the Chelomei bureau apparently suggested modifying the regional-range SS-11 for intercontinental tasks' (p. 76).
43. Wolfe, *Soviet Power and Europe*, p. 432.

8 Soviet strategic nuclear power at sea

1. Michael MccGwire, 'The Rationale for the Development of Soviet Sea-power', in John Baylis and Gerald Segal (eds.), *Soviet Strategy*, London: Croom Helm 1981, pp. 210–54; see particularly pp. 214–18.
2. For more detail see Michael MccGwire, *Military Objectives in Soviet Foreign Policy*, Washington DC: Brookings Institution 1987, p. 95.
3. For precise details on Soviet SLBM development, deployment and characteristics, see Robert P. Berman and John C. Baker, *Soviet Strategic Forces*, Washington DC: Brookings Institution 1982, pp. 106–08.
4. MccGwire, 'Rationale', p. 215.
5. For a description of the Soviet concept of a strategic reserve, see Bryan Ranft and Geoffrey Till, *The Sea in Soviet Strategy*, London: Macmillan 1983, pp. 167–70; for the Soviet response to the *Polaris* force, see MccGwire, *Military Objectives*, pp. 96–98.
6. George E. Hudson, 'Soviet Naval Doctrine, 1953–72', in Michael MccGwire (ed.), *Soviet Naval Developments*, New York: Praeger 1973, pp. 277–91; Ranft and Till, *Sea in Soviet Strategy*, pp. 145 f.
7. Berman and Baker, *Soviet Strategic Forces*, pp. 108 f.
8. Ranft and Till, *Sea in Soviet Strategy*, p. 167; for evidence of the greater assertiveness of the navy in the post-Khrushchev period generally see Hudson, 'Soviet Naval Doctrine', pp. 285–87.
9. *Izvestiia*, 31 July 1966.
10. Ranft and Till, *Sea in Soviet Strategy*, p. 167.
11. For evidence of dissent within the Navy towards Khrushchev's policies, see Hudson, 'Soviet Naval Doctrine', p. 283. Calls for a 'balanced' Navy reminiscent for a 'balanced' build-up of military forces generally.
12. Berman and Baker, *Soviet Strategic Forces*, p. 42.
13. Ranft and Till, *Sea in Soviet Strategy*, p. 167.
14. Berman and Baker, *Soviet Stragegic Forces*, pp. 106 f.
15. Laird and Herspring, *Strategic Arms*, pp. 55–58.

9 Strategic defence

1. Ghebhardt, *Soviet ABM Decisionmaking*, chapter 1; P. F. Batitskii, 'Voiska protivovozdushnoi oborony strany Part III, Moscow: Voenizdat 1968, p. 341.

2. Wolfe, *Soviet Power and Europe*, p. 185.
3. After the U-2 incident the confidence of Soviet strategic claims declined remarkably, presumably since it now appeared possible that the reality of Soviet capabilities might become clear. Cf. Wolfe, *Soviet Power and Europe*, pp. 86–89.
4. The performance of the SAM in Vietnam was not very impressive. In the first year of deployment, only one out of twenty-two missiles hit its target. By 1967 this had deteriorated to one in fifty. Low-level flying and other evasive techniques employed by American pilots were quite effective. See Wolfe, *Soviet Power and Europe*, p. 168.
5. Ghebhardt, *Soviet ABM Decisionmaking*, p. 14; see also a revealing recent account of the history of Soviet ballistic missile defence by Lieutenant Colonel A. Dokuchayev, *Krasnaia Zvezda*, 5 October 1990.
6. Freedman, *US Intelligence*, p. 87.
7. Ghebhardt, *Soviet ABM Decisionmaking*, p. 40.
8. I. V. Viktorov, 'Protivoraketnaia Oborona', *Vestnik Vozdushnogo Flota*, no. 4, 1958, pp. 93–96; V. A. Velokhvostov and N. I. Sizov, *Voevoe Snariazhenie protivraket'*, *Vestnik protivovozdushnoi oborony*, no. 7, 1961, pp. 21–24; B. M. Antsiferov, 'Protivoraketa "Naik-Zevs"', *Vestnik protivo-vozdushnoi oborony*, no. 6, 1961, pp. 25–26; V. N. Anuitin, 'Issledovaniia v oblasti protivoraketnoi oborony v S Sh A', *Vestnik protivovozdushnoi oborony*, no. 12, 1961, pp. 25–28. The frequency with which articles on BMD appeared in *Vestnik Protivovozdushnoi oborony* in 1961 has to be compared with the rarity in the late Sixties and early Seventies. For a classic book on the subject from 1961, see Nikolaev, *Snariad*.
9. *Izvestiia*, 9 September 1961, pp. 5–6, p. 6; Dokuchayev, *Krasnaia Zvezda*.
10. *Pravda*, 25 October 1961, p. 4.
11. *New York Times*, 17 July 1962, p. 1.
12. It was not entirely clear to Western intelligence at first whether the *Griffon* system was intended for air defence or anti-missile defence. The Soviets did, however, claim ABM capabilities for the *Griffon* deployed around Leningrad. The missile was later deployed along the 'Tallin Line' from Archangelsk to Riga, generating a great deal of controversy with regard to the question whether it was an air defence or an ABM system. Eventually a consensus developed in the US intelligence community that it was designed against aircraft and not ballistic missiles. See Freedman, *US Intelligence*, pp. 90–94.
13. Ghebhardt, *Soviet ABM Decisionmaking*, p. 17.
14. Ghebhardt, *Soviet ABM Decisionmaking*, p. 23. Ghebhardt also attempts a construction of a connection with the Cuban missile crisis, arguing that the PVO supported the placing of missiles into Cuba, since it then had the task of providing the anti-air defence. However, this argument is rather tenuous since Ghebhardt provides no direct evidence of any kind to back it up.
15. *Izvestiia*, 8 November 1963, p. 2.
16. V. Sudets, 'Nadezhnyi shchit nashego neba', *Izvestiia*, 5 January 1964, p. 2.

17. Ibid.
18. Ghebhardt, *Soviet ABM Decisionmaking*, p. 30.
19. John R. Thomas, 'The Role of Missile Defense in Soviet Strategy', *Military Review*, May 1964, pp. 46–58. Walter F. Hahn and Alvin J. Cottrell, 'Ballistic Missile Defense and Soviet Strategy', *Orbis*, 9:2, pp. 316–37. John Erickson, '"The Fly in Outer Space": The Soviet Union and the Anti-ballistic missile', *World Today*, March 1967, pp. 106–14. J. I. Coffey, 'Soviet ABM Policy', *International Affairs*, 45:2, 1969, pp. 205–22.
20. Wolfe, *Soviet Power and Europe*, p. 188.
21. Thomas, 'Role of Missile Defense', p. 53. For a discussion of strategic defence in Soviet strategic doctrine, see Wolfe, *Soviet Strategy*, chapter 15.
22. Erickson, *Soviet Military Power*, p. 43.
23. Quoted from Wolfe, *Soviet Strategy*, p. 193.
24. Ibid.
25. Ibid.
26. Ibid., p. 191.
27. Ibid.
28. Ibid., p. 193.
29. S. Shtemenko, 'Nauchno-Tekhnicheskii Progress: ego vliani na razvitie voennogo dela', *Kommunist vooruzhennykh sil*, no. 3, February 1963, pp. 20–30, pp. 27 f. English translation quoted from Wolfe, *Soviet Strategy*, p. 193.
30. D. Kazakov, 'Teoreticheskaia i metodologicheskae osnova sovetskoi voennoi nauki', *Kommunist vooruzhennykh sil*, no. 10, May 1963, pp. 7–15; V. Konoplev, 'O nauchnom predvidenii voennom dele', *Kommunist vooruzhennykh sil*, no. 24, December 1963, pp. 28–34.
31. N. Krylov, 'Strategicheskie Rakety', *Izvestiia*, 17 November 1963, p. 4.
32. Erickson, *Soviet Military Power*, pp. 42. ff.
33. Erickson, *Soviet Military Power*, p. 43.
34. See, for example, the article by Cols. I. Zheltikov and V. Igolkin, 'Certain Tendencies in the Development of Antiaircraft and Antirocket Defenses', *Voennaia Mysl'*, no. 8, 1964, pp. 53–65, which will be discussed in more detail below.
35. N. Talensky, 'Anti-Missile Systems and Disarmament', *International Affairs* (Moscow), no. 10, October 1964, pp. 15–19; p. 16.
36. Talensky, 'Anti-Missile Systems', p. 17.
37. Talensky, 'Anti-Missile Systems', p. 19.
38. Ghebhardt, *Soviet ABM Decisionmaking*, p. 45; see also Garthoff, 'BMD', p. 293.
39. Ghebhardt, *Soviet ABM Decisionmaking*, p. 47. For a discussion of the Soviet laser research programme and its connections with the PVO, see Alexander, *Decision-Making*, pp. 37 f.
40. Ghebhardt, *Soviet ABM Decision-Making*, p. 47.
41. N. F. Shibaev, *Bor'ba Protiv Strategicheskoi Rakety*, Moscow: Voenizdat 1964. This book is an analysis of American ABM efforts, but the criticisms

with regard to the very principles of BMD technology clearly apply equally well to the Soviet ABM development and most likely were intended to do so.

42. Cols. Zheltikov and Igolkin, 'Antiaircraft and Antirocket Defenses', p. 64. With regard to the Soviet programme, the authors gave the usual reaffirmation: *'This work has permitted the solution to very important problems concerning the reliable defense of our native land not only from aircraft, but from various types of rockets'* (p. 65). It is a usual technique, however, to address controversies within the Soviet military by reference to American programmes, and the article is extremely critical. Note also that a defence capability is claimed against *various types of rockets*, leaving open the possibility that there are rockets against which the Soviet Union has no effective defence. It appears that this is the thrust of this article.

43. L. I. Brezhnev, 'Speech to Soviet Officers', Radio Moscow Domestic Service in Russian, 3 July 1965, quoted from Ghebhardt, *Soviet ABM Decisionmaking*, p. 60. This statement is also discussed in Erickson, *Soviet Military Power*, p. 10 and p. 43.

44. Talensky, 'The Late War'; Rybkin, 'O sushchnosti'.

45. Ghebhardt, *Soviet ABM Decisionmaking*, p. 69.

46. See, for example, Sokolovskii and Cherednichenko, 'O sovremennoi voennoi strategii', p. 62.

47. Engr. Col. V. Aleksandrov, 'The Search for a Solution to the Problems of Antimissile Defense in the US', *Voennaia Mysl'*, no. 9, September 1965, pp. 13–23, p. 19.

48. Aleksandrov, 'Antimissile Defense in the US', p. 20.

49. Ibid., p. 22.

50. *Pravda*, 3 April 1966, p. 3.

51. M. V. Zakharov, 'Report to the Armed Forces Concerning the Work of the 23rd Party Congress', *Tekhnika i Vooruzhenie*, no. 4, April 1966, p. 8; quoted in English translation from Ghebhardt, *Soviet ABM Decisionmaking*, p. 69.

52. Cf. Johan J. Holst, 'Missile Defense, the Soviet Union and the Arms Race', in Johan J. Holst and William Schneider (eds), *Why ABM?*, Elmsford: Pergamon Press 1969, pp. 145–86, p. 152.

53. Ghebhardt, *Soviet ABM Decisionmaking*, p. 76.

54. Deutsche Aussenpolitik, no. 10, East Berlin, Press Office, GDR Council of Ministers, October 1966, p. 1181; cited from Ghebhardt, *Soviet ABM Decisionmaking*, p. 76.
    Kurochkin may have been playing to his audience, since on another occasion he expressed strong support for the ABM, stating that it could reliably protect the USSR against enemy attack; cf. 'General Kurochkin's Press Conference', *Soviet News*, 24 February 1967, p. 98. This does not, however, disprove Ghebhardt's general point.

55. Heinz Hoffmann, 'Überlegene Militärmacht des sowjetischen Lagers', *Neues Deutschland*, 3 May 1966, p. 5.

56. Radio Moscow in Hungarian to Hungary, 2 June 1966. Quoted from Ghebhardt, *Soviet ABM Decisionmaking*, p. 77.

57. *Pravda ukrainy*, 28 October 1966, p. 3; also cf. Marshal Chuikov's television speech, TASS International Service, Moscow, 22 February 1967; Ghebhardt, *Soviet ABM Decisionmaking*, p. 78; Wolfe, *Soviet Power and Europe*, p. 439.

58. *Pravda*, 6 April 1966, p. 2; quoted from Ghebhardt, *Soviet ABM Decisionmaking*, p. 80.

59. Zakharov, 'Report to the Armed Forces', p. 2.

60. Ghebhardt, *Soviet ABM Decisionmaking*, p. 78. Zakharov's advocacy of strategic offensive capabilities versus strategic defence is also evident in an article he published a year later in which the possibility of any defence against long-range nuclear missile strikes carried out by the Strategic Rocket Troops is entirely denigrated. See M. Zakharov, 'The Increasing Role of Scientific Troop Leadership', *Voennaia Mysl'*, no. 2, 1967, pp. 11–23.

61. *New York Times*, 20 February 1971, p. 1; see also Wolfe, *SALT Experience*, pp. 1–8.

62. R. Ia. Malinovskii, 'Oktiabr' i stroitel'stvo vooruzhennykh sil', *Kommunist*, no. 1, January 1967, pp. 26–36; p. 34.

63. Quoted from Rebecca V. Strode, 'Space-Based Lasers for Ballistic Missile Defense: Soviet Policy Options', in Keith B. Payne, ed., *Laser Weapons in Space – Policy and Doctrine*, Boulder: Westview Press 1983, pp. 106–61; p. 133.

64. Michael Deane cites the following sources: *Izvestiia*, 23 February 1967 (statement by Marshal Grechko); R. Ia. Malinovskii, *Pravda*, 23 February 1967; I. I. Anureev, *Vestnik protivovozdushnoi oborony*, no. 4, April 1967, p. 11; Michael J. Deane, *Strategic Defense in Soviet Strategy*, Miami: Advanced International Studies Institute 1980, pp. 34–41. Deane disputes the interpretation placed on the Soviet sources here; he doubts that there was a 'debate' on strategic defence in the Soviet Union. This author does not accept Deane's critique, since Deane bases himself mainly on the various perceived different nuances on the effectiveness of the Soviet ABM system, whereas the evidence we have presented here for deep divergences of view in the Soviet leadership is based on much broader issues than that.

65. For discussion and analysis see Wolfe, *Soviet Strategy*, chapter 15; Wolfe, *Soviet Power in Europe*, pp. 437–41; Deane, *Strategic Defense*, pp. 34–41.

66. General P. F. Batitskii, Tass International Service, Moscow, 20 February 1967; General p. F. Batitskii, *Vestnik protivovozdushnoi oborony*, no. 11, November 1967, p. 12 (this reference is from Deane, ibid.); P. Batitskii, 'Vsegda v boevoi gotovnost', vsegda nacheku', *Kommunist Vooruzhennykh Sil*, no. 18, September 1967, pp. 25–31; p. 27; see also Kurochkin, 'Deutsche Aussenpolitik'; for an interesting article claiming that the United States is developing lasers for BMD purposes see P. F.

Pliachenko, 'Razvitie sistemy PRO v S Sh A', *Vestnik protivovozdushnoi oborony*, no. 8, 1966, pp. 86 f.

67. See Erickson, *Soviet Military Power*, p. 49.
68. Berman and Baker, *Soviet Strategic Forces*, p. 149; this is confirmed in I. I. Anureev, *Oruzhie protivoraketnoi i protivokosmicheskoi oborony*, Moscow: Voenizdat 1971, p. 196.
69. I. I. Anureev, *Oruzhie*. A detailed technical discussion which looks ahead to likely developments in US BMD technology to the end of the 70s; see p. 217.
70. Major General I. I. Anureev, 'Determining the Correlation of Forces in Terms of Nuclear Weapons', *Voennaia Mysl'*, no. 6, June 1967, p. 38; for discussion see Strode, 'Space-based Lasers', p. 140; for a discussion of later elaborations of Anureev's model, see Stephen M. Meyer, 'Soviet Strategic programmes and the US SDI', *SURVIVAL*, vol. 27, no. 6, November/December 1985, pp. 274–92; for the disappearance of ABMs from public parades see Michael Rühle, *Die strategische Verteidigung in Rüstung und Politik der UdSSR*, Cologne: Bundesinstitut für ostwissenschaftliche und internationale Studien 1985, p. 7.
71. See Anureev, *Oruzhie*, pp. 194, 196.
72. E. I. Rybkin, 'Kritika burzhuaznykh kontseptsii', p. 90.
73. *Krasnaia Zvezda*, 4 October 1968; for comment see Payne, *SALT*, p. 64. and Garthoff, 'BMD', p. 300. Payne points out, 'During the entire SALT I period, from 1969 to 1972, the Soviet military press maintained almost complete silence on the subject of SALT' (Payne, *SALT*, p. 64).
74. Garthoff, 'BMD', p. 301.
75. Ibid., p. 302.
76. 'Mezhdu Khel'sinki i Venoi', *S Sh A*, no. 1, January 1970, p. 60. Quoted in English translation from Payne, *SALT*, p. 61.

10 The military uses of space

1. Nicholas Daniloff, *The Kremlin and the Kosmos*, Alfred Knopf: New York 1972, pp. 53–57.
2. Its official title was: 'Interdepartmental Commission for the Coordination and Control of Scientific-Theoretical Work in the Field of Organization and Accomplishment of Interplanetary Communications of the Astronomical Council of the Agency of Sciences of the USSR'. See Daniloff, *Kremlin and Kosmos*, p. 56.
3. *Astronomical Journal*, 9 June 1957; TASS, 26 August 1958; see Daniloff, *Kremlin and Kosmos*, pp. 59. f.
4. It is not clear, however, to what extent the United States consciously joined the 'race' until after the launch of *Sputnik* (although the CIA had recommended to the NSC that this should be done). However, it was engaged in a satellite programme in connection with the IGY. In response to the launch of *Sputnik*, however, the United States attempted some apparently ill-prepared and overly hasty efforts to match the Soviet

exploit which went wrong. See Daniloff, *Kremlin and Kosmos*, p. 100; Arnold L. Horelick, 'The Soviet Union and the Political Uses of Outer Space', in Joseph M. Goldsen (ed.), *Outer Space in World Politics*, Pall Mall Press: London 1963, pp. 43–70, p. 46.

5. *Pravda*, 10 October 1957; translation published in the *New York Times* on 11 October 1957.

6. *Pravda*, 19 November 1957.

7. *Pravda*, 28 January 1959, p. 7.

8. *Krasnaia Zvezda*, 13 September 1961.

9. Horelick, 'Political Uses of Outer Space', pp. 53 f. Horelick quotes Khrushchev's statement at the UN General Assembly debate on disarmament in October 1960 when he said that 'rocket after rocket [type unspecified] is coming off our factory lines, like sausages from automatic machines'. (Horelick, ibid.) Original quotation from *Pravda*, 12 October 1960.

10. Quoted from Daniloff, *Kremlin and Kosmos*, p. 124. For a good example of the argument that Soviet space successes prove the superiority of the achievements of Soviet socialism over capitalism, see K. Gil'zin, 'Sovetskii narod uverenno shturmuet kosmos', *Kommunist Vooruzhennykh Sil*, no. 18, September 1962, pp. 35–39.

11. Sawyer, *Soviet Space Controversy*, chapter 4.

12. See Daniloff, *Kremlin and Kosmos*, p. 55.

13. Berman and Baker, *Soviet Strategic Forces*, p. 154.

14. Dwight D. Eisenhower, *The White House Years: Waging Peace 1956–61*, Garden City, New York: Doubleday 1965, p. 556; see also Paul B. Stares, *Space Weapons and US Strategy: Origins and Development*, London: Croom Helm 1985, p. 56.

15. *Krasnaia Zvezda*, 23 July 1961, p. 4; translation quoted from Sawyer, *Soviet Space Controversy*, p. 145.

16. Quoted from Stares, *Space Weapons and US Strategy*, p. 69.

17. G. P. Zadorozhnii, 'Basic Problems in the Science of Space Law', in E. Korovin (ed.), *The Kosmos and International Law*, Moscow: 1962, quoted from Lawrence Freedman, 'The Soviet Union and "Anti-Space Defence"', *Survival*, vol. 19 no. 1, January/February 1977, pp. 16–23, p. 16.

18. Quoted from Stares, *Space Weapons and US Strategy*, pp. 70 f.

19. Quoted from Stares, *Space Weapons and US Strategy*, p. 71.

20. Cf. Wolfe, *Soviet Strategy*, p. 209.

21. Stares, *Space Weapons and US Strategy*, p. 71.

22. Stares, *Space Weapons and US Strategy*, pp. 62–70; G. Steinberg, *The Legitimization of Satellite Reconnaissance: An Example of Informal Arms Control Negotiations*, unpublished Ph.D. Thesis, Cornell University, New York: 1981. The necessity of satellite reconnaissance was affirmed in an article by B. Aleksandrov and A. Yur'yev, 'Air and Space Reconnaissance in Armed Conflict', *Voennaia Mysl'*, no. 10, October 1965, pp. 1–14.

23. Quoted from Stares, *Space Weapons and US Strategy*, p. 74.

24. I. Baryshev, 'Chto takoe protivokosmicheskaia oborona', *Krasnaia Zvezda*, 2 September 1962, p. 3.

25. V. Siniagin, 'Sozdanie material 'no-tekhnicheskoi bazy kommunizma i ukreplenie oboronosposobnosti SSSR', *Kommunist Vooruzhennykh Sil*, no. 14, July 1962, pp. 8–16; p. 16.

26. Quoted from Stares, *Space Weapons and US Strategy*, p. 80.

27. S. Shtemenko, 'Nauchno-tekhnicheskii progress i ego vliianie na razvitie voennogo dela', *Kommunist Vooruzhennykh Sil*, no. 3, February 1963, pp. 20–30, p. 23.

28. See Stares, *Space Weapons and US Strategy*, pp. 99 f.; Peebles, *Battle for Space*, pp. 57–76.

29. For more details see Stares, *Space Weapons and US Strategy*, p. 86.

30. Ibid., p. 89.

31. Ibid., p. 90.

32. Ibid., p. 99. Some observers did dispute the question as to whether FOBS was compatible with the UNGA Resolution. It could be argued that since FOBS would only travel a fraction of an orbit and not complete an entire orbit, it would qualify as a weapon 'travelling through space' rather than a 'space-based weapon'.

33. Curtis Peebles suggests the following explanation, 'The SS-10 was evidently designed as a fall-back system alongside the more technically advanced and therefore more accident-prone SS-9. SS-10 drew on cryogenic propellents, entailing protracted pre-launch fueling. Because the liquid oxygen which it used would boil away soon after fueling, launching could not be delayed. With the success of the SS-9 program, the SS-10 was abandoned.' Peebles, *Battle for Space*, p. 67.

34. See Berman and Baker, *Soviet Strategic Forces*, p. 119.

35. For a detailed list of references, see the bibliography in Sawyer, *Soviet Space Controversy*. Two interesting references not mentioned by Sawyer are the articles by M. Pavlov, 'Akt agressii v kosmose', *Krasnaia Zvezda*, 5 June 1962 and by M. B. Keldysha, 'Kosmicheskoe prostranstvo dolzhno byt' zonoi mira', *Krasnaia Zvezda*, 7 June 1962, p. 1.

36. Sokolovskiy, *Soviet Military Strategy*, p. 251; for comment see Freedman, 'Anti-Space Defence', p. 18.

37. Quoted from Freedman, ibid.

38. While the concept of PKO is clearly part of Soviet military literature, Paul Stares has raised doubts as to whether a PKO existed as an organizational unit (Stares, *Space Weapons and US Strategy*, p. 150). It seems, however, that this is implied in an article by P. Batitsky, then Commander in Chief of the PVO, when he speaks of 'the operational art of the country's PVO troops which was divided into three distinct areas: Antimissile, antiaircraft and antispace defense'. P. Batitsky, 'Development of the Tactics and Operational Art of the Country's Air Defense (PVO) Troops', *Voennaia Mysl'*, no. 10, October 1967, pp. 28–41; p. 39.

39. See Stares, *Space Weapons and US Strategy*, pp. 136–40; Peebles, *Battle for Space*, chapter 4; Freedman, 'Anti-Space Defence', pp. 18–21.

40. Charles Sheldon, *Soviet Space Programs 1966–1970*, Washington: US

Government Printing Office 1971; Charles Sheldon, *Soviet Space Programs 1971–1975*, Washington: US Government Printing Office 1976.

41. Quoted from Stares, *Space Weapons and US Strategy*, p. 137.
42. Freedman, 'Anti-Space Defence', p. 20.
43. Sawyer, *Soviet Space Controversy*.
44. B. Aleksandrov, *Krasnaia Zvezda*, 23 July 1961, p. 3; for discussion see Sawyer, *Soviet Space Controversy*, p. 188. There was also an interesting article by Aleksandrov on the U-2 spyplane; see B. Aleksandrov, *Krasnaia Zvezda*, 6 September 1962, p. 3.
45. V. Liutii, 'Put' v kosmos', *Voenno-istoricheskii zhurnal*, no. 8, August 1961, pp. 25–36; for discussion see Sawyer, *Soviet Space Controversy*, p. 189.
46. Radio broadcast on 7 August 1961; translation quoted from Sawyer, *Soviet Space Controversy*, p. 170.
47. N. A. Varvarov, 'Dve liniy osvoneiia kosmosa', *Ekonomicheskaia qazeta*, 6 November 1961, pp. 38–39; this article is discussed at length in Sawyer, *Soviet Space Controversy*, p. 137.
48. *Krasnaia Zvezda*, 21 February 1962.
49. Sawyer, *Soviet Space Controversy*, p. 194
50. V. Larionov, *Krasnaia Zvezda*, 18 March 1962, p. 4 and 21 March 1962, p. 3; these articles are discussed in Wolfe, *Soviet Strategy*, pp. 203–5; see also Sawyer, *Soviet Space Controversy*, pp. 186 f.
51. Sawyer, *Soviet Space Controversy*, p. 194; Sawyer makes the point that Larionov implies that general and complete disarmament is a condition for cooperation in the exploration of space, thus putting himself in contradiction with Khrushchev. See Sawyer, *Soviet Space Controversy*, pp. 194 ff.
52. Freedman, 'Anti-Space Defence', p. 17.
53. *Krasnaia Zvezda*, 18 July 1962, p. 1.
54. See, for example G. Petrovich, 'Cherez blizhnyi kosmos vo vselennuiu', *Aviatsiia i kosmonavtika*, no. 6, June 1962, pp. 8–12; V. Vershchetin, 'Kosmos-na sluzhbu chelovechestvu'. *Aviatsiia i kosmonavtika*, no. 8, August 1962, pp. 22–25; these references are discussed by Sawyer, *Soviet Space Controversy*, p. 198.
55. I. I. Anureev, 'Imperialisticheskaia agressiia v kosmose', *Kommunist Vooruzhennykh Sil*, no. 15, August 1962, pp. 17–23.
56. Anureev, 'Agressiia v kosmose', p. 23.
57. A. A. Blagonravov, 'Chelovek shagaet k solntsu', *Ogonek*, vol. 40, August 1962, p. 25; translation quoted from Sawyer, *Soviet Space Controversy*, p. 199.
58. For further examples from the Soviet press, see Sawyer, *Soviet Space Controversy*, chapter 5.
59. Ibid., p. 184.
60. B. Aleksandrov, 'Problems of Space Defense and Means of Solving Them', *Voennaia Mysl'*, no. 9, September 1964, pp. 94–104, p. 94.
61. Ibid., p. 104.
62. Ibid., p. 102.

63. Ibid., p. 103.
64. See Batitsky.
65. See Peebles, *Battle for Space*, p. 10.
66. Aleksandrov, 'Problems of Antimissile Defense in the US'.
67. S. Shtemenko, 'Nauchno-tekhnicheskii progress', p. 30.
68. Anureev, Ibid.
69. See the discussion on Anureev's views on strategic defence in chapter 9.
70. Peebles, 'Battle for Space', p. 98.
71. See Alexander, *Decision Making*.
72. Sawyer, however, counts the Polet, Proton and Elektron programmes as having some relevance to the manned programme; see Sawyer, *Soviet Space Controversy*, chapter 6.
73. James Oberg, 'The Moon Race Cover-Up', in 'Man in Space', *New Scientist*, special edition, September 1986, pp. 21–22; see also Oberg, *Red Star in Orbit*, New York 1981, on which this article is based. The Soviet intention to land on the moon was affirmed in an article by K. Gil'zin in 1962 in which he responded to Kennedy's challenge to American scientists that the United States should land a man on the moon by 1970 by saying that many scholars abroad were unanimous in their view that the first men on the moon would be Russians: K. Gil'zin, 'Sovetskii narod uverenno shturmuet kosmos', *Kommunist vooruzhennykh sil*, no. 18, September 1962, pp. 35–39, p. 38.
74. Oberg, *Red Star in Orbit*. Nicholas Daniloff has suggested that Khrushchev was very enthusiastic about the moon programme and demanded results from Korolev that were impossible to achieve. The moon programme certainly was the kind of spectacular effort that fascinated Khrushchev; the military space programme thus may have found itself in intense competition with the moon programme for resources. See Daniloff, *Kremlin and Kosmos*, chapter 6.
75. Sawyer, *Soviet Space Controversy*, p. 223.
76. Stephen M. Meyer, 'Soviet Military Programmes and the New High Ground', *Survival*, 25: 5, September/October 1983, pp. 204–15; p. 212.
77. B. Aleksandrov and A. Yur'yev, 'Air and Space Reconnaissance in Armed Conflict', *Voennaia Mysl'*, no. 10, October 1965, pp. 1–14.
78. A. Krasnov, 'Space and Combat Readiness', *Voennaia Mysl'*, no. 4, April 1966, p. 32.
79. Yu. Subarov, 'Communication Through Space: Opportunities and Prospects', *Voennaia Mysl'*, no. 8, August 1966, pp. 56–70.
80. S. Vol'nov, 'Space and Electronics Warfare', *Voennaia Mysl'*, no. 9, 1966, pp. 74–86, p. 77.
81. Ibid.
82. Ibid., p. 78.
83. Ibid., pp. 78 f.
84. Quoted from Stares, *Space Weapons and US Strategy*, p. 103.
85. Ibid.

86. Ibid.
87. A. Vasilyev, 'Development of Space Systems of Armaments in the US', *Voennaia Mysl'*, no. 3, 1967, pp. 54–63.
88. Ibid., p. 59.
89. Ibid., p. 61.
90. Ibid., p. 63.
91. Ibid.
92. It has been argued, on the basis of the timing of satellite launches and orbit similarities, that the Soviet ASAT programme was significantly influenced by the Chinese satellite reconnaissance programme; see Freedman, 'Anti-Space Defence', pp. 22 f.; Peebles, *Battle for Space*, p. 109. This conclusion has been partially disputed by Stares, *Space Weapons and US Strategy*, p. 153, on the grounds that the Soviet ASAT project began before any Chinese satellites had been launched; Stares argues that certain orbital characteristics are imposed on Soviet satellites due to the geographical location of the launch sites. Nonetheless, even Stares acknowledges the possibilities that the Chinese programme may have influenced Soviet ASAT tests in 1976.
93. For more details and sources, see Christoph Bluth, *New Thinking in Soviet Military Policy*, London: Pinter 1990, chapter 5.

11 Conclusion

1. Easton, *Political Analysis*, p. 50; see also Dougherty and Pfaltzgraff, *Contending Theories*, chapter 4; Thomas Risse-Kappen, *Sicherheitspolitik*, Part A.
2. For more detail on the values underlying 'new political thinking' and the implications for military policy under Gorbachev, see Stephen Shenfield, *The Nuclear Predicament*, London: Routledge & Kegan Paul Ltd 1987; Bluth, *New Thinking in Soviet Military Policy*.

Bibliography

Soviet and other East European sources

Note: the names of authors are transliterated from Russian sources according to the transliteration system used throughout this book. The names of authors from translated sources are spelt as in the source. All publications by the same author are listed together even if the name is spelt differently in the various sources cited. Unsigned articles from journals are listed under the title of the journal.

Aleksandrov, B., 'Problems of Space Defense and Means of Solving Them', *Voennaia Mysl'*, no. 9, September 1964, pp. 94–104.

Aleksandrov, B., and A. Yur'yev, 'Air and Space Reconnaissance in Armed Conflict', *Voennaia Mysl'*, no. 10, October 1965, pp. 1–14.

Aleksandrov, V., 'The Search for a Solution to the Problems of Antimissile Defense in the US', *Voennaia Mysl'*, no. 9, September 1965, pp. 13–23.

Aniutin, V. N., 'Issledovaniia v oblasti protivoraketnoi oborony v S Sh A', *Vestnik protivovozdushnoi oborony*, no. 12, 1961, pp. 25–28.

Antsiferov, B. M., 'Protivoraketa "Naik-Zevs"', *Vestnik protivovozdushnoi oborony*, no. 6, 1961, pp. 25–26.

Anureev, I. I., 'Imperialisticheskaia agressiia v kosmose', *Kommunist Vooruzhennykh Sil*, no. 15, August 1962, pp. 17–23.

Anureev, I. I., 'Determining the Correlation of Forces in Terms of Nuclear Weapons', *Voennaia Mysl'*, no. 6, June 1967, pp. 35–45.

Anureev, I. I., *Oruzhie protivoraketnoi i protivokosmicheskoi oborony*, Moscow: Voenizdat 1971.

Arbatov, G. A., 'Amerikanskii imperializm i novye real'nosti mira', *Pravda*, 4 May 1971, p. 4.

Arbatov, G. A., 'Sila politika realizma', *Izvestiia*, 22 June 1972, p. 4.

Barsukov, Iu. 'Oposnoe reshenie', *Izvestiia*, 12 March 1970, p. 2.

Baryshev, I., 'Chto takoe protivokosmicheskaia oborona', *Krasnaia Zvezda*, 2 September 1962, p. 3.

Batitskii, P. F., Tass International Service, Moscow, 20 February 1967.

Batitskii, P. F., 'Voiska protivovozdushnoi oborony strany', *Voennoistoricheskii zhurnal*, 8, 1967, p. 26.

Batitskii, P. F., 'Vsegda v boevoi gotovnost', vsegda nacheku', *Kommunist Vooruzhennykh Sil*, no. 18, September 1967, pp. 25–31.

Batitsky, P. F., 'Development of the Tactics and Operational Art of the Country's Air Defense (PVO) Troops. *Voennaia Mysl'*, no. 10, October 1967, pp. 28–41.

Batitskii, P. F., *Vestnik protivovozdushnoi oborony*, no. 11, November 1967, p. 12.

Batitskii, P. F., *Voiska protivovozdushnoi oborony strany*, vol. 27, Moscow: Voenizdat 1968.

Baz', I. S., S. N. Kozlov, P. A. Sidorov and M. V. Smirnov, *O Sovetskoi Voennoi Nauke*, Moscow: Voenizdat 1964.

Baz', N., 'V. I. Lenin on the Basic Factors Determining the Course and Outcome of War', *Krasnaia Zvezda*, 19 February 1957.

Belokhvostov, V. A., and N. I. Sizov, 'Voevoe Snariazhenie protivraket', *Vestnik protivovozdushnoi oborny*, no. 7, 1961, pp. 21–24.

Biriuzov, S. S., 'Velikaia bitva na Volge', *Politicheskoe samoobrazovanie*, no. 2, 1963, pp. 33–41.

Blagonravov, A. A., 'Chelovek shagaet k solntsu', *Ogonek*, vol. 40. August 1962, p. 25.

Bondarenko, V., 'Sovremennaia revoliutsiia v voennom dele i boevaia gotovnost' Vooruzhennykh Sil', *Kommunist Vooruzhennykh Sil*, no. 24, December 1968, pp. 22–29.

Bondarenko, V., 'Voenno-tekhnicheskoe prevokhodstvo – vazhneishii faktor nadezhnoi oborony strany', *Kommunist Vooruzhennykh Sil*, no. 17, September 1966, pp. 7–14.

Bragin, E. K., and A. G. Kubayev, *Protivoraketnaia Oborony*, Moscow: Voenizdat 1966.

Brezhnev, L. I., 'Speech to Soviet Officers', Radio Moscow Domestic Service in Russian, 3 July 1965.

Bugayev, E., 'Istoricheskoe znachenie opyta KPSS v stroitel'stve sotsializma i kommunizma', *Kommunist Vooruzhennykh Sil*, no. 1, January 1969, pp. 17–26.

Burlatsky, Fyodor, 'Why Khrushchev Failed', *Encounter*, vol. 70, no. 5, May 1988.

Byely, B., et al., *Marxism-Leninism on War and the Army*, USAF Translation, Soviet Military Thought Series no. 2, Washington: GPO 1972.

Cherednichenko, M. I., and V. D. Sokolovskii, 'O sovremennoi voennoi strategii', *Kommunist Vooruzhennykh Sil*, no. 7, April 1966, pp. 54–66.

Chuikov, V. I., 'Osnova osnov voennogo stroitel'stva', *Krasnaia Zvezda*, 17 November 1962, pp. 3–4.

Chuikov, V. I., 'Sovremennye sukhopotnye voiska', *Izvestiia*, 22 December 1963, p. 5.

Chuikov, V. I., Television Speech, TASS International Service, Moscow, 22 February 1967.

Demin, B., 'Nenavisit' k vragu – neot"emlemaia storona patriotizma sovetskikh voinov', *Kommunist Vooruzhennykh Sil*, no. 13, July 1969, pp. 25–32.

Derevianko, P., 'Nekotorye osobennosti sovremennoi revoliutsii v voennom dele', *Kommunist Vooruzhennykh Sil*, no. 1, January 1964, pp. 15–25.

Dziuby, Ia. S., N. Ia. Syshko and S. A. Tiushkevicha (eds.), *Marksizm - leninism o voine i armii*, Moscow: Voenizdat 1968, pp. 218–21.

Epishev, A. A., 'Tverdo provodit' v zhizn' politiku partii v Vooruzhennykh Silakh', *Kommunist Vooruzhennykh Sil*, no. 19, October 1962, pp. 2–15.

Epishev, A. A., 'O Vozrastaiushchei roli KPSS v rukovodstve Vooruzhennymi Silami', *Voprosy istorii KPSS*, no. 2, February 1963, pp. 3–14.

Epishev, A. A., 'Leninism – osnova vospitaniia sovetskikh voinov', *Kommunist*, no. 6, April 1969, pp. 60–71.

Epishev, A. A., 'Politicheskim organam sovetskoi armii i voenno-morskogo flota – piat'desiat let', *Kommunist Vooruzhennykh Sil*, no. 7, April 1969, pp. 9–22.

Fedorov, G., N. Sushko and S. Tiushkevich, 'Razvitie marksistskoleninskogo ucheniia o voine v sovremennykh usloviiakh', *Kommunist Vooruzhennykh Sil*, no. 18, September 1961, pp. 19–29.

Filippov, N. T., and A. M. Larkov, *Edinonachalie v Sovetskikh Vooruzhennykh Silakh*, Moscow: Voenizdat 1960.

Gil'zin, K., 'Sovetskii narod uverenno shturmuet kosmos', *Kommunist vooruzhennykh sil*, no. 18, September 1962, pp. 35–39.

Golubvich, V. S., *Marshal Malinovskii*, Kiev: Izdatel'stvo politicheskoi literatury Ukrainy 1988.

Gorbachev, Mikhail., *Perestroika i novoe myshlenie*, Moscow: Politizdat 1987.

Grechko, A. A., 'V. I. Lenin i stroitel'stvo sovetskikh vooruzhennykh sil', *Kommunist*, no. 3, February 1969, pp. 15–26.

Grechko, A. A., 'Na strazhe mira i sotsializma', *Kommunist*, no. 3, February 1970, pp. 51–64.

Grechko, A. A., *Vooruzhenyie Sily Sovetskogo Gosudarstva*, Moscow: Voenizdat 1975.

Gromyko, A. A., 'O mezhdunarodnom polozhenii i vneshnei politike Sovetskogo Soiuza', *Pravda*, 28 June 1968, p. 3.

Gromyko, A. A., *Pamiatnoe*, Moscow: Izdatel'stvo politicheskoi literatury 1988 (2 vols.).

Gus, M., 'General'naia linia sovetskoi vneshnei politiki', *Zvezda* (Leningrad), no. 11, November 1953, pp. 106–25.

Gusakovskii, I., 'Zabota partii o podgotovke i vospitanii voennykh kadrov', *Kommunist Vooruzhennykh Sil*, no. 1, January 1969, pp. 27–33.

Hoffmann, Heinz, 'Überlegene Militärmacht des sowjetischen Lagers', *Neues Deutschland*, 3 May 1966, p. 5.

Igolkin, V., and I. Zheltikov, 'Certain Tendencies in the Development of Antiaircraft and Antirocket Defenses', *Voennaia Mysl'*, no. 8, 1964, pp. 53–65.

Il'ni, S., and E. Tarasov, 'Vsemerno sovershenstvovat' rabotu partiinykh komitetov akademii', *Kommunist Vooruzhennykh Sil*, no. 5, December 1960, pp. 36–42.

Iovlev, A., 'On Mass Armies in Modern War', *Voennaia Mysl'*, no. 10, October 1963, pp. 1–12, p. 8.

Ivanov, S., 'Soviet Military Doctrine and Strategy', *Voennaia Mysl'*, no. 5, May 1969, pp. 40–51.

Karaganov, S. A., A. V. Kortunov, V. V. Zhurkin, 'O razumnoi dostatochnosti', *S Sh A*, no. 12, 1987, pp. 11–21.

Kazakov, D., 'Teoreticheskaia i metodologicheskae osnova sovetskoi voennoi nauki', *Kommunist Vooruzhennykh Sil*, no. 10, May 1963, pp. 7–15.

Keldysha, M. B., 'Kosmicheskoe prostranstvo dolzhno byt' zonoi mira', *Krasnaia Zvezda*, 7 June 1962, p. 1.

Khrushchev, N. S., *Report of the Central Committee to the 20th Congress of the CPSU*, London: Soviet News Booklet 1956.

Khrushchev, Nikita S., 'Razoruzhenie – put' k uprocheniiu mira i obespecheniiu druzhby mezhdu narodami', *Pravda*, 15 January 1960, pp. 1–5.

Khrushchev, N. S., *The Present International Situation and the Foreign Policy of the Soviet Union*, New York: Crosscurrents Press 1963.

Khrushchev, Nikita S., *Khrushchev Remembers*, edited and translated by Strobe Talbott, vol. 1, London: André Deutsch 1971.

Khrushchev, Nikita S., *Khrushchev Remembers*, edited and translated by Strobe Talbott, vol. 2, London: André Deutsch 1974.

Kommunist Vooruzhennykh Sil, 'O rabote partiinogo komiteta i partorganizatsii shtaba i upravlenii tyla Ministerstva oborony SSSR', no. 5, March 1962, pp. 55–57.

Kommunist Vooruzhennykh Sil, 'O rabote partkoma i partiinykh organizatsii shtaba i upravelnii sukhoputnykh voisk', no. 15, August 1962, pp. 38–41.

Kommunist Vooruzhennykh Sil, 'Ideologischeskaia rabota partiinykh organisatsii', no. 4, February 1969, pp. 3–8.

Kondratkov, T., 'War as Continuation of Policy', *Soviet Military Review*, February 1974, pp. 19–21.

Kondratkov, T., 'Limited War of Imperialist Aggression', *Kommunist Vooruzhennykh Sil*, no. 8, April 1969, pp. 24–31; unpublished English translation available at the Soviet Studies Centre, Royal Military Academy, Sandhurst.

Konoplev, V., 'O nauchnom predvidenii voennom dele', *Kommunist Vooruzhennykh Sil*, no. 24, December 1963, pp. 28–34.

Kopytov, M. I., and V. I. Varfolomeyev, *Design and Testing of Ballistic Missiles – USSR*, translated by the Joint Publications Research Service, JPRS-51810), Washington, D.C.: 1970.

Kotov, V., 'Partiino-politicheskaia rabota v voiskakh nariadakh', *Kommunist Vooruzhennykh Sil*, no. 1, January 1969, pp. 44–48.

Kozlov, S. N. 'The Development of Soviet Military Science After World War II', *Voennaia Mysl'*, no. 2, February 1964, pp. 28–49.

Kozlov, S. N. (ed.), *Spravochnik Ofitsera*, Moscow: Voenizdat 1971.

Krasil'nikov, S., 'O kharaktere sovremennoi voiny', *Krasnaia Zvezda*, 18 November 1960.

Krasnov, A., 'Space and Combat Readiness', *Voennaia Mysl'*, no. 4, April 1966, p. 32.

Kruchinin, V., 'Contemporary Strategic Theory on the Goals and Missions of Armed Conflict', *Voennaia Mysl'*, no. 10, October 1963, pp. 13–24.

Kruzhkov, V., 'V. I. Lenin – korifei revoliutsonnoi nauki', *Kommunist*, no. 1, 1954, pp. 15–33.

Krylov, N., 'Strategicheskie Rakety', *Izvestiia*, 17 November 1963, p. 4.

Krylov, N., 'The Nuclear-Missile Shield of the Soviet State', *Voennaia Mysl'*, no. 11, November 1967, pp. 13–21.

Kulakov, V., 'Problems of Military-Technical Superiority', *Voennaia Mysl'*, no. 1, January 1964, pp. 1–14.

Kulikov, V. G. (ed.), *Akademiia General'nogo Shtaba*, Moscow: Voenizdat 1976.

Kuznetsov, N., and N. Vasendin, 'Modern Warfare and Surprise Attack', *Voennaia Mysl'*, no. 6, 1968, 69, p. 45.

Larionov, V., 'Rakety i strategiia', *Krasnaia Zvezda*, 18 March 1962, p. 4.

Larionov, V., 'Kosmos i strategiia', *Krasnaia Zvezda*, 21 March 1962, p. 3.

Larionov, V., 'Strategicheskie debaty', *S Sh A*, no. 3, March 1970, pp. 20–31.

Liutii, V., 'Put' v kosmos', *Voenno-istoricheskii zhurnal*, no. 8, August 1961, pp. 25–36.

Lomov, N. A., 'O sovetskoi voennoi doktrine', *Kommunist Vooruzhennykh Sil*, no. 10, May 1962, pp. 11–21.

Lomov, N. A., 'Vliianie sovetskoi voennoi doktriny na razvitie voennogo isskustva', *Kommunist Vooruzhennykh Sil*, no. 21, November 1965, pp. 15–24.

Lukonin, S., and N. Tarasenko, 'V. I. Lenin ob oboronoi funktsii sotsialisti-cheskogo gosudarstva', *Kommunist Vooruzhennykh Sil*, no. 10, May 1969, pp. 18–25.

Malinovskii, R. Ia., 'Programma KPSS i voprosy ukrepleniia Vooruzhennykh Sil SSSR', *Kommunist*, no. 7, May 1962, pp. 11–22.

Malinovskii, R. Ia., 'Nasushchnye voprosy vospitaniia lichnogo sostava Vooruzhennykh Sil SSSR', *Kommunist Vooruzhennykh Sil*, no. 11, June 1962, pp. 3–15.

Malinovskii, R. Ia., *Bditel'no Stroiat' na Strazhe Mira*, Moscow: Voenizdat 1962.

Malinovskii, R. Ia., *Krasnaia Zvezda*, 25 October 1962, p. 3.

Malinovskii, R. Ia., 'Za novyi moshchnyi pod"em ideologicheskoi raboty', *Krasnaia Zvezda*, 5 July 1963, pp. 2–3.

Malinovskii, R. Ia., 'Oktiabr' i stroitel'stvo vooruzhennykh sil', *Kommunist*, no. 1, January 1967, pp. 26–36.

Mel'kumov, T. M., 'Nekotorye problemy raketnoi tekhniki', *Vestnik Vozdush-nogo Flota*, no. 2, 1958, pp. 79–89.

Mikhailov, V. I., and G. Nazarov, *Razvitie tekhniki puska raket*, Moscow: Voenizdat 1976.

Nalin, Y., and A. Nikolayev, *The Soviet Union and European Security*, Moscow: Progress Publishers 1973.

Nenakhov, I. N., 'The Policy of the Communist Party in Strengthening the

Active Defence of the Soviet State', *Voennaia Mysl'*, no. 10, October 1953, pp. 3–18.

Nepodayev, Yuri, 'On the Nuclear Threshold in NATO Strategy', *Voennaia Mysl'*, no. 6, June 1966, pp. 77–79.

Nikolaev, M. N., *Snariad protiv snariada*, Moscow: Voenizdat 1961.

Pavlenko, N., 'Letopis' surovykh ispytanii i pervykh pobed sovetskogo naroda v Veliko Otechestvennoi voine', *Voenno-istoricheskii zhurnal*, no. 11, November 1961, pp. 93–103.

Pavlov, M., 'Akt agressii v kosmose', *Krasnaia Zvezda*, 5 June 1962, p. 3.

Pechorkin, V., 'The Problem of Preventing War', *International Affairs* (Moscow), no. 9, September 1960, pp. 3–6.

Petrov, Iu. P., *Partiinoe stroitel'stvo v Sovetskoi Armii i Flote, 1918–1961*, Moscow: Voenizdat 1961.

Petrovich, G., 'Cherez blizhnyi kosmos vo vselennuiu', *Aviatsiia i kosmonavtika*, no. 6, June 1962, pp. 8–12.

Piatkin, A., 'Some Questions of the Marxist-Leninist Science of War', *Voennaia Mysl'*, no. 3, March 1954, p. 16.

Pliachenko, P. F., 'Razvitie sistemy PRO v S Sh A', *Vestnik protivovozdushnoi oborony*, no. 8, 1966, pp. 86–87.

Pobezhimov, I., and P. Romanov 'Organizational and Legal Principles of the Structure of the Armed Forces', *Voennaia Mysl'*, no. 9, September 1964, pp. 12–25.

Rotmistrov, P. A., 'O roli vnezapnosti v sovremennoi voine', *Voennaia Mysl'*, no. 2, February 1955, pp. 14–25.

Rotmistrov, P. A., 'On Modern Soviet Military Art and Its Characteristic Features', *Voennaia Mysl'*, no. 2, February 1958; reprinted in abbreviated form in English translation in William F. Scott and Harriet Fast Scott, *The Soviet Art of War*, Boulder: Westview Press 1982, pp. 137–45.

Rotmistrov, P., 'Rukovodstvo partii – istochnik mogucheshestvo sovetskoi Armii i Flota', *Kommunist*, no. 4, March 1965, pp. 15–24.

Rybkin, E. I., 'O suschnosti mirovoi raketno-iadernoi voiny', *Kommunist vooruzhennykh sil*, no. 17, September 1965, pp. 50–56.

Rybkin, E. I., 'A Critique of the Book *On Peace and War*', *Voennaia Mysl'*, no. 7, July 1966, pp. 78–85.

Rybkin, E. I., 'Kritika burzhuaznykh kontseptsii voiny i mira', *Kommunist vooruzhennykh sil*, no. 18, September 1968, pp. 87–90.

Rybkin, E. I., 'Leninskaia kontseptsiia voiny i sovremennost'', *Kommunist Vooruzhennykh Sil*, no. 20, October 1973, pp. 21–28.

Shavrov, I. E., 'Principles and Content of Military Stragegy', *Journal of Soviet Military Studies*, vol. 1, no. 1, April 1988, pp. 29–53.

Shchapov, N., 'Chto takoe mezhkontinental'naia ballisticheskaia raketa?', *Voenni Vestnik*, no. 9, 1957, p. 60

Shibaev, N. F., *Bor'ba Protiv Strategicheskoi Rakety*, Moscow: Voenizdat 1964.

Shtemenko, S., 'Nauchno-tekhnicheskii progress: ego vliani na razvitie voennogo dela', *Kommunist vooruzhennykh sil*, no. 3, February 1963, pp. 20–30.

Shtrik, S. V., 'The Encirclement and Destruction of the Enemy During Combat Operations Not Involving the Use of Nuclear Weapons', *Voennaia Mysl'*, no. 1, 1968.

Sidorov, P., 'Neustanno krepit' oboronosposobnost' strany', *Kommunist Vooruzhennykh Sil*, no. 12, June 1961, pp. 59–65.

Siniagin, V., 'Sozdanie material'no-tekhnicheskoi bazy kommunizma i ukreplenie oboronosposobnosti SSSR', *Kommunist Vooruzhennykh Sil*, no. 14, July 1962, pp. 8–16, p. 16.

Sokolovskii V. D. (ed.), *Voennaia Strategiia*, Moscow: Voenizdat 1962.

Sokolovskii V. D. (ed.), *Soviet Military Strategy*, translated and introduced by Herbert S. Dinerstein, Leon Gouré and Thomas W. Wolfe, Englewood Cliffs: Prentice Hall 1963.

Sokolovskiy V. D. (ed.), *Soviet Military Strategy*, English language edition edited by Harriet Fast Scott, New York: Crane, Russal & Company Inc. 1968.

Strel'nikov, B., 'Iadernyi kot v meshke', *Pravda*, 10 June 1969, p. 5.

Subarov, Yu., 'Communication Through Space: Opportunities and Prospects', *Voennaia Mysl'*, no. 8, August 1966, pp. 56–70.

Sudets, V., 'Nadezhnyi shchit nashego neba', *Izvestiia*, 5 January 1964, p. 2.

Surikov, B. T., *Boevoe primenenie raket*, Moscow: Voenizdat 1965.

Svetlov, A., 'Razoruzhenie – nasushchnaia zadacha bor'by za mir', *MEIMO*, no. 7, July 1976, pp. 3–16.

Talenskiy, Nikolay A., 'On the Question of the Character of the Laws of Military Science', *Voennaia Mysl'*, no. 9, September 1953, excerpts reprinted in translation in Harriet Fast Scott and William F. Scott (eds.), *The Soviet Art of War*, Boulder: Westview Press 1982, pp. 127–31.

Talenskii, Nikolai, *Bol'shaia Sovetskaia Entsiklopediia*, 2nd edition, vol. 34, 1955, p. 257.

Talensky, N., 'On the Character of Modern Warfare', *International Affairs*, no. 10, October 1960, pp. 23–27.

Talensky, N., 'Anti-Missile Systems and Disarmament', *International Affairs* (Moscow), no. 10, October 1964, pp. 15–19.

Talensky, Nikolai, 'The Late War: Some Reflections', *International Affairs* (Moscow), no. 5, 1965, pp. 12–18.

Timofeechev, M., 'Edinonachalie – vazhneishii printsip stroitel'stva sovetskikh vooryzhennykh sil', *Kommunist Vooruzhennykh Sil*, no. 12, June 1962, pp. 44–56.

Timofeechev, M., 'Vazhneishii printsip sovetskogo voennogo stroitel'stva', *Kommunist Vooruzhennykh Sil*, no. 4, February 1969, pp. 12–19.

Tumkovskii, R. G., 'Bazirovanie raketnykh chastei VVS SShA', *Vestnik Vozdushnogo Flota*, no. 12, 1959, pp. 86–89.

Varvarov, N. A., 'Dve linii osvoeniia kosmosa', *Ekonomicheskaia gazeta*, 6 November 1961, pp. 38–39.

Vasilyev, A., 'Development of Space Systems of Armaments in the US', *Voennaia Mysl'*, no. 3, 1967, pp. 54–63.

Vershchetin, V., 'Kosmos – na sluzhbu chelovechestvu', *Aviatsiia i kosmonavtika*, no. 8, August 1962, pp. 22–25.

Viktorov, I. V., 'Protivoraketnaia Oborona', *Vestnik Vozdushnogo Flota*, no. 4, 1958, pp. 93–96.

Voennaia Mysl', Editorial, 'On Some Questions of Military Science', no. 3, March 1955.

Voennaia Mysl', Editorial, 'The World-Historical Victory of the Soviet People', no. 5, May 1955.

Volkogonov, D. A., et al. (eds.), *Voina i Armiia*, Moscow: Voenizdat 1977.

Vol'nov, S., 'Space and Electronics Warfare', *Voennaia Mysl'*, no. 9, 1966, pp. 74–86.

Yefremov, A. Y., *Nuclear Disarmament*, Moscow: Progress Publishers 1979.

Zakharov, M., 'The Increasing Role of Scientific Troop Leadership', *Voennaia Mysl'*, no. 2, 1967, pp. 11–23.

Zakharov, M. V. (ed.), *50 Let Vooruzhennykh Sil SSSR*, Moscow: Voenizdat 1968, pp. 522–25.

Zemskov, Vasiliy I., 'Characteristic Features of Modern War and Possible Methods of Conducting Them', *Voennaia Mysl'*, no. 7, 1969; excerpts reprinted in translation in Harriet Fast Scott and William F. Scott (eds.), *The Soviet Art of War*, Boulder: Westview Press 1982, pp. 211–15.

Western sources

Abel, Elie, *The Missile Crisis*, New York: Lippincott 1966.

Adomeit, Hannes, *Soviet Risk-Taking and Crisis Behavior*, London: George Allen and Unwin 1982.

Adomeit, Hannes, and Mikhail Agursky, *The Soviet Military-Industrial Complex and Its Internal Mechanism*, mimeographed.

Alexander, Arthur, *Decision Making in Soviet Weapons Procurement*, Adelphi Paper no. 147/48, London: IISS Winter 1978/79.

Allison, Graham T., *Essence of Decision*, Boston: Little Brown and Company 1971.

Alperovitz, Gar, *Atomic Diplomacy*, Harmondsworth: Penguin 1985.

Aspaturian, Vernon V., 'The Soviet Military-Industrial Complex – Does It Exist?', *Journal of International Affairs*, 26: 1, 1972, pp. 1–28.

Avidar, Yosef, *The Party and the Army in the Soviet Union*, London: Frank Cass & Co. 1983.

Baker, John C., and Robert P. Berman, *Soviet Strategic Forces*, Washington: The Brookings Institution 1982.

Ball, Desmond, *Politics and Force Levels*, Los Angeles: University of California Press 1980.

Baylis, John, and Gerald Segal (eds.), *Soviet Strategy*, London: Croom Helm 1981.

Berman, Robert P., *Soviet Air Power in Transition*, Washington: Brookings Institution 1978.

Beschloss, Michael R., *Mayday*, London: Faber & Faber 1986.

Bloomfield, Lincoln, Walter C. Clemens and Franklyn Griffiths, *Khrushchev and the Arms Race*, Cambridge: MIT Press 1966.

Bluth, Christoph, *New Thinking in Soviet Military Policy*, London: Pinter 1990.

Bottome, Edgar, *The Balance of Terror: A Guide to the Arms Race*, Boston: Beacon Press 1971.

Bowker, Mike, and Phil Williams, *Superpower Detente: A Reappraisal*, London: SAGE Publications for the RIIA 1988.

Boyd, Alexander, *The Soviet Air Forces Since 1918*, London: Macdonald and Jane's 1977.

Bull, Hedley, *The Control of the Arms Race*, London: Weidenfeld & Nicolson 1961.

Burin, Frederic S., 'The Communist Doctrine of the Inevitability of War', *American Political Science Review*, 57: 2, June 1963, pp. 334–54.

Carter, Ashton B., and David N. Schwartz, eds., *Ballistic Missile Defence*, Washington: Brookings Institution 1984.

Coffey, J. I., 'Soviet ABM Policy', *International Affairs*, 45:2, 1969, pp. 205–22.

Cottrell, Alvin J., and Walter F. Hahn, 'Ballistic Missile Defense and Soviet Strategy', *Orbis* 9:2, pp. 316–37.

Crankshaw, Edward, *Khrushchev*, London: Collins 1966.

Currie, Kenneth, 'Soviet General Staff's New Role', *Problems of Communism*, March–April 1984, pp. 32–40.

Daniloff, Nicholas, *The Kremlin and the Kosmos*, Alfred Knopf: New York 1972.

Deane, Michael J., *Political Control of the Soviet Armed Forces*, London: Macdonald and Jane's Publishers Ltd 1977.

Deane, Michael J., *Strategic Defense in Soviet Strategy*, Miami: Advanced International Studies Institute 1980.

Dinerstein, Herbert S., *War and the Soviet Union*, London: Praeger 1962.

Dornberg, John, *Brezhnev: The Masks of Power*, London: André Deutsch 1974.

Dougherty, James E., and Robert L. Pfaltzgraff, Jr.; *Contending Theories of International Relations*, New York: Harper & Row 1981.

Douglass, Joseph D., and Amoretta M. Hoeber, *Soviet Strategy for Nuclear War*, Stanford: Hoover Institution Press 1979.

Easton, David, *A Framework for Political Analysis*, Englewood Cliffs: Prentice-Hall 1965.

Eisenhower, Dwight D., *The White House Years: Waging Peace 1956–61*, Garden City, New York: Doubleday 1965.

Erickson, John, 'The "Military Factor" in Soviet Policy', *International Affairs*, 39:2, April 1963, pp. 214–26.

Erickson, John, '"The Fly in Outer Space": The Soviet Union and the anti-ballistic missile', *World Today*, March 1967, pp. 106–14.

Erickson, John, *Soviet Military Power*, London: RUSI 1971.

Fainsod, Merle, and Jerry F. Hough, *How the Soviet Union Is Governed*, Cambridge: Harvard University Press 1979.

Feshbach, Murray (ed.), *National Security Issues of the USSR*, Dordrecht: Martinus Nijhoff Publishers 1987.

Floyd, David, *Mao Against Khrushchev*, London: Pall Mall Press 1964.

Freedman, Lawrence, 'Logic, Politics and the Foreign Policy Process: A Critique of the Bureaucratic Politics Model', *International Affairs*, 52. no. 3, July 1976, pp. 434–49.

Freedman, Lawrence, 'The Soviet Union and "Anti-Space Defence"', *Survival*, 19:1, January–February 1977, pp. 16–23.

Freedman, Lawrence, *The Evolution of Nuclear Strategy*, London: Macmillan 1981.

Freedman, Lawrence, *US Intelligence and the Soviet Strategic Threat*, London: Macmillan 1986.

Gallagher, Matthew P., 'Military Manpower: A Case Study', *Problems of Communism*, 13: 3, May–June 1964, pp. 53–62.

Gallagher, Matthew, and Karl Spielmann, *Soviet Decision-Making for Defense*, New York: Praeger 1972.

Garthoff, Raymond L., *How Russia Makes War*, London: George Allen & Unwin Ltd 1954.

Garthoff, Raymond L., *Soviet Strategy in the Nuclear Age*, London: Atlantic Books 1958.

Garthoff, Raymond L., *The Soviet Image of Future War*, Washington: Public Affairs Press 1959, p. 24.

Garthoff, Raymond L., *Soviet Military Policy*, London: Faber & Faber 1966.

Garthoff, Raymond L., 'Mutual Deterrence and Strategic Arms Limitation in Soviet Policy', *International Security*, Summer 1978, pp. 114–33.

Garthoff, Raymond L., *Reflections on the Cuban Missile Crisis*, Washington: Brookings Institution 1987.

Gasteyger, Curt (ed.), *Strategic und Abrüstungspolitik der Sowjetunion*, Frankfurt: Alfred Metzner Verlag 1964.

Ghebhardt, Alexander O., *Implications of Organizational and Bureaucratic Policy Models for Soviet ABM Decisionmaking*, unpublished Ph.D. Dissertation, Political Science, Columbia University, 1975.

Gilpin, Robert, *War and Change in World Politics*, Cambridge: Cambridge University Press 1980.

Goldsen, Joseph M. (ed.), *Outers Space in World Politics*, Pall Mall Press: London 1963.

Gourevitch, Peter, 'The Second Image reversed: The International Sources of Domestic Policies', *International Organization*, 32: 4, Autumn 1978, pp. 881–911.

Gray, Colin, *The Soviet-American Arms Race*, Farnborough: Saxon House 1976.

Griffin, Kenyon N., and Alfred L. Monks, 'Soviet Strategic Claims, 1964–1979', *Orbis*, 15 : 2, Summer 1972, pp. 520–44.

Haas, Steven C., 'Reassessing Lessons From the ABM Treaty', *International Affairs*, 64 : 2, Spring 1988, pp. 233–40.

Harvey, A. McGehee, *Life*, 18 December 1970.

von Hassel, Kai Uwe, 'Organizing Western Defense: The Search for Consensus', *Foreign Affairs*, 43 : 2, January 1965, pp. 209–16.

Healey, Denis, 'NATO, Britain and Soviet Military Policy', *Orbis*, 13 : 1, Spring 1969, pp. 48–58.

Herspring, Dale R., and Robbin F. Laird, *The Soviet Union and Strategic Arms*, Boulder: Westview Press 1984.

Hoensch, Jörg K., *Sowjetische Osteuropa Politik 1945–1975*, Düsseldorf: Droste Verlag 1977.

Holloway, David, 'Technology and Political Decision in Soviet Armaments Policy', *Journal of Peace Research*, 11 : 4, 1974, pp. 257–80.

Holloway, David, *The Soviet Union and the Arms Race*, New Haven: Yale University Press 1984.

Holst, Johan J., and William Schneider (eds), *Why ABM?*, Elsmford: Pergamon Press 1969.

Horelick, Arnold L., and Myron Rush, *Strategic Power and Soviet Foreign Policy*, Chicago: University of Chicago Press 1966.

International Institute for Strategic Studies, *The Military Balance* (All editions from 1960–61 to 1970–71).

Jacobson, C. G., *Soviet Strategy-Soviet Foreign Policy*, Glasgow: Robert Maclehouse & Co. Ltd 1972.

Johnson, Nicholas L., *Soviet Military Strategy in Space*, London: Jane's Publishing Company 1987.

Juviler, Peter H., and Henry W. Morton (eds.), *Soviet Policy-Making: Studies of Communism in Transition*, New York: Praeger 1967.

Kintner, William R., and Harriet Fast Scott, *The Nuclear Revolution in Soviet Military Affairs*, Norman: University of Oklahoma Press 1968.

Kissinger, Henry A. (ed.), *Problems of National Strategy*, New York: Praeger 1965, pp. 361–75.

Kolkowicz, Roman, *The Soviet Military and the Communist Party*, Princeton: Princeton University Press 1967.

Krippendorf, Ekkehardt, 'Ist Außenpolitik *Außen*politik?', *Politische Vierteljahres-Schrift*, vol. 4, 1963, pp. 243–65.

Lee, Asher, (ed.), *The Soviet Air and Rocket Forces*, London: Weidenfeld & Nicolson 1959.

Lee, William T., and Richard F. Staar, *Soviet Military Policy Since World War II*, Stanford: Hoover Institution Press, 1986.

Light, Margot, *The Soviet Theory of International Relations*, Brighton: Wheatsheaf 1988.

Light, Margot, and A. J. R. Groom, *International Relations: A Handbook of Current Theory*, London: Pinter 1985.

Linden, Carl A., *Khrushchev and the Soviet Leadership: 1957–1964*, Baltimore: Johns Hopkins Press 1966.

Litherland, Pat, *Gorbachev and Arms Control: Civilian Experts and Soviet Policy*, Peace Research Report Number 12, Bradford: School of Peace Studies 1986.

Lynch, Allen, *The Soviet Study of International Relations*, Cambridge: Cambridge University Press 1987.

MacKenzie, Donald, 'The Soviet Union and Strategic Missile Guidance', *International Security*, 13: 2, Fall 1988, pp. 5–54.

Mackintosh, Malcolm, *Strategy and Tactics of Soviet Foreign Policy*, London: Oxford University Press 1962.

Mackintosh, Malcolm, 'The Soviet Military – Influence on Foreign Policy', *Problems of Communism*, Sept.–Oct. 1976, pp. 1–12.

MccGwire, Michael, *Military Objectives in Soviet Foreign Policy*, Washington: The Brookings Institution 1987.

McNamara, Robert S., 'Statement of Secretary of Defense Robert S. McNamara before a Joint Session of the Senate Armed Services Committee and the Senate Subcommittee on Department of Defense Appropriations on the Fiscal Year 1966–70 Defense Program and the 1966 Defense Budget', declassified (US Department of Defense, 1965).

McNamara, Robert S.,The dynamics of nuclear strategy', *Department of State Bulletin*, 57: 9 October 1967.

Medevedev, Roy A., and Zhores Medvedev, *Khrushchev*, Oxford: Oxford University Press 1977.

Meyer, Stephen M., *Soviet Theatre Nuclear Forces*, Adelphi Paper no. 187/88, London: IISS 1984, p. 547.

Meyer, Stephen M., 'Soviet Military Programmes and the New High Ground', *Survival*, 25 : 5, September/October 1983, pp. 204–15.

Meyer, Stephen M., 'Soviet Strategic Programmes and the US SDI', *Survival*, 27 : 6, November/December 1985, 274–92.

Miller, Mark E., *Soviet Strategic Power and Doctrine: The Quest for Superiority*, Advanced International Studies Institute 1982.

Morgenthau, Hans J., *Politics Among Nations*, New York: Knopf 1967.

Myrdal, Alva, *The Game of Disarmament: How the United States and Russia Run the Arms Race*, Manchester: Manchester University Press 1977.

Nuclear Weapons Databook, 'Soviet Nuclear Weapons' (Working Paper), Washington: National Resources Defense Council 1986.

Oberg, James, *Red Star in Orbit*, New York 1981.

Oberg, James, 'The Moon Race Cover-Up', in 'Man in Space', *New Scientist*, special edition, September 1986, pp. 21–22.

Odom, William E., 'The Party Connection', *Problems of Communism*, Sept.–Oct. 1976, pp. 12–16.

Payne, Keith B. (ed.), *Laser Weapons in Space – Policy and Doctrine*, Boulder: Westview Press 1983.

Payne, Samuel B., *The Soviet Union and SALT*, Cambridge: MIT Press 1980.

Peebles, Curtis, *Battle for Space*, Poole: Blandford Press 1983.

Pipes, Richard, 'Why the Soviet Union Thinks It Could Fight and Win a Nuclear War', *Commentary*, 64 : 1, July 1977, pp. 21–34.

Pipes, Richard, 'Soviet Strategic Doctrine: Another View', *Strategic Review*, Fall 1982, pp. 52–57.

Pope, Ronald R. (ed.), *Soviet Views on the Cuban Missile Crisis*, Washington: University Press of America 1982.

Potter, William, and Jiri Valenta (eds.), *Soviet Decisionmaking for National Security*, London: Allen & Unwin 1984.

Prados, John, *The Soviet Estimate*, Princeton: Princeton University Press 1986.

Ranger, Robin, *Arms and Politics 1958–1978*, Toronto: Macmillan 1979.

Revel, Jean-Francois, *How Democracies Perish*, London: Weidenfeld & Nicolson 1985.

Rilkin, Alois, *Weltrevolution oder Koexistenz?*, Zürich: SAD 1969.

Risse-Kappen, Thomas, *Die Krise der Sicherheitspolitik*, München: Christian Kaiser Verlag 1988.

Rühl, Lothar, *Mittelstreckenwaffen in Europa: Ihre Bedeutung in Strategie, Rüstungskontrolle und Bündnispolitik*, Baden-Baden: Nomos Verlagsgesellschaft 1987.

Rühle, Michael, *Die Strategische Verteidigung in Rüstung und Politik der UdSSR*, Cologne: Bundesinstitut für ostwissenschaftliche und internationale Studien 1985.

Sawyer, Herbert L., *The Soviet Space Controversy, 1961–1963*, unpublished Ph. D. Dissertation, Fletcher School of Law and Diplomacy, Massachusetts, May 1969.

Schelling, Thomas C., *The Strategy of Conflict*, New York: Oxford University Press 1960.

Schick, Jack M., *The Berlin Crisis, 1958–1962*, Philadelphia: University of Pennsylvania Press 1971.

Scientific American, *Progress in Arms Control?*, San Francisco: W. H. Freeman 1979.

Scott, Harriet Fast, and William F. Scott (eds.), *The Soviet Art of War*, Boulder: Westview Press 1982.

Scott, William F., and Harriet Fast Scott, *The Armed Forces of the USSR*, Boulder: Westview 1979.

Seaborg, Glenn T., *Kennedy, Khrushchev and the Test Ban*, Berkeley: University of California Press 1981.

Sheldon, Charles, *Soviet Space Programs 1966–1970*, Washington: US Government Printing Office, 1971; Charles Sheldon, *Soviet Space Programs 1971–1975*, Washington: US Government Printing Office, 1976.

Shenfield, Stephen, *The Nuclear Predicament*, London: Routledge & Kegan Paul for the Royal Institute of International Affairs 1987.

Shevchenko, Arkady N., *Breaking with Moscow*, London: Jonathan Cape 1985.

Singer, J. David, *A General Systems Taxonomy for Political Science*, New York: General Learning Press 1971.

Slusser, Robert M., *The Berlin Crisis of 1961*, Baltimore: Johns Hopkins University Press 1973.

Speilmann, Karl F., 'Defense Industrialists in the USSR', *Problems of Communism*, Sept. – Oct. 1976, pp. 52–69.

Speilmann, Karl, *Analyzing Soviet Strategic Arms Decisions*, Boulder: Westview Press 1978.

Stares, Paul B., *Space Weapons and US Strategy: Origins and Development*, London: Croom Helm 1985.

Steele, Jonathan, *The Limits of Soviet Power*, Harmondsworth: Penguin 1984.

Steinberg, G., *The Legitimization of Satellite Reconnaissance: An Example of*

Informal Arms Control Negotiations, unpublished Ph.D. Thesis, Cornell University, New York, 1981.

Stent, Angela, *From Embargo to Ostpolitik,* Cambridge, Cambridge University Press 1981.

Stockholm International Peace Research Institute, *Armaments and Disarmament in the Nuclear Age,* Cambridge: MIT Press 1976.

Tatu, Michel, *Power in the Kremlin,* London: Collins 1969.

Thomas, John R., 'The Role of Missile Defense in Soviet Strategy', *Military Review,* May 1974, pp. 46–58.

Vladimirov, Leonid, *The Russian Space Bluff,* New York: Dial Press 1971.

Warner, Edward L., *The Military in Contemporary Soviet Politics: An Institutional Analysis,* New York: Praeger 1977.

Wassmund, Hans, *Kontinuität im Wandel,* Köln: Böhlau-Verlag 1974.

Watt, D. C., *Survey of International Affairs 1961,* London: Oxford University Press 1965.

Wheeler, Nicholas J., *The Roles Played by the British Chiefs of Staff Committee in the Evolution of Britain's Nuclear Weapon Planning and Policy-Making, 1945–55,* Ph.D. Thesis, University of Southampton, 1988.

Wolfe, Thomas, *Soviet Strategy at the Crossroads,* London: Oxford University Press 1964.

Wolfe, Thomas W., *Soviet Power and Europe 1945–1970,* Baltimore: Johns Hopkins Press 1970.

Wolfe, Thomas, *The SALT Experience,* Cambridge: Harper & Row 1979.

York, Herbert, *Race to Oblivion: A Participant's View of the Arms Race,* New York: Simon & Schuster 1971.

Yergin, Daniel, *Shattered Peace,* Harmondsworth: Penguin 1977.

Index

continued from page iv

22 JAMES RIORDAN
    Sport in Soviet society
    Development of sport and physical education in Russia and the USSR

The following series titles are now out of print:

 1 ANDREA BOLTHO
    Foreign trade criteria in socialist economies

 2 SHEILA FITZPATRICK
    The commissariat of enlightenment
    Soviet organization of education and the arts under Lunacharsky, October 1917–1921

 3 DONALD J. MALE
    Russian peasant organisation before collectivisation
    A study of commune and gathering 1925–1930

 4 P. WILES (ED.)
    The prediction of communist economic performance

 5 VLADIMIR V. KUSIN
    The intellectual origins of the Prague Spring
    The development of reformist ideas in Czechoslovakia 1956–1967

 6 GALIA GOLAN
    The Czechoslovak reform movement

 7 NAUN JASNY
    Soviet economists of the twenties
    Names to be remembered

 8 ASHA L. DATAR
    India's economic relations with the USSR and Eastern Europe, 1953–1969

 9 T. M. PODOLSKI
    Socialist banking and monetary control
    The experience of Poland

10 SHMUEL GALAI
    The liberation movement in Russia 1900–1905

11 GALIA GOLAN
    Reform rule in Czechoslovakia
    The Dubcek era 1968–1969

12 GEOFFREY A. HOSKING
    The Russian constitutional experiment
    Government and Duma 1907–1914

13 RICHARD B. DAY
    Leon Trotsky and the politics of economic isolation

14 RUDOLF BIĆANIĆ
    Economic policy in socialist Yugoslavia

15 JAN M. CIECHANOWSKI
    The Warsaw rising of 1944